1984

DRAMA
IN THE
TWENTIETH
CENTURY

AMS Studies in Modern Literature, No. 11

ISSN: 0270-2983

Other titles in this series:

1. Richard E. Amacher and Margaret F. Rule. *Edward Albee at Home and Abroad: A Bibliography, 1958 to June 1968.* 1973.

2. Richard G. Morgan, ed. *Kenneth Patchen: A Collection of Essays.* 1977.

3. Philip Grover, ed. *Ezra Pound: The London Years, 1908-1920.* 1978.

4. Daniel J. Casey and Robert E. Rhodes, eds. *Irish-American Fiction: Essays in Criticism.* 1979.

5. Iska Alter. *The Good Man's Dilemma: Social Criticism in the Fiction of Bernard Malamud.* 1981.

6. Charles Lee Green. *Edward Albee: An Annotated Bibliography, 1968-1977.* 1980.

7. Richard H. Goldstone and Gary Anderson. *Thornton Wilder: An Annotated Bibliography of Works By and About Thornton Wilder.* 1982.

12. Siegfried Mews, ed. *"The Fisherman and His Wife." Gunter Grass's* The Flounder *in Critical Perspective.* 1983.

DRAMA
IN THE
TWENTIETH
CENTURY

Comparative and Critical Essays

EDITED BY

Clifford Davidson
C. J. Gianakaris
John H. Stroupe

PREFACE BY

John H. Stroupe

AMS PRESS
NEW YORK

Library of Congress Cataloging in Publication Data

Main entry under title:

Drama in the Twentieth Century.
  (AMS Studies in Modern Literature, ISSN 0270-2983;
no. 11)
  Includes bibliographical references and index.
  1. Drama—20th Century—History and Criticism—
Addresses, Essays, Lectures. 2. Literature, Comparative
—Addresses, Essays, Lectures. I. Davidson, Clifford.
II. Gianakaris, C.J., 1934-   .   III. Stroupe, John H.
IV. Series.
PN1861.D65 1984   809.2   83-45289
ISBN 0-404-61581-3

MANUFACTURED IN THE UNITED STATES OF AMERICA

Contents

Notes on Contributors   *vii*

Preface   *xi*

Entropy and the "Death" of Tragedy: Notes for a
    Theory of Drama   1
    GEORGE KURMAN

The Retrospective Technique and Its
    Implications for Tragedy   23
    CHARLES A. HALLETT

Myth and Neurosis in Ibsen's Mature Plays   43
    MARGOT NORRIS

The Demons of *John Gabriel Borkman*   57
    BRIAN JOHNSTON

Strindberg's Historical Imagination: *Erik XIV*   73
    MICHAEL W. KAUFMAN

The *Skogsrå* of Folklore and Strindberg's
    The Crown Bride   87
    LARRY E. SYNDERGAARD

The Playwright as Perfect Wagnerite: Motifs from the
    Music Dramas in the Theatre of Bernard Shaw 101
    ARTHUR GANZ

Paterian Aesthetics in Yeats' Drama   125
    F. C. MCGRATH

"Body's Image": *Yerma, The Player Queen,* and the
    Upright Posture   141
    MURRAY BAUMGARTEN

The Antichrist Ubu   151
    JAMES H. BIERMAN

Anouilh's Little Antigone: Tragedy, Theatricalism,
    and the Romantic Self   173
    MICHAEL SPINGLER

Brecht's Quarrel with God: From Anti-Theodicy
to Eschatology 185
EDWARD M. BERCKMAN
Brecht's Contacts With the Theater of Meyerhold 203
KATHERINE EATON
Defeated Sexuality in the Plays and Novels of
Samuel Beckett 223
KRISTIN MORRISON
Krapp's Last Tape and Critical Theory 241
SUE ELLEN CAMPBELL
Genet's *The Blacks* and *The Screens:* Dialectic of
Refusal and Revolutionary Consciousness 255
W. F. SOHLICH
Dance to a Cut-Throat Temper: Harold Pinter's Poetry
as an Index to Intended Audience Response 275
CHRISTOPHER C. HUDGINS
Time and Memory in Pinter's Proust Screenplay 295
ENOCH BRATER
The Sound of a Poet Singing Loudly: A Look at
Elegy for Young Lovers 301
MARC A. ROTH
Edward Bond's *Lear* 323
LESLIE SMITH
Verse Drama: A Reconsideration 345
WILLIAM G. MCCOLLLOM
The Mirror as Stage Prop in Modern Drama 363
THOMAS P. ADLER
Index 383

Notes on Contributors

GEORGE KURMAN, author of two books on Estonian language and literature, is also active as a translator; he has completed an English rendition of *Kalevipoeg*, the Estonian national epic. Professor Kurman (Western Illinois University) has contributed to such journals as *Comparative Literature*, the *Journal of Baltic Studies, Comparative Literature Studies*, and *Canadian Slavic Studies*.

CHARLES A. HALLETT, Professor of English at Fordham University, has published two books on renaissance drama: *The Revenger's Madness: A Study of Dramatic Motifs in Revenge Tragedy* and *Middleton's Cynics*. With Kenneth Frost, he is co-author of *Poetry and Reality: The Zetema and Its Significance for Poetics*. He has contributed to such journals as *Studies in Philology, Philological Quarterly*, and *Journal of English and Germanic Philology*.

MARGOT NORRIS is author of *The Decentered Universe of Finnegans Wake* (Johns Hopkins University Press) as well as other essays on Joyce, Kafka, Nietzsche, and Max Ernst. She teaches at the University of Michigan and is at work on a book about the deconstruction of anthropocentrism in the Modern period.

BRIAN JOHNSTON, who has taught at various universities in England, Norway, and the United States, now lives in Irbid, Jordan, where he teaches at Yarmouk University. Professor Johnston is author of two books on Ibsen: *The Ibsen Cycle* (1975), and *To the Third Empire: Ibsen's Early Drama* (1980).

MICHAEL W. KAUFMAN has published on modern dramatic literature in such journals as *Modern Drama, The Shaw Review, James Joyce Quarterly*, and the *Educational Theatre Journal*. Currently, he is Assistant Dean at Brandeis University (Heller Graduate School for Advanced Studies in Social Welfare) and working on a study of the family in drama.

LARRY SYNDERGAARD, Western Michigan University, works primarily in the areas of medieval English literature, medieval and modern Scandinavian literature, and folk literature and mythology. Professor Syndergaard has served as co-editor of *Studies in Medieval Culture*, published by the Medieval Institute of Western Michigan University; his current research is on Scandinavian folk ballads.

ARTHUR GANZ has published numerous articles on modern playwrights (Ibsen, Wilde, Chekhov, Synge, Giraudoux, Williams, Miller) in *PMLA, Modern Drama, The American Scholar*, and other journals. Professor Ganz (The City College of CUNY) is the editor of the volume on Pinter in the Twentieth Century Views series and the author of *Realms of the Self* (New York University Press, 1981).

F. C. MCGRATH teaches at Rutgers University and is working on a book-length study of key Modernist values. Professor McGrath has published essays on Pater, Yeats, and Eliot in such journals as *The Canadian Journal of Irish Studies, Irish University Review, Yeats-Eliot Review*, and *Modern British Literature.*

MURRAY BAUMGARTEN, Professor of English and Comparative Literature at the University of California, Santa Cruz, has published extensively on nineteenth- and twentieth-century English literature in such journals as *Comparative Literature, Victorian Studies*, and *The Yale Review*. His current research is on the impact of Yiddish on certain modern Jewish writers, and a book on Yeats and Lorca.

JAMES H. BIERMAN teaches in the Department of Theater Arts and is Fellow of Cowell College at the University of California, Santa Cruz. He has published essays on the theater in such journals as *The Yale Review, The Drama Review*, and *The Soho News*, and is also a practicing playwright.

MICHAEL SPINGLER is currently at work translating Ionesco with particular emphasis on performance values. Professor Spingler (Clark University) has contributed essays to *Modern Drama* and *The Village Voice*, and he has also directed numerous plays.

EWARD M. BERCKMAN, Communications Officer for the Episcopal Diocese of Indianapolis, is also Vicar of St. Stephen's Episcopal Church, Elwood, Indiana. He has a Ph.D. in Religion and Literature from the University of Chicago, and his articles on Brecht have also appeared in *Brecht Heute/Brecht Today, Essays in Literature*, and *Modernist Studies.*

KATHERINE EATON has a Ph.D. in Comparative Literature from the University of Wisconsin, Madison, and teaches in the Communications Department of Richland College, Dallas. Her latest publication, *"Der kaukasische Kreidekreis* und *Feld-Herren.* Bemerkungen zu Brecht und Tretjakow," appeared in the *Brecht-Jahrbuch,* and she is completing a book on Meyerhold and Brecht.

KRISTIN MORRISON, co-author of *Crowell's Handbook of Contemporary Drama,* has published articles on both modern drama and modern fiction in *Texas Studies in Literature and Language, Nineteenth-Century Fiction, Western Humanities Review,* and *American Imago,* among others. Professor Morrison (Boston College) has recently completed a book on the use of narrative in the plays of Beckett and Pinter.

SUEELLEN CAMPBELL is interested in the relationships between critical theory, practical criticism, literature, and the visual arts. She teaches at Bowling Green State University, and is at work on a study of Wyndham Lewis's criticism, novels, and paintings.

WOLFGANG F. SOHLICH teaches courses in modern French and European theater at the University of Oregon. His publications include studies on Genet, Giraudoux, Audiberti, and French cooperative theater troupes; currently he is working on metatheater, audience response theory, and Paris theater productions.

CHRISTOPHER C. HUDGINS has published articles on Pinter emphasizing audience response theory and the influence of Pinter's work in other media on his theatrical techniques. Professor Hudgins (University of Nevada, Las Vegas) is working on David Mamet and Stanley Kubrick.

ENOCH BRATER teaches at the University of Michigan. In addition to his work on Pinter, he has written extensively on Beckett, Ionesco, Brecht, Stoppard, Arthur Miller, film, and modern and contemporary art. Before beginning his academic career, Professor Brater was on the staff of the Loeb Drama Center at Harvard and the New York Shakespeare Festival in Central Park.

MARC A. ROTH, Department of Dramatic Art, University of California, Berkeley, is working on a book on Wagner, Ibsen, and Strindberg. His most recent publications include articles on Strindberg (*Scandinavico*), Wagner and Appia (*Theatre Research International,*) and essays for *Opera News* and the *San Francisco Opera Magazine.*

LESLIE SMITH is Principal Lecturer in English at the Polytechnic of North London. His publications include articles on Bond, Isherwood, Orton, and Pinter in such journals as *Modern Drama* and *Adam International Review.* His current research is on British farce from Pinero to Orton.

WILLIAM G. MCCOLLOM, Professor of English at Case Western Reserve University, is author of two books on drama: *Tragedy* (Macmillan, 1957) and *The Divine Average: A View of Comedy* (Case Western Reserve University Press, 1971). He has also directed productions of some thirty plays by authors ranging from Sophocles to Ionesco.

THOMAS P. ADLER, Purdue University, has published widely on such modern playwrights as O'Neill, Williams, Albee, and Pinter, with articles in *Modern Drama, Arizona Quarterly*, and *Renascence*, among others; a book on Robert Anderson; and chapters in several collections of essays, including one recently on Williams's short fiction.

JOHN H. STROUPE, co-editor of *Comparative Drama,* is professor of English at Western Michigan University. He has published widely on Shakespeare, O'Neill, Coleridge, D. H. Lawrence, Edgar Allan Poe, Jean Genet, Anouilh, Archibald MacLeish, and many others in such publications as *Comparative Drama, Modern Drama, Studies in Short Fiction,* and *Tennessee Studies in Literature.*

Preface

THIS BOOK brings together a group of twenty-two essays on drama of the last one hundred years. The emphasis is on critical writing—on writing that sharpens vision and understanding—rather than on writing designed primarily to inform. The critical modes of the essays are deliberately various and have been selected (with the frustrations usual to anthologizing) not only for intrinsic excellence and for their coverage of many desired works and authors, but because they well illuminate the richness and diversity of modern and contemporary drama.

Importantly, the editors have also chosen essays which explore drama in relationship to other disciplines and other literary forms, for example, the two pairs of framing essays (on "Entropy," "Retrospective Technique," "Verse Drama," and "Mirror as Stage Prop"). George Kurman argues that tragic theory may best be understood by our attention to "a concept well known to the physical sciences and to mathematics, but seldom thought of in connection with the drama—namely that of entropy." Charles Hallett explores the parallels between the retrospective plots of such plays as *Oedipus Rex, Ghosts, Death of a Salesman*, and *Equus* and the mystery stories of popular culture: "In fact, the archetype of the retrospective plot is the detective story." William McCollom attempts to "map the terrain shared by poetry and verse" and reassesses twentieth-century verse drama, including the "poetry" of Samuel Beckett, William Alfred, John Heath-Stubbs, John Arden, and Howard Nemerov, among others. And Thomas Adler examines the "use of the mirror as an important stage prop" not only in the works of Pirandello, O'Neill, Camus, and Genet, but also in three recent major musicals—*Man of La Mancha, Cabaret*, and *A Chorus Line*.

In other essays, Arthur Ganz discusses Shavian drama via the "misty grandeurs of the Wagnerian universe," while Enoch Brater studies

Pinter's cinematic adaptation of Proust's *À la recherche du temps perdu* and concludes that it provides "the cinematic analogue for Pinter's own recent experimentation with the games Time plays with Memory on his stage." Marc Roth decries the "critical neglect of the bulk of Auden's operatic collaborations," and Kristin Morrison argues that "throughout Beckett's career, the fiction with its greater explicitness has provided an important context for words and phrases which appear in the plays."

In these and in the selection of many of the other essays included here, the editors have attempted to provide new perspectives for the reader— perspectives which are suggestive, challenging, and stimulating.

The essays included in this volume are reprinted from *Comparative Drama* and appear as originally printed except for minor corrections requested by several authors.

JOHN H. STROUPE
Kalamazoo, Michigan

Entropy and the "Death" of Tragedy: Notes for a Theory of Drama

George Kurman

I

Recent commentators agree that tragedy as an art form has undergone an irrevocable transformation. Some critics date this change at around the first decade of our century, while others would have it begin as far back as the era of Racine. In any case, within a year or two of each other, during the early 1960's, George Steiner wrote eloquently of the "Death of Tragedy," Martin Esslin tellingly coined the term "Theatre of the Absurd," and Lionel Abel contrasted older tragedy to "Metatheatre."[1] Later in the same decade, Walter Kaufmann took issue with portions of Steiner's argument and terminology, but nevertheless conceded the decline of tragedy, linking this decline to the sense of despair occasioned by the horrors of modern history.[2] Similarly, and in the same year, Geoffrey Brereton agreed that "all critics have experienced the same real difficulty in deciding what happened to dramatic tragedy in the present century. Merely to say that it died is unsatisfactory. No doubt it did die [however] as a single body. . . ."[3] To sum up the views of the critics cited above (together with the opinion of many other observers), it would be just to say that while there existed a coherent notion of tragedy among the dramatic stages of fifth-century Athens, Elizabethan England, and seventeenth-century France, the contributions to tragedy by Goethe, Ibsen, Strindberg, Chekov and other writers since Racine are either problematic or transitional, and during the last seventy years it has been at best questionable and at worst mere nominalism to apply the epithet "tragic" to modern dramatic literature. The purpose of this essay is to suggest that the apparent disappearance of or disjunction in the notion of tragedy can be parsimoniously accounted for in terms of a concept well known to the physical sciences and to mathematics, but seldom thought of in connection with the drama—namely that of entropy.

Entropy (Greek *entropia* "transformation," cf. *trope* "turning") was introduced into the modern languages by the German physicist R. Clausius (who had based much of his thinking in this area on the earlier work of S. Carnot) at the middle of the nineteenth century.[4] Not long thereafter, with the subsequent development of thermodynamics as a branch of physics, the concept of entropy was co-opted into what has since come to be known as the Second Law of Thermodynamics, mathematically expressed in 1872 by L. Boltzmann as the formula for thermodynamic entropy.[5] One year earlier, however, J. C. Maxwell, in his *Theory of Heat*, had followed Clausius by stating that the entropy of a closed system cannot decrease in the long run: that eventually any closed system will tend toward the leveling of energy potential, increasing disorganization and randomness. In short, Maxwell postulated the gradual evolution of cosmos into chaos. As Wylie Sypher puts it:

> Technically entropy is spoken of as a drift toward thermo-dynamical equilibrium—a squandering of energy into a permanent state where no observable events occur. Every isolated system increases in entropy until it reaches a condition of rest.[6]

In other words, the rise in entropy is a measure of the irreversibility of certain processes, all of which contribute to a decrease of available energy or order or structure in the system in question.

Now, as the universe itself may be thought of as a closed system (in addition to being composed of a plurality of systems), and as the universe, like all closed systems, exhibits—in the long run—rising entropy (the degradation of energy, ending in an eventual "heat death"), some scientists have extrapolated from the Second Law of Thermodynamics a statement of the only demonstrable purpose of the universe, namely that the only observable *telos* of creation is to contribute to the rise in entropy. Nevertheless, the Second Principle of Thermodynamics applies, by definition, only to closed systems, while man and other living organisms have been termed "open systems" by current system theory.[7] The *telos* of the metabolism of living organisms (open systems) can be said to be *not* a rise in entropy but homeostasis, or equilibrium; "open systems can maintain themselves in a state of high statistical improbability, of order and organization";[8]

that is to say, living things tend toward a steady state of energy. Yet the Second Law is not contradicted by the existence of apparently homeostatic open systems such as man. Even if living organisms do maintain an equilibrium within their system, they nevertheless contribute to the rise in entropy of their surroundings. And in any case, all living organisms die. "Therefore the laws of nature are not violated, because the end result of the interaction between a living [i.e., open] system and its environment is still a contribution to rising entropy."[9] Thus, in spite of the seeming generality of the law of rising entropy, this universal trend remains counterpoised by—however short-lived they may be—regions of stable or falling entropy in the form of open systems such as living organisms, along with certain of their groupings or their products.[10] And as the physicist Arthur Eddington observes usefully: "entropy, as it is treated today, is 'an appreciation of arrangement and oganization' and therefore deserves to be placed 'alongside beauty and melody'."[11]

If we turn now to theories of tragedy, the applicability of the concept of entropy becomes readily apparent.[12] For example, G. Brereton defines "the archetypal tragic situation" as "that of the individual or the community going down a slope which leads to destruction" (p. 267). Clearly, Brereton's metaphorical slope intersects with the rising entropy of Boltzmann's equation. Without specific reference to sudden entropy rise, Brereton also observes that "the death of a great man in an air-crash qualifies for tragedy unequivocally; if he is killed in a sports-car, the tragic quality becomes more dubious; if by falling off a bicycle, the whole conception is endangered" (p. 18), and Brereton goes on —when speaking of the "tragic flaw"—to refer to

> a different notion, for which there is no exact word. . . . A society—or, for that matter, a species—dies out on account of some defect which prevents it from adapting itself to changed conditions. A hereditary flaw or a defect of character (the commonest instances in tragedy) leads an individual to disaster. (pp. 40-41)

The intent of the present essay is to associate this defect or flaw observed to be central to tragedy with the concept of entropy as known to science and mathematics—in short, to furnish the lacking "exact word" referred to by Brereton in the quotation above. Max Scheler is even more metaphorical, but no less in accord with his fellow critics. "The tragic," Scheler suggests, is "an essential element in the universe itself. The material appropriated by artistic presentation and the tragic poet must contain the dark ore of this element."[13] One more quotation should suffice to illustrate my point:

> Tragic drama tells us that the spheres of reason, order, and justice are terribly limited and that no progress in our science or technical resources will enlarge their relevance. Outside and within man is *l'autre*, the "otherness" of the world. Call it what you will [*and I propose to call it rising entropy*—G.K.]: a hidden or malevolent God, blind fate, the solicitations of hell, or brute fury of our animal blood. . . . It mocks and destroys us. (Steiner, pp. 8-9)

II

In the sixth century before Christ, Greek science, radically different in concepts and approach from earlier Egyptian and Babylonian science, suddenly emerged. "It was in Ionia that the first completely rationalistic attempts to describe the nature of the world took place."[14] It was in Athens during the following century that the first completely theatrical attempts to describe the nature of the human condition occurred. Such a sequence was hardly fortuitous.[15] There is little doubt that Athenian tragedians were aware of the philosophical and scientific speculations of the Presocratic philosophers. Indeed Kirk and Raven (p. 212) have remarked on the stylistic similarities between the choral parts of Aeschylus' *Oresteia* and the writings of Heraclitus. But is there any evidence that the Presocratic philosophers of the sixth and fifth centuries dealt with notions akin to entropy? The concepts of *chaos* and *kosmos* are central to Presocratic thought. *Chaos,* a condition of unbound energy, disorder, and randomness is clearly a limit to rising entropy. It is commonly given (as early as in Hesiod's *Theogony* and as late as in Parmenides' "Poem") as the condition preceding creation, as well as (albeit less often) eschatologically cited as the final condition of man and the universe. Anaximander (fl. 547), for example, postulates a necessary return of all things to the "Indefinite" from which they came. And the possibility has been considered that Anaximander envisaged

> an even greater cycle, in which the appearance of this differentiated universe out of the Boundless would itself be periodically balanced by the return of all things, including the elements, back into their original source. This doctrine is ascribed to Anaximander by some doxographers. . . .[16]

Clearly, the view that the world is returning to a primordial chaos is an anticipation of the Second Law of Thermodynamics. *Kosmos,* already used by the Pythagoreans to denote the orderliness of the universe, plainly describes a situation of stable or falling entropy. It is no accident that for Heraclitus, in the early fifth century, *kosmos* "is perhaps best translated as 'organism'."17 In addition, the "philosophic sense of this term [i.e., *kosmos*] is as familiar to Heraclitus and Parmenides as it is to Anaxagoras, Empedocles, and Diogenes" (Kahn, p. 111). Furthermore, Hippocratic texts contemporaneous with the Attic tragedians "employ the word *kosmos* for the universal order, and apply this notion in detail to the structure and function of men's bodies" (Kahn, p. 112). Clearly, then, not only are the concepts of *chaos* and *kosmos* isomorphic with the limit of rising entropy and a condition of falling or stable entropy, respectively, but the application of *kosmos,* "order," to a living organism anticipates the entropic distinction between closed and open systems.

The Presocratic anticipation of the Second Law of Thermodynamics is further evident in Heraclitus' well-known identification of fire (cf. heat energy, rising entropy) as the central process (or ubiquitous presence) of the universe.18 Heraclitus further asserts that the soul of man is composed of fire, a fire related to the world fire and subject to the same laws (Kirk and Raven, p. 205). Finally, Parmenides anticipates application of the concept of entropy to human life in his observation that "Old age rises from the loss of heat."19 Or as an early fifth-century thinker, Alcmaeon of Croton, phrased it: "Men die because they cannot join the beginning to the end" (Hussey, p. 76).

Having established the existence, among the Presocratic thinkers, of concepts much like the thermodynamic application of the idea of entropy, and assuming the already indicated link between such thinkers and the Athenian dramatists, it should suffice, in the interest of brevity and for the broad purposes of the present essay, to discuss two instances of the awareness of thermodynamic entropy in the drama of Aeschylus.

It was Prometheus who gave mankind not only fire, according to Aeschylus, but civilization and history as well. "Hear what troubles there were among men," the chained Titan tells the Chorus,

> how I found them witless and gave them the use of their wits
> and made them masters of their minds. I will tell you this,

not because I would blame men, but to explain the goodwill
of my gift. For men at first had eyes but saw to no purpose;
they had ears but did not hear. Like the shapes of dreams they
dragged through their long lives and handled all things in bewilderment and confusion. They did not know of building
houses with bricks to face the sun; they did not know how to
work in wood. They lived like swarming ants in holes in the
ground, in the sunless caves of the earth. For them, there was
no secure token by which to tell winter nor the flowering spring
nor the summer with its crops; all their doings were indeed
without intelligent calculation until I showed them the rising
of the stars, and the settings, hard to observe. And further I
discovered to them numbering preeminent among subtle devices,
and the combining of letters as a means of remembering all
things, the Muses' mother, skilled in craft.20

But all of these gifts would have been without value, indeed
fraught with peril, had not Prometheus also "caused mortals to
cease foreseeing doom" by having "placed in them blind hopes"
(ll. 250, 252). Indeed Aeschylus' text can be interpreted as an
instance of the tragic poet's cautioning his public about the consequences of culture-heroes bearing gifts; for not only must
Prometheus be spectacularly tortured, but *Prometheus Bound*
ends with Hermes' stern admonition to the chorus:

> Remember then my warning before the act:
> when you are trapped by ruin don't blame fortune.
> Don't say that Zeus has brought you to calamity
> that you could not forsee: do not do this:
> but blame yourselves: now you know what you're doing:
> and with this knowledge neither suddenly
> nor secretly your own want of good sense
> has tangled you in the net of ruin, past
> all hopes of rescue.   (ll. 1071-79)

This statement of the consequences of cultural revolution ending
in man's self-awareness is followed by Prometheus' own tableau
of the necessary end of historical existence—the last word in
the play:

> Now it is words no longer: now in very truth
> the earth is staggered: in its depths the thunder
> bellows resoundingly, the fiery tendrils
> of the lightning flash light up, and whirling clouds
> carry the dust along: all the wind's blasts
> dance in a fury one against the other
> in violent confusion: earth and sea
> are one, confused together: such is the storm
> that comes against me manifestly from Zeus

to work its terrors. O Holy mother mine,
O Sky that circling brings the light to all,
you see me, how I suffer, how unjustly.   (ll. 1080-92)

Yet Aeschylus does not leave his readers entirely without consolation. One of his seven extant tragedies does not end in destruction. *The Eumenides,* the final play of Aeschylus' Orestes-trilogy, has justly been termed "a grand parable of progress," a triumphant vision, and so forth.[21] As we have seen, the concept of bounded system is central to any notion of entropy, and the *Oresteia* can be regarded as transitional between the family (or clan) and the *polis* as the governing conceptual (and thermo-dynamic) bounded system: even if the house of Atreus is fraught with internecine murder, the city of Athens can provide legal (and psychological) absolution; blood-ties and blood feuds beget only mayhem, while the city personified by Athene can render justice and peace. The Eumenides, who ". . . have chosen overthrow/ of houses, where the Battlegod/ grown within strikes near and dear/ down . . ." must necessarily—albeit temporarily —lose their *agon* to Athene, the patron of the *polis* in which "Time/ in his forward flood shall ever grow more dignified/ for the people of this city."[22] Calarco anticipates the temporary nature of this progress by observing that although

> the vision [of *The Eumenides*] is a triumphant one, . . . it con-
> tains distressing overtones reminiscent of *Prometheus Bound.*
> The polis has established its priority over an earlier social unit—
> the family—with a new promise of order, a new cosmos. But
> that cosmos, like the one which preceded it, carries the seeds of
> its own disintegration. (p. 40)

Even if by the end of the fifth century the promise of Athene once more had to yield to the dire prophecy of Aeschylus' Hermes and the vision of Prometheus cited above; even if by the turn of that century the historical ruin of Athens was not only fact as well as being portrayed in Thucydides' account (and in the destruction of Pentheus' Thebes in the *Bacchae* by Euripedes), Aeschylus had nevertheless tempered his tragic vision with hope, however temporary.[23]

Now Lancelot L. Whyte asks: "What is the relation of the two cosmic tendencies; towards mechanical disorder (entropy principle) and towards geometrical order (in crystals, molecules, organisms, etc.)?"[24] Whatever the relation, we can see these opposite "cosmic tendencies" reflected in tragedy and comedy, in plays ending in destruction or in increasing order; that is to say, in dramas of rising and falling entropy respectively. Furthermore, classical tragedy will demonstrate, will "reënact" the inevitability of eventual disorder and destruction while itself being supremely ordered and *repeatable,* just as what has been termed "The Theatre of the Absurd" (see below) will *communicate* the supreme difficulty of communication in a most economical and persuasive manner. Both types of theatre gain aesthetic resonance from their apparent ambivalence—but actual economy—of purpose and method. Meanwhile, comedy, whether the happy ending—falling entropy—is a product of the town or of the nuclear family conceived of as system (Cf. the marriage typically celebrated at comedy's end), will counterpoise the relentless doom of tragedy with the very "blind hopes" proffered by Prometheus, which are realizable for an indeterminate but nevertheless limited time by organic and inorganic structures. What could be a better portrayal of "order," after all, than the discovery by token, the dramatic demonstration that your old scar or locket, my birthmark or ring is not an accidental possession at all, but an identity card, a passport to lasting happiness!

The ambivalent figure of Dionysus, patron of Athenian drama, offers confirmation of the inverse relationship of comedy to tragedy suggested above. In so far as Dionysus is a god of vegetation and fertility he is living testimony to the power of living, growing, multiplying things to hold off rising entropy; but in so far as Dionysus is capable of wreaking destruction, in so far as he (or his sacrificial substitute) must die with winter, Dionysus is the enforcer of the tragic in the human condition. The unity of Greek thought and art in this respect is shown in the fact that even before the rise of Attic drama Heraclitus had recognized that ". . . Hades and Dionysus . . . are the same" (Kirk and Raven, p. 211).25

Whether or not Marshall McLuhan is correct in asserting that alphabetic literacy in Greece during the time of Plato brought about a destruction of "tribal awareness," we can keep in mind the importance of "system"—whether defined as the clan or the city, the individual or the species—for the determination of entropy and note that the great periods of tragedy after the Greek occurred in ages where the monarch and royal family held sway over the minds and bodies of men, on the stages of Shakespeare, Racine, and their contemporaries.

III

There is general agreement that Shakespearean tragedy had something quintessential in common with Greek tragedy. The plays of Racine are also linked—in the opinion of most critics— by the spirit of true tragedy with the above two. Thus, if tragedy in fact is dead, the cause for its demise must be sought somewhere during the last three centuries. And George Steiner is certainly correct in asserting that

> It is the triumph of rationalism and secular metaphysics which marks the point of no return. Shakespeare is closer to Sophocles than he is to Pope and Voltaire. . . . The modes of the imagination implicit in Athenian tragedy continued to shape the life of the mind until the age of Descartes and Newton. It is only then that the ancient habits of feeling and the classic orderings of material and psychological experience were abandoned. With the *Discours de la méthode* and the *Principia* the things undreamt of in Horatio's philosophy seem to pass from the world. (Steiner, p. 193)

Indeed the central feature of the "natural philosophy" of Descartes, Kepler, and Newton lies in its emphasis on the mechanical rather than the thermal aspects of nature. For these natural philosophers, in other words, animals are machines; the heavens are a mechanism; man is comparable to a clock-works. Rising entropy is no longer inevitable and inevitably fatal; rather, heat loss is irrelevant in view of the apparent *reversibility* of a mechanical universe. The resultant rationalism, philosophical optimism, and belief in progress are well known. Less well-known is the fact that belief in progress, faith in the possibility of new beginnings, is linked to the view of the world as a mechanism that can as well operate in reverse. Human perfectability had found its analogue, by the end of the seventeenth century, in the ideal of the *perpetuum mobile*; and any age fascinated by the latter can not also create tragedy. There is simply nothing dramatic about a machine that runs forever.

The rise of modern science spelled the decline of tragedy, the dissipation of what might be termed the tragic sense of life, in the face of the attractive, honorable, even splendid enterprise of unlocking the secrets of nature and turning the world into an Eden that would endure forever and in which no one need really die, and from which only entropy would be banished. "Eddington called entropy 'the arrow of time' . . . . it is the irreversibility of physical events, expressed by the entropy function, which gives

time its direction" (von Bertalanffy, p. 151). Even in the nineteenth century, when entropy was being rediscovered, this time
from a quantified thermodynamic rather than a cosmic or anthro-
pomorphic perspective,[26] we can see in the literature of the
period attempts to reverse entropy, to turn back the "arrow of
time." Consider, for example, the saliency of such otherwise
apparently diverse nineteenth-century literary subject matter as
Mary Shelley's Frankenstein, the ubiquitous literary utopia,
various vampirisms, and the prolific literary double—all of
which have in common the turning back of rising entropy, the
challenging of the inevitability of death for the individual or of
dissolution for the society, by means of science, or geographic
remove, or magic, or the interchangeability of human beings,
respectively. What is more, it can hardly be regarded as coincidental that the final project of Goethe's Faust is the reclamation
of low-lying land and the damming of the sea, resulting in an
increase in order and a decrease in the entropy of the region.[27]
It is hardly an accident, either, that the soul of Faust is redeemed
by a mystical, eternal principle. As George Steiner phrases it:

> "Near-tragedy" is precisely the compromise of an age which
> did not believe in the finality of evil. It represents the desire
> of the romantics to enjoy the privileges of grandeur and in-
> tense feeling associated with tragic drama without paying the
> full price.[28]

In connection with the nineteenth century it should also be
pointed out that alongside the re-emergence of entropy as a
theoretical and mathematical concept, the striving of organisms
toward greater complexity (as perceived from the perspective
of evolutionary theories) served to maintain optimism, to turn
aside for a moment the "arrow of time," to blur the harsh finality
of rising entropy. Indeed what have been termed the key intellectual currents of the first half of the twentieth century, Darwinism and Marxism, both can be seen to have their roots—will
they or nill they—in this nineteenth-century tendency to frustrate time and promise a means to allay the terrible awareness
of entropy inevitably rising. As a result, we see that Darwinism
and Marxism have in common with Christianity and nineteenth-
century bourgeois mentality an essentially anti-tragic orientation.
     If in the hundred years after the publication of Thomson's
important article in 1849, tragedy did not particularly distinguish itself, the notion of entropy during this period nevertheless

was finding new applications in diverse realms.29 Statistical mechanics adopted the concept of entropy (and defined it by an equation almost identical to Boltzmann's) as a measure of order, or probability. An increase of entropy was regarded as a decrease in order, a decrease in our knowledge, or an increase of randomness. Exactly a century after the publication of Kelvin's paper, in their groundbreaking and seminal book on information theory, Shannon and Weaver based the concept of information on a definition expressed in a way formally identical to that of the negative entropy of thermodynamics.30 The entropy of communication theory increases as the number of messages among which the sources may choose increases; it also increases as the freedom of choice (or the uncertainty of the recipient) increases. The entropy of communication decreases as the freedom of choice and uncertainty are restricted.31

Now not only are the mathematical expressions for rising entropy isomorphic in thermodynamics, statistical mechanics, and communication theory, but, subjectively speaking, among many observers in the West, awareness of increasing "freedom and uncertainty" had replaced awareness of "degradation of energy" as a suitable subject for tragedy. In other words (and from a different perspective), classical tragedy has been *justly* supplanted by the Theatre of the Absurd.

IV

Wylie Sypher convincingly argues that

> there is some reciprocity between what scientists are thinking and what artists are doing. . . . artists often are working along with scientists, in the same direction, even if they may not know they are doing so; and they are likely to be as sensitive as scientists to what is really contemporary. (pp. 4-5)

Yet why should there be a link between—on the one hand—modern drama, or "Metatheatre" or "The Theatre of the Absurd" or "The Death of Tragedy," and—on the other hand—changing applications of the concept of entropy from Presocratic thought to the rise of modern science, and on through nineteenth-century thermodynamics and contemporary information theory? The answer is far from obvious and what follows might be construed merely as a structuring, an attempt at decreasing uncertainty, an effort directed against rising entropy. Yet if I am right, there will be a certain advantage in regarding classical tragedy as a re-enactment of the "heat-death" of individuals, families, and cities, and seeing absurdist dramas as mimicking the "communications death" of modern man; both modes portray the inevitability of their respective rising entropies, but both, through the ritual of mimesis, tacitly deplore and, to a certain extent, neutralize this rise. In a world of irretrievable heat-loss, we are all doomed; yet if we can articulate—in tragedy—our doom in a *repeatable* process (i.e., in the dramatic performance), we have blunted the arrow of time, taken a token step toward salvation. Similarly, we cannot avoid uncertainty and confusion, yet if it proves possible to *communicate* the near-impossibility of communication via drama—in the theater of the absurd—then the Eumenides have, once more, been cheated of their impending victory.32

At the date of this writing, absurdist dramas number in the hundreds, and the secondary literature on modern drama is, of course, prodigious. Nevertheless, there is general agreement that the plays of Samuel Beckett and Eugène Ionesco are seminal to—and representative of—absurdist drama. Thus, a glance at *Waiting for Godot* and *The Bald Soprano* should serve to illustrate the connection between the entropy of communication theory and the theater of the absurd, and, by extension, demonstrate the advantage of the concept of entropy in revealing the essential unity of Western theater from Aeschylus to Ionesco. For just as Attic drama proclaimed the tragedy of rising entropy in a thermal or vital sense, the plays of Beckett and Ionesco proclaim impossibility of communication, the tragedy of entropy rising to frustrate human understanding. That both *Waiting for Godot* and *The Bald Soprano* are about the impossibility of communication is generally accepted by critics.33 Indeed, "When Alan Schneider, who was to direct the first American production of *Waiting for Godot,* asked Beckett who or what was meant by Godot, he received the answer, 'if I knew, I would have said so in the play'."34 Drama is the most mimetic of genres. It can truly show—as well as tell—how our solitary and mute destruction is certain in spite of our most ingenious efforts to communicate or sidestep death, and how it is useless to ask the universe "Why?" And by showing rather than telling, drama does not contradict its premises. Like the universe itself, the theater of the absurd has no encodable (or decodable) message. And the insight into the impossibility of communication (or the absence of meaning) allows the theater of the absurd only one ontological option, the same as the one enjoyed by reality—*to be.*

Thus even though the rise of science and a belief in progress led to the triumph of a technological rationalism by our century, the tragic sense simply responded by assuming a new form: tragedy remained subversive and cautionary, but modern tragic poets stressed the difficulty of communication rather than the unavailability of immortality. And just as the sudden rise in entropy embodied in the tragic downfall of a hero or town "purged" the audience, so the rapidly rising entropy evident during an absurdist play serves as a *catharsis* for the public, if not for everyone involved in the theatrical enterprise.[35]

Martin Esslin gives a fascinating account of how, in 1948, Ionesco became a playwright almost in spite of himself (pp. 109-15). Significantly, Ionesco, having penned *The Bald Soprano,* believed himself to have written a very serious piece— "the tragedy of language," as the author put it.[36] And appropriately, *La Cantatrice chauve* had almost no audience for many performances during its first run. Just as appropriate was Ionesco's avowed aim for his drama: "to put everything to paroxysm, to the point where the sources of the tragic lie" (Esslin, p. 113). Ionesco's second play, *The Lesson* (1950), is concerned, like *The Bald Soprano,* with language and the impossibility of communication. Indeed, as Esslin and other critics convincingly demonstrate, the problematic nature of communication is the central and uniting theme of what has come to be known as the theater of the absurd.[37] The fact that such a trend is not confined to French and English playwrights is well illustrated by a recent Czech absurdist play, *The Memorandum* (1965), by Vaclav Havel.[38] In fact, at one point Havel uses the term "entropy" in the communication-theory sense, while defining redundancy in communication.[39]

The universe is a message, but a badly garbled one. Post-Einsteinian science will seek patterns or structures in this message, or decode it in terms of whatever theory happens to be available and appears congenial. Dramatists of the absurd will recreate the lack of clear message, stage the apparent absence of meaning, dramatize the steady increase of disorder and confusion, mimic the failure of the universe (or message) to communicate a god, a nation, a family, progress, hope. Classical tragedy's faith in *logos* is not shared by the modern tragedians,

nor can absurdist drama concern itself with the inevitability of
death and destruction; yet even without coherent content, the
medium remains, in our age, to transmit the only thing it *knows:*
a badly garbled message.

V

There are a number of interesting considerations stemming
from the view of the drama in terms of the concept of entropy
that might be advanced. First, there is the well-known transition
from verse to prose between classical tragedy and modern drama.
Because of the restrictions (meter, often rhyme, also diction)
inherent to verse (cf. German *gebundene Rede*), the entropy of
a message in verse is lower than that of the "same" message in
prose; poetry is more ordered, prose less structured. Thus it is
entirely suitable that classical tragedy, dealing with "heat-death,"
should frame its presentation in the structured mode of verse,
while tragedy showing the death of meaning should employ only
prose. Walter Kaufmann comments on playwrights who

> rarely risk a sequence of a few lines that might haunt our
> memory. They are afraid of ridicule and seek security in large
> numbers of small words. More and more writers serve notice
> that no words can bear the burden of their offering. . . . After
> the retreat from poetry comes the retreat from prose, and finally
> the retreat into darkness. (p. 353)

(George Steiner [pp. 241ff] offers an analysis of the shift to
prose that differs from that of the present essay. Steiner's observations, however, on the relationship of money to prose in
tragedy [pp. 263ff] are entirely compatible with my hypothesis. Money appears in literature, treated realistically, at the end
of the seventeenth century—at about the time when the tragic
sense is thought to disappear. It is as though for a couple of centuries since that time men thought it possible to fend off rising
entropy with banknotes or precious metals. Absurdist drama, on
the other hand, is concerned with money only to demonstrate the
silliness of the proposition: "money talks.")

In view of the inappropriateness of verse to "tragedies of
communication," it is of course no accident that the twentieth-
century verse dramas of the "conservative" poet T. S. Eliot have
not had much impact on modern drama. Nevertheless, Eliot was
among the first modern dramatists to realize that "the poetic
pattern and the dramatic pattern must subsist together as integral
products of one act of imagination."[40]

Eliot's rejection of the prosaic in drama and his attempts at modern classical tragedy are but one instance of the sustained, albeit heretofore veiled, link between the history of drama and the various notions of entropy. The problem of communication was well-known to Greek tragedians just as modern dramatists are of course aware of the spirit of classical tragedy. Thus it is interesting to note that Presocratic philosophy was not beyond mistrusting communication. Parmenides' "Doxa" already speaks of "the deceptive *kosmos* of words."41 Aeschylus' Cassandra is already in the quintessentially absurdist situation of knowing what she knows but not being understood at all when she attempts, frantically, to communicate it to the Chorus of the elders of Argos. Furthermore, the oracle of Apollo at Delphi is traditionally obscure with respect to the meaning of its pronouncements. Examples of absurdist awareness in Attic tragedy could readily be multiplied. Similarly, it is gratifying to note, in Beckett's *Waiting for Godot,* the bare single tree of the first act making its compulsory obeisance to the vegetation *daimon* (and to the falling entropy characteristic of living organisms) by the simple expedient of sprouting four or five leaves for the second act. Pozzo may have gone blind and Lucky been struck dumb between the acts, but Dionysus still presides! Beckett's aging Krapp strives to fight both variants of entropy with the aid of his tape recorder in *Krapp's Last Tape.* And Havel's *Memorandum,* in spite of being an absurdist (as well as socio-political) drama, cannot entirely escape the ethos of Sophocles' *Oedipus Rex*: "Why can't I be a little boy again?" asks Gross, the protagonist of Havel's piece, and continues: "I'd do everything differently from the beginning." His antagonist's reply is devastating for all concerned: "You might begin differently, but you'd end up exactly the same—so relax!" (p. 80).

VI

The concept of entropy is also readily applicable to other literary genres as well as to the other arts. For example, if we consider the Homeric poems as precursors of Attic tragedy, the fate of Achilles can be regarded as a statement of the sensed problem: whether Achilles' life is long and undistinguished or short and glorious, the choice is of little importance; we last see Achilles in the land of the dead, longing to be alive, even if as an undernourished farmhand.42

In the realm of the plastic arts, the ambiguity with respect to picture plane, light source, depth, etc., evident in cubism can likewise be interpreted as a pictorial statement of the problematic nature of visual communication. One critic, Rudolf Arnheim, is of the opinion that modern art reveals ". . . an almost desperate need to wrest order from a chaotic environment, even at the most elementary level; and the frank exhibition of bankruptcy and sterility wrought by that same environment" (p. 55). The current disorganization of the plastic arts surely reflects the uncertainty of artists and their public and critics.

As a final example, this time from the realm of psychedelic drugs and choral music, consider Aldous Huxley's impressions, while under the influence of mescaline, of the madrigals of Gesualdo. Huxley remarks on the "psychological disintegration" of the music, and goes on to say:

> and yet it does not matter that he's [i.e., Gesualdo is] all in bits. The whole is disorganized. But each individual fragment is in order, is a representative of a Higher Order. The Highest Order prevails even in the disintegration. The totality is present even in the broken pieces. More clearly present, perhaps, than in a completely controlled work. At least you aren't lulled into a sense of false security by some merely human, merely fabricated order. You have to rely on your immediate perception of the ultimate order. So in a certain sense disintegration may have its advantages. But of course it's dangerous, horribly dangerous. Suppose you couldn't get back out of the chaos. . . .[43]

Thus not only tragedy but all of the arts are grasped in the vision that we have pursued chiefly from the point of view of drama, which, as a form, is able to focus this vision best because it is, sometimes in spite of itself, the art most imitative of life. And if we were to move beyond the arts to consider two apparently disparate schools of thought, Christianity and Marxism, rivals for modern man's allegiance, we would, still aided by the unifying concept of entropy, be able to perceive a common denominator. "The anabolic tendency . . . makes its symbolic entrance in the Book of Genesis when the creator separates the waters from the dry land. Thermodynamics refers to it as negative entropy."[44] In fact, Christian myth can be interpreted in terms of entropy, from creation out of chaos to an entropy-free Eden, to the Fall as the start of rising entropy, to the negnetropic, anabolistic miracles of Christ turning water into wine and stone into bread, to the Second Coming, where the sheep are to be transported beyond entropy to paradise while the goats are condemned to a spectacular (and, paradoxically, eternal) entropy rise in the flames of Hell.

While Christianity offered salvation to some, Marxism would force it upon us all, and just as the possibility of Christian tragedy is problematic, "Marx repudiated the entire concept of tragedy."[45]

> The Marxist world view, even more explicitly than the Christian, admits of error, anguish, and temporary defeat, but not of ultimate tragedy. Despair is a mortal sin against Marxism no less than against Christ. Lunacharsky, the first Soviet commissar of education, proclaimed that one of the defining qualities of a communist society would be the absence of tragic drama. Convinced that the powers of reason can master the natural world and give to human life a complete dignity and purpose, a communist can no longer recognize the meaning of tragedy. . . . The tragic theatre . . . is founded on the assumption that there are in nature . . . uncontrollable forces able to madden or destroy the mind. The Marxist knows . . . that there is no such thing as . . . the blind necessity which overwhelms Oedipus.[46]

The optimism inherent in Marxism precludes tragedy. Marxist aesthetics (along with Marxist history) is tailored to deny the consequences of rising entropy; Marxism can be seen as an ingenious—and at its best, a noble—attempt to expand the open system capable of indefinite homeostasis beyond the individual organism through the chosen social class into the classless society in order to avoid the grim consequences of historical existence. (Unfortunately, in practice the open system with falling entropy in the Communist world turns out, of course, to be the Party and its elite members.)[47]

However well and good all of the above may be, it is important also to keep in mind that the concept of entropy, both in thermodynamics and in communication theory, is a mathematical function, an intellectual construct. To impose such a construct upon a universe as wide as that constituted by drama from Aeschylus to Ionesco would appear to be sheer folly, were it not for the fact that, as system theory recognizes in theory, and as interdisciplinary study confirms in practice:

> The number of simple mathematical expressions which will be preferably applied to describe natural phenomena is limited. For this reason, laws identical in structure will appear in intrinsically different fields. The same applies to statements in

ordinary language; here, too, the number of intellectual schemes
is restricted, and they will be applied in quite different realms.
(von Bertalanffy, p. 82)

Furthermore, if we regard dramatic art as itself a system, or as a
group of systems; if we take literally the drama's status as imitating life, there is no reason why the stage should not be per-
ceivable in term of the same categories as nature.[48] And finally,
just as open systems in the form of living organisms manage to keep rising entropy at bay for a longer or shorter
period, so theoretical systems such as the present one, and
including all types of structuring and hierarchization of the
perceived world, generate negentropy—the condition necessary
for communication.

Whether or not ontogeny recapitulates phylogeny, the enterprise of *knowing* does recapitulate ontogeny; that is, man's
desire to discover unity in the environment is a logical consequence of his earlier discovery of the essential unity of the self.
B. G. Walter defines a "pattern" as

> Any sequence of events in time, or any set of objects in space,
> distinguishable from or comparable with another sequence or
> set. The [main] attribute of a pattern is that you can remember
> it and compare it with another pattern. This . . . distinguishes
> it from random events or chaos. For you cannot remember
> chaos or compare one chaos with another; there is no plural of
> the word. Pattern is a quality of familiar things. . . . Man seeks
> patterns . . . and . . . can boast himself a *pattern-making ani-
> mal.* . . . The sciences derive from pattern-seeking, the arts from
> pattern-making.[49]

Should we abandon the search for patterns, for unities, the best
that we, as men, could hope for in this life, with a dying universe
presided over by a dead god, would be a mutual stalemate, an
unlikely *Zugzwang* of sorts (cf. Beckett's *Endgame*) in the game
between man and the perceived world: whoever moves first
loses! That is to say, either the universe must move and betray
its secret, or man must move to betray his ignorance, and resultant despair.

Western Illinois University

NOTES

1 See George Steiner, *The Death of Tragedy* (New York: Knopf, 1961); Martin Esslin, *The Theatre of the Absurd* (New York: Doubleday, 1961); and Lionel
Abel, *Metatheatre: A New View of Dramatic Form* (New York: Hill & Wang, 1963).

The Retrospective Technique and Its Implications for Tragedy

Charles A. Hallett

"Mystery is a great embarrassment to the modern mind."
—Flannery O'Connor

Structural elements can play a determining role not only in the way a work of art renders experience but also in what experiences are rendered. This is as true in drama as it is in poetry. The specific aim of this paper is to examine the kinds of experience that can be rendered by the retrospective plot. It will be argued first of all, that the retrospective plot implies a rational universe, one in which the past possesses and under pressure will yield answers to problems of the present and, second, that this radical assumption of the retrospective plot (i.e., that the human condition, with all its attendant problems, is at least potentially comprehendible by the mind of man) makes it imperative that the playwright choosing the retrospective plot as the form for a tragedy separate himself from its assumptions. The separation is essential, for a rational universe becomes a tragic one only when its rationality is seen to be an illusion.

Because such distancing rarely occurs between the contemporary playwright and the rational world of his drama, the retrospective plot, with its denial of mystery, is partially responsible for the failure of today's serious drama to achieve tragic stature. Many scholars and critics have speculated on the causes for the nearly universal inability of the modern realistic theater to produce tragedy and, while some of their findings are both provocative and insightful, they have largely overlooked the implications arising from the fact that playwrights time and again choose the same plot technique.[1] This seemingly arbitrary choice of form reflects a certain cast of mind, a cast of mind which both marks these men as modernists and reveals a temperament unsuited to a tragic vision, and it is thus a determining factor in the success or failure of the playwright to render the experience of tragedy.

These are strong assertions. Can they be supported? Let us look more closely at the nature and implications of retrospective plotting.

Essentially there are only two methods for introducing into a play material which is outside the time span of the plot but necessary to our understanding of that plot. The first is generally regarded as the less sophisticated method of handling this problem. In it the exposition is hardly disguised as such and is served up unabashedly in huge hunks in the opening scenes, to be digested by the audience almost before they are comfortably settled in their seats. This is the only method of exposition practiced by the Elizabethan-Jacobean dramatists, and perhaps one of the most familiar examples of the type is provided by the Chorus in Shakespeare's *Henry V,* where, because of the violent time and place shifts between the acts, fresh exposition is required at each act division:

> Now we bear the King
> Toward Callice; grant him there; there seen,
> Heave him away upon your winged thoughts
> Athwart the sea. Behold, the English beach
> Pales in the flood with men, wives, and boys,
> Whose shouts and claps out-voice the deep-mouth'd sea,
> Which like a mighty whiffler 'fore the King
> Seems to prepare his way. So let him land,
> And solemnly see him set on to London.
>
> (V.i.6-14)

The exposition is presented, and the action, which unfolds in the *future,* takes up from that point.

The second kind of exposition, that which came strongly to the fore with Ibsen and the other practitioners of modern realistic drama, is known as retrospective exposition. In the retrospective technique there is no single scene of exposition; rather, the exposition is woven through the fabric of the entire play. In such plays exposition is not something to feed the audience as quickly and dexterously as possible; it is the very meat of the play.

Ibsen's own *Ghosts* is perhaps one of the best known and purest examples of this form. The play opens the day before the dedication of the orphanage Mrs. Alving has built to the

2 See *Tragedy and Philosophy* (New York: Doubleday, 1968).

3 *Principles of Tragedy* (London: Routledge & Kegan Paul, 1968), p. 213. In the same decade, R. J. Kaufmann discussed the career of tragedy in western dramatic literature, maintaining—contrary to the above-mentioned critics—that the late nineteenth and early twentieth centuries did in fact create tragedy comparable to fifth-century Athens and seventeenth-century England (see Kaufmann's "Tragedy and Its Validating Conditions," *Comparative Drama*, 1 [1967], 3-18).

4 See R. Clausius, "Über die bewegende Kraft der Wärme und die Gesetze welche sich daraus für die Wärmelehre selbst ableitan lassen," *Ann. Phys.*, 73 (1850), and "Über verschiedene für die Anwendung bequeme Formen der Hauptgleichungen der mechanischen Wärmetheorie," *Ann. Phys.*, 125 (1865), by the same author. Also S. Carnot, *Reflexions sur la puissance motrice du feu et sur les machines propres à dévéloper cette puissance* (Paris, 1824). In his article of 1865 Clausius devised the term *Entropie* as a designation for the "transformation-contents" (*Verwandlungsinhalt*) of a system. By 1875 the term was employed by Maxwell in English, according to the *Oxford English Dictionary*.

5 See Boltzmann's "Weitere Studien über Wärmegleichgewicht unter Gasmolekülen," *Wien. Ber.*, 66 (1872), 275.

6 *Loss of the Self* (New York: Random House, 1962), pp. 73-74.

7 The thermodynamics of open systems is an object of fairly recent study and lies beyond the present author's scope. For further reading see I. Prigogine, *Etude thermodynamique des phénomènes irreversibles* (Paris: Dunod, 1947), J. R. Meixner and H. G. Reik, "Thermodynamik der irreversiblen Prozesse," *Handbuch der Physik*, Bd. III/2, ed. S. Flügge (Berlin: Springer Verlag, 1959), pp. 413-523, and Ludwig von Bertalanffy, *General System Theory* (New York: Braziller, 1968), p. 39 et passim.

8 Von Bertalanffy, p. 143.

9 Walter Rand, "Diversiteedist looduses ja ühiskonnas" (On Diversity in Nature and Society), *Mana*, 40 (1974), 27.

10 Such as families, cities, and species, all of which might tend, even over increasingly longer periods of time, toward increased order, organization, and energy—in brief, toward a falling entropy.

11 Cit. Rudolf Arnheim, *Entropy and Art* (Berkeley: Univ. of California Press, 1971), p. 22.

12 Wylie Sypher has written of the sense of entropy as evidenced in modern (chiefly non-dramatic) literature, and Rudolf Arnheim has made a provocative attempt at reconciling the apparently universal *telos* of entropy rise with the striving for order evident in art, organisms, and evolution (without, however, saying anything specific about the relationship of the concept of entropy to tragedy). In a few paragraphs on the entropy of literary texts, P. T. Landsberg, in *Entropy and the Unity of Knowledge* (Cardiff: Univ. of Wales Press, 1964), has confined himself to counting the number of syllables in Shakespeare's *Othello* (pp. 18-19); see also W. Fucks, "Mathematical Theory of Word Formation," in *Information Theory, Third London Symposium* (London: Butterworth, 1956), p. 154 and D. A. Bell and A. S. C. Ross, "Negative Entropy of Welsh Words," ibid., p. 149—cit. Landsberg, p. 27.

13 "Zum Phänomen des Tragischen," in *Abhandlungen und Aufzätze* (1915), p. 1. Again, Scheler's "element" can be associated with rising entropy.

14 G. S. Kirk and J. E. Raven, *The Presocratic Philosophers* (Cambridge: Cambridge Univ. Press, 1960), p. 73.

15 The rise of historiography in Athens in the fifth century is also pertinent to much of the argument that follows.

16 Charles H. Kahn, *Anaximander and the Origins of Greek Cosmology* (New York: Columbia University Press, 1960), cit in *The Pre-Socratics*, ed. Alexander P. D. Mourelatos, (New York: Anchor/Doubleday, 1974), p. 107. Kahn, in a footnote on Anaximander, continues: "The destruction of the world (or worlds) appears in DK A10, A14, A17." See also Kirk and Raven, p. 118.

17 G. S. Kirk, "Natural Change in Heraclitus," *Mind,* 60 (1951), cit. in *The Pre-Socratics,* ed. Mourelatos, p. 192.

18 See Edward Hussey, *The Presocratics* (London: Duckworth, 1972), p. 48.

19 Kahn, p. 106 n. 17. Cf. also "a man is hottest on the first of his days, coldest on the last" (Hippocrates, *Nat. Hom.*, 12, Loeb Classical Library, IV, 36).

20 Aeschylus, *Prometheus Bound,* trans. David Grene in *Aeschylus II* (New York: Washington Square, 1967), ll. 441-62.

21 See Richmond Lattimore, *Aeschylus I* (New York, Washington Square, 1967), p. 35 and N. Joseph Calarco, *Tragic Being* (Minneapolis: Univ. of Minnesota Press, 1968), p. 40. According to Walter Kaufmann (p. 176), "In *The Eumenides . . .* we encounter in absolutely climactic form that rationalism and optimism of which tragedy are said to have died—and find them at the culmination of the greatest work of the so-called creator of tragedy." It should be noted that Kaufmann's obvious disagreement here with ˙Steiner's *Death of Tragedy* can readily be resolved in terms of the theory advanced in the present essay.

22 Aeschylus, *The Eumenides,* trans. Richmond Lattimore, ll. 366-69 and 852-54.

23 See also Calarco, p. 80. The hope referred to of course resides in the possibility of the individual's becoming part of a larger negentropic system, such as the city-state.

24 "Atomism, Structure, and Form," in *Structure in Art and Science,* ed. Gyorgy Kepes (New York: Braziller, 1965), pp. 20-28.

25 In connection with these speculations and what follows, the reader might also consider Northrop Frye's prodigious *Anatomy of Criticism* for a different analysis.

26 These earlier perspectives were of course the province of Presocratic science discussed above. It is of further interest to see the anti-humanistic application of this discovery in nineteenth-century conceptions of the human organism "as a *heat engine,* a notion which led to caloric calculations and other things" (von Bertalanffy, p. 140).

27 Contrast Faust's project with Prometheus' apocalyptic vision cited above: ". . . earth and sea/ are one, confused together . . ." (also Goethe's play on *Graben* "trench" and *Grab* "grave" in Mephistopheles' speech).

28 P. 133. Indeed Steiner's book makes repeated use of terms such as "disorder," "energy," "confusion," and the like. Many of Steiner's seminal ideas can be more parsimoniously arranged under the hypothesis of the present essay.

29 Thomson's (later Lord Kelvin's) article is entitled, "An Account of Carnot's Theory of the Motive Power of Heat," *Trans. R. S. Ed.,* 16 (1849).

30 See C. S. Shannon and W. Weaver, *The Mathematical Theory of Communication* (Champaign: Univ. of Illinois Press, 1949). Doede Nauta, Jr., however, claims that "the physicist Szilard was the first one to recognize that a MAXWELL-DEMON is an idealized construction or thought model which relates (physical) entropy to information. . . . In fact Szilard (1929) NOT SHANNON, was the first one who applied Boltzmann's S-formula to AMOUNT OF INFORMATION" (*The Meaning of Information,* vol. 20 of Approaches to Semiotics, ed. Thomas A. Sebeok [The Hague: Mouton, 1972], p. 188).

31 I am indebted to the books by von Bertalanffy and Nauta for portions of the above discussion.

32 It can be pointed out that the above view is reconcilable with Brereton's notion of tragedy as an "insurance premium" paid by society (see p. 73), as well as with the more radical view of the stage as an altar on which actors are ritually sacrificed in order to ward off what is most feared. (Mardi Valgemae's discussion—soon to appear in book form—of how and why *opsis* has supplanted *lexis* in the modern theatre is also clearly relevant here.)

33 See e.g., Seiner, p. 350 or Esslin, p. 63 et passim.

34 Esslin, p. 24. Some of these ideas on the impossibility of communication are already evident in Beckett's early (1931) monograph on Proust.

35 An analysis of absurdist drama via communication theory should prove interesting. One possible paradigm would distinguish between the dramatist, audience, and stage with actors, thereby allowing three channels of communication while also recognizing three additional "monologue" channels. A second, less structured analysis, in the spirit of the so-called "happening," could include casual passers-by, mounted police, newspaper reporters, and the like.

36 In "The Tragedy of Language: How an English Primer Became my First Play," *The Tulane Drama Review,* 4, No. 3 (1960), 10-13.

37 Cf., e.g., Esslin's discussion of the early plays of A. Adamov or his remarks on R. Pinget's *Lettre Morte.* John Russell Brown, in an article on the drama of Harold Pinter, also cites the term "Theatre of Non-Communication" as an alternative to "The Theatre of the Absurd" (see *Essays in the Modern Drama,* ed. Morris Freedman [Boston: Heath, 1964], p. 352).

38 Trans. Vera Blackwell (New York: Grove Press, 1967). Havel satirizes bureaucracy and totalitarianism as well as addressing himself to the problems of communication and the dehumanization of language.

39 P. 16. "Entropy" is also the title—and relevant to the content—of a story by Thomas Pynchon; see *The Kenyon Review* (1960), 300-13. (I am indebted to Charles R. Smith, M.A., for calling this item to my attention.)

40 F. O. Matthiessen, "The Plays of T. S. Eliot," in *Essays in the Modern Drama,* p. 264. Interestingly enough, Steiner characterizes modern verse tragedies as "attempts to blow fire into cold ash" (p. 305).

41 Alexander P. D. Mourelatos, "The Deceptive Words of Parmenides' 'Doxa'," in *The Pre-Socratics,* ed. Mourelatos, p. 316.

42 As further examples of the applicability of the perspectives advanced in this essay to non-dramatic literature, consider Voltaire's *Candide,* where the various "gardens" can be interpreted as the central metaphor for entropy-free existence (and where the problem of communicating the nature of the world has a central place), or the concepts of *Liebestod* and *Götterdämmerung* as conceived by Richard Wagner.

43 *The Doors of Perception* (New York, Harper & Row, 1970), pp. 50-51. Clearly, only a book-length discussion could begin to do justice to the breadth of the material implicated.

44 Arnheim, p. 31. Cf. also the references to Aeschylus' Prometheus and Goethe's Faust in note 27.

45 Steiner, p. 4. For Christian tragedy, see e.g., Laurence Michel, "The Possibility of a Christian Tragedy," *Thought* (1956); and Reinhold Niebuhr, *Beyond Tragedy: Essays on the Christian Interpretation of History* (New York, 1965).

46 Steiner, pp. 341-42. Compare also Steiner's astute observation that "The

Marxist conception of history is a secular *commedia*" (p. 343) with the remarks on comedy and entropy made earlier in the present essay.

47 Beyond Christianity and Marx, but well within the orbit of the present essay, it might be opportune to ask—in passing—whether the intuitive terminology of thinkers such as McLuhan ("hot" and "cold" media) and Levi-Strauss ("hot" and "cold"—also "thermodynamic"—societies) should eventually be incorporated into the conceptual scheme afforded by definitions of entropy.

48 After all, as Landsberg points out, ". . . *with any probability distribution whatever* one can associate an entropy" (p. 16).

49 *The Living Brain* (New York: Penguin, 1965), p. 68. I wish to thank the Department of English, Western Illinois University, for released time helpful in the preparation of the present essay.

The Retrospective Technique and
Its Implications for Tragedy

Charles A. Hallett

"Mystery is a great embarrassment to the modern mind."
—Flannery O'Connor

Structural elements can play a determining role not only in the way a work of art renders experience but also in what experiences are rendered. This is as true in drama as it is in poetry. The specific aim of this paper is to examine the kinds of experience that can be rendered by the retrospective plot. It will be argued first of all, that the retrospective plot implies a rational universe, one in which the past possesses and under pressure will yield answers to problems of the present and, second, that this radical assumption of the retrospective plot (i.e., that the human condition, with all its attendant problems, is at least potentially comprehendible by the mind of man) makes it imperative that the playwright choosing the retrospective plot as the form for a tragedy separate himself from its assumptions. The separation is essential, for a rational universe becomes a tragic one only when its rationality is seen to be an illusion.

Because such distancing rarely occurs between the contemporary playwright and the rational world of his drama, the retrospective plot, with its denial of mystery, is partially responsible for the failure of today's serious drama to achieve tragic stature. Many scholars and critics have speculated on the causes for the nearly universal inability of the modern realistic theater to produce tragedy and, while some of their findings are both provocative and insightful, they have largely overlooked the implications arising from the fact that playwrights time and again choose the same plot technique.[1] This seemingly arbitrary choice of form reflects a certain cast of mind, a cast of mind which both marks these men as modernists and reveals a tem-

23

perament unsuited to a tragic vision, and it is thus a determining
factor in the success or failure of the playwright to render the
experience of tragedy.

These are strong assertions. Can they be supported? Let us
look more closely at the nature and implications of retrospective
plotting.

Essentially there are only two methods for introducing into
a play material which is outside the time span of the plot but
necessary to our understanding of that plot. The first is generally regarded as the less sophisticated method of handling this
problem. In it the exposition is hardly disguised as such and is
served up unabashedly in huge hunks in the opening scenes, to
be digested by the audience almost before they are comfortably
settled in their seats. This is the only method of exposition
practiced by the Elizabethan-Jacobean dramatists, and perhaps
one of the most familiar examples of the type is provided by
the Chorus in Shakespeare's *Henry V,* where, because of the
violent time and place shifts between the acts, fresh exposition
is required at each act division:

> Now we bear the King
> Toward Callice; grant him there; there seen,
> Heave him away upon your winged thoughts
> Athwart the sea. Behold, the English beach
> Pales in the flood with men, wives, and boys,
> Whose shouts and claps out-voice the deep-mouth'd sea,
> Which like a mighty whiffler 'fore the King
> Seems to prepare his way. So let him land,
> And solemnly see him set on to London.
>   (V.i.6-14)

The exposition is presented, and the action, which unfolds in
the *future,* takes up from that point.

The second kind of exposition, that which came strongly to
the fore with Ibsen and the other practitioners of modern realistic drama, is known as retrospective exposition. In the retrospective technique there is no single scene of exposition; rather,
the exposition is woven through the fabric of the entire play.
In such plays exposition is not something to feed the audience
as quickly and dexterously as possible; it is the very meat of
the play.

Ibsen's own *Ghosts* is perhaps one of the best known and
purest examples of this form. The play opens the day before the
dedication of the orphanage Mrs. Alving has built to the

memory of her husband. Her son, Oswald, who has not been home for years, has returned for the celebration. Everything at the opening of the play points toward a reverence for the past, a past which will be celebrated in this monument. As the play unfolds, however, we learn that Mrs. Alving has constructed the orphanage not as a tribute to the past but as a way of freeing herself from it. In truth she hated her husband, a drunken profligate, whose reputation she protected so that her son would not be injured by his father's scandalous adventures. Mrs. Alving, too, learns about the past during the course of the play. She learns, among other things, that it was her prudishness that perverted her husband's quest for the joy of life. It eventually comes out that she herself is responsible for the father's profligacy and thus for the fact that his son is dying of congenital syphilis. All of this information, that needed for the learning process of Mrs. Alving as well as that needed by the audience, is worked in through the retrospective technique.

The retrospective exposition provided by Ibsen does not merely give the audience information. It is also the means used by the playwright to render the experience through which Mrs. Alving is living. The significance of that experience is described by Mrs. Alving in the second act when she describes what she has learned about the way the past has shaped her present life:

> I am half inclined to think we are all ghosts, Mr. Manders. It is not only what we have inherited from our fathers and mothers that exists again in us, but all sorts of dead ideas and all kinds of old dead beliefs and things of that kind. They are not actually alive in us; but there they are dormant, all the same, and we can never be rid of them.

By using the retrospective technique in a play which has as its theme the devastating effects of the past on the present, Ibsen merged form and content to a superlative degree.

Much more is at stake, then, in the choice between the two types of exposition than simply how one is going to reveal the incidents of the past. It is not as if the same story could be told equally well either way, thus permitting one author—for reasons best known to himself—to choose the retrospective mode of telling that story while another chooses the Elizabethan plot form to dramatize it. Quite to the contrary, *how* a story is told largely *is* the story. Just as the language of a poem is not alterable without altering the poem, so the structure of a play cannot be changed without affecting the action. And when a playwright discovers the proper structure for his theme, as Ibsen found the ideal plot form for the theme of *Ghosts* in the retrospective plot, the work clicks together with the same finality Yeats saw in the poem that had found its proper language. Plot structures are rich in thematic implications.

The omnipresent implication of the retrospective plot, no matter what the ostensible theme of the individual play, is the unspoken assumption that *the past holds the answer*. The play is begun after the critical moment, and the action of the plot focuses upon the process of discovering that moment and its true significance. Action is no longer straightforward; it jumps from one unit of time to another, even, as in *Death of a Salesman,* from one mode of consciousness to another. With so convoluted a plot, one might be led to expect it to reveal a complicated universe. Not so, however. The logic of the retrospective plot prevents this. The plotting technique implies a world in which every action has a direct reaction. Getting back into the past is a process of studying the causes of given effects, and the world is assumed to proceed rationally. Thus, the universe of the play based on the retrospective plot becomes the monodimensional universe of nineteenth- and twentieth-century naturalism, where causes and effects are laid out like so many billiard balls nudging one another on one flat green surface. Closely examined, the complexity reflects only a dramaturgical ingenuity.

The retrospective plot yielded the realistic playwright two seemingly contradictory elements. First, the "mystery" necessary to his drama if it were to engage the interest of the audience. And second, paradoxically, a method of assuring the audience that there is in fact no such thing as a "mystery." There could not be, because there is no mysterious level to reality. The realm of the mysterious, the doubtful, and the uncertain is, in these dramas, regarded as an illusion. The "mysteries" of the retrospective plot are understood from the start to stem from ignorance and are susceptible to investigation and analysis. Human reason, the power which had conquered the physical world, is regarded as capable—if not of solving the problems of human experience—at least of comprehending them. Mystery dissolves before the searching light of critical intelligence. What seemed mysterious in the past was merely the unknown, not the unknowable.

In this regard, the realistic tragedies of the retrospective type resemble the mystery stories of popular culture. In fact, the archetype of the retrospective plot is the detective story. Though recognizably a species of sub-literature, the detective story has had such success as a popular genre that its widespread acceptance where other formulas have failed must point to some significance. Clearly successful formulas such as the detective story (and, say, the western) endure because they satisfy deeply felt but as yet unformulated needs in the audience. In this sense the popular formula is one of modern man's equivalents for ritual. However, unlike myth and ritual, which gave form and substance to insights into reality and the nature of being and on occasion could be quite chilling and uncompromising, the popular formulas tell modern man what he wants to hear about himself and his world. Unfortunately, contemporary man's willingness to believe in the world created for him in his popular culture is no guarantee that reality is in fact anything like what we find there. In the case of the detective story it seems that people are more than willing to believe in a world order quite at odds with the facts. This is the fascinating thing about the detective story; it so succinctly sums up contemporary man's attitude toward many of the key issues about reality.

I want to mention here only those attitudes found in the detective story which have their corollary in retrospective drama. Consequently, I will not be dealing directly with the attitudes toward crime and punishment found there; rather, in keeping to the intention of this paper, I wish to set forth six traits discoverable in the detective story which tie in directly to the retrospective plot and its implications. In the detective story it is assumed

(1)   that the world is essentially rational and non-mysterious;

(2)   that man's reason is adequate to unravel the problems of that world, all of which are, in all their dimensions, world-immanent.

(3)   that it is the dispassionate observer who, through his powers of investigation and analysis, is most capable of finding solutions to these problems;

(4)   that evil can be separated not only from the hero but from the entire community in the person of the villain;

(5)   that the villain deserves to be treated as he has treated others;

(6)   that with the elimination of the villain, evil is purged from the community and order is restored.

These, then, are the fundamentals from which the world of the detective story is constructed.

That this list of characteristics is drawn from a form of sub-literature and not from the works of any one of a number of nineteenth- or twentieth-century philosophers, sociologists, or men of letters is at first surprising. That the culture of the marketplace should so well reflect what was supposed to be the advanced thinking of the age is disconcerting, until one realizes that though they have been expressed differently by such men as Hegel, Marx, Nietzsche, Weber, Darwin, and Freud, the gnostic myths of progress and the perfectibility of man are (given internal variations which do not alter the essential configuration) the same,2 and that it has been these myths which have served as the foundations for not only much of what has been called advanced thinking but also for the very climate of opinion these advanced thinkers were supposed to be combating.

There was general agreement between the detective, the readers of the detective story, and the philosophers that the world was reasonable and man rational. Kingsley Amis has said of Poe's master detective, "however suspect Dupin's chain of inference may be at any particular link, what we are witnessing overall is a convincing demonstration of the power of the human mind to observe and to reason." These powers of observing and reasoning would be to little avail to Dupin and the other heroes of detective literature if the world created by their authors for them to be dazzlingly brilliant in was not susceptible to that kind of analysis. Obviously the world of detective literature is. The question remains, whether the world of detective literature bears anything more than a superficial resemblance to reality. Interestingly, this analytical attitude of the detective and his author is similar to that advocated for the playwright by Zola in his essay, "Naturalism in the Theatre" (1881). The playwright must be scientific; he must be a compiler of human data, an anatomist of human life. And because man is a social animal, the playwright must not only analyze man, he must also study society scientifically. Drama was no longer to educate through entertainment; it was to become a paradigm of the scientific method. Drama was to dissect life by means of investigation and analysis. And the realistic retrospective tragedies were designed to answer Zola's call for a scientific drama. Again, in the drama as in the detective story, such an approach to the world could only be fruitful if the world created in the drama was a place which would reveal its essence when subjected to scientific scrutiny. And again, just as in the case of the detective literature, we can answer in the affirmative. But the question that remains unanswered is, how well does a world which conforms to the demands of the retrospective plot comport with reality?

This brings us back to the parallels that exist between the detective story and the realistic "tragedy." So far we have pointed out that both use the retrospective plot and are written out of the same climate of opinion. These parallels could have been chance occurrences, explainable by the fact that they are products of the same culture at the same time. But there is another explanation. We spoke earlier of the detective story as a form of modern myth, a fable which tells contemporary man what he wants to hear about himself and his world. It seems probable that the playwrights have sensed in the detective story an archetype through which their own experience, their own vision of the world, could be expressed. Realistic drama is one example of the prevalence of the notion in the modern world that life can be regarded in terms of a detective story. It is fascinating to discover how many erstwhile "detectives" stalk through the drawing rooms of the British or American stage, searching diligently for clues to some domestic, psychological or socioeconomic "mystery."

The retrospective technique in many modern plays unabashedly takes the form of the straight detective plot. *Equus* might be taken as the paradigm of a "tragedy" which is structured around the detective story. The psychiatrist, Martin Dysart, is certainly in the role of the detective. The "mystery" he is to solve is why Alan Strang has blinded six horses. The methods of the psychiatrist lend themselves particularly to drama of this type; Dysart is the detached observer applying the scientific method to analyze life's problems. For him, as for the detective, the proper approach to a problem is to search for clues to the past that will explain the mystery. Dysart uncovers many clues fairly quickly (the mother's emphasis on religion, the substitution of a portrait of a glaring horse for a portrait of

Christ) and other clues later (the boy had been given a stimulating ride across the beach on horseback; had come, through his worship of horses, to confuse horses with Jesus; had made Equus his god). The final clue that permits Dysart to solve the mystery—why Alan blinded the horses—comes when the psychiatrist discovers that guilt feelings had arisen in Alan after the girl Jill had tempted him to sexual intercourse in the sacred precincts of the stable. For Dysart, as detective, the search is over when all the clues lead him to this event. The detective has solved the mystery. The implication is that with this knowledge of the past Dysart can restore Alan to sanity. Though Dysart questions the *value* of normality, there is no doubt that the knowledge he has obtained gives him, the rationalist, the power to remove the "mystery" that had disordered the world.

Most frequently, however, the detective story aspects of the retrospective plot are more subtle, and the protagonist is only latently a detective. We might think of Chris in *All My Sons* or Bernie Dodd in *The Country Girl* as latent detectives. Robert Anderson's *Tea and Sympathy* is typical of this type of play. The truth about the past lies clouded for the protagonist Laura Reynolds. Yet at a critical moment, without ever consciously scouring the past, she puts together the events of the past in such a way that they become clues, clues that alter her understanding, and she has what the author wants us to believe is a tragic illumination. Throughout the play, Laura receives hints about the past that in the end lead her to discover that her husband is a homosexual. Like the detective, she solves a mystery, and having found the source of the disorder in her life, escapes from it.

There are many plays employing the retrospective technique, plays like *Hedda Gabler,* in which the *audience* becomes the detective. In such plays no one of the *dramatis personae* is actively seeking clues to the mystery, yet hints are thrown out by the author to the viewers: the audience itself functions as the sleuth, weighing evidence and making judgments about events in the past. For example, Ibsen presents us with a discontented Hedda Tesman. Because no one on stage is privy to Hedda's secret, we have to piece together, from hints dropped as various characters discuss the past in retrospect, the cause of her discontent. Primarily in those scenes with Thea in which Lovborg is described, we discover not only the past of Hedda and her expectations for the future but her desire to control people. Hedda herself has been no detective; she understands nothing further about the world from the events in which she participates, coming only to the conclusion that life as Judge Brack paints it for her would be intolerable. By the time Hedda decides to commit suicide, however, *we* are adequately prepared to determine the cause, for like the observant Holmes or the persistent Marlowe, we the audience have unraveled the "mystery" of the past that made Hedda what she is.

These three methods of approaching the retrospective plot do not always occur in isolation. Plays which have actual or latent detectives in central roles may, especially where the mode of dramatic irony is strong, also ask the audience to play detective. Conversely, in plays of the objective type, in which the viewer must solve the mystery, it is not uncommon to find, in a subordinate role, a "latent detective" who voices on stage the discovery the audience is presumed to make—witness Biff in *Death of a Salesman* or Zan in *The Little Foxes*.

Whatever the method of presenting the detective and however it is combined with other methods of presentation, the fact remains: in structure, retrospective drama closely resembles the archetypal detective story. In all of these cases there is a "mystery," and a probing into the past to get at the cause of this mystery. The mystery is not so much an unsolved crime as some variation of the question, "why is life in the present unsatisfactory?", and the solution always hinges on the discovery of what it was that went wrong in the past. As a consequence, the action of the play involves a search into the past, whether it is carried out by a detective-like protagonist or not—a search similar to one that might be instituted by Holmes, Dupin, or any of their colleagues. Moreover, as both the modern play and the detective story grow out of the same climate of opinion, the world order we see in each is similar. The assumption most generally is that the world is reasonable and that evil can be ferreted out and order restored. There cannot in the true sense of the word be anything "mysterious" in the world, only temporary ignorance.

Ironically the detective story itself is not, nor was it intended to be, a tragedy. Not only is the detective traditionally the embodiment of abstract intellect with "character" rather pasted on by the author in the form of irrelevant idiosyncrasies;

there is also never any doubt that crime and its punishment is strictly a logical problem—find the murderer and make him pay for his crime. The criminal is guilty by virtue of his act, whereas the detective is free of guilt no matter what he does in the pursuit of the criminal because he stands for logic and law. There is no recognition—nor is there any place in the retrospective plot for the recognition—of ambiguities and tensions inherent in the situation of crime and punishment. It is out of these ambiguities and tensions that tragedy grows. But tragedy requires a world view which has within it the possibility of transcendence. The detective story, with the answer to the problem securely located on the same plane of reality as the problem itself, denies the protagonist the opportunity for true knowledge.

In contrast to the detective story, let us look at a genre of drama which has a recognizable plot structure of its own but a genre which has been conspicuously successful in producing tragedies. Coincidentally this genre has frequently been referred to as the Renaissance's detective story—the revenge tragedy. This designation is a misnomer because there is truly no similarity between the genres at all, and, significantly, what separates them is what allows the revenge tragedy to raise to the heights of tragedy and restricts the detective story to a subliterary genre.3

Take *Hamlet* as an example of the former. The play is not a whodunnit, nor is Hamlet a dispassionate observer. Hamlet is responding to the situation as a total human being, and as a revenger he is walking on the line between focusing on Claudius as a murderer and recognizing at the same time that the problem of killing the murderer of his father is not merely that of eliminating an evil man. Yet while he partially recognizes that in its widest dimensions the problem is not world-immanent but rather has a metaphysical dimension to it, he is continually stymied in his efforts to give full formulation to the problem. As frequently as he tries, his symbolism can't get hold of the magnitude of the problem. Nor should this be surprising, as the problem of evil in the world and what is to be done about it ultimately is not formulable in rational terms. Therefore, the fact that the revenge hero is related to the murdered man and that he is emotionally involved in the pursuit of evil has just the opposite effect from what one might expect. Normally one would expect him to be a more virulent pursuer than the disinterested detective whereas because of his total involvement Hamlet is able to intuit the complexity of the situation, and it is this complexity which makes the directness and ferocity of the detective impossible for the revenge hero. The detective responds to the problem of the murder as a rational problem admitting of a world-immanent solution—get the murderer and restore order to the community. In the revenge tragedy the problem has a metaphysical dimension which precludes the restoration of an edenic order through the simple act of killing an evil man. Consequently, the problem transposes itself in revenge tragedy to a tragic meditation for which there is no simple solution and in some instances no solution at all. The tragic situation the hero of a revenge tragedy finds himself in is that he is wrong if he seeks to bring the murderer to justice and wrong if he doesn't. It is a situation that admits of no rational solution, yet paradoxically it leads to the most illuminating of insights. Because this is true, the revenge tragedy is at the other pole from the detective story, a fact which makes it very ironic that though the detective story is commonly referred to as a "mystery story" the term could be used with equal justification to describe that which is its very antithesis. Could, that is, if one is quite aware of a subtle but significant shift in definition. When speaking of the mystery in revenge tragedy, one is not merely referring to a perplexing situation requiring a keen mind for its solution but to a truth that is undiscoverable through the discursive process, a truth that is unknowable except at those luminous moments when man is raised out of himself.

The reader may object to my insistence that the retrospective plot is devoid of tragic implications by pointing out that though Ibsen may have been the first to use this technique in modern times he was not the inventor of the retrospective plot and that though it is the traditional plot form used in the detective story it is not the exclusive property of detective-story writers. After all, Sophocles used it in a play which for 2,500 years has been universally regarded as perhaps the most successful tragedy ever written. True, but as every reader of *Oedipus Rex* knows, Sophocles not only invented the retrospective plot in that play, he also created the prototype of the detective story.[4] The six characteristics of the detective story listed above are all present in *Oedipus*. But most important, Oedipus *sees himself* in the role of the detective. He thinks of himself as the outsider whose cool dispassionate approach to the problems of Thebes is exactly what has been lacking among its citizens. He intends to solve the problem through the application of "the power of the human mind to observe and reason." Oedipus is quick to point out to Teresias that all of his augury and soothsaying was incapable of solving the riddle of the sphinx whereas Oedipus himself, through the use of his reason alone, unaided by divine powers, was capable of solving that problem, and, he predicts, his powers will also be capable of ridding Thebes of the plague. As detective, Oedipus also hopes to sever the murderer (whom he does not connect with himself or his fate) from the community, an act which will restore order. Clearly Oedipus regards himself as a detective, views the world as rational, and denies that human life has anything mysterious within it.

However, though Oedipus regards himself as a detective and the plot structure is the one traditionally associated with the detective story, *Oedipus Rex* is not a detective story. And it is just that dimension in which it departs from the detective motif which raises it to the level of tragedy. The supreme irony in this play, a play noted for its ironies, is that Oedipus's reason finally reveals to him its own inadequacy and Oedipus realizes that the world is not merely metaphoric and mysterious but mysterious in its very essence, that its rhythm and order are and must remain mysterious to man. In short, the contrast between *Oedipus* on the one hand and the detective literature on the other is that where the latter assumes that the world that is discoverable at the level of the retrospective plot comports to a high degree with reality, the former assumes just the contrary. In *Oedipus* the level of the retrospective plot, the level at which Oedipus conducts his life, is discovered to be the realm of illusion. This is the tragic illumination he gains.

Scholars have frequently compared Hamlet to Oedipus, and certainly there are numerous similarities between the two. However, the comparison most often made is one which finds an Oedipal element in Hamlet. In fact, the truth is just the opposite: Oedipus is more like Hamlet than Hamlet like Oedipus. Oedipus discovers through the course of the play in which he is a hero that he is not a detective but rather the hero of a revenge tragedy. Where he thought of himself as a disinterested investigator, he finds that he is both the pursued and the pursuer.

And where he believed the world to be reasonable, he ends up learning what Hamlet sensed at the beginning,5 that life is tragic, and it is tragic because it is ultimately mysterious.

What raises *Oedipus* to the tragic level is that long before there ever was such a thing as a detective story Sophocles knew he wasn't writing one. But he gave us a man whose view of the world was that of the detective—which leads one to speculate that though the detective story had to wait over two thousand years to be invented, any rationalist age is on the brink of its discovery. In a sense, it is exactly the myth the rationalist seeks in order to justify his world view. Sophocles, no rationalist himself, saw his detective as a man whose view of reality was inadequate but who, in pursuing his view, comes face to face with the real under circumstances which both illuminate and overwhelm him:

> I tell you, king, this man, this murderer
> (whom you have long declared you are in search of,
> indicting him in threatening proclamation
> as murderer of Laius)—he is here.
> In name he is a stranger among citizens
> but soon he will be shown to be a citizen
> true native Theban, and he'll have no joy
> of the discovery: blindness for sight
> and beggary for riches his exchange,
> he shall go journeying to a foreign country
> tapping his way before him with a stick.   (448-57)

The detective is revealed to be figuratively blind. When he at last attains sight, the discovery of his own folly causes him to put out his eyes.

To create a dramatic situation which would render symbolically the rationalist in the world as he saw and experienced it, Sophocles invented the retrospective plot. In it the realm of mystery is apparently missing. But only apparently. And when Oedipus realizes the limitations he has imposed upon his own understanding, he not only frees himself from a monodimensional view of reality, he also shatters the retrospective plot which could not encompass his new insight. That form implied that truth would be found in an investigation of the past. All that the investigation of the past teaches Oedipus is his profound ignorance. Oedipus had to learn to break the form his life had taken and transcend his philosophy if he was to find meaning.

It is this ironic distancing of the author from his hero which allows Sophocles to transform the detective story into tragedy, and it is just this distancing which is not only lacking from the popular formula detective stories but also from the modern dramas that are written in the retrospective manner. The authors of both the detective story and the dramas see no more of the world than their heroes do.

Modern plays which have used the retrospective technique in plotting have not by and large had as their theme crime and its punishment, the ubiquitous theme of the detective story. Nevertheless, these plays follow the same general patterns which we saw in the detective story and for this reason fall short of tragic stature. They lack that ironic distancing found in Sophocles. Let us conclude with an examination of the nature of the tragic illumination commonly found in the retrospective plot and of the relationship between the playwright's awareness and that of his "detective."

Ironically, the frequent choice of the retrospective plot as the form for realistic tragedy may have been determined as much by traditional as by modernist considerations. If one examines the body of realistic tragedies from Ibsen to Shaffer, it seems obvious that to a man our dramatists would have agreed with Shakespeare and Sophocles that the essence of tragedy is the action that carries the protagonist to illumination through suffering (this movement from suffering to illumination being based on the assumption, fundamental to any tragic vision, that suffering has the power to illuminate). That is, modern dramatists write as if they share the conviction that reversal can produce recognition. No other plot structure has so immediately available to it the opportunity for reversal and recognition as the retrospective plot. As the "mystery" surrounding the past gives way to knowledge, the fortunes of the characters are altered. At the end there is recognition—the "mystery" is solved.

Now while this may on the surface resemble tragedy, it is a uniquely modern notion of the tragic vision to imply that the pain and suffering found in the human condition is composed of solvable "mysteries"—that life is comprised of sets of problems that are fully analyzable in socio-economic terms, as Arthur Miller seems prone to suggest, or in terms of one or another psychological theory, as Shaffer suggests in *Equus*. Or even less tragic is the notion that recognition and analysis of

the problem can be followed by a solution located at the level
of human action, as when Nora walks out of her home.

Briefly stated, the reason the retrospective play falls short
of tragic stature is that it fails to make experience luminous. I
will explain what I mean by making experience luminous by
examining the tragic vision of two seemingly quite different
plays, *A Doll's House* and *Death of a Salesman.* If one regards
Death as Willy's play from beginning to end, as Arthur Miller
did in the article he wrote in defense of his play as a tragedy,[6]
it would fall into that type of play we have called objective in
which the audience is the detective, for despite Miller's claims
to the contrary, there is no illumination, therefore no change of
character, for Willy. Willy ends the play by succeeding in doing
what he was trying to do before it began—kill himself. Watching him, the "sleuths" in the audience learn that society had
taught Willy the wrong values and destroyed him for remaining
faithful to those values. This resolution to Willy's mystery
hardly points in the direction of tragedy. An alternate reading
of the play is frequently offered by critics who enjoy the play
and want to salvage its reputation as tragedy. They see Biff as
a "latent detective," the character in the play who has the insight
Willy is unable to have, that is, that he, like his father, is "a
dollar-an-hour." Of course such a realization can be a staggering blow to one's self-esteem, and there is something to be said
for the man who can come to terms with his mediocrity. Yet
can it be seriously maintained that such knowledge constitutes
the kind of passing from ignorance to knowledge that is the
hallmark of a tragic recognition?

As with Biff so with Nora. Through her suffering Nora may
have raised her consciousness and thereby found the courage to
slam the door in Torvald's face. Yet it seems a bit hyperbolic
to claim that her new self-knowledge constitutes a transfiguration. And though it is at least plausible that she could not learn
the truth of her marriage short of its falling apart—reversal
followed by recognition—her new knowledge is nothing more
than a clever observer like Mrs. Lind could see from the start.
Ibsen has managed to obscure the limited dimension of Nora's
enlightenment by the inflated rhetoric he has used to mask
Nora's rather banal insight that she has been a silly woman
pampered by a doting father and husband:

Our home has been nothing but a playroom. I have been your

> doll-wife, just as at home I was papa's doll-child; and here
> the children have been my dolls. I thought it great fun when
> you played with me, just as they thought it great fun when I
> played with them. That is what our marriage has been, Torvald.

That this kind of rhetoric is currently enjoying a vogue does not alter the fact that it is inflated. Nothing in the new Nora is transfigured—unless that word is to be used so loosely as to lose its meaning. While she may be the prototype of the new woman, she is no Oedipus, no Lear, no Duchess of Malfi. Rather, one is haunted by the terrible suspicion that had Nora slammed that door in the 1970's instead of the 1870's she would have found her way to Vermont, where she would have quickly "gotten her head together" once she was "into" either pottery or photography.

There is no attempt here to deny that both plays have been extremely influential works. In fact, they were deliberately chosen because of their historical impact. *Doll's House* has long been regarded as a sort of *Uncle Tom's Cabin* of the feminist movement, and *Death* has been used time and again as an indictment of the exploitation that lies at the heart of the capitalist system. In each case the impact the play has had on the public is directly connected to what Nora and Biff learn. Yet this very aspect that has given the plays considerable sociological significance is the aspect in which they fail to rise to tragic stature. For what is it, after all, that Nora and Biff learn? First, the knowledge they struggle to is already known by others who are not particularly set apart by either their insightfulness or their heightened spirituality. Nor can this new knowledge be said to profoundly alter the direction of their lives. Their new knowledge leaves them on the same plane of being they were formerly on when they were in error; they have simply been turned around. It is as if they were going north previously and now have realized that their goal actually lies to the south.

The distance between either Nora or Biff's state of ignorance and state of knowledge is no greater than the distance traveled by the detective from his first erroneous suspicion to the time when he discovers the clue that unravels the "mystery." Nevertheless, this new understanding is presented as a revelation obtained by the hero only through pain and suffering. But the fact that this knowledge was available to others as well as to the hero, *without* the suffering, indicates that the need for suffering is not in the nature of the knowledge gained. That the hero could only learn it through suffering tells us something about the psychology of the hero but nothing about reality.

It might be commented that after all the shepherd and the messenger also knew what Oedipus only learned through suffering, that in his role as detective he discovers a secret which reveals that the things of the past are not what they seemed to him to be. If that were all that Oedipus learned—which is all the knowledge available within the structure of the retrospective plot—*Oedipus Rex* would also fall short of tragedy. Had *Oedipus Rex* ended there, it would have been not one of the first tragedies but the first detective story. The discovery that he has killed his father and married his mother is terrifying news indeed, but no more tragic than the discovery made at the end of the average detective story—or the discoveries made in *Doll's House* and *Death of a Salesman*. In fact, Sophocles' point is to show that, far from leading to the sublime heights of tragedy, this kind of thinking reveals a mind which has, through willfulness, cut itself off from its most potent resources; it must therefore either destroy itself in its own ignorance or submit itself humbly to those powers beyond itself which it cannot understand but from which it can hope for illumination. At this point Oedipus ceases to be a rationalist and the plot ceases to be retrospective. There is no more for Oedipus to learn from the past. He gouges out the eyes that have deceived him for so long; now, Oedipus needs only insight.

Another defense offered not only Nora and Biff but many of the heroes of retrospective plays is that (as with Oedipus) the particular facts they learn concerning the past are actually unimportant. Nor is it of any importance that (unlike Oedipus) they seem to learn nothing of the nature of the universe. What is important is that through their painful exploration of the past they have "found themselves." Finding oneself. Ironically that is exactly what Oedipus at its profoundest is about. And to find himself, Oedipus must first understand what it means to be a man. To do that he must perceive how man fits into the scheme of things. Slamming doors or riding the range, though wonderfully theatrical gestures, can hardly be said to lead directly to finding oneself, except in the flabby and inexact manner in which that expression has come to be used in the media.

Tragedy has always implied the act of finding oneself, but

that act has never been seen as the result of a program of personal rehabilitation. The tragic hero finds himself when his suffering turns his eyes inward and he descends into himself. That is the tragic author's concept of the function of suffering, of which Richard Sewall said in his *The Vision of Tragedy:*

> For all its inevitable, dark and destructive side, suffering could lead under certain circumstances not only to growth in the standard virtues of courage, loyalty, and love as they operate on the traditional level, but also to the discovery of a higher level of being undreamt of by the standard (or choric) mentality.[7]

The standard mentality represented in the Greek plays by the chorus has in the retrospective tragedy taken stage center. It has, in fact, become the climate of opinion out of which the plays are written. This fact has an ironic dimension to it in that most of these plays could be called problem plays, in which the author means to berate society for its twisted values. Yet we find that in matters of supreme importance—what does it mean to say one has found oneself?—the author exhibits the most commonplace of views. The fact is that Nora and Biff are not tragic figures for the same reason that the plots of *A Doll's House* and *Death of a Salesman* are not tragic; they do not transcend themselves. What is learned is only what has always been there. It had merely been overlooked.

Where the values of Sophocles and Shakespeare were quite different from the values of Oedipus and Lear as we find them in Act I of their respective dramas, the only thing that separates Ibsen's view of the world from Nora's, Miller's from Biff's, at the opening of the play is merely a question of the interpretation of facts. In this regard Ibsen and Miller more nearly resemble the authors of detective fiction than the authors of tragedy.

The detective story writer and his hero share a common view of the world—at least for the purposes of the story. They are both rationalists who accept the perimeters of the material universe as the limits of reality. The sole distinction is that the hero is ignorant of facts that are known to the author. Once the detective discovers the clues to the hidden secrets of the past, once he has unlocked the mystery, he knows all that the author knows. The same is true of Nora and Biff. There is a mystery in each of their lives which they must uncover and, as in the detective story, once that mystery is solved they are one with the author and ready to move into a more richly fulfilling life in the future.

The problem here is the notion of tragic ignorance and tragic knowledge. The "mystery" is an absence of information or an erroneous interpretation of facts. On this level suffering plays no integral part in the movement from ignorance to knowledge. Suffering in tragedy allows, even forces, something to happen—transcendence—which cannot happen in the retrospective tragedy because the author has accepted for himself and imposed on his characters the rationalist's universe, where nature never gets beyond nature.

The action of the retrospective tragedy is the peeling away of the errors that shroud the mystery in the past. In fact, the mystery itself is nothing more than these errors which have obscured the hero's access to the truth. Therefore, the movement from ignorance to knowledge in the retrospective tragedy more nearly imitates the movement in the detective story than in the tragedy. For, as in the detective story, the problem is to solve the mystery, which implies a movement into a more perfect future. Mystery is also the center of tragedy; however, it is mystery in the old-fashioned sense of the word, that is, something beyond human comprehension. Consequently, the tragic movement toward mystery is quite different. In tragedy the movement is toward the discovery and recognition of the presence and existence of the mystery which, far from being searched for by the hero, is initially not believed to exist.

Fordham University

NOTES

1 See, for example, George Steiner, *The Death of Tragedy* (New York: Knopf, 1961), 284-355; Moody E. Prior, *The Language of Tragedy* (Bloomington: Indiana Univ. Press, 1966), 291-311; Dorothea Krook, *Elements of Tragedy* (New Haven: Yale Univ. Press, 1969); R. J. Kaufmann, "Tragedy and Its Validating Conditions," *Comparative Drama*, 1 (1967), 3-18; George Kurman, "Entropy and the 'Death' of Tragedy: Notes for a Theory of Drama," *Comparative Drama*, 9 (1975), 283-304; John von Szeliski, *Tragedy and Fear: Why Modern Drama Fails* (Chapel Hill: Univ. of North Carolina Press, 1971).

2 On the subject of modern gnosticism, see Eric Voegelin's *Science, Politics, and Gnosticism* (South Bend, Ind.: Gateway Editions, 1968).

3 See Charles A. Hallett, "Andrea, Andrugio, and King Hamlet: The Ghost as Spirit of Revenge," *Philological Quarterly*, 74 (1977), 43-64.

4 Francis Fergusson, *The Idea of a Theater* (Garden City, N. Y.: Doubleday, 1949), p. 28.

5 There are more things in heaven and earth, Horatio/Than are dreamt of in your philosophy (I.v.166-67).

6 Arthur Miller, "Tragedy and the Common Man," *The New York Times*, 27 Feb. 1949, II, pp. 1, 3; and "Introduction" to *Collected Plays* (New York: Viking, 1957), pp. 23-38; both reprinted in *Death of a Salesman*, ed. Gerald Weales (New York: Viking Press, 1967).

7 Richard Sewall, *The Vision of Tragedy* (New Haven: Yale Univ. Press, 1959), p. 48.

Myth and Neurosis in Ibsen's Mature Plays

Margot Norris

I

Myth and realism are quite incompatible, we suppose. Their curious marriage in Ibsen's plays, in which mythic patterns are enacted by the Norwegian burghers and their matrons, poses problems which call the nature of modern myth criticism into question. The case is not unique, of course. Eliot praised Joyce's use of myth in *Ulysses,* and described its function as that of a template, imposing form on the chaos of modern life.[1] But Ibsen, writing earlier, depicts not a chaotic world which needs shaping, but a highly structured world in the process of unravelling.

Orley Holtan's important study of mythic patterns in Ibsen's plays[2] employs a method borrowed from Jung, Frye, Cassirer, and other proponents of the archetype, who classify myth semantically, according to content.[3] Holtan therefore looks for archetypal myth structures in Ibsen's work—Frye's quest pattern and Campbell's monomyth, for example—and for myth content, such as the inclusion of supernatural beings and improbable events. This method prompts him to conclude that only the early and the late plays of Ibsen are mythic in nature. He classifies the "social dramas" of the middle period in terms borrowed from Frye, as myth displaced in favor of realism: "They operate in a human world in which the supernatural is absent and causes and effects are, in large part, realistically determined."[4] By aligning myth with the sacred and realism with the secular, Holtan fails to avail himself of those critical tools which would allow him to overcome the dichotomy of myth and the real, and to analyze simultaneously the compelling structural principle which governs Ibsen's last twelve plays.

Contemporary structuralism, particularly the myth criticism of anthropologist Claude Lévi-Strauss, offers a way of looking for repetitions, similarities, differences, and other relationships

43

between elements, as clues to the "deep structure" of the myth,5 which reveals the unconscious conflict at its source. Because this method recognizes the psychological component of myth, and even treats myth and neurosis as homologous manifestations of psychic trauma,6 Lévi-Strauss' myth study suggests a particularly promising approach to Ibsen's "mature" plays. Ibsen's plays share with Freud's case histories—Dora, little Hans, the Wolf Man, Schroeber, the Rat Man—the same fine sense of the dramatic emerging from the formal elements: buried secrets, ancient guilts, physiological symptoms and inexplicable compulsions, remembrances and revelations.

Not only the causes of neurosis, but its manifestations, and the process by which the patient effects either his cure or his destruction, can be found in the dramas of Ibsen. Observing that neurotics are enthralled to private myths which crystallize around the painful and guilty experiences of their past, Ibsen forces his protagonists into crises when their myths are challenged.7 These crises take the form of a ritual which re-enacts the guilty myth— a process essentially therapeutic in nature. "Myth and action form a pair always associated with the duality of patient and healer,"8 writes Lévi-Strauss. It is probably no accident, then, that Ibsen, the erstwhile pharmacist's apprentice, peopled his plays with patients and healers: the dying Lyngstrand, Osvald Alving, Ella Rentheim, Beata Rosmer, myopic Hedvig, crippled Eyolf, assorted madmen and madwomen, and the doctors Stockmann, Wangel, and Rank.

Insofar as it is prompted by guilty acts, even physical sickness in Ibsen is both moral and psychological, as many of his characters are quick to point out. The ailments of children are usually hereditary in nature, and serve as manifestations of the "sins of the father"—either by direct infection or indirect causality, as in the case of Eyolf and the Solness twins. This theme of inherited sin reflects the Christian redemption myth, which itself recapitulates the process of neurosis: an ancient mythic crime, an Original Sin, must be expunged by a ritualistic re-enactment, the Redemption with its numerous Old Testament parallels, and its dramatic re-enactment in the sacrifice of the Mass. As in the Christian cosmology, the original sin is committed by the parents, and the redemption often requires the sacrifice of a child, of an innocent—a motif reflected in the *Kindermord*9 of many Ibsen plays, such as the obvious cases of Hedvig and Eyolf.

Ibsen's familiarity with the Bible is well-documented,[10] as is his curious aesthetic appreciation of the fall: "Raphael's art has never really moved me," he writes of his visit to Rome, "His people belong to a period before the fall of man."[11]

Lévi-Strauss' model for structural myth study provides a method which would allow the various plays to be studied in relation to one another by comparing their "mythemes," the constituent units of the myth which Lévi-Strauss describes as "bundles of relations."[12] Such "mythemes" have, of course, been variously discovered in Ibsen's works, as, for example, in Richard Schechner's study of "The Unexpected Visitor in Ibsen's Late Plays."[13] Schechner interprets this phenomenon with Jungian tools, explaining the unexpected visitors as "personified thoughts" —an interpretation which forces him to neglect such important surprise visitors in the earlier plays as Lona Hessel and Johan Toennesen in *Pillars of Society,* Kristine Linde in *A Doll's House,* Thea Elvsted in *Hedda Gabler,* and Ulrik Brendel in *Rosmersholm.* Again, Daniel Haakonsen isolates another "mytheme" in his study of the sacrifice motif, a study which he confines to the realistic dramas, and to considerations of the conflict between individualism and idealism.[14] Yet these mythemes—surprise visitors, sacrifice, *Kindermord,* sickness and healing—occur in virtually each play, relating to each other not just as elements of plot, but as finely connected figures and events in the neurotic process.

II

A mythic pattern which exemplifies the structure of neurosis underlies all of Ibsen's mature plays from *Pillars of Society* to *When We Dead Awaken.* Believing they are well, or even about to have some good fortune, the characters are troubled by symptoms which are shortly explained as manifestations of a suppressed sin or crime from the past. This revelation of the ancient crime is often triggered by a visit from someone in the past who prompts a reinvestigation of the buried sin. The protagonist then re-enacts the ancient crime in some symbolic fashion, thereby effecting either his forgiveness and redemption or his penitent destruction.

The myth which serves as a structural model for the condition of neurosis is, of course, the Oedipus myth. A guilty trauma, an ancient sin, is repressed until a symptom, the plague, forces its reinvestigation. This reinvestigation clarifies Oedipus' status as a guilty man, and allows him to acknowledge his guilt in authentic self-recognition. This process of reinvestigation requires the reliving of the repressed trauma of the past, and therefore corresponds to the rememoration of the psychoanalytic patient, who must remember the ancient trauma and deal with it anew in order to cure his neurosis.

A contemporary popular dramatizer of this neurotic process is filmmaker Alfred Hitchcock, whose psychological thrillers trace such symptoms as amnesia ("Spellbound") or kleptomania and fear of thunderstorms ("Marnie") back to the original childhood trauma (the impalement of the brother on the fence, and the murder of the mother's lover, respectively). Ibsen also uses this structure to create suspense in his earlier plays, in which the visitors such as Lona Hessel, Krogstad, or Gregers Werle threaten to expose the crimes which have been so steadfastly suppressed for many years. In the later plays, however, Ibsen foregoes suspense and tragic exposure in a decided shift of focus from plot complication to psychological unfolding.

Far from destroying the time-honored distinctions between the "realistic" and "symbolic" dramas of Ibsen, the concept of a single mythic structure as basic to the mature plays clarifies the significance of these distinctions. For example, the famed "symbols" of the later plays serve as analogues to the symptoms of the earlier plays precisely because symptoms, as visible effects of invisible causes, are symbolic by nature, as we see when Stockmann himself designates the poisoned baths as symbols of the polluted sources of the community's life. However, Bernick's rotten boat and Osvald's syphilis are more than synechdoches or shorthand notations for the capitalistic or sexual excesses that produced them. They are involuntary and therefore ironic signs that betray the sinner—effects which dramatize a hidden sin against all efforts to conceal it, as old Werle's deceptive altruism is undone by Hedvig's incipient blindness. Although, unlike a symptom, the White Horse of *Rosmersholm* is an arbitrary representation of Beata's murder, its function is the same: an involuntary reminder of Beata's haunting presence, like the neurotic phobia which prohibits Rosmer from crossing the foot-bridge over the mill-race. Thus, while their functions remain the same, the symbols of the later plays become more arbitrary while the symptoms become more purely psychological—Solness' vertigo,

Ellida's malaise, and Rubek's artistic impotence, for example. The many animal-like symbols of the later plays—White Horse, Wild Duck, Rat-Wife, Dying Mermaid, the sculptures of Rubek —all carry the pall of death as surely as do the symptoms of the earlier plays—the unseaworthy *Indian Girl*, the syphilis of Osvald, the polluted baths. Symbols and symptoms both serve as harbingers of death occasioned by an illness whose source is moral and spiritual.

Although the ancient crime in Ibsen's dramas is not the Freudian sexual trauma of the child, the sins in the plays are sometimes guilty wishes rather than deeds—wishes to remove an obstacle to happiness, like Solness' wishing for the fire to destroy Aline's home, and Rita Allmers wishing Eyolf away. Yet the original sin in all the mature dramas appears to be an act of sacrifice, whose crux is the resolution of a conflict by a guilt-ridden choice between two inescapable evils or two desired goods. This creates the great variety of motivations found in the plays, which range from the generous self-sacrifice of Nora to Rubek's callous sacrifice of Irene.

The precise nature of the choice varies as well, although *the sacrifice of love by marriage for money* may be considered as a mytheme recurring not only in several of the realistic dramas but in such later works as *The Masterbuilder, Little Eyolf,* and *John Gabriel Borkman* as well. In fact, two plays as widely different in their thematic issues, atmosphere, imagery and resolution as *Ghosts* and *Little Eyolf* are structured very much alike when their basic conflict is explored as a sacrifice. Both Helene Alving and Alfred Allmers marry their respective spouses for money—Helene pressured by relatives and at the cost of her love for Manders, Alfred Allmers in order to provide for his beloved half-sister Asta. Both Captain Alving and Rita Allmers make unwelcome sexual demands on their marriage partners which result in damage to their children: driven to syphilitic prostitutes by Helene's coldness, Alving infects his son, while little Eyolf is crippled by his fall from the table during his parents' love-making. The theme of disturbed family and sexual relationships is further exemplified in both plays by confused sibling loves; the incipient lovers Osvald and Regine are revealed to share a father, while the supposed siblings Alfred and Asta are revealed to not share a father. Finally, the protagonists in both plays seek redemption by constructing orphanages in reparation for their injury to their own sons—Helene, unwittingly and disastrously, but the Allmers, perhaps successfully so.

Illegitimacy, a prominent mytheme in many Ibsen plays, is usually a consequence of *sacrifice of love by marriage for money* rather than an original sin in itself. Despite the tantalizing material from Ibsen's biography, his begetting a bastard with a servant in Grimstad and the rumor of his own illegitimacy by the poet Tormod Knudsen,[15] Ibsen's plays lack the signs of confessional catharsis, particularly since spiritual illegitimacy shares identical functions with its social counterpart. In *Lady from the Sea,* Ibsen develops the theme of spiritual adultery almost on the model developed in Goethe's *Elective Affinities:* Ellida's child, legally and presumably biologically the child of Wangel, has the Stranger's eyes to betray its spiritual illegitimacy. Ibsen, like Goethe, sacrifices the child, thereby interlocking the sin of betrayed love with the redemptive and retributive sacrifice of the innocent. Although Ellida's child is not drowned, like Charlotte/Ottilie's, Hedvig, another illegitimate child, becomes a sacrificial victim when she dies symbolically in "the depths of the sea," like a shot wild duck. Little Eyolf, of course, is also drowned—another spiritual bastard since Allmers' true love is his sister Asta, Eyolf's namesake, whose security he provided by marrying Rita. The betrayed love disclosed by illegitimacy is as readily manifested by a spiritual "child" as by a physical one in Ibsen's plays. Hedda Gabler marries dull Tesman for security, leaving Løvborg to beget the spiritual "child" with the dull Thea. Hedda's legitimate pregnancy has as little to do with her as her husband's boring treatise on medieval handicrafts, and she therefore destroys the spiritual bastard, Løvborg's brilliant book. Like Hedda, Ella Rentheim claims Erhart Borkman, the "spiritual bastard" of John Gabriel Borkman and her sister, whom he married for money. As John Gabriel's true love, Ella receives his fortune and his child upon his fall, and years later tries to formalize her claim by asking to adopt and give him her name—like Eyolf, who received Asta's nickname.[16] One further variation of the configuration "marriage for money—illegitimacy—death of child" may be seen by comparing *Pillars of Society* and *Ghosts,* plays in which a legitimate and an illegitimate child are harbored under the same roof by the guilty parent. The immolation of the innocent is here displaced from the illegitimate to the legitimate child, so that it is Olaf Bernick who is feared drowned on the

Indian Girl, and Osvald who contracts the disease, while their illegitimate siblings, Dina Dorf and Regine Engstrand, escape to freedom.

Buried in the near or distant past, the ancient crime is forgotten save for betraying symptoms, and the protagonists are well and facing hopeful futures as the plays open. This condition is threatened by the arrival of a surprise visitor whose effect is that of a psychoanalytic free association which awakens painful memories of the ancient trauma, like Oedipus' messenger. Most shocking is the arrival of those visitors who are themselves the victims of the ancient crime, particularly the betrayed true loves such as Lona Hessel, Ella Rentheim, Irene deSatow and Ellida Wangel's Stranger. Some of the unwelcome guests threaten to expose the ancient crime, like Johan Toennesen and Gregers Werle, others come to lay claims on the protagonists, like Ella Rentheim and Ellida Wangel's Stranger. Still other surprise visitors are school friends, or tutors of the protagonists who serve as foils or object lessons for them. Kristine Linde illustrates to Nora both a wasted life of sacrifice and a brave retrieval of lost happiness, Ulrik Brendel serves as a cautionary example of the fate of freethinkers for Rosmer, and Thea Elvert, who has risked her security and respectability for love, serves as a foil for Hedda. The Rat-Wife, an animal catcher like Ulfheim in *When We Dead Awaken,* appears on the scene as a fearful metaphor of sexual predation. Both the Rat-Wife, who once lured men and drowned them like rats, and Ulfheim, who hunts women along with his usual game of eagles, wolves, and elk, send frightful warnings to Rita and Maia, whose sexual passions have been dangerously exaggerated by the neglect of their cold, indifferent husbands.

The arrival of the visitor triggers an eventual crisis in the play which is essentially psychological in nature. The unearthing of the buried sin creates a situation in which the protagonist is forced to re-enact a critical moment from his past. It is the nature of this re-enactment which most sharply divides the middle plays from the later plays. The protagonists must confront their original choice again in *Pillars of Society, A Doll's House, An Enemy of the People, Ghosts, Lady from the Sea,* and *Little Eyolf.* In the rest, the protagonists re-enact the myth, the real or imaginary moment from the past which has become symbolic and their sinful idealism.

Both Bernick of *Pillars of Society* and the citizens of *Enemy of the People* must re-enact their original choice between honesty and prosperity, only this time dishonesty involves potential murder: the drowning of the passengers on the unseaworthy *Indian Girl* and the infection of the tourists in the pestilent baths. Ibsen allows the outcome to vary; Bernick chooses honesty and salvation, but the citizens are damned by their greed.

Nora must choose once more between the protection of her husband's pride or her own personhood, and she also chooses differently than she did eight years before. Helene Alving, who denied herself many years before, chooses the "joy of life" for Osvald, when she sees him dally with Regine, like a ghostly mime from the past. But her choice is too late to undo the fatal effects of the original error. *Ghosts* is the only play in which reformation, a worthy choice, is unrewarded—the reason, perhaps, why *Ghosts* has been selected for discussions of modern tragedy.17

Ibsen introduces a curious twist into the development of *Lady from the Sea* and *Little Eyolf,* in which he gives his protagonists the opportunity to return to the original true loves whom they had betrayed in order to marry for money and security. The marriages to Wangel and Rita have produced ill-fated children, and the critical choices must be made as the Stranger and Asta are about to depart by steamer. But to redeem themselves, the protagonists need not follow them, for Wangel and Rita are good people. Instead, the marriages must be renewed for worthier motives, and the protagonists must adopt children not their own, as Ellida agrees to provide a real home for Wangel's daughters, and Alfred agrees to help Rita care for the orphaned boys.

In each of the plays from the middle period, the neurosis is cured when the protagonists accept their original guilt, and re-enact the original dilemma to their moral credit. The cycle is mythic: Adam damns the human race by aspiring to be like God; Christ redeems the human race by condescending to become like man. In the later plays Ibsen gives no more second chances, and the re-enactments are mere gestures, symbolic and doomed, of the flawed ambitions that brought the protagonists low.

The later plays have the same mythemes as the earlier plays: marriage for money, the framing of the innocent, the sharp business practice, illegitimacy and the paid-off wedding to conceal illegitimacy, and the peculiar Ibsenite murder which takes the form of a provocation to suicide by an idealist. Hedvig dies this way, inspired by Gregers Werle, Beata Rosmer by Rebekka West, and Løvborg by Hedda Gabler.

Hedvig's suicide, shooting herself in the attic she thinks of as "the depths of the sea," recapitulates the shooting of the wild duck—Old Werle's literal act and figurative sin against old Ekdal, of whom he says, "there are people in this world who plunge to the bottom when they've hardly been winged." *The Wild Duck* is the first of the dramas in which the neurotic myth that dominates the lives of the characters emerges in a single obsessive image—a violent, dynamic fantasy which occurs once, either in reality or in the imagination,[18] and which must be re-enacted if the obsession is to be disarmed. Whatever its violent motions, diving into the water as in *The Wild Duck* or *Rosmersholm,* climbing impossible heights as in *The Masterbuilder* and *When We Dead Awaken,* or shooting with guns as in *The Wild Duck* and *Hedda Gabler,* the obsessive image depicts the deadliness of idealism which replaces the bourgeois greed and destructive self-sacrifice of the earlier plays as the dominant sin.

Hedda is obsessed by the image of refined debauchery, Løvborg as vine-leaved Bacchus, and by the dangerous gun play which she compulsively repeats throughout the play until she provokes Løvborg to suicide before taking her own life. Rebekka West's murder of Beata, another suicide provoked in the interest of an intellectual ideal, is re-enacted precisely when she and Rosmer plunge from the bridge into the mill-race—Rebekka even shrouded in Beata's shawl. The Babelian sin of Solness, the challenge of God by climbing the tall church spire, is also suicidally re-enacted at the goading of the thrill-seeking Hilde Wangel. John Gabriel Borkman's obsessive fantasy of conquering the cold, metal kingdom is elliptically re-enacted when at his death "a freezing hand of metal" seizes his heart. Like that of Solness, the original sin of Rubek and Irene is biblical, a parody of the temptation of Christ as Rubek shows Irene the glory of the world from the mountain top and she falls to her knees and worships and serves him. In fatal re-enactment, they climb the mountain again.

III

Ibsen's mature plays transcend mere psychological case histories precisely because the mythic patterns underlying neurotic illness reverberate with philosophical implications for modern man. Writing in the late nineteenth century, Ibsen saw the moral struggle to fulfill "Human Responsibility" or answer the "summons of the ideal" undermined by unconscious hypocrisies and lies, by that fatal lack of self-recognition which in the next century would be formalized as Sartrean "bad faith" or Heideggerean "inauthentic being." He therefore depicted his bourgeois protagonists as trapped in a morally ambiguous universe in which the double valences of every action, the repressive nature of self-control, or the destructive nature of moral license, for example, damn them to ineluctible guilt. Ibsen responded to this moral entrapment with sympathy. "Who is the man among us," he once asked his young followers, "who has not now and then felt and recognized within himself a contradiction between word and deed, between will and duty, between life and theory in general?"19

In exploring the status of guilt in a morally ambiguous universe, Ibsen confronted a technical problem first manifested in the early dramas, *Brand* and *Peer Gynt*. These early heroes, too, are trapped between the double valence of idealism, so that in their laudable effort to achieve transcendence they inevitably pass from the human to the non-human. It makes no difference whether the movement is upward or downward, toward god or toward animal: Brand and Peer Gynt are freaks alike, whether monstrous saint or troll-like beast. But this very freakishness, which makes of Brand and Peer Gynt singular pathological cases, fails, in the end, to shed light on the universal moral dilemma which Ibsen clearly sought to explore. "*Brand* has been misconstrued," he wrote to Georg Brandes in 1869, "The misunderstanding has evidently arisen from the fact that Brand is a priest and that the problem is presented as a religious problem. But both these circumstances are quite unimportant. I could just as easily have constructed the same syllogism about a sculptor or a politician as about a priest."20 The syllogism was reconstructed in later plays—with businessmen, housewives, architects, doctors, and scholars—but this professional diversity alone did not universalize the thematic moral dilemma. Before Brand's fault could rise above the miscalculation of the worth of ideals, Ibsen conjoined moral blindness with psychological compulsion, thereby bringing the moral dilemma within the purview of human inevitability. Unlike Brand's existential responsibility for his actions, Rosmer's inhuman righteousness will be triggered by irrational forces quite beyond his control. "At this pass the inner truth of the situation comes out," Shaw writes of Rosmer's asking Rebekka to prove her honor by killing herself, "What is really driving Rosmer is the superstition of expiation by sacrifice."[21]

Ibsen conjoined psychology and morality in mythic patterns, which, as Freud also discovered, trace the ambiguous responsibility of human actions.[22] Oedipus proceeds to his doom by pursuing vigorous moral imperatives which prove to be unconscious enactments of patterns pre-ordained at his birth. The revelation at the end of *Brand* lacks resonance because it proves Brand merely wrong; the revelation at the end of the later plays is the ironic recognition that, like Oedipus, the figures incurred guilt by evading it—like Mrs. Alving, whose "virtue" is the source of her family's doom. If Brand's actions are extreme and freakish, it is because they lack the psychological justification of the symmetry between conscious and unconscious behavior. In the mature plays, the characters often indulge in various kinds of seemingly "innocent" or trivial play, which becomes fraught with significance at the moment of revelation. The bizarre behavior which follows is a logical, conscious re-enactment of earlier unconscious behavior: Hedvig's shooting in the Ekdal fantasy forest or Solness' ascent to his "castles in the air," for example. Just so, Oedipus self-inflicts physical blindness in recognition of his moral blindness. There are no more Button Moulders in Ibsen's mature plays, where the characters punish or heal themselves.

Ibsen will remain famous as the Father of Dramatic Realism, whose natural dialogue and contemporary themes relegated Scribean dramaturgy to oblivion. But the dramatic power of his mature dramas springs from sources deep below the surface of bourgeois life, in the compulsive rituals by which man copes with his own irrationality—the shamanistic cure, the psychoanalytic rememoration, and the religious sacrament.

University of Tulsa

NOTES

1 T. S. Eliot, "Ulysses, Order and Myth," *James Joyce: Two Decades of Criticism*, ed. Seon Givens (New York: Vanguard Press, 1948), p. 201. First printed in *Dial*, 75 (1923), 480-83.

2 Orley Holtan, *Mythic Patterns in Ibsen's Last Plays* (Minneapolis: Univ. of Minnesota Press, 1970).

3 Ibid., pp. 8-14.

4 Ibid., p. 34.

5 See "Structural Study of Myth," in *Structural Anthropology*, trans. Claire Jacobson and Brooke Grundfest Schoepf (New York: Doubleday, 1967), chapt. 11.

6 Myth, dream, and the neurotic symptom are all structured by the unconscious, which Lévi-Strauss regards not as a thing, or a place, but as the "symbolic function." *Structural Anthropology*, p. 198. Anthony Wilden writes: "If 'primitive' myths are the public cosmological and conscious memory of a society which simply repeats its unconscious synchronic structure through time, then any important dream or symptom can be regarded as a similarly symbolic conscious private memory of the original system of relationships which the subject also repeats synchronically and unconsciously." *The Language of the Self* (Baltimore: Johns Hopkins Univ. Press, 1968), p. 208.

7 John Northam describes these crises of the Ibsen protagonists in philosophical terms as a renewed struggle between the "essential" and the "social" self—in other words, as a crisis of character rather than a psychoanalytic confrontation. *Ibsen, A Critical Study* (Cambridge: Cambridge Univ. Press, 1973), p. 225-26.

8 Lévi-Strauss, p. 196.

9 Holtan, p. 84. Also James E. Kerans, "Kindermord and the Will in Little Eyolf," in *Modern Drama: Essays in Criticism*, ed. Travis Bogard and William I. Oliver (New York, 1965), pp. 192-93. See also Charles Lyons, "Some Variations of *Kindermord* as Dramatic Archetype," *Comparative Drama*, 1 (1967), 56-71.

10 During his work on *Brand*, Ibsen wrote to Bjørnstjerne Bjørnson, "I read nothing but the Bible—it has vigor and power." (Letter dated September 12, 1865). *Ibsen, Letters and Speeches*, ed. Evert Sprinchorn (New York: Hill and Wang, 1964), p. 44.

11 Letter to Georg Brandes, dated July 15, 1869. *Letters and Speeches*, p. 86.

12 Although I am taking great liberties with Lévi-Strauss' method, a concept such as the "mytheme," which Lévi-Strauss treats as a constituent unit of a system—analogous to the phoneme or sememe in language—suggests a practical method for rigorously treating elements in Ibsen's plays in terms of their relationship to each other and to the larger structure, rather than as mere symbols or archetypes. See *Structural Anthropology*, pp. 206-07.

13 *Ibsen, A Collection of Critical Essays*, ed. Rolf Fjelde (Englewood Cliffs, New Jersey: Prentice-Hall, 1965), p. 158.

14 Daniel Haakonsen, "The function of sacrifice in Ibsen's realistic drama," *Contemporary Approaches to Ibsen*, ed. Daniel Haakonsen (Oslo: Universitetsforlaget, 1966), p. 21.

15 Hans Heiberg, *Ibsen, A Portrait of the Artist*, trans. Joan Tate (London: George Allen and Unwin, 1969), pp. 34 and 22, respectively.

16 Rebekka West is another bastard who takes the name of the real or biological parent.

17 See Francis Fergusson, *The Idea of a Theater* (Princeton: Princeton Univ. Press, 1949), pp. 148-60.

18 Hermann J. Weigand makes the case that Hilda Wangel's fantasy of the events at Lysanger is evidence of psychopathic abnormality: "The ability to intermingle fact with fancy to this extent, however, is characteristic only of small children and of adults who have never outgrown the mental habits of childhood; hence our supposition can stand as plausible only if other features of Hilda's conduct yield traces of an abnormal infantilism." *The Modern Ibsen* (New York: E. P. Dutton, 1960), p. 289. But the mythologizing of traumatic experiences is just that fundamental process in neurosis which gives to memories the power to dominate psychic life. Lévi-

Strauss writes, "For the neurotic, all psychic life and all subsequent experiences are organized in terms of an exclusive or predominant structure, under the catalytic action of the initial myth." *Structural Anthropology*, p. 198.

19 Speech to Norwegian students in Christiania, September 10, 1874. *Letters and Speeches*, p. 151.

20 Letter dated June 26, 1969. *Letters and Speeches*, pp. 83-84.

21 Bernard Shaw, *The Quintessence of Ibsenism* (New York: Hill and Wang, 1957), pp. 104-05.

22 Leo Aylen dismisses Ibsen as a poor playwright and a "bad moralist" precisely because he fails to recognize the psychological/moral nexus implicit in Ibsen's use of the dual structure of ancient sin (past) and ritual re-enactment (present) in his plays: "But its chief deficiency is the moment of decision. This Ibsen avoids. We never see the moment of the most important decision the hero makes in his life; it has always happened sometime before the play begins. The retrospective method enables Ibsen to avoid facing up to the question as to whether human beings are free or not. . . . It is likely therefore that writer who did not make it clear whether his hero was right or wrong, would not be able to understand the problem of freedom. . . . Because of this lack of moral insight on Ibsen's part, we are shown pathetic studies of people who have gone wrong." *Greek Tragedy and the Modern World* (London: Methuen, 1964), p. 237.

The Demons of *John Gabriel Borkman*

Brian Johnston

Theatre is the art of apparitions. The curtain rises and suddenly the presences manifest themselves. Their appearance is their whole life. The actor, waiting in the wings, is a wholly different creature from the character who enters onstage. The great dramatist is the artist who most boldly and effectively presents us with memorable and forceful apparitions which then take on life by feeding off of our captive imaginations: a form of transfusion takes place in which we "enter into" the fictive characters and endow them with substantial life while they in turn take possession of us.

In Ibsen's *John Gabriel Borkman* this "vampyric" relation exists not just between the fictive characters and the audience but also between the fictive characters and their world. The elder trio, Borkman, Gunhild, and Ella Rentheim, all are figuratively dead and have been discarded by the world: but they seek to live once again in the world, to take possession of it by taking possession of the will of the young man, Erhart Borkman. He is to ensure their continuation in life. As Gunhild proclaims:

> Erhart has an obligation, before all else, to achieve a brilliance [aa lyse saa höyt] of such height and scope that not one person in this country will still recall the shadow his father cast over me—and over my son.[1]

Ella, who wishes to "open a path for Erhart to be happy here on earth," nevertheless demands that the young man take on her name—Rentheim—and so perpetuate her existence beyond her imminent death. Even Borkman, the most self-sufficient of the trio, will urge Erhart to join him and help him "win this new life."

For Gunhild, Erhart's "mission" is the "oppreisning" of the Borkman name and honor. Oppreisning implies not only restitution but also resurrection and the idea of Erhart resurrecting a dead and discredited world, and, by his brilliant light dispelling the darkness, recalls the Scandinavian myth of the resurrection of the destroyed northern world by the young god Baldr, a regeneration of the world free from the guilt of the older gods.

Silence and sound are telling metaphors in the play. The superbly uncanny sound of Borkman pacing up and down in his room overhead, which the audience is made to hear, then forget, suddenly to be startled into awareness of its significance when Gunhild explains its origin, is itself a rich blend of sound and silence:

> GUNHILD   Always hearing his footsteps up there. From early morning till far into the night. And so loud, as if they were in this room.
> ELLA   Yes, it's strange how the sound carries.
> GUNHILD   Often I have the feeling that I have a sick wolf pacing his cage up in the salon. Right over my head. *(Listens, then whispers)* Hear that, Ella! Listen! Back and forth—back and forth, the wolf pacing.

The wolf is one of the identities, or manifestations, of the god Odin, and the manner in which Ibsen introduces this identity in this passage causes the audience to "register" it with maximum force. In the silence of winter sound does seem to become more clear and to carry further, and Gunhild's whispered injunction to Ella to listen makes the hearing of the audience, too, more thrillingly acute. Act I opens with the metallic sound of sleigh bells and closes with the swelling sound of the piano hammers striking the metallic strings. Deep within Borkman's imagination, we will learn, is the sound of a ghostly hammer striking at and releasing the metal ores within the mines, a sound that punctuates the silence of his lonely exile. In the last Act, just before he dies, Borkman not only sees his ghostly kingdom but hears the thousands of hammers and machines creating a new world out of metal.

The "apparitional" quality of the play is enhanced by a pattern of startling entrances and exits repeated in each Act. The play opens with Ella's unprecedented entrance into Gunhild's living room and she as dramatically exits from it, to appear, for the first time, in Borkman's upper salon. After Gunhild briefly and fatefully invades the salon, Ella brings off the *coup* of getting Borkman, for the first time in eight years, to exit from his room. Borkman then descends to Gunhild's room, terrifying the maid and startling his son. At the end of this third Act he abruptly exits from the house, to the consternation of Ella; and, in the last Act there is a general exodus when all the characters leave the house, either to follow Borkman up to his Pisgah height where he glimpses his lost promised land and dies, or to follow Mrs. Wilton south, to warmth and a new life. In one particularly memorable apparition, in Act I, Mrs. Wilton enters the grey and cold living room and, with her entrance, a lamp is lit in the rear garden-room which comes alive with the green hues of a lusher nature, as if the winter scene itself were being invaded by a nature deity from the south. Silence and sound, immobility and movement, drabness and color, spaces forcefully occupied and vacated, all are tellingly employed to create a theatric poetry of compelling "presence" unusual even for Ibsen.

The description of Mrs. Wilton makes her stand in the strongest contrast to the two elderly, greying women, for she is extremely attractive with a *ripe* (yppig) figure, full red lips, playful or mischievous eyes, and rich, dark hair. The word "yppig" can be applied to vegetation with the meaning of lush and luxuriant, to the earth meaning fertile and rich, and to a woman, carrying these meanings over in the terms "buxom" and "ample."[2] It is only after Mrs. Wilton has thus appeared, establishing her rich presence, that Erhart, "elegantly dressed," adds his youthful and subordinate male presence to hers. Mrs. Wilton, in her richly furnished sleigh with its chiming silver bells, will take her two youthful companions, Erhart and Frida, south with her just as Borkman will draw his two companions, Ella and Gunhild, up to the cold of the hilltop. Such symmetrically contrasting grouping and movement has the formal quality of a dance, a dance of life versus a dance of death, where, in one direction, we feel the urgent pull of earthly life with its seductiveness and instigation to sexual fulfilment, while in the other direction we feel the equally as imperative pull of a visionary and spiritual world with its poignant lure of transcendence. There is no right and wrong way here, but an imaginative and compelling grasp of the paradox of human existence with its long dialogue between the flesh and the spirit.

Between these two contradictory realms there is a curious nebulousness, a lack of specific social and familial detail very unusual in Ibsen's writing. The aspirations of the sensuous and the spiritual egos simply put aside this arena of social/familial

conflict upon which the earlier dramas had been fought, and
this partly accounts for the often stark and melodramatic nature
of the characters' speeches and gestures. They communicate at
a level of hortatory injunction that would be impossible within
the subtle complexities of shared familial and social consciousness:

> GUNHILD *(in passionate agitation)* You want to leave me! To
> be out with those strangers! With — with — no, I won't even
> think of it!
> ERHART   There are so many shimmering lights down there.
> And young, happy faces. And there's music there, Mother!
> GUNHILD *(pointing toward the ceiling)* Upstairs there's also
> music, Erhart.
> ERHART   Yes, it's that music *there*—that's what's hounding
> me out of this house.
> ELLA   Can't you allow your father a little chance to forget
> himself?
> ERHART   Yes, I can. I can allow it a thousand times over—
> if I don't have to hear it myself.
> GUNHILD *(looks reprovingly at him)* Be strong, Erhart!
> Strong, my son! Don't ever forget you have a great mission!

It is a testimony to the power of the play that it is able to
survive lines such as these (and I am quoting from the best
available translation — Rolf Fjelde's). The heavily handled
references to the music are bathetic: Gunhild's solemn upward
pointing towards what even she must recognise as hardly an
inducement to stay at home, Erhart's melodramatically agonized
reaction, and Ella's oddly inconsequential piece of pious solicitude, the exchange ending with Gunhild's grotesque injunction
to Erhart and his mission, all create a movement or pattern of
exaggerated response not rooted in any plausible psychological
situation. Ibsen intentionally makes the situation grotesque, and
this is typical of the bold stylistic incongruities he develops in
this play, but even so, one cannot help but sympathize with the
dilemma of the actors who have to speak lines of such emphasis
with so little support from any basis of conventionally plausible
reality. The characters as Ibsen has conceived them, uniquely
to this play, live only at the level of ultimate confrontation: it is
the heroic mode of *The Vikings at Helgeland* transposed almost
without change to a modern bourgeois drawing-room where it
can be both mocked and honoured. These are the awkward
conditions the author accepts in order to rise to the movingly
authentic visionary height of the last Act, for only such odd

instruments as these will be capable of the final poignant harmonies.

It is because these characters exist in so stark a medium that their "demonic" aspect becomes apparent to us, and that the struggle the play presents can be seen as one between "forces" that have taken on alarming human identity. Mrs. Wilton, for example, radiates not only vitality and warmth but also a formidable power which enters into open battle, and victory, against the cold force of Gunhild. With Erhart she plays the game of casting a spell over him, suggesting magical as well as natural powers and though, within the realistic convention, this might be discounted as a mere pleasantry, we notice that the spell, nonetheless, works. Treating Erhart as if he were the young and subservient male consort of her female divinity, she warns him that her spell will command him and that he help-lessly will obey:

> When I'm going along, I'll talk to myself—right out of my innermost will, I will say; student Erhart Borkman,—take your hat at once! . . . he'll pick up his hat straight away.

Erhart, a little later, after her exit, desiring to leave the house, looks about the living room asking, "Where did I leave my hat?" The vitality and power emanating from Mrs. Wilton make us the more aware of the ghostly and "finished" nature of the older trio. For these elders to possess the will of Erhart, as they wish, would be the vampyric invasion of his youthful life by forces that wrongly seek to perpetuate themselves among the living, and it is only when they are brought, painfully, to recognize that their drama is finished that they can escape the incongruities of their long dance of death and attain to tragic dignity and poignancy.

With Erhart's rejection of the "mission" Gunhild had pro-jected onto him, the sisters recognize that their mutual hatred is greater than their attachment to Erhart:

> ELLA Better her than you.
> GUNHILD *(nodding slowly)* I understand that. I say the same.
> Better her than you.
> ELLA Whatever the end result for him—
> GUNHILD That scarcely matters now, I think.

The passionate struggle to possess Erhart now subsides into the conclusion that it scarcely matters what happens to him: it is almost as if two spirits that had sought to occupy a human being

and had urgently gestured to him all the time they thought they
might succeed, now relapse into a resigned abandonment of
him, as if he were of no interest. This is not, in fact, the end of
the struggle for Erhart. The ghosts are to be brought to a more
agonizing relinquishment of him as a preparation of their final
release.

The struggle of the passions, in the first act, had been played
out in the lower realm of the house. In Act II we ascend to Borkman's intellectual realm where that extraordinary figure, pacing
up and down over the lives he has devastated, waits, like a
brooding god, for the repentant world to return to him so that
he might live again in the world. At this height of consciousness
Borkman three times attempts his self-vindication: to Frida, to
Vilhelm Foldal, and to Ella, the successive accounts increasing
in depth and complexity. The first apparition of Borkman, with
Frida, is the most impressive and simplistic: the miner's son and
visionary who with his hammer that sounded like the midnight
bell would free the metallic spirits of the earth from their
enchantment. He urges upon poor Frida, whose mind he fear-
fully overburdens, his own attitude of proud exile, of holding
to a consciousness of containing a music within which the par-
ticipants in the dance of life never will attain to. Borkman's
impressiveness is abetted by the scenic background: walls decor-
ated with tapestries depicting hunting scenes, shepherds and
shepherdesses, and, in the rear wall, a door that blends in with
the tapestry so that it is invisible until it opens and closes—as
if this faded pastoral landscape both took and gave characters.
Frida will disappear into this tapestried landscape when she
exits by the concealed door and both Ella and Gunhild will
startlingly emerge from it, so that it is the female characters
who are associated with this dim and faded but once vividly
natural scene just as in Act I Mrs. Wilton had been visually
associated with the lush green of the garden room. The tapestries, which belong to Ella, may suggest the natural world that
Borkman had blighted with his crime against love, thus effecting
a visual extension of Ella's accusation, while the "hunting" *motif*
they depict might supply a hunter-identity, associated with Odin/
Wotan, to Borkman.

The juxtaposition of Borkman, the would-be monarch of the
kingdom he created, and of Foldal, the would-be tragic poet of
this kingdom, is one of the boldest grotesqueries of the play. The

ruin of Borkman's projected empire brought down with it, like
the satanic disgrace, a host of lesser figures, and Foldal, who
each night brings the manuscript of his one tragedy in the vain
hope of reading it to Borkman, supplies to Borkman's aborted
king-identity his own aborted identity of the king's skald and
the king's fool. Like the fool, Foldal must suit the moods of his
master and, if he oversteps the mark, may be dismissed as
Borkman does finally dismiss him when Foldal at last calls into
question the very basis of Borkman's proudly sustained identity.
Foldal, bathetically "imitating" Borkman (like Borkman he is
isolated within his family, the passionate hatred which Borkman
inspires from Gunhild becoming the contempt which Foldal
earns from his wife; Borkman loses a son to Mrs. Wilton and
Foldal loses a daughter to her), most endangers the heroic stance
Borkman assumes before us. The dramatic method whereby
Borkman is mocked, passionately condemned and ultimately
honored is among the most intriguing things in all Ibsen: it
maintains the apparition of Borkman in a condition of extreme
uncertainty, now farcical, now monstrous, and now heroic, until
the final magnificent assertion of his visionary identity.

Borkman's aborted project had been on a Faustian scale.
"Trade routes and shipping lines girdling the globe." It had
foundered through the betrayal of a friend, Hinkel, whose medi-
ocre rise depended on Borkman's spectacular fall and was caused
by rivalry over a woman, Ella. Borkman loftily dismisses this
love-rivalry ("Enough of these old, idiotic stories") but the
history will repeat itself, in accordance with the Marxian formula, now as farce: for the friendship of Borkman and Foldal
will break down over merely the *theme* of "woman" as Borkman ridicules Foldal's most cherished poetic ideal. This is a
farcical rehearsal, too, for the more terrible confrontation of
Ella and Borkman that will follow when Ella resurrects the "old,
idiotic story" and exposes the great crime of which Borkman is
guilty.

With the dismissal of Foldal Borkman now reconciles himself to total solitude until death. He puts out the lamp and stands
in semi-darkness, a Hamm-like figure of impressive but heart-
rending loneliness; but his silence and solitude are abruptly
ended by a knock on the tapestry door, and Ella emerges, the
candle she is carrying making her a center of moving light in
the room. The effect of the rear tapestry wall opening up for

Ella's luminous entrance into the darkened Borkman realm gives her the appearance, I think, of a figure emerging from Borkman's own subconscious. The room remains in semi-darkness, lit only by the candle, for the rest of the scene, so that the faded tapestries and the pastoral and natural world they depict supply a now darkened visual extension of Ella's accusation that Borkman has destroyed the natural and instinctual forces of life.

Ella had been Borkman's spiritual companion, the sole person who divined his desire to "wake all the slumbering spirits of the gold," in the depths and able, also, to soar with him in his loftiest projects. Falsely, however, he allowed himself to abandon Ella (whom one might see as his Jungian anima in its beneficent aspect, as Gunhild might be its malign aspect) and be deceptively lured by Hinkel "towards the enticing heights I longed for" until Hinkel "toppled me into the abyss." Just as Borkman's height-depth metaphors evoke mythic and archetypal actions (at one point he likens his boldest project to a balloon voyaging, a god-like aerial freedom), so Ella describes her drama in natural and cosmic terms that take on archetypal overtones. Borkman has killed the natural joy in her so that she lives under an "eclipse," unable to give love to humans, animals, or plants, like the desolate Demeter or the goddess Freia whose love was cynically bartered for gold and power by Wotan. The account she gives of her coldness of heart itself sounds like an episode from folk-tale:

> I've never known any compassion—since you left me, I'm wholly incapable of that. If a poor, starving child came into my kitchen, freezing and weeping, and begged for a little food, then I left it up to my cook. I never felt any urge to take the child in myself, warm it at my own hearth, and enjoy sitting by, watching it eat its fill. And I was never like that in my youth; I remember so clearly. It's you who've made this sterile empty desert within me—and around me, too.

The generalizing effect of the syntax "If a poor starving child . . . then I left it up to my cook. . . . I never felt . . ." implies not a single episode but a universal situation, suggesting that Ella was a force of potential natural warmth and love in the world that has been destroyed and made into a sterile desert. This "universalizing" phrasing is similar to that in which Borkman depicts his ambitions that take on the dimensions of total world-conquest far beyond the potentialities of any actual nineteenth-century Norwegian industrial financier. On the purely psychological level of interpretation one would have to dismiss such phrasing by Ella, Gunhild, and Borkman as symptoms of multiple megalomania—one of the reasons why the still prevalent psychological interpretation of Ibsen is so unrewarding. It is far more rewarding to respond to the immensity of these metaphors and to invest the dramatic characters with archetypal presence in a drama of universal forces that once fought for dominion over the world itself, as in Wagner's *Ring of the Nibelungs.*

We should experience the play as a psychic ritual where the forces of our spiritual life are resurrected to be re-experienced by us in terms larger than psychological limitation or moral judgment. To attempt to judge Borkman, for instance, in conventional terms is to prevent the power of the figure to work fully upon us, for he is one of our own gods or demons projected onto the stage. Instead of trying to cut the play down to the size of our psychological and moral limitations, we should respond to the gods and demons of Ibsen's dramas with the same fearful excitement, the same ambivalence of feeling toward these alarming forces that the spectator of oriental theater, with its demonic masks and costumes, feels. The visionary longing for dominion over the earth and the transformation of it, the equally as urgent longing for a world transfigured by the power of love, and the desire for honor and glory, which are the animating principles of Borkman, Ella, and Gunhild, are the subjects not only of the earliest mythic expressions of the race, but also of the modern individual's inward dreams and fantasies which, like the mythic stories, exist outside the categories of moral judgment or psychological explanation. As an audience we must permit the presences on the stage to assert themselves to their full potential, and I believe that this does happen: that playgoers are moved and excited by the play even though, on the realistic level, it contains inconsistencies and absurdities that any critic can point to. For the playgoer is moved unconsciously, feels the operation of the larger, archetypal drama behind the realistic action, and this larger drama succeeds in imposing itself to such an extent that the visionary last actions of the play, of Borkman's ascent to the height, his address to his invisible kingdom and its spirits, the eerie emergence of the metal hand from this kingdom which fatally clutches his heart, and the final condition of the twin sisters as shadows over a dead man, are all taken in its stride by

an audience that could not have responded at this level at the
beginning of the play. Ibsen has "trained" his audience to rise
to this level of perception by making the mythic drama continually weave its pattern through the movement of the realistic
action until it is this mythic pattern, and not the realistic action,
that finally imposes itself upon us.

The primacy of the archetypal drama over the realistic one
is evident in the curious fact that the play sets up the scaffolding
of a larger *realistic* structure than it actually supplies, as William
Archer observed: for the play seems to abandon a major plot—
the role of Hinkel in the flight of Erhart, Mrs. Wilton, and Frida.
It is as if the larger than life rivalry of Borkman and Hinkel, and
Hinkel's success and effectiveness within the world from which
Borkman has exiled himself, were indispensable elements of the
mythic fable but that to integrate this story into the·realistic
structure would involve the minute and ingenious plotting of
Ibsen's earlier procedure that would remove much of the force
of the "demonic" and archetypal drama. The "realistic" plot of
Erhart's planned flight with Mrs. Wilton and its consequences
is treated with a similar unconcern for detail, and the "gestures"
of the older characters towards Erhart are strangely inappro-
priate. At Ella's impassioned request, Borkman permits Erhart
to adopt Ella's surname: at which point the tapestry door is
flung open as Gunhild, for the first time since her arrival in the
house, enters Borkman's room fiercely to oppose this project.
So desperate does Ella now consider Erhart's situation to be
("Erhart's bound to go down in this storm"), that she actually
persuades Borkman, also for the first time, to leave his realm
and descend to that of Gunhild. Yet, far from being in danger
of going down in the storm, Erhart is sunnily immune and
already has resolved to leave them.

The incongruity of this passionate gesturing toward Erhart
by the elders is continued in the third Act whose two unequal
sections involve Borkman's confrontation with Gunhild and
Erhart's flight with Mrs. Wilton. The first section has all the
fine demonic power of the best moments in the play as Borkman
proudly exonerates himself while Gunhild pronounces him already dead and adjures him to stay in the grave where he lies,
and over which she will create a monument that will erase the
memory of him for ever from the world. This monument, however, is Erhart, who now bursts into the room to oppose his youth

and vitality, his joy-of-life, against the manic idealism of his mother. The ghostly aspect of the play, where Ella, Gunhild, and Borkman beckon futilely towards Erhart like exiled spirits seeking to inhabit living flesh and blood, was noted by Bernard Shaw. "This melancholy household of the dead crumbles to dust at the knock of the younger generation at the door. . . . The fresh air and the light of day break into the tomb; and its inhabitants crumble into dust."[3]

Erhart's reactions to the overtures of the elders occupy a great deal of the action but, until Mrs. Wilton's appearance, these exchanges have a somewhat formal and mechanical quality so that Erhart's bid for freedom against the implorations of his elders to join them dutifully in love (Ella), honor (Gunhild), and power (Borkman) has the quality of a purely archetypal situation unfiltered through the mesh of familial reality (in striking contrast to the almost stifling familial intricacies of the preceding play, *Little Eyolf*). It is a deliberate artistic intention, for Ibsen has underscored Erhart's detachment from these elders: he has hardly seen his father, has been brought up for many years by his aunt, has lived in recent years with his mother but now lives away from the house. The dispassionate and dramatically slack nature of his responses, therefore, hardly is surprising, but it causes an uncomfortable drop in the play's level of intensity. The mechanical nature of his replies might also imply he is under Mrs. Wilton's "spell," as Gunhild actually charges: "There's some strange power that's over you. You're not under your mother's influence anymore. Nor your — your foster mother's, either." Erhart's "effortful" reply that he now knows his own strength is not entirely convincing.

This scene is somewhat like an ironic reversal of the legendary temptation of the young knight to be unchaste: here the young knight of Venus must withstand the three ghostly temptations of fidelity, honor, and power before he can claim his sensual prize, which he does at last by opening the door and calling Mrs. Wilton into the room. The life forces of Mrs. Wilton and Erhart now exit from the play and, after only the briefest wild agitation from Gunhild, the elders reconcile themselves to their loss. From this point onwards, their ghostly drama overcomes the incongruities that afflicted it all the time these figures attempted to participate again in life, and it rises to a height of poignant and majestic authenticity.

The play that began in late evening now ends, outdoors, in the dark of night, the moon shining through the scudding clouds making a continuous play of light and shadow upon the characters on the snow-covered ground. After Gunhild's final flurry of agitated action the play proceeds on a superbly *reflective* plane anticipating the mood of *When We Dead Awaken*. As the metallic sound of Mrs. Wilton's silver sleigh bells dies away in the distance, the older trio group for an at first sardonic, then visionary recapitulation and apotheosis of their painful history. Borkman *"as if awakening"* is transfigured to a level of conciousness that would seem mad if it were not so finely and deeply aware of its condition. His reaction to the incongruous figure of poor Foldal, who limps into view with a battered umbrella and without his spectacles to report that he has been run over by the sleigh, and his sardonic responses to the details of Foldal's story are those of a man to whom everything now is falling into perspective, to the extent that he even is able to appreciate the comedy, with all its sexual innuendoes, of Foldal's naive narration.

As the comic-pathetic figure of Foldal happily hobbles out of view, Borkman, who now has been enlarged rather than diminlished by his juxtaposition with the clerk and thus has overcome the earlier comic incongruity, collects himself for his grander departure. He resolves to look again on his "buried treasures" and to bring to life again, in his imagination, the world he once wished to create but which now lies lifeless under this world of snow. The scene around him changes to accord with his vision, the house and open land giving way to a wilder and wilder landscape until he reaches a height where, in the now clear moonlight, there is revealed "an expansive landscape, with fjords and high, distant mountain ranges towering one after another." Borkman, like a magician, now brings his whole ghostly kingdom to life, seeing smoke from the steamers that would have sailed out of the transfigured fjord to "make the whole round earth into one community." He hears the uncreated factories whirring as the night shift continues the unceasing activity of his empire which itself becomes infinite:

> Do you see those mountain ranges *there*—far off. One after another. They leap skyward. They tower in space. That's my deep, my endless, inexhaustible kingdom.

Borkman's religion had been to transfigure the world through means other than the human spirit itself: through mineral and metallic forces. This displacement of *love* from human to metallic values is an aberration, but, with Borkman, it is an impressively poetic one, and though Ella indicts this aberration, the indictment would have no force if Borkman's aberrant love had not been a tremendous thing. Borkman is a spiritual hero who can arouse love-hatred because his misdirected powers were so impressive. It is just such a displacement of powers that has created the most impressive achievements of history of which the tremendous industrialist-Capitalist civilization of the present, which Borkman would have transformed, is the latest manifestation. It is only the most visionary and energetic imaginations within the human herd, the "demonic" ones, who are capable of so magnificent an aberration. Every great culture that has made its decisive mark upon the world is an imaginative distortion of our basic humanity, what Reinhold Niebuhr, in *Beyond Tragedy*, has termed "a tower of Babel": an attempt by humanity blasphemously to attain to godhood. The act of self-indictment is only the culminating point of a great culture, creed, or ideology, the point at which it becomes most deeply self-reflective and is aware of its own demons. In *Civilization and its Discontents* Freud pessimistically saw this process of displacement and distortion of instinctual energies into repressive cultural forms as both essential and fatal to civilization.

Borkman's betrayal of the "warm, living human heart" of Ella for "the kingdom—and the power—and the glory" of his empire can stand for humanity's continual betrayal, or displacement, of its instinctual life for transcendent achievement, a betrayal that Erhart refused to make. "The kingdom—and the power—and the glory" are in traditional Christianity the province of God only, and the act of appropriating this province on behalf of humanity is a Faustian blasphemy to which a number of Ibsen heroes are impelled. Julian, for example, boldly appropriates the same words from the Christian paternoster and uses them against Christianity, and Ibsen's own professed goal of a "third empire of spirit" that would supersede Christianity is a blasphemous ambition to create heaven here on earth. Borkman's "crime" against Ella, therefore, is inseparable from his greatness (and, on the level of individual life-history, Ella's estimate of the enormity of her own suffering is as megalomaniacal as Borkman's ambition), and it would be difficult to deplore that greatness. In the most poetic and thrilling speech in the entire Cycle, Borkman, in what is simultaneously a prayer and a declaration of love, carries us into the very heart of his vision:

> That wind works on me like the breath of life. It comes to me like a greeting from captive spirits. I can sense them, the buried millions. I feel the veins of metal, reaching their curving, branching, beckoning arms out to me. I saw them before me like living shadows—the night I stood in the bank vault with a lantern in my hand. You wanted your freedom then—and I tried to set you free. But I lacked the strength for it. Your treasures sank back in the depths. *(His hands outstretched)* But I'll whisper to you here in the silence of the night. I love you, lying there unconscious in the depths and the darkness! I love you, you riches straining to be born—with all your shining aura of power and glory! I love you, love you, love you.

Although Rolf Fjelde has rendered this speech as finely as one can imagine in English, it finally defies translation. From underground comes a breath *(pust)* that acts upon Borkman like the "air of life" *(livsluft):* the vampire theme of the breath of the dead awakening the living. This breath is the greeting from the enslaved *(underdanige)* spirits, reminiscent of the slave workers who served Alberich before Wotan seized power over the gold. Borkman then senses or sees (the Norwegian *"fornemmer"* implies both) the bound *(bundne)* millions of ghost slaves. He feels the veins of ore stretching out their curving, branching, tempting/luring arms, with the sinister suggestion, here, not only of imploring release but also of luring the beholder into a ghostly trap, as in many fables of sirens or spirits who seek to trap the living.

Ella will urge that Borkman has betrayed the world of the living for that of the dead, and in this image of the ghost-slaves lifting imploring and tempting arms to Borkman, who then responds, we become aware of the appalling but magnificent perversity of Borkman who could be moved deeply by the enslavement of *metals* in a world where millions of humans still were enslaved. When he stood in the bank vault, contemplating his crime, these ghostly images appeared to him like animated shadows, the flickering light of his lamp making the shadows appear like spiritual shapes. The shadows begged to be set free from their slavery but Borkman "lacked the power" and they sank back into the depths and darkness. Yet now Borkman addresses this shadow world again in the stillness of the night with his poignant and perverse declaration of love — a demon addressing demons. He wished to bring these spirits or demons and all their shining train of power and glory into the world, using the limited riches of the bank to release the infinite hordes of life-craving riches *(livskrevende verdier)* which still lay unconscious/asphyxiated *(skinndöde)* needing to be roused to life by the air of the upper world in order to breathe. By betraying the living human world in order to serve this shadow-world, Borkman had converted the living into shadows, "a dead man and two shadows," as Ella will say.

As Ella accuses Borkman of killing the power of love "in the living human heart" that beat for him, and as she prophesies that "you will never ride in triumph into your cold, dark kingdom," a cold metallic hand eerily reaches upward and clutches at Borkman's heart in a form of demonic love-response. The action suggests more than the conventional infernal punishment for the sinner of dragging his soul down to hell, for the powers that Borkman sought to release into the world are not necessarily infernal, but potentially beneficent. "Borkman remains crippled," as Ronald Gray deprecates, but not, as Gray (Ibsen's most unremittingly carping critic) is eager to suggest, through some deficiency in Ibsen, but because the spirit of modern humanity, which Ibsen is accurately depicting, is fragmented into such separate, inadequate and often hostile parts so that even so magnificent an energy as Borkman's is guilty of betraying essential aspects of our humanity.

The major characters of Ibsen's plays unconsciously or consciously, willingly or unwillingly, are lured away from the condition of comfortable mediocrity with which our psychological and moral categories are at ease, to commitments of the spirit that entail guilt and unhappiness and even self-destruction: but the dramas they thereby instigate have value for lighting up and identifying essential aspects of our total spiritual life. Such moments as Ella's indictment, Borkman's self-exoneration, his declaration of love, his death, and the tragic reconciliation of the twin sisters over his dead body are epiphanies, means of "showing forth" the powers, both demonic and benign, within the spirit—powers which most of us shrink from seeing. Such spiritual heroes, for all their ambiguous and alarming qualities, move in a circle far beyond the range of our moral and psychological sharp-shooting, that range in which we keep ourselves secure at the price of being insignificant.

Vancouver, British Columbia

NOTES

1 All English quotations of the play are from Rolf Fjelde's translation, *Ibsen: The Compete Major Prose Plays* (New York: Farrar, Straus and Giroux, 1978).

2 I have used, I hope not too injudiciously, Einar Haugen's *Norwegian English Dictionary* (Madison: Univ. of Wisconsin Press, 1907) as the basis for my speculations on alternative meanings to Norwegian words.

3 Bernard Shaw, *The Quintessence of Ibsenism* (New York: Hill & Wang, 1957), pp. 135-36.

Strindberg's Historical Imagination: *Erik XIV*

Michael W. Kaufman

I

At the end of the nineteenth century to study history was still to believe that the historian's highest commitment was to Truth, and that invariably the right historical method would disclose the formal coherence of man's life in time. To be sure, by the 1890's methods of attaining truth and discovering universal principles of order were anything but uniform. Positivists like Ranke, Comte, Marx, and Mill argued that history was merely another branch of natural science and that the past should be studied from a sound basis of experimentally verifiable laws. For Idealists like Hegel, Croce, and Dilthey, on the other hand, history was a human not a mathematical science, and thus the historian had to get "inside" the past, to write history in Leopold von Ranke's term "as it actually was" by reliving or rethinking what happened and why. Still, no matter what differences in methodology or philosophy existed, nineteenth-century European historical thought "represented an effort to constitute history as the ground for a 'realistic' science of man, society, and culture";[1] almost without exception men accepted that history was proceeding in a more-or-less coherent direction toward some teleology, and that historical events could be made to yield their ultimate meaning.

Strindberg's position at century's end made it possible for him to know all the important developments of nineteenth-century historiography. Indeed, he was remarkably well read in history, an interest he maintained right up to his final years.[2] Early in his life Henry Thomas Buckle's *History of Civilization in England* had made a profound impression upon Strindberg when it first appeared in Swedish in 1871. It was with Buckle's book before him that Strindberg revamped his early drafts and produced his first significant drama, the prose *Master Olof* (1872). During the eighties Strindberg undertook a comprehensive study of Swedish history partly because of his dissatisfaction with the official versions which he felt had reduced Sweden to the history of its kings.3 By 1881-82 Strindberg published his own two volume *Kulturgeschichte, The Swedish People.* The next decade produced his seige of profound depression and now history became something of a therapy to ameliorate his psychic pain. As Strindberg later wrote to his German publisher, Emil Schering, about his Inferno crisis, "as a means of killing time I read right through world history."4 After he had completed his series of royal historical dramas, Strindberg published a long essay, "The Mysticism of World History" (1903), which combined a Swedenborgian mysticism with the Schopenhauerean theme of Conscious Will in the form of higher powers that mysteriously govern the universe.

Almost always Strindberg's interest in history and its meaning led him to accept an ultimate design evident in the course of events. The very scope of his planned historical cycle, stretching from St. Erik to Gustav Adolph IV, some seven and a half centuries of Swedish history, attests to Strindberg's interest in discovering causal pattern amidst complex chains of events. This reason alone makes *Erik XIV* (1899) a striking exception in Strindberg's historical canon. Contrary to the dominant thought of his age and his own inclinations to embrace a providential destiny for mankind, *Erik XIV* emerges as an ironic critique of traditional nineteenth-century historicism in its skepticism about coherent designs in history and its extreme doubt about whether any light or shape pertains to human existence at all. The plot of *Erik XIV* appears tantalizingly simple: the play records the last years of the reign of Gustav Vasa's heir, depicting Erik's struggles with his half-brothers and the powerful Swedish nobles, climaxing with his deposition and the ascension of John III.5 But in the course of its chronicle *Erik XIV* progresses to the brink of the grotesque, broaching a nearly apocalyptic confrontation of Erik with his role, and by extension, of Strindberg with history.

In a deeper sense it is Strindberg's other historical works which are anomalies and *Erik XIV* which marks the essential continuity with the rest of his dramatic canon. This play, to a far greater degreee than *The Saga of the Folkungs* and *Gustav Vasa,* reveals the same irreconcilable conflicts that had characterized Strindberg's early Naturalistic works and that reappear in his later expressionistic plays. *Erik* also looks back to *The Father, Miss Julie, Comrades,* and *The Bond* where Time is perceived as the inevitable falling away from a golden age of innocence, and forward to the late plays where the shifting, complex transitions between dream and waking express Strindberg's sense of fluxing, unstable reality. Yet *Erik XIV* exhibits the artistic control and the "irony" that R. J. Kaufmann rightly finds missing in most of Strindberg's dramas.[6] This is because history offered Strindberg a perspective distant enough to enable him to view his personal agonies with detachment, yet still close enough to exploit their imaginative possibilities. In the Vasa trilogy history becomes a convenient metaphor for Strindberg's life-long struggle between faith and skepticism, between his desire to believe that human existence has meaning and his suspicion that chaos and absurdity are man's existential fate. If *Gustav Vasa* expresses Strindberg's faith in supernatural powers who chastize men but eventually lead them to the right path, *Erik XIV,* written only months afterward, dramatizes a history stripped of all illusions of providential order, emptied of teleology or regeneration.

Strindberg's conventional attitude toward history collapsed in *Erik XIV* because the cast of his mind was fundamentally unhistorical.[7] The kind of temperament that habitually attempted to transcend time and transmute matter, that steadfastly refused to adopt a simple view either of self or of reality, that persistently elevated the authenticity of its own imagination over that of the empirical world was apt to feel uncomfortable with a materialistic interpretation of history. Because Strindberg perceived with special intensity the ambiguous nature of human experience, the historian's tendency to crystallize human personalities and to account systematically for the structure of events violated his sense of the impenetrable complexities of existence. For Strindberg, as for Pirandello a generation later, history reflects the tragic conflict between life which is always moving and form which attempts to fix the process immutably.

Specifically, this essay suggests that a better approach than reading *Erik XIV* as a historical drama is to read it as a drama about history; to appreciate that the events of Erik's reign were not facts Strindberg wished to recover from the past, but rather imaginative actions he wished to used to controvert the idea of history as a valid, complete determination of past actuality. History, as Strindberg conceives it in *Erik XIV,* is the product of blind wills and ironic reversals that challenge the providential and Hegelian notions of time as a linear or dialectical advance toward some destined goal. In its place *Erik XIV* projects history as discontinuous, fragmented, and chaotic where the only principles of order inhere in the mind of the individual perceiver. Such an idea was not new to Strindberg; in 1888 he had declared that the laws of nature are "merely subjective perceptions of our brains, which love order and work to find purpose everywhere."[8] Seen from the perspectives of its subjectivity, absurdity, and dysteleology, *Erik XIV* is more than the final link in the Vasa Trilogy; it is a clear anticipation of some crucially modern traditions that trace their line of descent to Pirandello, Sartre, Kafka, and contemporary existential historicism.

II

Erik XIV confronts the mystery of human actions, the bewildering contrarieties in human nature. But unlike the historian, Strindberg never attempts to schematize perplexing dichotomies into a unified resolution. Nor will he allow his audience explanations of psychological motivations or of causal coherence of action. Not only is human action unpredictable, but it is played out in a universe so opaque that it remains doubtful whether any governing purpose exists. "I don't understand how what has happened could happen. Why, it's against all logic, against all calculation, against all justice. Is there a God who . . . makes black white,"[9] Göran asks late in the play, and his incomprehension reflects our own. The meaning of the dramatic action lies in its involutions which probe the world beneath recorded chronicles where reality remains confusing and where the possibility of exercising volition is severely limited. "Don't you see," Göran explains late in the play, "how events take place without our being able to do anything about them? . . . I can't move a finger and can only wait, asking: what is going to happen next?" (310-11).

That sense of human complexity finds fullest expression in Erik. Later in his life, in a letter to the Intimate Theatre, Strindberg referred to Erik as "the characterization of a characterless human being."[10] Strindberg's meaning, similar to that which he elucidated in the preface to *Miss Julie* written more than a decade before, is that Erik is characterless in the sense that he is far too protean to be confined within the Procrustean bed the historian assigns him. "Do you like Erik," Mother Persson asks her son, and Göran's response—"Yes and no"—reveals the vital ambivalences a complex human being evokes. Conflicting evaluations of Erik proliferate in the play; we see him through the refracting vision of most of the characters. To Karin, Erik is like a weak child who demands pity and needs caring. Her father, in contrast, sees in him an unscrupulous profligate, a libertine lord who abuses his status by trifling with the common people. The dowager Queen who contemptuously speaks of Erik as "more pitiable than wicked" (269), later speaks of him as "a raging madman who still wears the crown" (301), unfit to rule or to live. But Göran Persson comes to understand Erik as a weak, sensitive soul tormented by agonies of a guilty conscience. His brother John thinks him a "madman"; his other brother, Charles, agrees his action is not wise, "but it isn't crazy either" (315). Strindberg's insistence on these opposing attitudes creates a complex view of Erik which Peder Welamson summarizes when he insists to Mans that "the king's a human being all the same" (312). Erik becomes a vivid symbol in whom conflicting impressions and attitudes merge; as an expression of opposites Strindberg suggests the multiplicity of his nature.

Such a multiple view of human character is consistently advanced during the play in the way that pairs of minor characters mirror the dichotomies within Erik. Between Göran and Karin (and to some degree within each of them) oscillate the contrary forces of public obligation and private fulfillment, the former depending on crafty and callous action, the latter nurturing tender sentiments of guilt and compassion. Nils Gyllenstjerna represents the conservative world of courtly ritual and feudal loyalty while Prince John epitomizes political subterfuge and broken oaths. The ensign, Max, is naively honest and innocent, but the soldier, Peder Welamson, is crassly pragmatic and seasoned in political treachery. In contrast with Queen Katarina's vengeful hatred of her step-son is Mother Persson's tender solicitude for Göran. The tensed contrasts between characters reflect the confusion in Erik's mind. Erik's emotional instability and mercurial temperament may have some basis in fact; but in Strindberg's hands they are reasons for disputing historical accuracy since they emphasize dramatically the illogical, incongruous, and capricious elements that elude historical scholarship. Although one of the initial impetuses for Strindberg's interest in historical drama came from his reading of Shakespeare's chronicle plays, what he produced finally owes more to Shakespeare's understanding of human personality; the inspiration behind *Erik XIV* is not so much the *Henriad* as it is Hamlet, "made up of apparent contradictions, evil and good, hating and loving, cynical and enthusiastic, cruel and lenient, strong and weak; in a word: a human being, different at every moment as human beings are, of course."11

If reality and personality are random and unstable, then the structure of drama, if it is to imitate life, should be similarly fragmented and disintegrated. *Erik XIV* with its continually alternating scenes is, formally, the antithesis of the structurally well-made *Gustav Vasa*. The action shifts at an astonishingly rapid pace from Stockholm to Uppsala, from a bridgehead to a tower room, from Göran Persson's home to Mans Knekt's home. Structurally the episodic scenes stress the lack of causality and coherence that the baffling characterizations and elliptic action suggest on a deeper level. Private scenes alternate with public ones, frequently merging to depict the conflict between the demands of the Self and those of governing authority as merely another manifestation of the maddeningly irreconcilable opposites that characterize Strindberg's world-view. The interpenetration of private and public is stressed from the play's opening. Instead of the splendid scenes of ceremonial ritual that Strindberg frequently used to introduce his history plays, *Erik XIV* begins with an outrageously intimate scene where a furious Erik heaves a keg of nails at his mistress and her lover. Yet even this private scene is qualified by the "pair of ears behind the hedge," belonging to Göran Persson who brings news of Erik's failed courtship of Elizabeth.

The opening scene is highly effective not only for its whimsical rearrangement of historical materials, but more significantly, for its disturbing mode of presentation. "This is too crazy," (267) says Karin, and we are inclined to agree. The ludicrous action has the effect of reducing the historical sublime to a kind of farcical ludicrousness, providing, as we shall see, a comical vision of great historical matters that pervades the play. The farce serves to diminish both sides of the conventional conflict between private impulses and public obligations: on the one side appears the political world of skulking eavesdroppers, ambitious power-hungry lords; on the other is the world of romance played out as silly slapstick. And Strindberg emphasizes that these warring opposites may never be reconciled, nor even firmly distinguished, for affairs of state and affairs of the heart blend so imperceptibly that our impression must be either that history is created by quixotic emotional urges or that an individual's emotional life is dictated by public events; or both at once.

Strindberg's concern with the complexities of being as the ultimate reality also expresses itself in the compressed swiftness of the dramatic action and the changes he made in his sources. Of the eight eventful years of Erik's reign (1560-68), Strindberg chose to concentrate on the last four. The final acts particularly compress into a whirlwind of action the last two years of his rule—the massacre at Uppsala, Erik's fit of guilt, the meeting of the Estates, the marriage and Coronation of Karin, the rebellion and the deposition. Chronologically, the imprisonment of the Stures and their massacre took place in 1567 and not until a year later were Erik and Karin married. Only after the wedding did John begin his rebellion and not until three months later did Erik step down. Dramatically, Strindberg compresses all of this action in a virtual simultaneity of time during the fourth act.12 Such techniques as the telescoping of events, the compression of time, and the continual interpenetration of the past on the present (Vasa's golden reign is kept continually before our minds) and the present on the future (characters frequently prophesy accurately, such as Göran's warning that as long as John lives there will be no peace in the realm) work to destroy any notion of a linear temporal order progressing from past through present to future; the episodic structure of *Erik XIV* suggests instead a universe in which the flow of time is neither continuous nor orderly. Even more noteworthy is the way Strindberg brings back a character like Agda who was introduced in an earlier play and explicitly emphasizes that *Erik XIV* open on "the same setting as in the fifth act of *Gustav Vasa*" (263). Instead of history as an intellectual inquiry into a completed past, these techniques suggest the intricacies of organic process, contemplating history as a seamless, unending web.

Rapid fluctuation in mood is the basic rhythm of the play and is everywhere apparent: in Erik's volatile, manic-depressive fits, in the sudden rise and fall of political and personal fortunes, in the rapid chops and changes in action and setting. The alternations and the mysterious world they manifest are given fullest expression during the final act where amidst bewildering reversals Erik and Göran desperately try to comprehend the mad world in which they have been condemned to live. In such an unstable world irony becomes the appropriate artistic method to portray a reality which is not fixed, and personalities who seem a succession of roles in a continually shifting scenario. In the preceding plays of the trilogy what irony appears is prophetic, anticipating the destined fulfillment of events. Olof's early re-mark, for example, that "one man can't set himself against the current" (36), prepares for his later compromises between reforming idealism and political necessity. In a similar manner the insistent references to past treacheries during the opening scene of *Gustav Vasa* lay the foundation for the bloodbath of the Dalesmen. The political conflicts dramatized in the first act lead us to anticipate a future, climactic meeting between the king and the Dalecarlians. The expectation is fulfilled, but ironically, in the final scene when the Dalesmen approach Vasa not in vengeance but in friendship.

Both *Master Olof* and *Gustav Vasa* are energized by a providential conception of history depicting "the giant hand, which one never sees, only feels" (189), working its will through human agents. But in *Erik XIV* not even "the finger of God" is apparent and human existence is never redeemed. From the first act when Erik gives Catherine of Poland to his half-brother, John, after "mature consideration," only to renege moments later and decide to marry her himself, to the end of the play when he magnanimously pardons the lords immediately after the Estates declare them guilty, Erik's impetuous regal moves ironically nullify his royal power. Such plotting more than simply ensures focus on Erik's erratic temperament, though it does that; it provides Strindberg's sardonic assessment of a universe that promotes such ironies. "There's only one person I don't want to see," Erik declares, "That's Karin's father. The soldier,

Mans" (289), at which point Göran opens the door revealing the thing itself.

The mainspring of the plot is a bewildering series of reversals that sends crashing all expectations of political and private fulfillment the first three acts had hinted at. It is Karin's naive hope of preserving peace at her wedding and preventing blood-guilt from falling on her children that prompts her to warn the nobles of the Estates' decision. From the depth of her affection for the childlike Erik, Karin acts in love; yet her act shatters the political scheme that Göran had so assiduously erected, which in turn destroys the marriage Karin had so long anticipated, and sends Erik and Göran to their deaths. Throughout the play characters are hoist with their own petard. Not only do political plots foil their engineers, but intimate relations capriciously turn against men and fall far shy of their promised potential. Göran, whose former life gains a purity of inspiration through the love of a woman, inexplicably loses that love and the "old devilish Göran" re-emerges in the final act a broken, cynical man. Göran who alone "knows all the secret ways in [Erik's] soul," and Erik who is tied to Göran by "invisible bonds," cannot create a lasting relationship because of their conflicting natures and the social differences between them. And Karin who is afraid of Göran "but yet must be friends," who loves Max but lives with Erik because of her maternal affection and public obligation, indirectly causes Max's death and directly precipitates Göran's and Erik's.

Still, the sense of irony and the utterly chaotic complexity it mirrors are clearest in Erik. Erik seems purposeless in the political scenario in which he is merely an actor—a "theatre king" as he tells his children. The contrast with Strindberg's *Queen Christina* in this respect is striking and instructive. Like Eric, Christina is presented as a "crowned actress," but here Strindberg provides information that *explains* her character. Her early separation from her mother, her rearing by a cold, affectionless aunt, her training for a masculine role help to answer why her struggle to emerge a woman is so difficult, and why she expressed such hatred toward her own sex. In *Erik XIV*, by contrast, the relatively slight attention given to the naturalistic details of the characters' past suggests that we are not meant to look for understandable patterns of behavior. What is characteristic of this play, as in *Charles XII*, is that Strindberg never exhibits the origins of the characters' motivations. Instead of dialogue of retrospection or scenes of analysis of the past, Strindberg thrusts at us sudden and unexpected changes.

It is a psychological drama without any attempt to explain psychic etiology. (We never know what motivates Göran's solicitude for Agda, or Karin's concern for Erik, or Erik's volatile fits of jubilance and frenzy.) If anything, Strindberg teases us with naturalism only to turn its deterministic premises into an ironic confirmation of life's inscrutability. The knowledge (gained from *Gustav Vasa*) that Erik was an unwanted product of a loveless home might explain his paranoiac suspicions and insecurity; but it does not explain why this comical mutation, so spectacularly unfit to rule, has been placed on the throne. In the play's own terms, this irony is best expressed by Göran when he remarks, "I wasn't born to wear a crown, but to rule" (281). Late in the third act, after his humiliating debacle before the Estates when he learns that Karin and his children have abandoned the palace, Erik picks up Sigrid's toy doll. "Her name's blind paleface," he tells Göran, the line recalling Karin's speech of the first act where she confides to Max that she pities Erik, "call[s] him my blind paleface for the last doll I ever had—he looked like her" (263). Now as he stands helplessly confused, the limp toy presents a grotesque image of Erik, which finally comes to encompass the whole of his disastrous career: an abandoned doll, passively borne by forces he can neither control nor understand.

If Erik is mad, his madness is a brilliant metaphor for the disturbing ambiguities of existence. The madman, traditionally, represents the annihilation of conventional foundations of logic and order. His madness attests to the terrifying diversity of perspectives and therefore presents to us the very embodiment of the relativity of truths. In this spirit Erik assures Mans Knekt that his actions seem eccentric only "because you who consider yourself sane are convinced that you wouldn't act as I if you were in my place" (314). Moreover, Erik's paranoiac suspicions are at once expressions of his instability as well as ironic commentaries on the slipperiness of objective truth. "You think all people are your enemies," Karin chides; "Yes," Erik replies, but only "because they hate me" (271). There is a kind of method to the madness that fears the violent and vicious world Erik must rule. Even more significantly, Erik's madness emerges from his vivid imagination, the result of confusing his own fantasies of reality with objective truth. With characteristic ease Erik transforms Elizabeth's refusal of his proposal to his own dismissal of that "whore." This is, one must conclude, part of Strindberg's point. Erik's failure to distinguish his imaginative projections from actuality is hardly unusual and certainly not insane; such *gestalts* are an integral part of human experience.

If the historian's greatest error is to accept appearances for reality and go on to transform living complexity into fixed simplicity, it is fallacious precisely because, as Erik says, "reality's never quite what I anticipate" (308). This realization of the ludicrous disparity between simple expectation and the complex reality is projected through the play's oscillating rhythms of tragedy and comedy. No other of Strindberg's history plays has so many comic moments which move it perilously close to farce. In *Erik XIV*, history subtly turns into comedy, and comedy, willy-nilly, transforms itself into tragedy as the Renaissance prince is revealed to be a court jester, a bumbling buffoon who turns to tragic shambles Göran's calculated schemes and dies for his buffoonery. The great historical moment is delivered as vaudeville when Erik enacts a hilarious charade of ineffectuality:

> You know I'm no speaker; that's why I had it written. I thought I had my speech in my pocket and opened fire against the traitors impromptu. Then I reached for my speech, but at the same moment I saw the Redbeard grinning at me as only John can. And I couldn't find the paper! Then I got wild, rushed on, mixing up names and figures, and it was as if someone had stirred up everything in my head and picked the mechanism of my tongue to pieces; this someone whom I hesitate to call Satan, made me say Svante Sture instead of Peder Welamson, and vice versa; I said the lords had decorated the bridge with garlands instead of wreaths, and all the old suspicions of the Stures that I've surpressed I blurted out, and a lot of accusations I can't prove. (303-04)

Strindberg's mixing of modes is at once funny and profound. As he uses a fragmented structure to point at experiences beyond the scope of coherence, so he uses a mixture of modes to point to complexities of human reality that lie beyond the scope of dramatic conventions. This structural technique stands in direct relationship to Strindberg's understanding that if drama is to reflect life accurately, it cannot simply resort to the reductive generic categorizations of art. Because history reduces men to characters, the complex past to events, it remains blind to the hidden forces that shape men's private lives, which in turn direct their public destinies. To fix and classify life, as history does, is unreliable because, as Erik and Göran so absurdly discover, categorization cannot contain the eccentricities, fluidity, and unpredictability of living. "Is life more to be laughed at than to be wept over?" Erik asks Göran in the closing moments of the play. Göran's answer expresses the essential ambiguities Strindberg finds beneath the historical chronicles: "as much the one as the other, I suspect" (323-24).

Strindberg's early title for Master Olof—"What is Truth?"—reveals that he was preoccupied with the epistemologic as well as the historiographic difficulties of comprehending actuality. But what receives a degree of emphasis in the earlier play, permeates the entire fabric of *Erik XIV*. The play seems to illustrate with a relentless thoroughness the pervasive relativity that renders all attempts to categorize and classify absurd. *Erik XIV* presents a world in which all of the old absolutes have ceased to have meaning, where the bases for judgment of right from wrong, sanity from insanity have been obliterated. News is bad or good depending only "on how you can make use of it" (286). Once murder was indeed murder, but now such simplistic reductions are "nonsense" (312). It is a world in which man's moral sentiments are in deadly combat with practical necessity, where what one plans to do "might not be legal, but certainly is just" (307). Even the intriguing Charles seems aware that Erik's pardon of the lords "isn't wise, but it isn't crazy either" (315). And Peder Welamson echoes this sentiment when he confesses that what Erik has done is "nice" but it "isn't wise" (312). In such a state ambiguities are so pervasive that they penetrate the cosmos: "The best life has to give is the worst of all. Hell lies in paradise; the angels are devils. Satan is a white dove and the Holy Spirit . . ." (307), Göran says, vividly depicting a world in which justice and order are warped. It is finally and most significantly a world in which multiplicity of perspectives denies the possibility of authoritative assessment. "I have always thought my acts were right," says Göran; "I too," responds Erik, "and most likely others do too" (323). From this perspective Erik's actions must be judged simultaneously as "his weakness and his strength" (328), and we are likely to share Göran's pessimism when he declares "I know absolutely nothing, understand nothing" (323).

By the final act Erik's assertion that the world is mad has a force of conviction; even the pragmatists, John and Charles, have come to believe it. But the play's reductive pessimism is most apparent in the way Strindberg's trilogy differs so radically from previous uses of this dramatic form. Aeschyus' *Orestia* and Shakespeare's *Henriad* both are dramatic groupings that proceed through a clear sequential pattern of cause and effect, with each play preparing for the following and where the final play (*The Eumenides* and *Henry V*) brings the entire group to a satisfactory resolution by projecting the fulfillment of justice, good government, and order. In their hands the idea of a trilogy (or tetralogy) becomes the most complete dramatic statement about teleology; the plays depict the final realization of a purposeful, beneficent goal worked out through time. Strindberg, on the other hand, allows the three plays of his *Vasa Trilogy* to unfold only to conclude *Erik XIV in medias res* where the power struggle is still unresolved, and the misery and despair still very much a mystery.

The dramatic action ceases with Göran and Erik condemned to death, leaving John and Charles to struggle for the throne. Charles's summary remark with which the play concludes comes near to Strindberg's own cynical response to the overall significance of the events the trilogy dramatizes. To the child's question regarding when the conflicts of interest and the clash of personalities will be over, Charles responds: "the struggles of life are never over" (328). In fact Strindberg perceives that the deadly contention is, if anything, eternal in its historical recurrences, now looking back to the end of Act I where Erik had prophetically warned that "the strife between brothers, the game of the Folkungs, isn't over" (279), and now forward to the fraternal enmity yet to come. Two points emerge from Strindberg's conclusion. First, in *Gustav Vasa* where Strindberg dramatizes a divine design working through *Vasa* to "unite Swedish men and Swedish lands into one" (221), the conclusion, reconciling historic antimonies, dramatizes the purposeful order behind the chaotic flux of events. But in *Erik XIV* the circular pattern of events reveals a history endlessly repeating itself. The inconclusive ending suggests a temporal pattern devoid of redemptive meaning, indifferent to the meaning and value of human life and consequently unable to justify the terrors of existence. And this pessimism in a beneficent providential order parallels its distrust in historicism itself. For the open-ended structure is intended to leave the impression of irresolution. It serves to remind the audience that human actions can never be judged as completed, for they generate causes and consequences that reach well beyond the scope of individual lives or epochs.

State University of New York at Albany

NOTES

1 Hayden White, *Metahistory: The Historical Imagination in Nineteenth Century Europe* (Baltimore: Johns Hopkins Univ. Press, 1973), p. 432. See also White's Introduction and first two chapters, pp. 1-131; Maurice Mandelbaum, *History, Man, and Reason: A Study of Nineteenth Century Thought* (Baltimore: Johns Hopkins Univ. Press, 1971).

2 Martin Lamm, *August Strindberg*, trans. Harry Carlson (New York: Benjamin Blom, 1971), p. 328, reports that Strindberg frequently borrowed books from the literary historian, John Mortensen, and goes on to list the principal volumes Strindberg used extensively.

3 Lamm, p. 327.

4 Letter to Schering, Dec. 12, 1902; quoted by Walter Johnson, *Strindberg and the Historical Drama* (Seattle: Univ. of Washington Press, 1963), p. 3.

5 See Johnson's succinct historical background to the play in his introduction to *Erik XIV* in his edition of *The Vasa Trilogy* (Seattle: Univ. of Washington Press, 1959), pp. 246-50.

6 "Strindberg: The Absence of Irony," *Drama Survey*, 3 (1964), 463-76; rpt. in *Strindberg: A Collection of Critical Essays*, ed. O. Reinert (Englewood Cliffs: Prentice Hall, 1971), 57-70.

7 See Birgitta Steene, "Shakespearean Elements in the Historical Plays of Strindberg," in Reinert, *Strindberg*, pp. 125-36.

8 Harry V. E. Palmblad, *Strindberg's Conception of History* (New York: AMS Press, 1966), p. 24.

9 Johnson, *The Vasa Trilogy*, p. 308. All quotations are from this edition and will subsequently be incorporated into the text.

10 *Open Letters to the Intimate Theatre*, trans. Johnson (Seattle: Univ. of Washington Press, 1966), p. 256.

11 *Ibid.*, p. 85. In another passage Strindberg compares Erik with Hamlet:

Erik XIV is a Hamlet, Stepmother (=stepfather; murders) Sture (=murders Polonius): Ophelia=Karin Mansdotter; Erik XIV dies poisoned as Hamlet does; insane or simulating insanity like Hamlet, vacillating, judges and rejects his judgment; his friend Horatio= Erik's friend Goran Persson—faithful unto death; Fortinbras= Dukes John and Charles; Hamlet was loved by the uncivilized masses. Erik, too, a hater of the lords and the people's king.

12 Joan Bulman, *Strindberg and Shakespeare* (London, 1933), p. 146 reports that Strindberg's earlier notes for *Erik XIV* indicate that he had planned a five act structure in which Erik's wedding and his deposition would each be given an entire act. That *Erik XIV* is the only play of this period to break with the traditional five act structure, and that Strindberg compresses his initially conceived fourth and fifth acts suggests that he consciously sought to produce the effect of breakneck, chaotic speed.

The *Skogsrå* of Folklore and Strindberg's *The Crown Bride*

Larry E. Syndergaard

Strindberg seems to have a folklore element at every turn in *The Crown Bride (Kronbruden):* herders' calls and songs, the wild hunt, riddles, the castle submerged in a lake, curses, the child-haunt, horn-calls, the despairing riverman (*forskarl* or *näck*), the bridal crown itself—even a ballad-like interrogation at the beginning of the play. But the most surprising and perplexing folk element appears when the midwife turns her back. Suddenly we are aware that Strindberg has given us a hybrid: not just an old crone, but the fox-tailed *skogsrå* or wood-nymph as well. This is the erotically tempting but later derisive "courtesan of the forest" who, when she wears no animal tail, is foul and hollow behind.[1]

Granted, her most general associations fit the play. The *skogsrå* is an ominous figure in Swedish folklore,[2] and the midwife-*skogsrå* is a direct accessory in the two basic transgressions of the play: Kersti's bearing an illegitimate child, and its death. The very reappearances of the midwife-*skogsrå* help build the atmosphere of lurking evil. And her delivering the illegitimate child, her insisting on attending the wedding as payment, her helping get rid of the child, and her appearing to Kersti at the wedding support the theme of the evolution and inescapability of sin.

Yet these points alone can hardly explain Strindberg's grafting of the *skogsrå* onto the midwife. The wood-nymph of folklore, after all, preys on *men;* in the play she pursues Kersti. And there is a visual anomaly in fusing the normally young and seductive *skogsrå* with the older midwife. There were alternatives. A midwife alone would seem to have been ominous

87

enough.[3] Strindberg might also have chosen a witch,[4] or he might have constructed a troll-midwife, the success of whose blandishments on Kersti would reflect trolls' abilities to bewitch humans.[5] Clearly, however, the *skogsrå* figure seemed more useful—enough so to compensate for the anomalies.

In this paper I will seek to sketch the way in which the *skogsrå* is useful to the dramatist and essential to the play, and hence to suggest a possible rationale for Strindberg's choice. I will proceed by examining the way he adapts the qualities inherent in the *skogsrå* of the folklore sources available to him,[6] and by analyzing his dramatic use in general of the midwife-*skogsrå* figure.

I

Certain factors may have played a specific if limited role in Strindberg's choice and use of the *skogsrå*. For example, the raucous and wanton *skogsrå* provides a better figurative counterweight to the bridal crown, an emblem of virginity, chastity, and decorum, than could witch or midwife alone. The *skogsrå* was sometimes identified as the quarry of the wild hunt, another of Strindberg's folk motifs.[7] Even one bit of the play's auditory embellishment, the thunder in the stove into which the midwife has ducked at the wedding celebration, seems suspiciously like an adaptation from legends in which thunder can strike down the heathen *skogsrå*[8]—particularly when we note that the Christlike White Child issues forth immediately afterward in apparent symbolic victory. The problems of fusing *skogsrå* and midwife may have seemed less formidable in view of the minor tradition of *skogsrå* as shapeshifter who was known to appear as an old crone.[9] And Strindberg may have inferred what later statistical studies show: the *skogsrå* tradition is associated with the old "summer-dairy culture" or "chalet culture" generally and with the region of Dalarna in particular. These form, of course, the setting of the play.[10]

Such factors, however, are not deeply organic to the play. More important is the fact that, in contrast to the other creatures we have mentioned, only the *skogsrå* is always finally inimical to man.[11] The midwife of folklore can help as well as hurt, and trolls can often treat men fairly.[12] Neither leaves as strong an impression of an actual malevolent principle at work as does the *skogsrå*. And, this is exactly one of the functions Strindberg has given his midwife-*skogsrå*—both generally, as evil symbol, and specifically, in tempting Kersti into crime. Even the common expression of this malevolence, the *skogsrå's* derisive laughter,[13] seems to carry into the play in the midwife's raucous exits: "A! Dsi! A Dsi!" she cries, as she lopes off threatening to inform on Kersti to the sheriff,[14] and she riddles gleefully as she makes off with the baby.

But it is the temptress quality of the *skogsrå* that genuinely pervades the play, ranging from near-symbolic associations to the direct subornation of Kersti by the midwife. And intimately connected with temptation in both folklore and play is a basic duality: attractiveness and foulness; alluring promise and ugly aftermath. Temptation and duality are in turn inseparable from the general theme of fall from grace that Strindberg has established for the lovers.

The simple presence of a *skogsrå* figure points up important parallels between the patterns of play and of folklore. One of the most common accounts of the *skogsrå* as temptress is the *vakna i kärret* (waken in the mire) type: she entices men far off into the woods, or to bed in her hut—and the victims awaken in the cold and muddy reality of a morass or pool.[15] This is strongly parallel to Mats and Kersti's awakening to a world of doubt, regret, and increasing despair. "Wretched us and a wretched wedding!" realizes Mats in the first scene (p. 297), a cry prophetic both for the pathetic "wedding before God alone" (with its hungry marriage feast of two pipes of tobacco) and for the public wedding which will reveal Kersti's guilt in full. We are watching the awakening in the mire; the play presents little of the earlier, allurement side of the process. (As we shall see below, the *skogsrå* associations also seem to provide the psychological pre-history of the unhappy awakening we see.) The repeated refrain from the lament of the *forskarl* is an exact musical counterpart: "Brave was it then; how ugly it is now!" (p. 302).

This ugly awakening parallel is much more extensively worked out for Kersti than for Mats. She enters a nightmare world in the dank and starkly white mill, which is at once an expressionistic extension of conscience[16] and a sought-after reality that turns rotten when achieved. "I have what I asked for," Kersti says in despair, as what seemed to be a part of the prize along with the crown is finally seen to be part of the price for it (p. 305). She has sought to buy the mill with the life of the baby; it becomes a cross to bear in payment for that crime. And the mill-morass in which Kersti awakes is stifling in other ways as well. Its hollowness comprises everyday responsibility and the demands of family and society (the bridal crown is the mill-folks' price for the mill, and Kersti must take over the symbolically ugly furnishings unchanged), as well as the inherited curse of family feud. Brita, received with the mill as sister-in-law and in one sense the torturing absoluteness of Kersti's conscience, is also her personal Fury, family hatred distilled.

The final stages of Kersti's awakening come during her second experience in the mill, the oppressive wedding celebration. As soon as Kersti is alone the midwife-*skogsrå* glides in, and we infer that the crime now fully dominates Kersti's mind. But more important is Kersti's final, full realization of what she has sacrificed, as she embraces the *myling* (the apparition of the baby) and feels a pain strike to her heart. In fact the minor motif of the affection between Kersti and Lill-Mats has functioned as a pathetic-ironic preparation for this moment.

The sheriff's well-meant predictions, during bride's-eve, about Kersti's new life become a kind of dialogue locus for her final steps from anticipation to reality. Figuratively, the *skogsrå's* hollow back is nearly turned. But it is a locus for more than dashed hopes. When the sheriff echoes Kersti's own plaint over her lost fields and sun and defines the future in gray terms of duty and toil, there are clear overtones of the original fall and the expulsion from Eden. And in this connection we recall that in the mill Kersti finds herself suddenly "under *forsen* [the stream, the rapids]," where slime grows on the wheel; she has entered the realm of the *forskarl* (river-man or nix), the angel also fallen from grace.[17] The simple "waken in the mire" pattern of *skogsrå* legend here reaches its final dramatic extension.

We also find a set of parallels between *The Crown Bride* and the tendency in *skogsrå* legend for the victim to suffer permanently from his experience even after he has physically escaped. He may be mentally injured or may fall into a long illness, or even die.[18] Such fates are like Kersti's: despite the physical reprieve, her suffering for the crime is ineradicable, and the end is death. Mats' failure to recognize Kersti after she has been shorn and stripped of her veil is more than an expressionistic contribution to the hallucinatory atmosphere, for it acknowledges in visible action the inner deterioration, the moral defectiveness into which the audience has already seen Kersti fall. The temptation is past; a transformed or *bergtagen* Kersti remains, just as in the legends. Strindberg carries Kersti on to a final death, but he goes well beyond the simple death pattern of folklore. If in Kersti there is no tragic illumination, there is at least acceptance of responsibility; if not tragic exaltation, at least resignation, moral amendment, and conventional salvation.

Of course, parallel with folk legend as Strindberg's plot is, we should not assume that it is *the* source for the play. There are other important sources for the patterns the play follows: *Romeo and Juliet* (for death as reconciler of families), and Strindberg's own preoccupation with the themes of purification through suffering, conversion, sacrifice for family, and punishment growing out of crime (e.g., *A Dream Play*, *To Damascus*, *Easter*, and *Crimes and Crimes*). The folklore provides as much enrichment as source.

A third important association drawn upon from the legend is the sexual nature of the temptation in the legends of the *skogsrå*. At times this can be blatantly specific. Less heroic methods failing, the *skogsrå* may simply hoist her skirt over her head.[19] The parallel between folklore and play is of course not literal. Patently, sex appeal is not among the weapons in the arsenal of the midwife-*skogsrå*. Nor does the presence of a *skogsrå* in the play provide, as we might expect, associative guilt for the protagonist as seducer. Strindberg makes Kersti and Mats jointly responsible.

What we find instead in the *skogsrå* aspect of the midwife is a kind of character-shorthand (through her general associations with sexual attraction and sexual fall) for the *pre-history* of Mats and Kersti's predicament, their reaction, and their disillusion. For example, the physical and psychological isolation of Kersti's situation corresponds strongly with the isolation of the victim so common in the legends.[20] An even more important correspondence is with the youthfulness of so many of the victims.[21] These are the exact effects Strindberg is concerned with at the beginning of the play: isolation, evoked in the talk of the woods and its creatures and in the communication through field-songs; and youthfulness, in Kersti's half-frightened defiance of her mother and in the pathetic "wedding" of two youngsters who, true to the fall of man, understand so few of the implications of their acts. The *skogsrå* provides an associative glimpse backward into the psychological climate of the initial sexual temptation, where Mats and Kersti could see only the alluring side.

The beast-tail begins to slip into sight rather early, however. When Strindberg chooses to create neither Mats nor Kersti as seducer, he gains the advantage of presenting a sympathetic protagonist and universalizing the predicament. There is a more fundamental culprit; it culminates Mats' summary of the course of their attraction: "affection, love, lust" (p. 298). Again the parallel is with the folklore *skogsrå's* essence more than her acts, with the general power of sexual allure and with the revulsion and emptiness once it is satisfied. Symbolically she is, I suspect, the only figure Strindberg could find to suggest both past sexual excitement and present ugly result.

Finally, the play is similar to the folk material in evoking a sense of duality, attractive surface over corrupt reality. In folklore the means are straightforward: a creature fair before and foul behind. The play is more complex. The audience gradually comes to feel that in the play world the truth (sin, then crime) is hidden and yet not hidden, that it is coiled barely below the surface ready to overturn the false rituals of bride's-eve and crown wedding. Kersti's mother can't know and yet seems to know of the baby; Brita knows and yet shouldn't know of the baby and its death. The stark silence of the chorus of bridesmaids after the bath and the savagery of Brita's attack begin to establish a nightmare atmosphere in which all somehow know the truth before they can and are simply waiting for Kersti to acknowledge it. The perverted wedding—gloom for merriment—and the immediate, unsurprised acceptance of the truth by the families provide the final intensifications of this atmosphere. Strindberg here evokes both sides of the duality at once, figuratively showing the rump of the *skogsrå* through the front.

Duality—appearance and reality—is at the heart of the folk concept and it is placed near the heart of the play as a common denominator of the interwoven themes of the fall and of crime, concealment, and guilt.

II

Our discussion thus far has focused on the sometimes tenuous matters of parallel and analogue. It must be admitted that such associational enrichment would generally be provided even by a figurehead presence of the *skogsrå*. But exactly like her cousin of the countryside, Strindberg's *skogsrå* has the ability to bring about evil, not just to reflect it.

The temptations of the midwife-*skogsrå* are aimed exclusively at Kersti, and they operate on two levels: the criminal and the spiritual. Strindberg, of course, modifies folk tradition by making the victim not a man but a girl with an unwanted child.22 Thus the midwife role is particularly consistent with and appropriate for the seductress function of the *skogsrå*.

The crucial crime is causing or at least allowing the death of the baby. The midwife could hardly be more directly involved. She first threatens to appear at the wedding, and then offers the basic trade: bridal crown and respectability for baby. Whether Kersti is literally guilty of deliberate murder or whether she acquiesces in an unspoken agreement that the baby will die in the midwife's hands, the indisputable thing is her crime of intent under the lure of pride and Mammon, like Maurice's in *Crimes and Crimes*.23 In that play the child bars the triumphal chariot; in this, the crowned procession to the mill. The guilt, at least of intent, is finally acknowledged by Kersti in her confession to the sheriff, just as by Maurice in his to the Commissaire.

It is important here to see that Strindberg makes things much more complex than they are in the folk legends, where the *skogsrå* is the simple villainess. The midwife-*skogsrå* is not altogether serpent to Kersti's Eve; she panders to, and expresses, an impulse already there. Kersti's guilt of intent is clear from her first outburst of names for the child: "Burden, foul luck, necessity, crown-thief" (p. 298). The pattern is the same after the wedding when Kersti, frantic from guilt and the appearance of the *myling* apparition of her baby in the mill, is perhaps almost ready to admit the deception and crime. But the midwife represents the opposing, concealing impulse; she replaces the *myling* in the trap door under the mill. Thus the *skogsrå* in each episode becomes the expressionistic extension of the girl's human propensity toward deception, pride, and sin—i.e., of temptation from within Kersti herself.

The third temptation of Kersti is the natural aftermath of these first two, but the stakes are now explicitly spiritual. Kersti is prisoner outside the church, and the midwife-*skogsrå* arrives

to close the soldiers' eyes and to tempt her to escape.24 Some
of the issues for Kersti are again ethical: self-preservation, and
accepting the child as responsibility, not liability. But now
Strindberg makes clear that, within the context of the play,
preserving the soul will involve accepting the death of the person. Kersti now realizes that in addition to having the grace of
Christ, earlier represented by the White Child in the mill, she
must be willing to atone with her own life. It becomes virtually
the *skogsrå* against Christ:

MIDWIFE.   I can help you out of this.
KERSTI.   I have found my helper! He is Christ.

Or immediate life against eternal:

MIDWIFE.   Fly, fly, fly!
KERSTI.   No! I want to come into the keeping of the living
           God. (p. 317)

Here Strindberg escalates the legendary *skogsrå's* antipathy
to Christianity into direct temptation of the state of the soul.25
And for Kersti's defenses he employs the same safeguards that
many a quarry in folk legend uses: the sign of the cross, God's
name, and the church bell.26

This third and most vital temptation is not an abrupt inter-
position. It culminates a "peril to soul" theme that, beyond the
obvious connections with the fall of man motif, has been carried largely by folklore associations. It is implicit in the opening
situation: the unbaptized baby and the mother not yet
"churched" were felt to be uniquely vulnerable to evil forces.27
The presence of the *myling* apparition evokes a whole class of
legends in which an unbaptized, murdered child cannot rest because it is a lost soul.28 This widens the implications of Kersti's
guilt by reminding us that she is responsible for another soul.
Even the will-'o-the-wisps seen by Kersti in Scene I probably
predict this situation.29

Kersti's "awakening in the mire" in the mill is partly her
realization that she has descended into the *forskarl* or river-man's
domain. In addition, his ubiquitous refrain—"I am hoping, I
am hoping, that my redeemer still liveth"30—is a constant musical reflection of Kersti's own state as a lost soul and of her most
vital need. The substitution of "thy" for "my" in his refrain as
Kersti is accused and discovered is both an intensification of
this reflection and an ironic gesture of grace from one lost soul

to another. Finally, Brita's chilling earth-baptism of Kersti as she enters the mill suggests a ritual entry to the lost state. "He who has mould over his head is [as] dead and shares the lot of the dead."31 The third temptation by the midwife-*Skogsrå* is essentially an attempt to block Kersti's climb back out of the riverman's realm of the spiritually lost.

III

The *skogsrå* figure has yet another major significance for *The Crown Bride*. Kersti, who has been general victim of the midwife-*skogsrå* along with Mats, and specific victim of specific wiles, also becomes very like a *skogsrå* herself.

Strindberg bypasses the obvious possibility of making Kersti a sexual seductress. But he does make her the deceiver and ethical seductress of Mats, immediately following her own ethical seduction by the midwife. It is a tripartite campaign beginning with sophistry. Kersti must first convince Mats that the bridal crown stands for nothing and that the crown bride is she who wears it, not she whose chastity deserves it. In the second stage, she is both persuader and deceiver; she convinces Mats that they should give the baby into the care of the midwife (whom she knows to be evil) and yet says nothing of the fact that she has already done so. And in the third stage she adopts the bleakest of rationalizations for a crime already committed in the will, the "whatever may happen is fated by God" argument.

How complete this *skogsrå* identification is to be for Kersti is hard to decide. Most unlike the folklore temptress, Kersti gives her subject timely warning and a preview of what she will later attempt.

KERSTI.   You are good, Mats; I am not. If only I were!
MATS.   Become good!
KERSTI.   Mats, be evil; try and see if you can.
MATS.   You don't mean that! (p. 298)

But she does, at least when she has become desperate, and Mats does become her accomplice. Even less like the real *skogsrå,* Kersti is tortured by conscience, as evidenced in her feverish attempt to shift to Mats the responsibility for suggesting the midwife and in the turning and clicking of wheels and loom as expressionistic extensions of her agitation in the mill. The effect is even stronger in her reactions to the repeated ironic reassurance that the baby "is sleeping, far, far off in the forest." And her attraction for the touchstone, Lill-Mats, is certainly meant to suggest that she has been more desperate than demonic.

Un*skogsrå*-like as they are, these features probably represent the minimum necessary to make Kersti a believable human who carries the seeds of her own later rehabilitation. And other points suggest that Strindberg does create at least a strain of the *skogsrå* within Kersti. There is, for example, a whole sub-genre of legends in which the *skogsrå* appears to her victim in the guise of his fiancée.32 But the strongest similarity to the folklore material is in Mats' "awakening in the mire" to the reality of what Kersti has done. This appears at the wedding, where all Mats' reactions are concentrated into one last despairing (and his first understanding) repetition of the choruses, "How brave was it then; how ugly it is now," and "The little one sleeps in the forest." And by the time he comes bearing the little coffin to the church he has a full indictment; it is not just murder, but the murder of an unbaptized soul over whom the priest cannot even read. He has seen the hollow back in full, while we have seen the infectiousness of evil as the temptation has passed from the midwife-*skogsrå* to Kersti and from Kersti-*skogsrå* to Mats.

IV

The *skogsrå* thus has four principal uses in *The Crown Bride*. Plot: the midwife-*skogsrå* triggers the central actions by successfully tempting the main character, Kersti. Character: Kersti is partially and temporarily converted to the *skogsrå*-temptress pattern, illustrating and exploring the power of evil to spread under psychological and moral stress. Expressionism: the midwife-*skogsrå* darts in and out as a reflection of Kersti's guilt and the diseased state of her conscience, and as a reminder of the crime. Theme: by means of her associations from legend, the *skogsrå* figure symbolically reinforces principal themes. These are sexual and ethical temptation, mental transformation, spiritual peril, and above all, duality—suffering after license, and nightmare reality behind the attractive surface. This duality underlies most of the other themes, even temptation, which can be seen as an attempt to bring about the ugly side of the duality.

None of these uses is inconsistent with the essence of the folklore *skogsrå*. And if we recall our initial observation, the fact that Strindberg chose to put a *skogsrå* tail on his midwife even though he might have fused other folklore figures with her more smoothly, it seems valid to conclude that he worked with a general conception of the essence of the *skogsrå* and that he used the figure because his play is concerned with the same essentials: attraction and repulsion, disillusion and recognition, guilt, and danger to the soul.

What is involved here is more than a chance discovery of a family of legends that happens to suit a particular drama. In various ways the *skogsrå* figure and legends reflect and even sum up many of Strindberg's major preoccupations of the post-inferno period: guilt of intent in *Crimes and Crimes, To Damascus,* and *The Burned Site;* eventual revelation of crime in *The Burned Site* and *The Ghost Sonata;* deterioration and resuscitation of the soul in *To Damascus, Easter, A Dream Play,* and *Crimes and Crimes;* and the awakening from sleepwalking into an ugly reality in *A Dream Play, Crimes and Crimes, The Burned Site, The Ghost Sonata, The Pelican,* and *The Highway.* Indeed this duality, so consistent a preoccupation of Strindberg's drama from 1898 until his death, is at the heart of the entire concept of the *skogsrå* and may be Strindberg's central consideration in using that figure.

Western Michigan University

NOTES

[1] *Skogsrå* is the wood-nymph's most usual name in Sweden; others include *skogsnu(f)va, skogsfru,* and *rå.* Similar enticing and deceiving creatures are called *huldre* in Norway and *skovfru* or *ellepige* in Denmark. Gunnar Granberg, *Skogsrået i yngre nordisk folktradition,* Skrifter utgifna av Gustav Adolfs Akademien för folklivsforskning, No. 3 (Uppsala, 1935), pp. 6, 79, 210-18. H. F. Feilberg, *Bjærgtagen; Studie over en gruppe Træk fra Nordisk Alfetro,* Danmarks Folkeminder, No. 5 (Copenhagen, 1910), p. 32.

[2] Feilberg, p. 32.

[3] In Swedish folklore the midwife is commonly versed in the black arts and is just as able to bring evil over child and family as to forestall it. Tobias Norlind, *Svenska allmogens lif i folksed, folktro och folkdiktning* (Stockholm, 1912), p. 555.

[4] The dramatic possibilities of witches could easily have been on Strindberg's mind since his treatment of them in *Svenska Folket i Helg och Söken, i Krig och i Fred, Hemma och Ute; eller Ett Tusan Ar af Svenska Bildningens och Sedernas Historia* (Stockholm, 1882), I, 423-25; II, 147-49.

5 Trolls could make humans *trolltagen* or *bergtagen*. The state implied ranges from being "touched" to being addle-brained to being stolen away. See especially pp. 7-11 in Feilberg, who is concerned throughout with such bewitchment.

6 I have not tried to survey all of Strindberg's potential sources. Norlind, pp. 684-94, lists about 120 books and major articles before 1900 that can have contained important folk material. I have relied heavily on Feilberg's survey of such sources. I rely on Granberg's *Skogsrået*, a work which rests more scientifically on later *skogsrå sägn* (legend) collections, for confirmation of patterns in earlier sources.

7 Gunnar O. Hyltén-Cavallius, *Wärend och Wirdarne: ett försök i svensk ethnologi* (Stockholm, 1864-68), I, 208, as cited in Granberg, pp. 251-52. (Hyltén-Cavallius is one folklore source Strindberg cites—with praise—in *Svenska Folket*, I, 208, and II, 21, 172.) Eva Wigström, *Folkdiktning, visor, sägner, sagor, gåtor, ordspräk, ringdansar, lekar ock barnvisor* (Copenhagen, 1880), p. 238. Strindberg may also have in mind a parallel tradition in which the quarries of the wild hunt are lost or tormented souls—a natural foreshadowing of the peril to come for Kersti's and the baby's souls. See Norlind, p. 641.

8 Granberg, pp. 202-04.

9 Granberg, p. 90.

10 Granberg, p. 47 and map no. 11.

11 Feilberg, p. 32, states flatly: "Association with her is always dangerous" (my translation). The exception noted by Granberg, p. 43, her rare helpfulness to legitimate dwellers of the forest such as charcoal burners, does not apply to the situation Strindberg has created. Pride of place in this malevolence is even a point of dispute between *skogsrå* and mermaid. Herman Hofberg, *Swedish Folk-lore*, trans. W. H. Myers (Chicago, 1888), p. 136n. *Runa*, 4 (1845), 29, cited in Norlind, p. 642.

12 Hofberg, pp. 55-59. Norlind, p. 642.

13 Leonard F. Rääf, *Beskrifning ofver Ydre härad i Östergötland*, I (1856), p. 65, as cited in Feilberg, p. 33. Granberg, pp. 101-05.

14 *Skrifter av August Strindberg*, ed. Gunnar Brandell, XI (Stockholm, 1962), 298. Subsequent page references to the play are from this edition. Translations are mine except where otherwise noted.

15 Granberg's term: pp. 205-09; Wigström, p. 130; Feilberg, pp. 35-36.

16 Richard B. Vowles, "Strindberg and the Symbolic Mill," *Scandinavian Studies*, 34 (1962), 111-19.

17 Wigström, pp. 135-36.

18 Wigström, p. 212; Feilberg, p. 33.

19 Feilberg, pp. 35-36; Wigström, p. 130. For full discussion see Granberg, pp. 243-54.

20 Feilberg, p. 35, and especially Granberg, p. 247.

21 Granberg, pp. 247-48.

22 A *skogsman* sometimes lures and deceives women in legend, but he is rare. Granberg, pp. 20-29, 36-37.

23 Brita M. Mortensen and Brian Downs, *Strindberg: An Introduction to His Life and Work* (Cambridge, 1949), p. 135, and Elizabeth Sprigge, *The Strange Life of August Strindberg* (New York, 1949), p. 193, vote for the unvarnished term "murder." But does Kersti smother the child, or does her piling clothes on the cradle reflect her wish that the child were gone? And does the White Child's regret speak to an accomplished deed or does it anticipate the baby's death and respond to Kersti's criminal intent?

24 Granberg, pp. 92-93, mentions several reports in which the *skogsrå* clouds a human's vision. But the episode in the play may owe as much to the close of Goethe's *Faust*, Pt. I.

25 In some legends it is the victims' Christian faith that makes them so satisfying for the *skogsrå* to seduce. Rääf, I, 65, as cited in Feilberg, p. 33; Granberg, p. 245.

26 Wigström, p. 130; Feilberg, pp. 58-60.

27 Norlind, pp. 555-61; Wigström, pp. 170, 229-30.

28 Hofberg, pp. 105-06; Wigström, p. 221; Norlind, p. 638.

29 Norlind, p. 637.

30 As translated in Edwin Björkman, ed., *Plays by August Strindberg. Fourth Series: The Bridal Crown* (London, 1927).

31 Feilberg, p. 117 (my translation).

32 Granberg, p. 244; *Runa*, 3 (1844), 44, cited in Feilberg, p. 42.

The Playwright as Perfect Wagnerite: Motifs from the Music Dramas in the Theatre of Bernard Shaw

Arthur Ganz

Let us begin with some hypothetical circumstances—for the moment dissociated from the names of the persons whom in fact they concern. A young man, brought up in a musical household and especially knowledgeable about opera, determines upon a career as a writer. As he makes his way in the literary world, he becomes a music reviewer, the liveliest and most perceptive of his day. He also becomes the champion of a musico-dramatic artist, the grandiosity of whose conceptions and the novelty of whose techniques make him, even at the culmination of his career, a figure of controversy. So passionate does the young writer's advocacy of his hero become that he produces a book explicating the composer's major work (ingeniously if somewhat perversely in terms of the socialism to which our writer has become committed). He then turns to dramatic criticism and at last finds his true métier as a playwright. Nevertheless—and here we come to the crux of our hypothesis—despite the young writer's long public admiration for an artist who was not only a composer but one of the seminal dramatic theorists and practitioners of the age, the older composer-dramatist has no discernible influence on the young playwright's work.

What is there to say of such a hypothesis except that it is preposterous? Surely it is hardly reasonable to argue that a dramatist at an impressionable and formative stage of development could admire, and even champion, an already famous composer of theater pieces without the older artist's work having a significant, even profound, effect on that of the younger. Nevertheless, the paucity of critical references to the relations

101

between Wagner and Shaw—the figures here described—suggests that some such assumption has been widely made. That this assumption, however improbable, should have stood for so long is hardly surprising: two bodies of dramatic work more disparate than those of Wagner and Shaw are, after all, not easy to imagine. Between Wagner's vast and solemn evocations of Germanic legend and Shaw's sharp and witty dissections of the modern world an impassable gulf would seem to be fixed. (Even if we take into account the humane comedy of *Meistersinger* or the heroic tragedy of *Saint Joan,* we will hardly have established any equivalences.) The one work of Shaw's, *Man and Superman,* that admittedly derives from an opera owes its origin not to Wagner but to Mozart; nor are we surprised that *Don Giovanni* with its pace, its wit, and its rebellious hero defying the demands of authority should appeal to the brilliant socialist playwright.

It is, in fact, helpful to remind ourselves that Shaw's operatic allegiances extend beyond Wagner. Not only is there a sense of musical organization and the balancing of various voices in Shaw's style (Shaw himself proudly quoted Granville-Barker's appeal to the actors at a rehearsal of one of Shaw's plays: "Ladies and gentlemen: will you please remember that this is Italian opera")[1] but familiar "operatic" situations are not unknown in his work (in the first act of *Arms and the Man* the heroine herself points out the analogy between the hero's situation and that of *Ernani*). More important still Wagner himself has similar allegiances. Part of the operatic tradition that stimulated the drama of Bernard Shaw had also fostered the work of Wagner. "Not only *Rienzi,*" as Robert Gutman shows us, "but also *Tannhäuser, Lohengrin, Meistersinger, The Twilight of the Gods,* and *Parsifal* reveal in their mixed heritage strains that descend, as does Verdi's *Aida,* from Meyerbeer's Parisian grand opera."[2] Moreover, a crucial part of this operatic structure was, beyond its grandiose historical spectacle, the Scribean dramaturgy that formed its foundation. When we recall that much of Shaw's work consists of ingenious inversions of Scribean and other kinds of conventional nineteenth-century dramatic formulas, we recognize the point at which the Shavian and Wagnerian ancestries merge.

A further recognition comes in considering the Shavian reworking of *Don Giovanni.* Aside from the "Don Juan in Hell" third act—a sort of verbalized, vastly extended operatic quartet —there is very little of *Man and Superman,* at least in terms of character and action, that directly echoes the original. Without the third act and Shaw's testimony in his introductory letter, we would hardly realize that what its creator himself called a "trumpery story of modern London life" was in fact a treatment of material from Mozart's masterpiece. When we see that even the conscious recasting of an earlier operatic work involves modernization and changes sufficiently drastic as to leave the original hardly discernible behind the new work, we recognize that the Wagnerian echoes that might be expected to resonate in Shaw's plays will have modulated to keys quite remote from the originals.

There is, after all, no reason to suppose that Shaw will necessarily be conscious of the note he is sounding. By the time he had entered upon his career as a playwright, the material of the Wagnerian poems had been fully absorbed, and when it surfaced again, it would be transformed into the glittering stuff of Shavian drama. And though this drama is marked by a realistic depiction of its creator's world (even history is whimsically modernized), by the play of a supreme comic imagination, and by a concern with immediate social issues—all of which would seem to separate it absolutely from the misty grandeurs of the Wagnerian universe—it has relations with that universe, whether Shaw was aware of all of them or not, that help reveal a significant, though not always conspicuous, aspect of Shaw's own work.

What that aspect is can best be discerned by examining a work whose Wagnerian ancestry Shaw did, in fact, recognize. Although *Candida* is built on the familiar husband-wife-lover triangle, one could hardly claim that it is descended from *Tristan und Isolde* if Shaw had not maintained in a letter to James Huneker that at the end of the play, when Marchbanks exclaims "Out, then, into the night with me" and leaves, rejecting the limited domestic happiness of Candida and Morell, he is going out into "Tristan's holy night."[3] The "heil'ge Nacht" in which Wagner's lovers mingle their ecstasy might seem a far cry from the atmosphere outside a lower middle-class parsonage in an unfashionable district of Edwardian London, but Tristan and his curious descendant breathe very much the same air. Even though Shaw's Isolde, in what is a domestic comedy rather than a tragic opera, decides to remain with King Mark on the grounds that he needs her and that Tristan is too young for her, she has glimpsed the truth Marchbanks has fully apprehended, that what he seeks are not the comforts and coddling of the ordinary human "happiness" Candida provides for Morell but a bliss not to be realized in this world. It is the longing for transcendence that breaks through the comic transmutations and social detail or *Candida*, linking it firmly to *Tristan*.

These works thus provide us with a paradigm of the Wagnerian-Shavian relationship. As Wagnerian material works its way into the Shavian drama, circumstances will, of necessity, change radically, plot and character will alter to some degree, but a central and deeply significant thematic similarity will bind two works to each other. It is illuminating to consider another work, which even more decisively links these two masters, summarizing it generally. A beautiful maiden of the royal family finds that her rule over her kingdom is imperiled. However, a great warrior, whose identity is not at first known, comes over the waters, discomfits her enemies, and rescues her. (The maiden, in fact, dreams of a beautiful warrior and longs for him to come to her.) The rescuing warrior is of an exalted spiritual nature and makes certain demands on the maiden who, though she attempts to do so, cannot finally live up to them. In the ensuing action, the maiden's enemy, who had openly accused her, is slain; the slayer demands public judgment and is exonerated. The warrior explains his true nature. Toward the end of the work the rights of the maiden's younger brother to the throne are finally settled. At last, amid much public grief the great warrior leaves the maiden behind and returns across the water to the land from whence he came.

All faithful Wagnerians will easily recognize this account as a presentation, perhaps somewhat elliptic, of the action of *Lohengrin*—just as any good Shavian will realize at once that it is a summary of *Caesar and Cleopatra*. Considering the depths of Shaw's commitment to Wagner, the recurrence of the *Lohengrin* pattern of action in Shaw's play is not likely to be a pointless coincidence, just as it is not likely to be a deliberate echo meant to be recognized by the initiate. If this Wagnerian material has become part of Shaw's sensibility and has risen to the surface of his consciousness recreated in the new form of *Caesar and Cleopatra*, it would only have done so because Shaw found in it a meaning as central to him as to Wagner.

This meaning becomes clearer when we observe that the conclusion of this play is essentially the same as that of *Candida*. In both plays Shaw has created heroes—Marchbanks and Caesar —whose courage, discernment, and refinement of feeling are superior to those of the people about them and who, at the end of the play, withdraw from the world of human affairs, resposibilities, and passions to a realm more suited to their own nature. Although both plays are ostensibly comedies, in both the withdrawal has a morbid aspect: Marchbanks' associations with Tristan's kingdom of Night are no less suggestive than Caesar's prescient sense of his approaching death. Ultimately the Lohengrin material attracted Shaw as a myth of withdrawal, an exemplar justifying the impulse to retreat from human involvements. Even as Shaw's puritan conscience demanded that he do useful social work in the world, a more severe and elusive desire led him to create in his works persistent images of dissociation and removal.4

All of the early Wagner operas must have offered support for this desire: the Dutchman's return to the sea after his fancied betrayal by Senta; Tannhäuser's death after his rejection by the Pope; and finally Lohengrin's departure after Elsa's failure of faith. Of these operas we may guess that *Lohengrin* made the deepest effect. It was, after all, the first Wagner opera Shaw knew, as his autobiographical letter to Archibald Henderson reveals.5 More significant, however, because the guilt that haunts the Dutchman and Tannhäuser is here conveniently shifted to a lesser figure, Telramund, Shaw was able to discern in Lohengrin a kind of unconscious model for the superman as saint, the figure he was shaping in Julius Caesar.

The first words that Caesar utters, in fact, suggest that like Lohengrin he has come into the mortal world from a happier place. As Caesar, alone in the desert, greets the Sphinx, he tells it that he has "wandered in many lands, seeking the lost regions from which my birth into this world exiled me" and contrasts himself with the great statue that has remained "looking out— out of the world—to the lost region—the home from which we have strayed" (p. 374).6 In these words Shaw evokes the romantic vision of the lost homeland also suggested by Lohengrin's opening words as he addresses his "lieber Schwan," "Kehr' wieder nur zu unserm Glück!" [beloved swan,—return but to our happiness].7 That vision revives when Lohengrin, attempting

to silence Elsa's questions, says—perhaps somewhat tactlessly—
"Denn nicht komm' ich aus Nacht und Leiden,/ aus Glanz und
Wonne komm' ich her" (p. 104) [For I do not come from night
and suffering/ from brightness and bliss I come here]. At the
end of the opera, however, a different element is recognized: the
land that Lohengrin left is not only one of "brightness and bliss"
but of holiness as well. Although he has been greeted as a God-
sent hero, "du gottgesandter Held" (p. 73), only in the revelations of "In fernem Land" (p. 109) [In distant land] that his
power stems from the Grail and that he is the son of Parsifal,
ruler of Monsalvat, do we fully realize Lohengrin's identity. And
similarly, only in a grand declamation near the end of the play
do we come to understand the source of Caesar's power and the
nature of his presence. After all of Caesar's friends have agreed
that Cleopatra was justified in ordering the assassination of
Pothinus, she turns to Caesar and triumphantly promises to
have herself crucified on the door of her palace "if one man in
all Alexandria" says she did wrong. "If one man in all the
world," Caesar replies, "can be found, now or forever, to know
that you did wrong, that man will have either to conquer the
world as I have, or be crucified by it" (pp. 456-57). As Caesar
goes on to denounce the morass of blood and murder in which
those about him are mired, we recognize how much his Lohen-
grin-like sense of separateness derives not only from his superior
intelligence and energy but from the moral, even spiritual, remoteness suggested by his anticipatory identification with Christ.[8]

Yet, though we may see a significant similarity in the
spiritualized warrior figures of Lohengrin and Caesar, we will
not recognize an equivalent resemblance in Elsa and Cleopatra.
No ingenuity will be able to equate the temperaments of the
radiantly dreamy maiden of Brabant and the childishly passionate queen of Egypt. Indeed, Telramund's slanderous taunt after
Elsa describes her visionary knight, "sie schwärmt von einem
Buhlen!" (p. 70) [she babbles about a lover!] is far more appropriate to the Cleopatra who dreams of Mark Antony's "strong,
round arms." But however different their temperaments, Elsa
and Cleopatra are alike in their connection with the central
figures and the nature of their strivings. In both cases the connection is broken by the women's actions, and, more significant
still, the relation is far from being essentially erotic.

Even in the bridal chamber scene when Lohengrin and Elsa

are alone before the nuptial bed, their protestations are full of religious imagery, as in Elsa's first words:

> Wie wär' ich kalt, mich glücklich nur zu nennen
> besitz' ich aller Himmel Seligkeit!
> Fühl' ich zu dir so süss mein Herz entbrennen,
> atme ich Wonnen, die nur Gott verleiht!   (p. 101)
> [How cold I were, to call myself merely happy
> Should I possess all heavenly bliss!
> I feel my heart burn so sweetly for you,
> I breathe delight, which only God bestows!]

And Lohengrin's most impassioned compliment to Elsa is, "Deine Auge sagte mir dich rein von Schuld" (p. 101) [Your eye pronounced you to me pure of guilt]. Similarly, in the very Prologue by the god Ra, Shaw teased his first audience, which no doubt hoped for a drama about the temptress of the Nile: "Do ye crave for the story of an unchaste woman? Hath the name of Cleopatra tempted ye hither? Ye foolish ones; Cleopatra is as yet but a child that is whipped by her nurse" (p. 361). What happens between "the old Caesar and the child queen" is not so much a story of love as a struggle for power. In having Pothinus murdered, Cleopatra has, as Caesar says, "taken the powers of life and death" upon herself; that is to say, she has taken Caesar's powers. Pothinus had been killed because his accusation that Cleopatra desired to replace Caesar was true, and Caesar leaves partly because his business in Egypt is finished and partly because, if he stays, he will have to kill Cleopatra. And because one's name symbolizes one's self, and to know that name is to possess power over that self, Lohengrin confronts something of the same dilemma. (Consider the relevant tale of Rumpelstiltskin: when the troll's name is known, his power is lost. In stories even more directly analogous—those of Psyche and Eros, Semele and Jupiter—the erotic element in the woman's struggle for knowledge and power, repressed in *Lohengrin,* is immediately evident.)

Ostensibly Elsa expresses her love in images of humility and sexual submission:

> Da wollte ich vor deinem Blick zerfliessen,
> gleich einem Bach umwinden deinen Schritt
> als eine Blume, duftend auf der Wiesen,
> wollt' ich entzückt mich beugen deinem Tritt.   (p. 102)
> [Here would I melt before your glance,
> Like a brook winding about your step,

Like a flower exhaling fragrance over the meadow,
Would I rejoice bowing myself before your tread.]

However, she soon demands of Lohengrin not only trust but
knowledge of his masculine self and power over it that he will
not, cannot, yield her. A warning of the danger is visibly present
in the figure of Telramund, an honorable man who has fallen
prey to the wiles of the same sorceress woman who tempts Elsa
to walk forbidden paths. One can hardly avoid the symbolism of
Telramund's anguished cry that they have taken the very weapon, "die Waffe selbst" (p. 81)—the sword with which he could
kill Ortrud. And similarly, one comes to realize that Cleopatra
too is watched over by a passionate votaress of the pagan gods
and that Pothinus, Cleopatra's accuser, is, as Shaw mentions
quite casually in the stage directions introducing him, a eunuch.

The emasculation of these lesser characters is a clue to the
meaning behind the de-eroticizing of the central stories. Ultimately these are accounts of the dangers of eroticism and of the
necessity of withdrawing the self from such dangers. (That the
act Elsa is accused of—killing her brother—is first threatened
by Cleopatra and then, through Caesar, brought about, suggests
that the woman is as dangerous a sibling as a lover.)9 In both
cases, the peril is heightened by the strength of the attraction.
The faith and pathos of Elsa's longing and the powerful choral
surge that sweeps Lohengrin onstage drawn by his phallic swan
and leaning upon his sword (memories of Jupiter and Leda are
surely relevant here) both testify to the impelling force of desire
that Wagner has captured. But, however genuinely impassioned,
the desire must be resisted and ultimately rejected. The woman
who is its object demands to know her lover's name, that is to
know his self and thus to acquire power over it, to possess it.
(In this regard, observe Elsa's quite conventional possessiveness
in the bridal chamber scene: "Soll ich die Tage zählen,/ die du
mir bleibest noch?" (pp. 102-03) [Shall I count the days,/ in
which you still remain to me?]. And, for the Shavian view,
consider in the third act of *Man and Superman* Don Juan's
description of his celebrated conquests as a series of narrow
escapes.) Moreover, and more significantly, the woman can
never fully realize her dual image, for she is desired both as a
source of erotic gratification and of spiritual transcendence. It
is no accident that Lohengrin is a servant of the Grail, that image
at once archetypally feminine and supremely spiritual. But what

may be conveniently combined in an artistic symbol is hardly to be realized in an actual, or a viably imagined, person.

Similarly Caesar, even with his wisdom and exalted morality, is deeply attracted to Cleopatra, whose grace and charm are genuine. He admits that he is drawn to women and that he idealizes them. "Their eyes dazzle him," he says of himself, "and he sees them not as they are, but as he wishes them to appear to him" (p. 379). Cleopatra is a particularly troublesome presence, "the most dangerous of all Caesar's conquests" (p. 383). Like Elsa, but even more directly, she desires to partake of her warrior's power. Moreover, like Elsa she possesses a double aspect: she is passionate yet apparently asexual. Though Cleopatra has nothing of Elsa's ethereal quality, she is to Caesar a child, "a divine child," and thus not, to him as least, an object of erotic interest. Nevertheless, as she matures, emotionally as well as intellectually, during the play, even acquiring a gallant in Apollodorus, Caesar realizes that he must withdraw himself and send her the sensualist, Mark Antony.

The servant of the higher morality, like the servant of the Grail, cannot linger for long in the ordinary world. Neither the squabbles of the Egyptians nor even the wars of King Henry are his real concerns. He has come for a moment to irradiate the human world by his presence, to be an exemplar of a condition not yet attained by men. In this world, however, he encounters creatures attractive in their childlike radiance and yet disturbing in their demands. Recognizing the dangers they present, he has no choice but to board his ship and return to the country from which he came.

That this theme of withdrawal from the engagements of the sensual world tends to evoke Wagnerian echoes in Shaw is suggested not only by *Candida* and *Caesar and Cleopatra* but by a play whose operatic allegiances, as we have already noted, seem to lie elsewhere. Although *Man and Superman* dispenses with the *mille e tre* ladies and most of the paraphernalia of the Don Juan legend, in the "Don Juan in Hell" third act, when what we think of as the Mozartean material appears most openly, Shaw is—paradoxically—most profoundly Wagnerian. In this regard the discourse on the Superman, whatever its Wagnerian-Nietzschean resonances, is not fully relevant, for it is not part of the immediate theatrical circumstance. (Eventually, of course, Shaw will come around to creating an innocent child of nature, full of strength and energy, who longs for weapons, knows no fear, ignores the dignity and power of the elder generation, and even obeys the injunctions of air-borne voices; but pursuing parallels between Joan and Siegfried will not ultimately be fruitful, for Wagner's youthful hero, as we will see, finds his Shavian reflection in quite a different figure.) The dramatic action here in *Man and Superman* lies in Juan's decision to leave Hell, the illusory world of love and beauty, in his rejection of those who defend its virtues, and in his ultimate departure for a realm of sterner realities and of greater spiritual richness. But these circumstances are not other than those of Tannhäuser as he withdraws himself from the embrace of the goddess of love and accepts again the lures and dangers of the mortal world. Both the great seducer and the Minnesinger, lover of Venus, turn from the delights of sensuality, real or imaginative, to something both grander and darker. Juan's vision of heaven as a place where "you live and work instead of playing and pretending. You face things as they are; you escape nothing but glamor; and your steadfastness and your peril are your glory" (p. 617) lacks something of the romantic enthusiasm of Tannhäuser's "nach Freiheit, Freiheit, dürstet's mich;/ zu Kampf und Streite will ich stehen,/ sei's auch auf Tod und Untergehen" (p. 10) [For freedom, freedom I thirst;/ to battle and strife will I turn,/ be it also to death and dissolution]. It suggests, however, the acceptance of struggle and loss common to both figures. And if Wagner's sentimental religiosity ("Mein Heil liegt in Maria" [My salvation lies in Mary] the knight abruptly exclaims when Venus becomes too passionately appealing) is hardly genuinely Christian, neither is Shaw's exalted vision of the Life Force. Moreover, both writers take their heroes out of Hell with a similar stage effect: as the *"furchtbarer Schlag" [fearful crash]* signals the disappearance of the Venusberg and its replacement by the Thuringian hillside, the shepherd boy, and the pilgrims, so Ann's cry marks the obliteration of Hell and the reappearance of the Sierra, the sleeping Tanner, and the band of revolutionaries.

This similarity in the circumstances of the theatrical moment, though it reinforces the sense that Juan's departure from Hell involves a reminiscence of *Tannhäuser*, may in itself be no more than a suggestive coincidence. There are, indeed, other Wagnerian evocations in Shaw where the connections, however intriguing, remain at best indirect. For instance, although Shaw offers us a passionate and saturnine sea captain who is released from a life-long compulsion through the mediation of a beautiful woman, it is hardly reasonable, in this connection, to make any Wagnerian claim for Captain Brassbound except that, though he appears—somewhat disconcertingly—in a Shavian comedy, he reflects the traditions of the "fatal man" and the "accursed wanderer" of which the Flying Dutchman is both an example and a source. But if we are to argue for a rich congruence between Wagner and Shaw, we must place beside the comparison of *Lohengrin* and *Caesar* something equally specific, and we must deal with that work of Wagner's which held the greatest conscious fascination for Shaw, *Der Ring des Nibelungen.*

There is no single work in the Shavian canon that holds as central a place as *The Ring* does in the Wagnerian, but many students of Shaw would, if pressed, suggest *Major Barbara,* whose prophetic social vision, comic vitality, and extraordinary range of characterization may make it the representative Shavian masterpiece. That in fact we find in *Major Barbara* Shaw's analogue to *The Ring* is at the least a pleasing conjunction; it may even illustrate the power of one great work to evoke another. (And, less happily, it may suggest the power of one work to transmit its problems to another: Shaw complained that *Götterdämmerung* was an operatic irrelevance tacked on to the end of *The Ring;* the last act of *Major Barbara* is unquestionably its problematic section.) By now we are not surprised to find Shaw translating a grim Germanic myth into a comedy of London life, but we still need to discern the terms of the translation. Fortunately, Shaw is prepared to assist us in doing so.

In 1907, when Shaw published *Major Barbara* (produced two years earlier), he also wrote for the German translation of *The Perfect Wagnerite* (first published in 1898) a short additional chapter explaining what he felt to be *Götterdämmerung*'s lack of significant social and intellectual content. Shaw did so on the grounds that by the time Wagner was completing its scoring for the first *Ring* festival of 1876, his faith in the naive Socialism embodied, according to Shaw, in Siegfried had eroded as a result of the movement's squabbles and failures, which reached a climax in the collapse of the Paris Commune of 1871. In the midst of this very Shavian recapitulation of Wagner's intellectual development—the justness of which need not, for-

tunately, be considered here—Shaw presents a whimsical view
of the true development of modern economics in terms of
Wagner's characters. In order to get a decent income Fafner
has had to invest his treasure in the capitalist enterprises of
Alberich, who finds that in accumulating wealth "to turn thousands into hundreds of thousands requires economic magna-
nimity and a will to power as well as to pelf. And to turn
hundreds of thousands into millions, Alberic must make himself
an earthly Providence for masses of workmen, creating towns,
and governing markets. . . . Consequently, though Alberic in
1850 may have been merely the vulgar Manchester factory
owner portrayed in Friedrich Engels' *The Condition of the
Working Class in England in 1844,* in 1876 he was well on his
way towards becoming exoterically a model philanthropic employer and esoterically a financier."10 (In the edition of *The
Perfect Wagnerite* published in Leipzig in 1913 this passage
ends with references to particular industrialists, among them the
munitions manufacturer "Krupp of Essen.") It is difficult to
read here about a powerful munitions maker, or indeed capitalist, who has created towns in the course of making "an earthly
Providence for masses of workmen" without seeing the shadow
of Andrew Undershaft fall across the page—though one feels
that the force and dignity of the proprietor of Perivale St.
Andrews find their equivalent not in the Niebelheim dwarf but
in Wotan, who is like Undershaft the lord of a noble citadel.

So persuasive are these parallels that they have already convinced one commentator, J. L. Wisenthal, who cites this passage
and goes on to link Siegfried and Adolphus Cusins,11 quoting
in support Shaw's suggestive sentence, "The end cannot come
until Siegfried learns Alberic's trade and shoulders Alberic's
burden." Oddly, Wisenthal does not refer to a passage in this
same section of *The Perfect Wagnerite* that offers not merely a
thematic but very nearly a verbal connection with *Major Barbara.* Commenting on Alberich as the "dominant sort of modern
employer," Shaw remarks:

> Wotan is hardly less dependent on him than Fafnir: the War-
> Lord visits his works, acclaims them in stirring speeches, and
> imprisons his enemies; whilst Loki does his political jobs in
> Parliament, making wars and commercial treaties for him at
> command. And he owns and controls a new god, called The
> Press, which manufactures public opinion on his side, and
> organizes the persecution and suppression of Siegfried. (p. 91)

In Undershaft's contemptuous dismissal of Stephen's admiration for British politics, one hears the same voice:

> Do you suppose that you and half a dozen amateurs like you, sitting in a row in that foolish gabble shop, can govern Undershaft and Lazarus? No, my friend: you will do what pays us. You will make war when it suits us, and keep peace when it doesnt. You will find out that trade requires certain measures when we have decided on those measures. When I want anything to keep my dividends up, you will discover that my want is a national need. When other people want something to keep my dividends down, you will call out the police and military. And in return you shall have the support and applause of my newspapers, and the delight of imagining that you are a great statesman. (p. 416)

But in themselves these passages demonstrate only that *Major Barbara* was in the front of Shaw's mind when he added new material to *The Perfect Wagnerite*. A deeper equation must be established if we are to agree that *The Ring* was at least in the back of Shaw's mind when he wrote *Major Barbara*. Professor Wisenthal suggests that the central point of connection lies in the limitations of Undershaft and Wotan. Pointing out that Wotan, bound by his contracts, must have a hero free of his control to express his will and that Shaw stresses this idea (a passage from the "Wagner as Revolutionist" section of *The Perfect Wagnerite* is quoted here: "Meanwhile, let us not forget that godhood means to Wagner infirmity and compromise, and manhood strength and integrity" [p. 30]), Wisenthal goes on to claim that the Andrew Undershaft of the play, unlike the confident personage of the Preface, is like Wotan a very limited figure. "Although he has a stronger grasp of the actual world than Barbara or Cusins," Wisenthal writes, "he is less highly evolved than either of them. His religious vision does not extend as far as Barbara's, and his political vision does not extend as far as Cusins'" (p. 59). But the problem with Wisenthal's view is that it contravenes not only the Undershaft of the Preface but the Undershaft of the play as well. When he answers Cusins' question about what drives Perivale with the reply, "A will of which I am a part" (p. 431), Undershaft means not the will of society (as Wisenthal, astonishingly, says) but the Life Force and thus offers Barbara a glimpse of a religion nobler than her previous one. And it is Undershaft who offers to Cusins the vision of Perivale as a center of revolutionary force. "Poverty and slavery," he tells Cusins, "have stood up for centuries to your sermons and leading articles: they will not stand up to my machine guns. Dont preach at them: dont reason with them. Kill them." And a moment later he exclaims, "Come and make explosives with me. Whatever can blow men up can blow society up" (p. 435-36). Wisenthal quotes these passages but offers no real comment on them except to say that they are "impassioned"—as indeed they are.

Nevertheless, though we may have reservations about Wisenthal's view of Undershaft as a characterization, we need not doubt that he is correct in equating the master of Perivale and the lord of Walhall. Moreover, we must grant him the observation that "Wotan's wife Fricka, the main representative in *The Ring* of conventional attitudes, is rather a close counterpart to Undershaft's wife Lady Britomart; and both marriages are strained by the wife's disapproval of her husband's disreputable behavior" (p. 62) The words "conventional attitude" may not quite do justice to Lady Britomart's charm and assurance nor to Fricka's devotion to the hierarchy of godhead and to her horror at incest, but they do perhaps suggest that both are guardians of the hearth and of the familial relations of parents and children.

It is in this area of emotive connections—rather than in doubtful comparisons between Wagnerian and Shavian economics or in attempts to equate the limiting effects of Wotan's contracts and Undershaft's capitalism—that one may discern the themes and patterns that bind these works together. Although Wisenthal refers once to "Cusins/Siegfried," he makes no attempt to relate these figures; and yet they have similarities, especially in regard to their progenitors. Both, after all, are orphans. Siegfried is a child of incest, brought up by a hostile and untrustworthy parent substitute; the comic equivalent in *Major Barbara* is Cusins' claim that he is a foundling because his mother is his "father's deceased wife's sister" and her marrage is thus illegal in England. Remote as these circumstances are from each other, they remind us that the youthful hero's ultimate destiny is a reunion with a lost parental figure. Cusins' happy absorption into Undershaft's munitions factory stands in obvious contrast to the grandiose conflagration that unites Siegfried and Wotan at the end of the *Ring*. But, though the differences between a social comedy and a mythic tragedy can hardly be evaded, neither need we evade their similarities. At the ends of both works the destinies of father and son figures converge.

Indeed, in the final confrontation that precedes this convergence there is an evocative moment that links these disparate episodes, yet emphasizes a crucial thematic distinction. To ascend the burning mountain to Brünnhilde, Siegfried must thrust aside its parental defender. "Schwing' deinen Speer:" he challenges Wotan, "in Stücken spalt' ihn mein Schwert" (p. 163) [Brandish your spear: in pieces my sword will split it]. But in *Major Barbara* the relations are reversed. As Cusins in the last act thrusts at Undershaft with the claims of conventional morality, the father remains master and confidently challenges the son, "Come! try your last weapon. Pity and love have broken in your hand" (p. 439). The metaphor is a natural one for Shaw, but its use reminds us that in both cases the subject is a generational conflict with a daughter as a prize.

Nor is this material the only point of similarity here. Siegfried's feelings find a curious echo in Cusins, for both of them have divided attitudes toward the noble warrior maiden to whom they are so profoundly drawn. Siegfried, who has been searching for the meaning of fear, finds it as he contemplates the sleeping Brünnhilde and calls upon his dead mother for help:

> Ist es das Fürchten?—
> O Mutter! Mutter!
> Dein mutiges Kind!
> Im Schlafe liegt eine Frau:—
> die hat ihn das Fürchten gelehrt!   (p. 165)
>
> [Is it fear?—
> Oh, Mother! Mother!
> Your brave child!
> In sleep lies a woman:—
> Who has taught him fear!]

And as Siegfried leans over the sleeping beauty about to awaken her to erotic life with the ritual kiss, Wagner's stage directions specify that he sinks *"wie ersterbend"* and places his lips to hers *"mit geschlossenen Augen."* (She is, one assumes, both too holy and too terrible to be looked upon.) Shaw, in contrast, offers none of Wagner's surging eroticism nor the immediate Freudian implications of Siegfried's equivocal appeal to his mother at the moment when he is about to consummate a sexual union with one who is almost inescapably her surrogate (his mother's half-sister), but he does give his Siegfried an awareness that the relationship he would undertake is dangerous. Even as Cusins tells

Undershaft, in their second-act colloquy, that he loves Barbara and that he and nobody else must marry her, he qualifies his feelings: "I don't like marriage:" he says, "I feel intensely afraid of it; and I dont know what I shall do with Barbara or what she will do with me." (p. 387). Barbara, fortunately, does not arrange for her hero's death, as Brünnhilde does, but after Bill Walker's warning that Cusins will be "wore aht" by her, Cusins exclaims meditatively, "Yes, my dear, it's very wearing to be in love with you. If it lasts, I quite think I shall die young" (p. 383). The humorous Shavian tone disguises but does not conceal the complex of feelings that the feminine presence evoked in Shaw and had evoked in his great mentor as well: for them women offered motherly comfort ("my dear little Dolly boy" Barbara calls Cusins; Wagner's women almost invariably offer the ultimate maternal gifts of total allegiance and death); however, their profound sexual allure— deriving in part from that very maternal component—was also deeply disquieting.

But the women in these works have significant relations not only to their lovers but also to their fathers. Both of them are women of exalted rank (Brünnhilde is a goddess, Barbara the granddaughter of an earl and the daughter of "the Prince of Darkness"); both are costumed in garments that suggest their quasi-military status; and most significantly both are seen as agents of their father's wills, extensions of their very selves. "Wer—bin ich," asks Brünnhilde, "wär ich dein Wille nicht?" [Who—am I, if I am not your will?]. And Wotan himself recognizes this identity:

> Was keinem in Worten ich künde,
>   unausgesprochen
>   bleib' es denn ewig:
>   mit mir nur rat' ich,
>   red' ich zu dir.—   (p. 37)
> [What I tell no one in words,
>   unspoken
>   may it remain forever:
>   with myself only I confer,
>   when I speak to you.]

Undershaft is more exuberant but no less certain of his daughter's relationship to him as he realizes that, like himself, she is wielded by an external power that expresses itself as an inner inspiration. "It is the Undershaft inheritance," he exclaims triumphantly. "I shall hand on my torch to my daughter. She shall make my converts and preach my gospel—" (p. 388). The very missions that the daughters perform suggest the intensity of their allegiance to their fathers. As Brünnhilde, along with her sisters, gathers up heroes fallen in battle and transports them to Walhall to become Wotan's guard, so Barbara is a gatherer of the souls of the fallen. And though she does not initially select heroes or devote them to her earthly father's service, when she comes to understand his aims, she makes it her mission to ennoble the inhabitants of Perivale and make them worthy citizens of her father's "heavenly city."

But however profound this devotion, both of these daughters have with the fathers a relationship that does not remain untroubled. Brünnhilde, after all, defies her father's injunctions in attempting to give victory to Siegmund, and by preserving Sieglinde she contributes to his downfall. By her work as a salvationist Barbara has supposedly been defying her father's values even before she challenges him to visit Canning Town. What is interesting here, however, is not merely the act of defiance by the daughter whose military accoutrements are—at least in part— the symbol of her affinity to her "warrior" father but rather the similarity in the nature of the defiance and in the fathers' reaction. Brünnhilde's disobedience of her father stems from her compassion for the sufferings of the mortal twins and particularly from her admiration for Siegmund's nobility and devotion. Shaw is hardly given to sentimentalizing romantic love (Bill Walker is, if anything, a reverse Siegmund, notable for his lack of chivalry), but Barbara's determination to succor the poor and her recognition of Bill Walker's moral independence have, in this context, a reminiscent quality.

But even more striking than the act of rebellion itself is the nature of the father's feeling toward his daughter and the punishment he visits upon her. Brünnhilde is Wotan's beloved favorite: "du kühnes/ herrliches Kind!" (p. 82) [you bold, magnificent child!] he calls her as he bids her farewell in the great arioso at the end of *Walküre,* "Du meines Herzens heiliger Stolz!" (p. 83) [You my heart's holy pride]. In a moving passage he envisions the hero upon whom her eyes will shine when he breaks through the bridal fire to possess her; then Wotan kisses away her divinity:

Dem glücklichern Manne
glänze sein Stern:

dem unseligen Ew'gen
muss es scheidend sich schliessen.
Denn so kehrt
der Gott sich dir ab,
so küsst er die Gottheit von dir!   (p. 84)
[Upon the happier man
may your star shine
upon the unhappy immortal
must it departing set.
For thus turns
the god away from you,
so he kisses the godhead from you!]

The intensity of feeling suggested at this moment is only increased by our knowledge that the foreordained hero who will
come to Brünnhilde is Wotan's grandson—an extension of himself.

Though the incest fantasy here implied is far more deeply
submerged in *Major Barbara,* Cusins admits, after Undershaft
says he has come to love Barbara "with a father's love," that such
a love is "the most dangerous of all infatuations" (reminding us
that Cleopatra is "the most dangerous of all Caesar's conquests")
and denigrates by comparison his own "pale, coy, mistrustful
fancy" (p. 387).12 And just as significant as the nature of the
father's love in these works is the similarity in the punishment
they administer for the daughter's defiance. As Wotan kisses
away Brünnhilde's godhead, so Undershaft, kindly but firmly,
with a stroke of his pen and a flourish of his checkbook takes
from Barbara her faith in the Army and thus her sense of divine
mission. As Brünnhilde, her armor removed, appears before
Siegfried *"in einem weichen, weiblichen Gewande"* (p. 165) [in
a soft, feminine garment], so Barbara, having discarded her uniform, must sit disconsolately in her mother's drawing room "in
this vulgar silly dress." In each case, however, the devoted father
mitigates his act and restores to the daughter something of her
lost status, Wotan by the protective fire, Undershaft by his suggestion to Barbara, who had complained of the loss of Bill
Walker's soul, that she could not "strike a man to the heart and
leave no mark on him" (p. 420).

Both fathers are thus ambiguously affectionate, severe yet
protective. Moreover, they have at least two other elements in
common. They descend to a nether world to perform their acts
of power (though Niebelheim is less suggestive of the shelter

than of Barbara's fantasy of Perivale—in a passage also cited by Wisenthal—as "a sort of pit where lost creatures with blackened faces stirred up smoky fires and were driven and tormented by my father" [p. 418). More important still, Wotan and Undershaft are both absent parents, fathers who have deserted their offspring but who at crucial moments return to offer succor. If Wotan has been kind to Brünnhilde, he seems to have been cruel to her half-sister. As Sieglinde sleeps restlessly while Siegmund goes off to meet his death in battle, she dreams of paternal desertion: "Kehrte der Vater nur heim!/ Mit dem Knaben noch weilt er im Forst" (p. 55) [If only Father would return home!/ With the boy he still lingers in the forest]. Barbara too has grown up without the presence of a male parent. "She has," says Lady Britomart rebuking Undershaft, "no father to advise her" (p. 359). But in fact Sieglinde's father has not been without affection for her and appears at her wedding with a sword intended for the rescue of her future lover. Nor has Undershaft deserted his daughter; he, too, though he has been an absent parent, has nevertheless remained a beneficent guardian. He has saved her soul, he tells Barbara in their climactic confrontation, for his wealth, which has allowed her to be "wasteful, careless, generous," has "saved her from the crime of poverty" (pp. 433-34).

Though Barbara and her father are reconciled, Shaw's sense of childhood anger lingers in Stephen Undershaft's rejection of his father's values and his peevishness with his mother, just as the sense of grief lingers in Sieglinde's anguished cry. Characteristically, Shaw presents this emotional relationship between father and son in social and economic terms, but it remains an emotional one nonetheless.[13] Barbara's relationship, in fact, is a variation on the fantasy already referred to of the distant but beneficent parent of exalted status who will arrive to rescue the child, who in turn may even—like Barbara—go to live in the parent's castle. Both Wagner and Shaw, however, are deeply attuned to the ambiguities in these relationships, and by dividing the child figures into sibling groups they are able to express the child's angers (against the real parent for his failures, against the fantasy parent for his absence) as well as ultimate love and acceptance.

Although both Brünnhilde and Barbara finally come to such feelings, their temperaments and their creators' visions make for irreducible differences. At the end of *The Ring* and of *Major Barbara* each heroine is vouchsafed a transcendent understanding, but of a rather different sort. As she stands before Siegfried's body, contemplating her own imminent death and the obliteration of Walhall, Brünnhilde says that she understands all—"alles ward mir nun frei!" (p. 253) [all was now open to me!]—and sends her father a message of peace before his destruction. Although here she does not say what she knows but rather, expressing a desire for union with Siegfried in love and death, spurs her horse into the funeral pyre, originally as Shaw noted (in a passage that Wagner finally did not set) she had asserted a faith in the efficacy of love. Not surprisingly, Shaw is impatient with this passage, which he takes to be an exaltation of "vehement sexual passion" (p. 84).14 And yet, at the end of *Major Barbara* he gives his heroine a moment of transfiguration that is no less exalted than Brünnhilde's idealization of love and no less mysterious than her mingling of the morbid and the erotic. Resolving to work with the well fed citizens of her father's realm, Barbara says, "My father shall never throw it in my teeth again that my converts were bribed with bread," and continues:

> I have got rid of the bribe of bread. I have got rid of the bribe
> of heaven. Let God's work be done for its own sake: the work
> he had to create us to do because it cannot be done except by
> living men and women. When I die, let him be in my debt, not
> I in his; and let me forgive him as becomes a woman of my
> rank.   (pp. 444-45)

Like Brünnhilde, Barbara is elusive in her vision of death; she does not tell us what sin the Ultimate Parent has committed that requires her forgiveness (nor does she offer him Brünnhilde's "Ruhe! Ruhe, du Gott!" (p. 253) [Peace! Peace, you god!]). We cannot quite know why Barbara insists so absolutely on inverting the roles of parent and child, but we may wonder if the parental sin here is not Wotan's archetypal crime—of desiring gratification not for his child but for himself, of loving his offspring not for herself but as an extension of himself.

In this moment of transcendence that Barbara and Brünnhilde achieve we find not only a further link between the works in which they appear but a point of connection with those previously considered as well. At their final moments *Major Barbara* and *The Ring* also become myths of withdrawal. For Brünnhilde no less than Caesar turns away from the mortal world and gives herself over to death; Barbara no less than Lohengrin retreats to her father's citadel, there to pursue her spiritual mission.

But whereas in the relatively simple world of *Lohengrin* and *Caesar* is embodied the impulse to withdraw from the sensual world for fear of the loss of power and identity, in the greater richness of the *Ring* and *Major Barbara* is evoked a whole complex of relations both erotic and familial (terms which are by no means mutually exclusive) that lie behind the desire to transcend the ordinary human condition. There is not only the familiar male fear of erotic entanglement, explicit in Siegfried, hinted at in Cusins, but the ambiguous lure of the maternal as well. No less ambiguous is the portrayal of the father figure, absent yet beneficent, in conflict with the son yet yielding to his succession, intensely affectionate with the daughter yet punishing her defiance by removing her "godhead," that is her linkage to him. And that linkage is ultimately transcended by the daughter herself in the moment of illumination that finally comes to her.

Behind whatever teleological myth Wagner may have intended, behind the profound social vision that *Major Barbara* still offers to us we sense the presence of the personal elements that bind these two artists together despite their divergences of mind and temperament. It was his instinctive sympathy for the personal essence of the Wagnerian myth, for the transcending of certain human failures and entanglements, that made of Shaw a "more perfect" Wagnerite than he ever consciously realized. We will best understand what Wagner taught Shaw if we turn back for a moment to a play of Shaw's mentioned briefly near the beginning of this essay, to *Candida,* whose poet hero learned to live without happiness because "life is nobler than that." Whatever life indeed is, Shaw's sense of what one had to know to deal with it—and perhaps his own unconscious recognition of a master from whom he had learned—comes in a passage from *The Perfect Wagnerite* in which he is describing the events that occur between *Das Rheingold* and *Die Walküre.* Speaking of Wotan's life in the forest with Siegmund, and assuredly unconscious of the resonances of his words, Shaw writes, "With the son he himself leads the life of a wolf, and teaches him the only power a god can teach, the power of doing without happiness" (p. 35).

New York, New York

NOTES

1 Quoted in Martin Meisel, *Shaw and Nineteenth-Century Drama* (Princeton: Princeton Univ. Press, 1963), p. 40.

2 *Richard Wagner: The Man, His Mind and His Music* (Harmondsworth: Penguin, 1971), p. 113.

3 Bernard Shaw, *Collected Letters 1898-1910*, ed. Dan H. Laurence (London: Max Reinhardt, 1972), p. 415.

4 I have argued for the centrality of this theme in a number of Shaw's important plays in "The Ascent to Heaven: A Shavian Pattern," *Modern Drama*, 14 (December 1971), 253-63.

5 *Letters 1898-1910*, p. 505.

6 Quotations from Shaw's plays are taken from *Complete Plays with Prefaces* (New York: Dodd, Mead, 1962). *Caesar and Cleopatra* and *Man and Superman* are in Volume III; *Major Barbara* is in Volume I. Page numbers appear in parentheses after the quotations.

7 Quotations from Wagner's librettos are taken from the *Sämtliche Schriften und Dichtungen* (Leipzig: Breitkopf & Härtel [etc.], 1912-14). *Lohengrin* and *Tannhäuser* are in Volume II; *Das Rheingold* is in Volume V, and the other three texts of *The Ring* in Volume VI. Page numbers appear in parentheses after quotations; my translations, contained in square brackets, adhere as closely as possible to the structure of the original.

8 Not surprisingly, Wagner shared this identification and, indeed, sketched out a drama about Jesus within a year of finishing *Lohengrin*. Both he and Shaw, along with their desire to create a hero who would embody certain transcendent virtues, had personal reasons for identifying with the figure who, above all, exemplifies the common fantasy of being in reality the child of a far more exalted parent than his supposed one. Wagner's actual father bore a name, Geyer, which because it was common among Jewish families exposed his son to the suspicion—painful to him— of being thought to be Jewish (see Gutman, pp. 28-29). Shaw's father, with his tendency to drink and his lack of energy and competence, was a disappointing figure for his son.

9 Robert Donnington argues, in passing, that Elsa's asking the forbidden question ultimately brings her back her brother (in Donnington's Jungian view her "inner masculinity"), but Elsa's collapse at the end of the opera hardly supports his optimistic reading. *Wagner's 'Ring' and Its Symbols* (London: Faber and Faber, 1963), p. 120.

10 *The Perfect Wagnerite* (New York: Dover, 1967), p. 90. Page numbers for this and subsequent texts appear in parentheses after the quotations.

11 "The Underside of Undershaft: A Wagnerian Motif in *Major Barbara*," *Shaw Review*, 15 (May 1972), 57. Page numbers appear in parentheses after the quotations. A view similar to Wisenthal's is argued in Alfred Turco's *Shaw's Moral Vision: The Self and Salvation* (Ithaca, N.Y.: Cornell University Press, 1976), pp. 208-12, 215-17.

12 For further examples of this theme in Wagner and Shaw, consider the Sachs-Eva relationship in *Meistersinger* and that of Shotover and Ellie in *Heartbreak House*.

13 For this view of familial relations in *Major Barbara*, I am indebted to the comments on the play by Margaret Ganz in *The Enduring Voice* (New York: Macmillan, 1972).

14 (Shaw even expresses displeasure with the musical treatment of the end of *Götterdämmerung*, calling the major theme first "rapturous" and then "trumpery.") In regard to this omitted passage Shaw offers a grandly socialist translation of Brünn-

hilde's paean to love ("I believe not in property, nor money, nor godliness, nor hearth and high place, nor pomp and peerage, nor contract and custom, but in Love" [p. 83]), but he says nothing about another passage that Wagner intended to substitute for this one (though ultimately that text was not set either) and that Shaw may well have known. The omission is intriguing because the second text astonishingly anticipates aspects of Shaw's own dramatic vision, as a few excerpts demonstrate:

> Aus Wunscheim zieh' ich fort,
> Wahnheim flieh' ich auf immer;
>
> . . .
>
> nach dem wunsch und wahnlos
> heiligsten Wahland,
>
> . . .
>
> von Wiedergeburt erlöst,
> zieht nun die Wissende hin.   (pp. 255-56)

> [From the home of wishes I journey forth,
> The home of illusion I flee forever;
>
> . . .
>
> toward the wish and illusionless
> holiest land of desire,
>
> . . .
>
> redeemed from rebirth,
> the knowing woman now journies on.]

Both the departure from the home of wishes and illusions, so immediately evocative of Don Juan's disdainful withdrawal from Hell, and the longing to be "von Wiedergeburt erlöst," to escape from the endless cycle of mortal life, so suggestive of the Shavian dream of release at the end of *Back to Methuselah,* reveal that darker, tragic part of Shaw's temperament that he was usually at pains to conceal from the world, and from himself.

Paterian Aesthetics in Yeats' Drama

F. C. McGrath

The pervasiveness of Walter Pater's influence on English letters in the 1890's is canonical fact. Yeats and his friends in the Rhymers' Club had looked to Pater as the greatest contemporary prose stylist, and they had been infatuated with his philosophy of the flux. Like many literary styles in the nineties, Yeats' early experiments, such as "Rosa Alchemica" and *The Shadowy Waters,* were imitations of Pater's florid, languorous cadences. Partly as a result of his early stylistic failures, Yeats, with the help of the rigorous demands imposed by writing for the stage, began during the next decade to forge a new style that led to the lean, sinewy power of his mature verse. Writing plays gave Yeats' verse vigor, concreteness, and a sense of structure, and consequently brought it out of the "cloud and foam" of the Celtic Twilight and his 1890's aestheticism. It has long been a critical commonplace that Yeats' experience as a dramatist had a substantial impact on his later poetry, but what has not been recognized is that Pater played an even greater role in shaping the dramatic ideals that informed Yeats' new style than he had in influencing his earlier style. When Yeats went to Stratford-on-Avon in April of 1901 to study Shakespeare as part of his preparation to become a serious dramatist, he again turned to Pater for philosophy; only this time he was assessing not the philosophy of the flux but Pater's philosophy of aesthetic form, and not the accidentals of his style but the essence of his thought. As the revisions to *On Baile's Strand* and the development of Yeats' dramatic theory after 1901 indicate, Yeats' new style resulted not merely from a fusion of his early Paterian lyricism with a new interest in dramatic action and simplicity;[1] rather his new dramatic aesthetic was an expansion and refinement of a somewhat vague notion of *lyricism* into a more precise and profoundly Paterian concept *of lyric unity.* Moreover,

the direction of Yeats' subsequent refinements in his drama
continue inexorably toward perfecting Pater's lyric ideal. Far
from leaving Pater behind in the nineties, Yeats was not so
much transcending his aesthetic philosophy as arriving at a
deeper understanding of it and discovering its true meaning for
himself.

We cannot ignore, however, the very significant differences
between Yeats and Pater. Yeats' vision of reality was substan-
tially broader than Pater's: it encompassed a spiritual universe
in addition to the material, intellectual, and emotional. But once
this difference is granted, Yeats' affinities with Pater become
clearer. Even though Yeats says, "nothing is an isolated artistic
moment; there is unity everywhere," if we grant the metaphysical
chasm, Pater's statements on intense personal experience and
"life as the end of life" are appropriate to Yeats as well; and
Yeats' writings during the time when his theory of drama was
developing reveal that his broader metaphysical vision is not
exclusive of Pater's but inclusive of it. Although Paterian in
conception, Yeats' ideal of lyric unity was not subject to the
general neo-Kantian limitations of Pater's vision; for Yeats not
only incorporated it into his drama and poetry, but also extended its scope and application to his spiritual-aesthetic vision
of reality. The apparent difference between Yeats' new and old
styles and the tendency of his critics to emphasize the distinctions between him and Pater have obscured how Yeats incorporated Pater into his mature theory and practice; hence many
have been led to misunderstand Pater's influence on one of his
most successful disciples, for through Yeats' drama Pater's aesthetic subtly found its way into Yeats' poetry and into the literary
sensibility of the twentieth century.

Prior to his Stratford visit, Yeats' dramatic theory was inchoate. Most of his comments were either in praise of symbolist
drama, such as *Axël*, which had a strong influence on his own
Shadowy Waters, or critical of realist drama.[2] The earliest
statements suggesting the course his own drama would take,
however, were exaggerated encomiums of the plays of an Irishman, Dr. John Todhunter. His 1890 review of Todhunter's plays
cited an impersonal, religious, and austere beauty in which
"acting, scenery, and verse were all a perfect unity" (*LNI*, 113-
17). Todhunter's moderate success inspired hope in Yeats that
there would soon be a "genuine public, however small, for poetic

drama," a public which would appreciate "plays of heroic passions and lofty diction" (*LNI,* 217). By the end of the decade, in condemning the elaborate, spectacular costumes and scenery of contemporary realistic drama, Yeats was advocating a drama that remembered its origins in the "enchanted ode," that delighted our ears more than our eyes, and that would "appeal to the imagination alone." As models he admired the artifice and severe visual beauty of Greek drama and the poetry and oratory of the Elizabethans (*Ltrs.,* 309-10). His essay "The Theatre" (1899) summarizes these formative ideals: he felt that poetry in its highest moments would be out of place on the visually distracting realistic stage; he wanted to recall words to their "ancient sovereignty" by allowing only austere and simple gestures, costumes, and scenery and by subordinating everything to the verse. He declared that plays written under these principles would be "remote, spiritual and ideal" (*E&I,* 166-70). These early statements hardly constitute a coherent and comprehensive dramatic theory. However, they are not "merely random and sympathetic insights."[3] On the contrary, they indicate that as far as the essentials of poetic drama were concerned, Yeats knew what he was looking for and was moving consistently in the direction of a lyric unity. Nevertheless, by 1899 his theoretical formulation was not adequate to inform his own practice, as evidenced by the fruit of this early speculation, *The Shadowy Waters,* published after much revision in 1900.[4] Yeats himself soon recognized that this play was "obscure and vague" and "overgrown with symbolic ideas."

At this point in his career Yeats went to Stratford "to learn construction from the masters" (*Expl.,* 81). There he attended performances of Shakespeare's histories in the evening and he spent his days in the theatre library "reading all the chief criticisms of the plays" (*Ltrs.,* 349). Critical of most of the scholars, he said, "The more I read the worse does the Shakespeare criticism become and Dowden is about the climax of it. It came out of the middle class movement and I feel it my legitimate enemy" (*Ltrs.,* 349). In the nineties Yeats and his friends, most notably Oscar Wilde, had appealed to Pater's authority in their attacks on middle-class values and their attendant morality. In "At Stratford-on-Avon," published in 1901 as a result of his Shakespeare studies, Yeats again enlisted Pater as an ally against the middle-class sensibility, which chose Henry V as "Shakespeare's

only hero." Without mentioning Pater, Yeats quotes from his
"Shakespeare's English Kings" and draws from it and from his
essay on *Measure for Measure*.5 (Both essays appear side by
side in *Appreciations*.) From the essay on *Measure for Measure*
Yeats drew his elaboration on Shakespeare's sympathetic judgment of his characters, but "At Stratford-on-Avon" and "Shakespeare's English Kings" especially contain a number of significant parallels: both essays emphasize *Richard the Second* and
prefer Richard's poetic temperament to the "showy heroism"
of Henry V; both discuss the tragic irony with which Shakespeare treats his English kings; they both comment on the unity
of the English history plays and speculate on the hypothetical
possibilities of a completed cycle of English histories, had
Shakespeare chosen to complete such a venture (*E&I*, 109-10;
App., 105); and both comment adversely, though for different
reasons, on German Shakespeare critics (*E&I*, 104; *App.*, 202)
and on the vulgarity of contemporary London (*E&I*, 98-99;
App., 195). Much of Yeats' essay appears to be a direct reply
to Pater's interpretation of *Richard the Second,* and taken together the two essays constitute a fascinating dialogue on Shakespeare's tragic irony, sympathetic justice, and concept of the
hero in the history plays.

Although Yeats allies himself with Pater's preference for
the lyrical Richard, he also diverges in significant ways from
Pater's interpretation of Richard's character. Pater found Richard a specimen of quite ordinary humanity thrust by fate upon
greatness, his plight ennobled only by a poetic eloquence that
enabled him to "plead somewhat more touchingly than others
their everyday weakness in the storm" (*App.*, 186-87). Pater's
Richard was less a tragic hero than a world-weary aesthete,
whose defeat was "the great meekness of the graceful wild creature tamed at last . . . turning to acquiescence at moments of
extreme weariness" (*App.*, 200). Yeats, on the other hand,
could not accept Pater's remoteness from the tragic immediacy
of Richard's fate; and he required a lyric victory where Pater
found only passive resignation much like that of his own Marius.
Yeats found extravagant fantasy, noble passion, immense energy,
and a lyric wisdom in Shakespeare's "weak" king, who failed,
not because of his common qualities, but "more because he had
certain qualities that are uncommon in all ages" (*E&I*, 105).
For Yeats Richard's language was no mere "personal embellish-

ment," but a manifestation of his spiritual majesty. His triumph was a lyric victory over circumstance: Yeats claims Shakespeare saw

> in Richard II the defeat that awaits all, whether they be artist or saint, who find themselves where men ask of them a rough energy and have nothing to give but some contemplative virtue, whether lyrical fantasy, or sweetness of temper, or dreamy dignity, or love of God, or love of His creatures. He saw that such a man through sheer bewilderment and impatience can become as unjust or as violent as any common man, any Bolingbroke or Prince John, and yet remain that sweet lovely rose.
> (*E&I*, 106)

Despite their disagreement over Richard, Pater and Yeats were in fundamental agreement on the nature of Shakespeare's sympathetic judgments of his characters, a quality Pater characterizes as "the recognition of that which the person, in his inmost nature, really is"—a true justice that "lies for the most part beyond the limits of any acknowledged law" (*App.*, 183). Pater's analysis appealed to Yeats because, in opposition to the moralistic criticism of nineteenth-century scholars, Pater found Shakespeare's "moral" judgments to be based not on orthodox moral conventions in the ordinary sense, but on the discriminations of a detached aesthetic observer, who "knows how the threads in the design before him hold together under the surface" (*App.*, 183). Echoing Pater Yeats asserts that "behind the momentary self which acts and lives in the world, and is subject to the judgment of the world, there is that which cannot be called before any judgment seat . . ." (*E&I*, 102). As much an attribute of Pater as of Shakespeare, this sympathetic judgment—the ability to "watch the procession of the world with that untroubled sympathy for men as they are, as apart from all they do and seem"—was adopted by Yeats as the "substance of tragic irony" (*E&I*, 106).

As a result of this dialogue on Shakespeare, Yeats was able to build upon Pater's analysis, at points of both agreement and disagreement, to develop and refine his own sense of the tragic hero, sympathetic justice, and tragic irony.

But more remarkable to Yeats than anything else in "Shakespeare's English Kings" must have been the eloquent final passage on the "unities" of the drama, for it provided Yeats with a rich and passionate formulation of what he had praised in Todhunter's plays and sought for his own. In this passage Pater says that, like *Romeo and Juliet,* "that perfect symphony," the form of *Richard the Second* approaches the unity of a musical composition, "of a lyrical ballad, a lyric, a song, a single strain of music." In the opening paragraphs of "The School of Giorgione" Pater had argued that, in its continuous effort to obliterate the distinction between matter and form, "all art constantly aspires toward the condition of music," and that the goal of art is to "present one single effect to the 'imaginative reason'." Pater elaborates on this latter point in the concluding passage of "Shakespeare's English Kings" where he repeats his claim for the superiority of lyric poetry because it preserves, "in spite of complex structure," a perfect "unity of impression," the "unity of a single passionate ejaculation." Pater would substitute this lyric unity for the old Aristotelian unities. The passage concludes,

> It follows that a play attains artistic perfection just in proportion as it approaches that unity of lyrical effect, as if a song or ballad were still lying at the root of it, all the various expression of the conflict of character and circumstance falling at last into the compass of a single melody, or musical theme. As, historically, the earliest classic drama arose out of the chorus, from which this or that person, this or that episode, detached itself, so, into the unity of a choric song the perfect drama ever tends to return, its intellectual scope deepened, complicated, enlarged, but still with an unmistakable singleness, or identity, in its impression on the mind. Just there, in that vivid single impression left on the mind when all is over, not in any mechanical limitation of time and place, is the secret of the "unities"— the true imaginative unity—of the drama. (*App.,* 202-04)

Pater's emphatic phrases on the true imaginative unity of the drama must have resonated profoundly in Yeats' mind and struck him as a more highly developed expression of his own inchoate ideals. As he made no explicit mention of Pater in "At Stratford-on-Avon," he also made no comment on this passage; nevertheless, when later he not only recalls the origins of drama in choric song, but also says, "A writer of drama must observe the form as carefully as if it were a sonnet" (*V Plays,* 1294), we can reasonably suspect that his failure to mention Pater and his concluding passage was no indication of the depth of their impression. Before long Yeats was saying that he was beginning to "feel the unity of the arts in a new way" (*Ltrs.,* 360), and for several years after the publication of "At Stratford-on-Avon" Yeats' writing contains numerous echoes and further developments of issues raised in his dialogue with Pater. Moreover, the development of his drama in theory and practice began to move consistently in the direction of Pater's ideal lyric unity, a movement completed and perfected only in the last year of his life with the publication of *Purgatory.*

Over the next decade Yeats formally developed and refined his dramatic ideal mainly in *Samhain,* the official organ of his Irish Dramatic Movement. In these essays he continued to emphasize simplicity and unity and the subordination of everything to the spoken words; and as his theory crystallized it retained its strong Paterian bias. Drama, like all the other arts, Yeats says, is "a moment of intense life . . . reduced to its simplest form . . . an eddy of life purified from everything but itself" (*Expl.,* 153-54). The emphasis here on art as purified, isolated, intense experience and on simplicity of form are Paterian. Yeats' writing in these essays even reflected the cadences of Pater's own prose at times.

Occasionally Yeats appears to refute the Paterian basis for his ideal lyric unity. For example, in *Discoveries* (1907) he objects to Pater's identification of music as the type of all the arts (*E&I,* 267-68). This objective is understandable when we consider Yeats' personal musical disabilities and his lifelong antagonism toward the obliteration of the sounds of words by music in song. What bothers Yeats, though, is not the ideal unity of form and matter that music represented for Pater, but the use of music as the most appropriate expression of that ideal. Yeats preferred a symbol that expressed a joy of the whole being—body, intellect, and emotions—in that unity. Instead of music alone Yeats offered the example of a guitar player whose physical movements, as well as his fingers and mind, contributed to the total impact on the imagination (*E&I,* 268-69). The metaphor of the guitar player does not reject Pater's ideal, but typically incorporates it into a larger unity, a unity of the whole being which Yeats later embodied in his symbol of the dance.

Yeats had clearly learned his lessons on the true unity of form and matter. In his plays he no longer strove to unify them by making each voice speak as one voice, as he did in *The Shadowy Waters,* and he rejected the imitative Paterian style of his nineties writing: "I do not mean by style words with an air of literature about them, what is ordinarily called eloquent writing" (*Expl.,* 107-08). Instead he pursued another ideal more profoundly Paterian and eloquently treated in Pater's "Style"—

the art of precisely suiting language to thought and of their
inseparability in true art:

> The speeches of Falstaff are as perfect in their style as the
> soliloquies of Hamlet. One must be able to make a kind of
> Faery or an old countryman or a modern lover speak that
> language which is his and nobody else's, and speak it with so
> much of emotional subtlety that the hearer may find it hard to
> know whether it is the thought or the word that has moved him,
> or whether these could be separated at all. (*Expl.*, 107-08)

Yeats' advances in his ideal of lyric unity and stylistic
refinements were accompanied by an emerging conception of
the tragic hero. Here again Yeats appears to reject the passive
sensibility of Marius and the ineffectual lyricsm of Richard II
that Pater admired, and to prefer instead the vigorous, heroic
energy of his own Cuchulain. He was not rejecting passive lyricism for heroic energy, however, but searching for a larger unity
that would reconcile and complete them; and that larger unity
was as Paterian in essence as his earlier lyricism was superficially Paterian.

In spite of the obvious differences between the Paterian
hero and the Yeatsian hero of this period, there are some striking similarities that suggest Yeats was by no means repudiating
his predecessor. Yeats' heroes are not characterized solely by
their heroic commitment to action, for, as J. R. Moore explains,
the hero's role in a Yeats play is both active and passive, the
former being a prerequisite to the latter. In the passive state the
hero receives "a transcendent intuition of new possibility."[6]
This type of disposition, a readiness to receive transcendent
insight, is precisely where Pater leaves Marius at the end of
Marius the Epicurean. With his broader metaphysical vision
Yeats is able to make that transcendent leap, but his own exposition of what constitutes tragic passion in his heroes emphasizes
the ecstasy of contemplation rather than action: he says, "The
soul knows its changes of state alone, and I think the motives of
tragedy are not related to action but to changes of state"
(*Autob.*, 471). Yeats' plays are not in any sense an Aristotelian
action. That is why he uses the carefully chosen word *gesture*
to describe his own drama. *Gesture* is more related to the self,
more inward turning, than *action,* which relates the self to the
external world. Yeats was striving in drama for the equivalent
of symbol in poetry,[7] which, although passionate, is contempla-
tive rather than active.

The Yeatsian hero does not differ from the Paterian hero in being a man of action so much as in the broader metaphysical scope of his contemplation. If the Yeatsian hero embodies action at all, it is, as Moore suggests, in conjunction with impassioned contemplation, a very Paterian attribute. That Yeats himself recognized the attribute as Paterian in quality, if not in metaphysical scope, is apparent in his expression of this highest attribute of art in terms which echo Pater's famous statement in the "Conclusion" to *The Renaissance*. In "The Tragic Theatre" (1910) Yeats says that "tragic ecstasy," his dramatic equivalent for impassioned contemplation in poetry, "is the best that art—perhaps that life—can give" (*E&I*, 239; *V Plays*, 1302). Yeats' conception of the tragic hero, then, does not so much depart from Pater's ideal as incorporate it into a new unity by emphasizing *gesture*, which fuses action to contemplation.

During this decade Yeats was also striving to achieve a more masculine character in his work. Citing William Morris as an example, he saw contemporary literature as "monotonous in its structure and effeminate in its continual insistence upon certain moments of strained lyricism" (*Expl.*, 220). This could be said as well about his own "Rosa Alchemica" or *The Shadowy Waters*, both written in the vague and strained lyrical style of the nineties. He found the antidote for this effeminate lyricism in writing for the stage. When he was extensively revising his plays in 1906 he wrote, "every rewriting that has succeeded upon the stage has been an addition to the masculine element, an increase of strength in the bony structure" (*Expl.*, 22). Defending his preoccupation with the theatre against his friends who were encouraging him to stay with his lyric poetry, Yeats says, "to me drama . . . has been the search for more of manful energy, more of cheerful acceptance of whatever arises out of the logic of events, and for clean outline, instead of those outlines of lyric poetry that are blurred with desire and vague regret" (*V Poems*, 849). Yet, despite Yeats' rhetoric, his pursuit of a more masculine quality in his art was not a radical departure from Pater, whose ideal of culture Yeats said could "only create feminine souls" (*Autob.*, 477). Rather it was a reaction to what he regarded as an excess of femininity in art and an effort to bring the masculine and feminine characteristics of his own art into a unified balance. He still saw his new achievements as Paterian in quality, and even described them in Pater's terms and cadences: "All art is in the last analysis an endeavour to condense as out of the flying vapour of the world an image of human perfection, and for its own and not for the art's sake . . ." (*V Poems*, 849). Here Yeats rejects the offspring of Paterian aesthetics, the art for art's sake movement of the nineties, by yoking art to human values again; but the role of art to capture out of the flux of experience "a single sharp impression" is clearly Paterian. Art for Pater gave "nothing but the highest quality to your moments as they pass and simply for those moments sakes"; art for art's sake emptied Pater's ideal even of the fleeting moment's experience; Yeats not only restored that moment but gave it expanded significance by rooting its image in the *anima mundi*.

That Yeats' rhetoric about masculinity was only a temporary means to correct an imbalance in his early style and not a permanent departure from Pater is made clearer in his 1909 diary, where Pater becomes half of a revitalized cultural ideal. Here Yeats sees Pater's more feminine cultural ideal as the antidote for the overly masculine Irishman: "Culture of this kind produces the most perfect flowers in a few high-bred women. It gives to its sons an exquisite delicacy" (*Autob.*, 477). To complement his Paterian ideal Yeats proposes what he calls the "culture of the Renaissance," which "seems to me founded not on self-knowledge but on knowledge of some other self . . . not on delicate sincerity but on imitative energy" (*Autob.*, 477). This Renaissance ideal of culture, perhaps influenced by Pater's *Renaissance*,[8] is analogous to the masculine and intellectual character Yeats was striving for in his drama.

Yeats saw the contemporary culture inherited from the nineteenth century as degraded because it had lost what he calls "classical morality," a traditional, pre-Christian morality based on "certain heroic and religious truths, passed on from age to age" (*Autob.*, 490). According to Yeats classical morality, which he thought "not quite natural in Christianized Europe," dominated our cultural tradition during the Renaissance and "passed from Milton to Wordsworth and to Arnold, always growing more formal and empty until it became a vulgarity in our time—just as classical forms passed on from Raphael to the Academicians" (*Autob.*, 490). The aesthetic revolt of the Decadence, which separated art from all but the senses, he saw as a reaction to an empty and formal popular morality; but he predicted that the arts were "about to restate the traditional morality" (*Autob.*, 489-90). His masculine Renaissance ideal would restore fundamental human values to his feminine Paterian ideal. Far from scrapping his inherited culture, what Yeats wished to do was to reassert traditional values in the arts and resurrect a decadent culture into unity.

In terms of Yeats' system of antitheses, his Paterian ideal represents lunar beauty while the more masculine Renaissance ideal represents solar beauty. Beyond these ideal opposites, however, is the Yeatsian Unity of Being in which the opposites are fused. In striving for a masculine ideal he was striving for the opposite mask, "choosing whatever task's most difficult/ Among tasks not impossible"; and out of this struggle would result not the rejection of the feminine ideal, but its fusion with the masculine in unified beauty, or, in terms of culture, an empty feminine form rejuvenated by a masculine classical morality and both fused into a new modern cultural unity.

Precisely what Yeats learned from Pater's ideals and how he applied them in his stagecraft emerge with surprising illumination in the revisions to *On Baile's Strand,* which demonstrate Yeats' movement from superficial imitation of a Pater seen through the eyes of the *decadence* to a more profound achievement of Pater's ideal of lyric unity for the drama. Yeats began writing the play in the summer of 1901 and had finished the first version by April 1902 (*Ltrs.*, 353, 369). He revised the play a number of times and spent most of 1905 making extensive revisions.[9] Except for the hastily written *Where There is Nothing,*[10] it was the first play he wrote after his encounter with Pater at Stratford-on-Avon, and the first play in which he applied his recently developed theories.[11] He wanted to simplify his new play from the start, and his own satisfaction with it is testimony to how close he thought it approached his new theoretical standards (*Ltrs.*, 444).

On Baile's Strand contains several significant echoes of issues Yeats raised in his dialogue with Pater in "At Stratford-on-Avon." For example, the treatment of Cuchulain's character reflects a Shakespearean sympathy that places the hero's actions beyond the ken of mortal judgment; so Cuchulain's passionate dilemma is related to the concept of "tragic irony" which Yeats developed in his essay. These echoes indicate that Yeats had the issues raised with Pater clearly in mind while he was writing and revising the play.

Even more than these echoes, however, the importance of the essay is demonstrated in the revisions to the play, for through them Yeats began his inexorable development toward perfecting in practice Pater's ideal for poetic drama. The revisions generally move toward clarity of structure, austerity of style, and consequently toward Pater's unity of impression. Although the revised play does not achieve these aesthetic standards perfectly, it moves a long way toward them; and what Yeats learned in the process of revising shows up in his later plays. It is a tribute to Yeats' genius that in the aesthetic development of his drama toward clarity, austerity, simplicity, and unity he did not sacrifice complexity, another attribute of Pater's lyric ideal; rather the greater clarity enabled a greater complexity. Yeats' great achievement is his own self-determined goal to "arrange much complicated life into a single action" (*Expl.*, 108).

In his revisions to the first scene Yeats brought out more clearly the correspondences between the low and the heroic characters: as Conchubar needs Cuchulain's strength and Cuchulain needs his wisdom, so the Blind Man needs the Fool's eyesight and agility while the Fool needs the Blind Man's cleverness. He also made the foreshadowing of the main incidents more subtle. Instead of giving "the whole show away,"[12] by adding a mock play and a new speech for the Fool where he tries to puzzle out the relationships among all the central characters just before they begin to make their entrances, Yeats made this first scene of the Fool and Blind Man a microcosm of the play, yet at the same time withholding revelation of the outcome. This revision created a suspense that enhanced the unity of impression by sustaining an interest in the denouement throughout the play. Yeats also transformed Cuchulain's character from a lyrical tempered hero after the manner of Richard II in the first version to something harder—more "repellent yet alluring" (*Ltrs.*, 425). The long dilatory conversations and Cuchulain's flights of lyricism of the first version were replaced by passionate arguments in heated debate. An oath was introduced to strengthen Conchubar's hand against the more fierce Cuchulain and to internalize the conflict within Cuchulain by creating a destructive tension between his oath-bound allegiance to his king and his natural bond to his son. Yeats also introduced a new concern for heirs which heightened the confrontation between Cuchulain and Conchubar; and Conchubar's need for Cuchulain's military prowess (as opposed to his attempt in the first version to convert Cuchulain's energies to peaceful purposes) made the need for reconciliation more pressing as well as more organic to the plot and characterization.

Yeats made most of the major revisions of *On Baile's Strand* in the first half of the play. However, the impact of these revisions on the second half is no less significant than the revisions themselves. Conlaoch's entrance, for example, is greatly enhanced, since it follows immediately upon the consummation of Cuchulain's oath. And the debate and oath scene brings up a number of subjects and themes that are played out in the denouement.13

A particularly brilliant revision that moved the play considerably toward Pater's lyric ideal was made in the image patterns. Yeats eliminated the non-functional images of the seawoman and the dog's head, traditionally associated with Conchubar and Cuchulain respectively. In their stead the Sidhe and their domain of the sea became associated with Cuchulain's ruinous passions for unfettered freedom and for the Scottish warrior-woman Aoife; additionally, they were contrasted to two new, more appropriate images for Conchubar—the threshold and the hearthstone—which express his more domestic concerns for the succession of his heirs and the security of the realm. Together with the climactic gesture of the play—Cuchulain fighting the waves of the Sidhe and seeing "Conchubar's crown on every one of them"—these new images embody the conflicting forces of the play and establish a coherent pattern which enhances the play's improved structural logic. Yeats marshals all his new-found aesthetic simplicity and unity to support this final gesture. The dramatic gesture, equivalent to a symbol in poetry, captures both the unity and complexity of the play's action. In fighting the waves, fused in post-filicide frenzy with the crowns of Conchubar, Cuchulain is not merely taking on the "invulnerable tide" or the "unappeasable host," but committing his whole being to its tragic destiny in a unified image of the external forces that represent the internal destructive antinomies of his fate. With its impressively orchestrated build-up, this final gesture, which fuses heroic action with impassioned contemplation, achieves Pater's "true imaginative unity" of the drama—"that vivid single impression left on the mind when all is over."

Though these revisions contributed immensely to aesthetic simplicity and unity in the play, they also enhanced its complexity, a quality cogently articulated by Peter Ure, who sees the links between the two halves of the revised play as not "merely narrative connexions," but "vital antitheses" that lead to the lively interaction of the two episodes":

> Thus Yeats makes a double knot out of his singly knotted source. The two central episodes are interlocked by means of certain thematic links, so that the second episode draws meaning from the first. These links serve not only to make the tale more exciting; they also tighten by twisting, making the inward life of Cuchulain tenser by pulling it in different directions.[14]

The revisions of *On Baile's Strand* demonstrate the enormous advances in Yeats' dramatic practice at a time when Pater was freshly on his mind, and they indicate that at the center of his emerging aesthetic was Pater's ideal lyric unity for the drama. What Yeats learned in revising *On Baile's Strand* is that true lyric unity, as opposed to vague lyricism, lay not in the aesthetic temperament of the individual hero, but in the tightly wrought organic form of the play.[15]

If Yeats' application of Pater's principles produced an art quite different from Pater's in style as well as metaphysical scope, it is not because he rejected Pater or found his principles inadequate. On the contary, Pater's theories, especially those on unity and style, are sufficiently flexible and universal that the character of the art they produce depends entirely on the nature of the artist's input. Pater's lyric ideal applies to Shakespeare as well as Yeats. The failure of critics to recognize this flexibility in Pater has obscured the fact that Pater's theories and their offspring have produced so many different forms of excellence in twentieth-century art—for example, in the works of James Joyce, Virginia Woolf, and Wallace Stevens. Pater's limitations as an artist prevented him from realizing his own ideals, but this does not negate the value of his principles. Yeats' artistic genius, on the other hand, consummated Pater's ideals, and his development as a dramatist is less a process of weaning himself from Pater than of understanding Pater more profoundly, recognizing the universality of his theories, and realizing that the works of a disciple of Pater need not resemble Pater's own.

Pater's principles did not inform Yeats' drama only. Thomas

Parkinson and other critics have amply demonstrated how his dramatic aesthetics and experience as a playwright have shaped his mature poetry.16 *A Vision*, which systematically organizes Yeats' most developed views of human personality, history, and the afterlife, also has been characterized as a Paterian aesthetic reverie.17 Indeed, the culmination of earthly and spiritual experience for Yeats resembles Pater's lyric ideal: the ultimate aim of the soul in Yeats' system is to convert the experience of its many incarnations into knowledge by embodying it in a single, complex image such as Yeats' own dancer or Cuchulain fighting the waves. So Pater's presence, lodged at the core of Yeats' aesthetic vision, was not limited to his work in the nineties, but was much more enduring, pervasive, and profound. The same can be said of Pater's impact on other modernist writers, for Yeats, as the first major modernist to carry Paterian principles into the twentieth century, also provides an illustration of how Pater has become one of the most persistent influences on our literature.

University of Pennsylvania

NOTES

Abbreviations for works of Pater and Yeats cited in the text and notes are as follows:

Pater:

App.	*Appreciations*. London: Macmillan, 1910.
Renaissance	*The Renaissance*. London: Macmillan, 1910.

Yeats:

Autob.	*Autobiographies*. London: Macmillan, 1955.
E&I	*Essays and Introductions*. New York: Macmillan, 1961.
Expl.	*Explorations*. London: Macmillan, 1962.
LNI	*Letters to the New Island*. 1934; rpt. Oxford: Oxford Univ. Press 1970.
Ltrs.	*The Letters of W. B. Yeats*, ed. Allen Wade, New York: Macmillan, 1955.
UP	*Uncollected Prose*, vol. I, ed. John Frayne. London: Macmillan, 1970.
V Plays	*The Variorum Edition of the Plays of W. B. Yeats*, ed. Russell K. Alspach. New York: Macmillan, 1966.

1 A claim made by some critics: John Unterecker, "The Shaping Force in Yeats's Plays," *Modern Drama*, 7 (1964), 346-51; Eric Bentley, *In Search of Theatre* (New York: Knopf, 1953), p. 324; John Rees Moore, *Masks of Love and Death: Yeats as Dramatist* (Ithaca: Cornell Univ. Press, 1971), pp. xi-xii, 12.

2 For example see his 1894 reviews of Villiers de l'Isle-Adam's *Axël* and Ibsen's *Brand (UP*, 320-25, 344-46).

3 Leonard Nathan, *The Tragic Drama of William Butler Yeats: Figures in a Dance* (New York: Columbia Univ. Press, 1965), p. 43.

4 Nathan sees *The Shadowy Waters* as the culmination of Yeats' Paterian ideal of lyric unity, but it was conceived long before Yeats' contact with Pater's disciples in the Rymers' Club; he began writing it years before his encounter with Pater at Stratford; and he published the first version a year before he went to Stratford. For a detailed discussion and assessment of *The Shadowy Waters* and its revisions see Nathan, *Drama*, pp. 64-80, and Thomas Parkinson, *W. B. Yeats: Self-Critic* (Berkeley: Univ. of Calif. Press, 1951), pp. 59-75.

5 For other comparative studies of Yeats' and Pater's Shakespeare essays see Nathan, *Drama*, pp. 45, 104-05, and his "W. B. Yeats's Experiments with an Influence," *Victorian Studies*, 6 (1962), 66-74; and Rupin W. Desai, *Yeats's Shakespeare* (Evanston: Northwestern Univ. Press, 1971), pp. 32-33.

6 "The Idea of a Yeats Play," *W. B. Yeats, 1865-1965: Centenary Essays on the Art of W. B. Yeats*, ed. D.E.S. Maxwell and S. B. Bushrui (Ibadan: Ibadan Univ. Press, 1965), p. 55.

7 S. B. Bushrui, *Yeats's Verse Plays: The Revisions 1900-1910* (London: Oxford Univ. Press, 1964), p. 46.

8 In his "preface" to *The Renaissance*, Pater says that in the age of Lorenzo "artists and philosophers and those whom the action of the world has elevated and made keen do not live in isolation, but breathe a common air, and catch light and heat from each other's thoughts. There is a spirit of general elevation and enlightenment in which all alike communicate. It is the unity of this spirit which gives unity to all the various products of the Renaissance; and it is this intimate alliance with mind, this participation in the best thoughts which that age produced, that the art of Italy in the fifteenth cenury owes much of its grave dignity and influence" (p. xiv).

9 There are several analyses of the revisions to *On Baile's Strand* to which I am partly indebted for my summary: Bushrui, pp. 41-62; Nathan, *Drama*, pp. 108-29; Moore, *Masks*, pp. 110, 125; and Reg Skene, *The Cuchulain Plays of W. B. Yeats* (London: Macmillan, 1974), pp. 45-46, 154-200.

10 Yeats wrote *Where There is Nothing* in two weeks' time with the help of Lady Gregory and Douglas Hyde in order to copyright the plot before George Moore, with whom he had once planned to collaborate on the play (*Ltrs.*, 530). Yeats later revised the play and published it as *The Unicorn from the Stars*.

11 Nathan also agrees on the importance of *On Baile's Strand* as a product of Yeats' new theories (*Drama*, 116), but he does not acknowledge the Paterian basis for them.

12 Moore, *Masks*, p. 125.

13 Peter Ure, *Yeats the Playwright: A Commentary on Character and Design in the Major Plays* (London: Routledge and Kegan Paul, 1963), p. 65

14 Ure, pp. 65-69.

15 Peter Ure makes a similar observation about Yeats' later plays, written after 1915, where "the great Shakespearean moment of tragic ecstasy" is induced not by the individual heroic character, but by the Paterian unity of the play's form. "W. B. Yeats and the Shakespearean Moment," *Yeats and Anglo-Irish Literature: Critical Essays by Peter Ure*, ed. C. J. Rawson (Liverpool: Liverpool Univ. Press, 1974), p. 219.

16 See especially Parkinson's *W. B. Yeats: Self-Critic*.

17 See Harold Bloom's Introduction to Pater's *Marius the Epicurean* (New York: New American Library, 1970), p. xii.

"Body's Image": *Yerma, The Player Queen,* and the Upright Posture

Murray Baumgarten

Francis Fergusson has reminded us of the ways in which Lorca's theatre, of a piece with his poetry, brings the latent memory of the rich Andalusian folk-tradition to dramatic vivid life. Writing out of the revival of a national culture, which he in part helped to bring about, Lorca creates "significant art forms, filled with immediately relevant moral and spiritual content"; his poetic theatre responds to rather than evades "the crucial labor of the dramatic poet, faced with the modern stage and the modern crowd," by discovering and articulating his poetic vision as myth, ritual, and ceremony.[1]

Like Yeats, Lorca "felt the need of a story and form which should make the play itself (as distinguished from the language) poetic," seeking these "elements in myth and ritual. Yeats proceeded from Irish myths, to an English version of Oedipus, to forms based on the *No* play"; Lorca found the possibilities he sought among the gypsies and the (mythic) landscape of his native Andalusia. Yeats labored "to reincarnate a myth in our time," struggling to release "the suggestion of deep poetic insight" that tempted him in his reading into the dramatic life of his plays. Just as self-conscious a poet, Lorca found his own way into myth.

Lorca persuades us to suspend our modern disbelief in ceremony; making believe with him, we participate in the evocation of ancient stories, exploring and articulating their nonrealistic meanings. His magic lifts us out of our everyday world; his ritual becomes ours. If the story of *Don Perlimplín* is "not strictly a myth, it has the qualities our poets seek in myth: It seems much older and much more generally significant than any history which is literally true," Ferguson points out, "yet Lorca does not seem

141

to have thought it up, but rather to have perceived it, or heard it, in the most intimate chamber of his sensibility. In embodying it on the stage he is careful to preserve this oft-told feeling, like a song, or a tale told by a grandmother. This he does with the utmost confidence and simplicity," in a manner Yeats came to understand through his theoretical study of the theatre and struggled to embody in his own plays and theatrical company.[2]

Both men discover or invent versions of traditional tales which, rooted in their respective locales, come to form the structure of their theatrical practice. Like the stories of folklore, legend, and ballad, they are quick with a tragic intensity. These simple plots of desperation and love's loss are the vehicles by whose means Yeats and Lorca explore fundamental human questions. In examining an issue like the body's image—the center of *The Player Queen* and *Yerma*—both artists create works that in their dramatic fullness articulate a philosophical anthropology. As the protagonists of these plays encounter each other in theatrical dialectic, they realize their human destiny as beings determined by their upright posture, and work through a perspective similar to the one Erwin Straus has outlined in his famous essay.[3]

"I have long wanted to go there to lose my name and disappear,"[4] the real, but anonymous, Queen says at the crisis of *The Player Queen* as she dresses Decima for the royal part and makes her exit. Mild and meek, living a fantasy life, the Queen has visions of martyrdom. At the beck and call of the Prime Minister, she has closeted herself with her mystic visions for the seven years of her rule, striving to deny her body's call to love in order to be martyred like her patroness, Saint Octema.

Her encounter with Decima makes it possible for this real Queen to slip away to the convent and disappear. She fulfills her deepest wish just as Decima, the player queen, now has granted the fulfillment of Septimus' poetic prophecy. As her body accedes to the image of royalty and as she plays the royal part, Decima becomes in fact the queen her changeling was in name alone. "Man is nothing till he is united to an image," Septimus says, enunciating the secret his inspiration and drunkenness have brought him at the crisis of the play, as Decima fulfills his prophecy.[5] Body and image fuse to make the meaning demanded by this theatrical world.

The complications and turns of the plot serve to poise its

poetic truth, uttered by Septimus, against the superstitious politics of the mob and to fuse them in the revelation of Decima—united with the image of royalty—at the moment of *peripeteia*. Though a foundling and of illegitimate birth, she plays the Queen's role properly because her beauty has destined her for it; it is the role for which she was born. She fulfills her life in enacting the prophecy of Septimus' song—"the song of the mad singing daughter of a harlot. The only song she had," Decima comments. "Her father was a drunken sailor waiting for the full tide, and yet she thought her mother had foretold that she would marry a prince and become a great queen." And Decima recites one of Yeats' finest lyrical ballads, given here to Septimus, the poet-playwright's alter ego:

> 'When she was got,' my mother sang,
> 'I heard a seamew cry,
> I saw a flake of yellow foam
> That dropped upon my thigh.'
>
> How therefore could she help but braid
> The gold upon my hair,
> And dream that I should carry
> The golden top of care?

As she emerges from her poetic meditation, she dreams it has become her reality: "The moment ago as I lay here I thought I could play a queen's part, a great queen's part; the only part in the world I can play is a great queen's part."6

Decima's refusal to play the role of Noah's wife (and thus help the Prime Minister use the passions of male chauvinism to secure the throne for himself) is the dramatic knot that the plot first ties and then unravels. Her accession to queenhood allows her to rule and make the scheming politician subservient rather than, as he had hoped, the ascendant force in the kingdom. The image of a queen, she can become its majestic reality because image and body fuse in her being. We understand thus that her marriage to Septimus and her shabby treatment of him have served as her apprenticeship to the throne she now comes to possess.

As the play concludes, Decima, the new Queen, has the players dance before her, and banishing them she banishes her past as a player—"You are banished and must not return upon pain of death, and yet not one of you shall be poorer because banished. That I promise. But you have lost one thing that I will not restore." It is the price of transformation, which she shares with her company. "A woman player has left you. Do not mourn her. She was a bad, headstrong, cruel woman, and seeks destruction somewhere and with some man she knows nothing of; such a woman they tell me that this mask would well become, this foolish, smiling face! Come, dance!"7 Wearing the mask of the sister of Noah, she hides her past identity as one of them from the players, and is thereby enabled to play her new role.

Masking her face, Decima loses her identity in order to gain her royal body's image. This is an essential gesture of Yeats' plays, and a central strategy by which to evade the expectations of realistic drama. As the face is hidden and stylized by the mask, the essential lineaments of the body can stand forth and move through the ritual actions of the plot. *The Player Queen* thus celebrates the body of love, expressed in its moment of entrapment and participation in the pattern of history and the design of human life.

With the personages of this drama, the audience discovers—like the Prime Minister and the mob—to its astonishment the revelation of the majesty of the body's image. As Decima becomes one with her role playing, and the player queen is revealed as the true embodiment of royalty, the various strands of the play are fulfilled. Decima integrates—at a higher level than the scheming Prime Minister would have desired—the political demands he has expressed as a queen's look, gesture, and stance of command.

"Walk! Permit me to see your Majesty walk," he asks (Act I) of the real Queen whose only desire is to return to her self-abnegating prayers. "Be more majestic," he commands. He demands of her what she cannot fulfill but what the play discovers to be the essence of Decima's being. "Ah! If you had known the queens I have known—they had a way with them." They conquer if not by costume by "charm, dignity, royal manner." The Prime Minister's understanding of the fundamentals of human experience as well as his lust break out in his concluding comment, evoking real queens with the "morals of a dragoon, but a way, a way! Put on a kind of eagle look, a vulture look."8 What the hereditary ruler cannot assume is Decima's by right of birth, theatrical training, and personal experience.

The ecstatic moment of Decima's appearance as queen fuses the majestic stance of the royal body and its regal movement.

It sums up the dance which, along with the verse of the play, has enacted this central poetic image of the play. The final dance with which the play closes brings together the illusion-making skill of the theatre company and the royal habit of ruling by image projection. Yeats has captured in this the moment when dance gathers into itself its temporal dimension as it articulates space and brings both to ecstatic self-consciousnesss. In Valéry's words, *"L'instant engendre la forme, et la forme fait voir l'instant."*9

The first time Decima commands the company to dance, at the moment when she has discovered her husband's infidelity, she seduces the various male members of the company through the dance and her song. They dance for her; she is the posturing, play-acting queen as beloved, as available woman, almost as playful yet sacred harlot, and her beauty and desirableness command her suitors. This dance is interrupted by the advent of Septimus, her husband, bleeding, fleeing from the mob, and announcing its imminent arrival. The final dance, when the company performs for the newly minted queen, complements the earlier one, but now the sexual element of the former has been raised—through Decima's assumption of regal status—to the sublimated dance of a harmonious realm which she controls by the royal authority that, we have seen, is a function of her beauty and poise. The morals of a dragoon, which she displays in seducing the company, are now in kingly service, endowing her with the royal eagle's look. The earlier ritual of seduction is transformed into the later ceremony of investiture and the establishment of order, as the state finds its harmony in her assumption of the throne. So, too, Nona and Septimus are married and base their marital happiness in Decima's abandonment of the company for the higher realms of illusion making and performance. The threatened tragedy of state and players finds its happy conclusion in this festive, ironic, and comic moment.

We have been tracing the characteristic postures of the play in which theme and theatrical gesture meet. These postures proceed through a carefully delineated movement linking the fortunes of the body-politic and the physical space and being of the human body. The postures of the characters are choreographed: they articulate the mythic action of the body—shared by the polis and the individual—of seeking its true image and thereby coming to consciousness of itself as body. We have moved from the prone Septimus seeking a place to sleep, from the agon of verbal and physical confrontation and struggle, memories of lovemaking, the hide and seek of the search for a way to flee the enraged mob, through the demand for the culmination of the upright posture in the queen's stance, to the dance in which movement and music fuse in a performance that celebrates the gesture of royalty—of reward to her subjects and dignified fare-well to her former company of players. Yeats' drama has articu-lated the various meanings implicit in humankind's upright posture—the endless striving against gravity to maintain its dangerous equilibrium—which is also the condition for human choice. The real queen who denies her body's existence in search of martyrdom and self-abnegation lacks the will to assert her sexual being—the very center, as we have seen, of Decima's character. As we stand erect—the determinant in and of our human structure—we choose our being through our bodies. It is this act of intending and this posture of choosing our inclina-tions that is at the heart of *The Player Queen*.

To phrase it differently, Yeats has created a dramatic ver-sion and articulation of the upright posture in this story of a stooping queen, whose inclinations are to martyrdom and disap-pearance of self—suspected by the mob of unnatural (prone) coupling with a white unicorn—who is supplanted by the es-sence of royalty and natural transcendent beauty. As Erwin Straus notes, "with upright posture, an unescapable ambivalence penetrates and pervades all human behavior. Upright posture removes us from the ground, keeps us away from things, and holds us aloof from our fellow-men. All of these three distances can be experienced either as gain or as loss."[10] As we shall see, the question of the upright posture in this biological, anthro-pological, and philosophical signification is also the central issue of Lorca's *Yerma*.

The violence of the mob in *The Player Queen* is echoed in the relationships of the Prime Minister and the Queen, Deci-ma, Septimus, and Nona. Coercion and oppression are replaced through the magic of role playing which expresses the true nature of those involved. The reinstated *polis* finds its fulfillment in the relationship of condescension (so important to Renais-sance philosophers and poets) in whose observance the mutual obligations and rights of classes leads to the well-ordered organic state. Nona becomes Septimus' sensible wife, a just exchange for

Decima's dreadful persecution of her poet mate, while Decima now finds her true *métier* in queenly rule. There is a suggestion that her aristocratic habits of imperial rule over her husband will now find fit arena for exercise in her marriage to the Prime Minister. The mob accepts the new queen; the old one disappears happily into her convent where she can shed the body that has never expressed her spiritualism, and the new queen unites her theatrical, image-making and natural beauty to the regal image. The violence central to the play powers and energizes the transformation of roles and social functions crucial to this world's stability and survival in a way that echoes Shakespeare's later romances—even to the ambiguities and ambivalences that characterize the future of the reconstituted world with which the play concludes. Personal and public desperation have been transfigured in this dance, and life's choreography has brought us through a passionate revitalization of the value and meaning of the upright posture.

Yerma moves in the other direction. Its violence builds slowly, revealing Yerma's increasing personal desperation. In ironic counterpoint the sexual fulfillment of the verse interludes becomes more explicit and more profound in the course of the play, reaching its climax in the penultimate scene when, as Gustavo Correa puts it, *"La última canción con su mezcla de danza constituye una especie de ceremonial mágico del acto de la concepción."*11 From this ironic vantage point Yerma uncovers her own barren essence, for instead of having intercourse with Juan in a life-giving, life-renewing act, she strangles him in desperate response to his refusal to inseminate her, for he has requested that she perform oral intercourse with him instead. It is noteworthy that the recent Spanish production of *Yerma* took the opportunity of its Berkeley performance to balance the athleticism and abstract expressionism of its trampoline set with a nude portrayal of the murder—a possibility denied to it in Hispanic theatres by censorship and prurient morals.

In *Yerma,* the body's image thus finds a dialectic expression, enacting through dance, verse, music, and gesture both poles of possibility implicit in the existential situation of the upright posture. In its last two scenes, these dialectic opposites force each other to a dramatic explosion. Perhaps because these poles are articulated in more leisurely, less intense and charged a scale in *The Player Queen,* Yeats' play can end as a witty comedy while Lorca's is a fertility-ritual *manqué,* a bitter tragedy wrought out of emptiness of spirit. In both plays, the various personages are pitted against each other in a merciless agon, emerging as forces incarnate in dramatic figures rather than as realistic individuals. Juan embodies the pettiness of the crafty merchant, who refuses to spend—either his money or his semen —a masterly stroke by Lorca in which he fixes character on the ambivalence of a key word.

Using honor as his rationalization, Juan amasses a fortune while struggling to keep his wife in her place. His chauvinism is a way of avoiding the penetrating relationship for which Yerma hungers. While he complies with his husbandly duties in the rare occasions when he is not devoting himself body and soul to the increase of his flocks or vineyards, Juan's occasional sexual forays are either, as Yerma tells us, cold and dutiful, or, as we witness in the last scene, power plays and thus perverse. He refuses to choose the prone position, and it is this act of intentionality which is expressed in his preference for oral love at the conclusion of the play. It takes three acts for the willful barrenness of Juan's commitment to money-making at the expense of child-making to emerge with a force sufficient for Yerma to realize her situation and act upon it out of total desperation. Juan has become an upright puppet, unwilling and unable to participate in the fertile dance of nature and assume all those postures that make it possible for mankind to choose and renew their humanity in cosmic cycle.

While Yerma and Victor experience the possibility of fulfillment, this is a potential never able to be fulfilled because of the demands honor and duty have imposed upon their world. The first scene of the play, in which Yerma has lovingly patted Maria's pregnant belly, concludes with an exchange between Victor and Yerma about the need for children in the house. Together they affirm the value of the suffering children bring— in the pains of childbearing and childbirth—for the renewal of life they make possible. Victor is an image of potential sexuality for Yerma, both in her memories of their childhood encounters and in his advice for Juan. He is a Gary Cooper-like figure of strength and height, suggesting his possible choice of Yerma for fulfillment which has been denied by her marriage to Juan. Duty and honor bind him too; it is not until after he leaves their town, selling his flock to Juan, that Yerma comes to recognize her sterile isolation. Lorca clinches Yerma's need for Victor by concluding the first scene of the play with a crucial stage direction: "Yerma, who has risen thoughtfully, goes to the place where Victor stood, and breathes deeply—like one who breathes mountain air." Moving to occupy his bodily space, Yerma enacts a gesture of implied union with him in bodily fulfillment.12

It is their embrace as an intentional act and choice of human renewal that is the theme of the play, named after the figure who, despite her desires, lives to become the epitome of the meaning of her name—Yerma, the barren one. It is against the desperate force with which she seeks to be fruitful and multiply that we measure Juan's refusal.

The play enacts her search for fructifying, physical succor as she braves superstitions in search of remedies for her tragic situation. She will not allow herself to transgress the bourgeois code, even though urged to several times. The concluding ritual ceremony of pilgrimage and the fertility dances at the shrine cannot penetrate the armor of her morality, even though she is explicitly told and consciously knows that it is a rendezvous where married women encounter new partners in order to create new life. Despite the comments of her friends about the meaninglessness of marriage as well as her own bitter experience, Yerma finds it impossible to act outside its bounds. In the end, she can only destroy that individual who for her embodies the refusal to be body—and thus only can she renew the spirit of the flesh.

Hence in their poetic theatre Yeats and Lorca celebrate the body by articulating and enacting its image. Poetry, dance, and music are here woven together into dramatic wholeness. In both *Yerma* and *The Player Queen,* the upright posture becomes theme and vehicle, and its meanings at once philosophical, psychological, and theatrical are explored by means of mythic, ritual celebrations. Through this image of the body, Yeats and Lorca focus their plays and create new possibilities for the renewal of their respective national cultures as part of a universal— because humanistic—world-culture, rooted in the existential situation bestowed upon us by our human bodies.

Stevenson College
University of California, Santa Cruz

NOTES

1 "Don Perlimplín: Lorca's Theatre-Poetry," in *Lorca: A Collection of Critical Essays*, ed. Manuel Duran (Englewood Cliffs, N.J.: Prentice Hall, 1962), p. 174.

2 Ibid., pp. 172-73.

3 "The Upright Posture," in *Essays in Phenomenology*, ed. Maurice Natanson (The Hague, 1966), pp. 164-92.

4 I have used *The Collected Plays of W. B. Yeats* (New York, 1952); the citation is to scene II, p. 271.

5 Ibid., scene II, p. 267.

6 Ibid., scene II, p. 259.

7 Ibid., scene II, p. 273.

8 Ibid., scene II, p. 258.

9 Paul Valéry, "L'ame et la danse," quoted in Isolde von Bülows' *Der Tanz im Drama. Untersuchungen zu W. B. Yeats' Dramatischen Theorie und Praxis* (Bonn, 1969), p. 114.

10 Straus, p. 170.

11 "The final strophe, mingling dance [and song], constitutes a form of magic, a ceremony invoking the act of conception" (my translation of Gustavo Correa, *La Poesía Mítica de Federico García Lorca* [Madrid, 1970], p. 141).

12 Act I, scene 1. I cite the translation of *Yerma* by James Graham-Lujan and Richard L. O'Connell, in *Three Tragedies of Garcia Lorca* (New York, 1955), p. 110.

The Antichrist Ubu

James H. Bierman

And I will show wonders in the heaven above
and signs on the earth beneath,
blood, and fire and vapor of smoke;
the sun shall be turned into darkness
and the moon into blood,
before the day of the Lord comes,
the great and manifest day.
—Acts of the Apostles, 2.19-20

Alfred Jarry's *Ubu Roi* has received considerable recognition
and acclaim in recent years for its role as a parent play to twentieth-century *avant-garde* drama. Its appearance in Barbara
Wright's translation, in George Wellwarth and Michael Benedikt's *Modern French Drama,* and in several more recent anthol-
ogies has augmented an interest created by Roger Shattuck's
extraordinary portrait of Jarry in *The Banquet Years* and Martin
Esslin's praise of the play as "a landmark and a forerunner."
Coupled with the ongoing efforts of the *Collège de 'Pataphy-
sique,* Jarry enthusiasts have become acquainted with the remarkable diversity of his work, which includes art criticism,
mystical and occult writings, pornography, and science fiction as
well as drama and poetry. The aim of this study is twofold and
it is thus divided into two corresponding sections. The first contends with notions such as Michael Benedikt's that *Ubu Roi* was
a maverick work with no consistent development behind it. It
explores the play within the context of Jarry's earlier epic drama
Caesar Antichrist[1] and presents a wealth of formerly unexposed
material which can contribute enormously to our understanding
of *Ubu Roi* and of the author's intentions in writing it. The second part deals with the obvious gulf between the intentions of
the Ubu drama within the context of *Caesar Antichrist* and the
reality of the separated *Ubu Roi.* In understanding that gulf,

151

one becomes aware of the fact that Jarry had a clear vision of an *abstract* theatre and that he consciously worked to implement that vision in his dramaturgy.

I

Caesar Antichrist is an epic portrayal of the Antichrist universe in the form of a four-act play. Its symbols are crowded into an amazingly dense complex of images, and its stylistic diversity would seem unbelievable to one who knew Jarry only though the later Ubu cycle. It has all the imagistic complexity of a James Joyce novel and all the open fantasy of Marvel comic books. In the work, the Antichrist universe is divided up into four levels that correspond to the mirror reversals of the celestial, astral, terrestrial, and transitional realms. The play takes the reader from a Christian world through the Antichrist cycle, starting with the birth of the Antichrist by a process of inverse resurrection, then following his development into a terrestrial form, and finally through the transition by crucifixion back to the Christian world. During that period, the Antichrist universe is characterized by a complete reversal, both literal and figurative, of the Christian universe and its values. Thus there is continual reference to upside down creatures such as the antipode or the sciapode, and characters such as the Saint Peter Humanity of the first act are depicted upright despite the fact that Saint Peter was commonly held to have been crucified upside down. In comparison, Christ and the thieves on Calvary are upside down in that act. Throughout the play, there are endless reversed images which support the pataphysical process by which Jarry takes a statement such as the life of Christ, and reverses one of the terms by substituting Antichrist, and then carries that statement to its conclusion, leaving us with a radically new statement to consider.

One of the most obviously relevant aspects of the new statements comes from the presence of the third act, which dramatizes the monumental blunderings of the Antichrist incarnate in the form of King Ubu as he stumbles through his earthly existence. That third act became *Ubu Roi.* It is not all of what eventually became *Ubu Roi,* but it does include Act I, scenes vi and vii; Act II, scenes i, ii, and iv; Act III, scenes i through viii; and Act IV, scene iii, of the final play. When one year later

Jarry took *Ubu Roi* out of the context of *Caesar Antichrist,* what he did to make it stand as a play in itself was to broaden its base, giving it stability of its own. Almost all the scenes he added take the focus off Ubu by strengthening the role of other characters, particularly Mère Ubu. The added scenes introduce Mère Ubu's prodding of Ubu, a banquet given by her and Ubu (at which fine sheit is served), her attempts to abscond with Ubu's "phynance," her affair with Gyron, and her flight to France with Ubu, Pile, and Cottice. Only two speeches from the terrestrial act have not been included in the later play.

Since the other three acts of *Caesar Antichrist* are strongly symbolist in style, an iconographic approach to *Ubu Roi* can be seen as fitting within the context of the larger drama. The extent of Jarry's involvement with the second generation symbolists at the time of the genesis of *Ubu Roi* has been little discussed and generally underestimated. The interests which inform *Caesar Antichrist* reflect the fads of symbolist literary circles at that time, particularly of the Tuesday gatherings of the *Mercure de France* group. They are interests in graphic iconography, mysticism, the occult sciences, and heraldry. His erudition in these fields, as much as his eccentricities, earned him the admiration of many of his contemporaries. In many respects, *Caesar Antichrist* represents a veritable *tour de force* of such erudition and, unless the reader shares some of Jarry's background, the intelligibility of the work is greatly reduced.

The relationship of symbolism to the occult sciences or mysticism is by definition a close one. Since the truth of the mystic lies outside the realm of normal human experience and since language is insufficient to convey that truth directly, it is necessary to describe it by analogy or through the use of metaphor. The occult is obscure because its truth (the analogue) is hidden on the other side of the veil of metaphor. It is not the aim of the occult sciences to remove that veil, but to provide a means of seeing through it. The world of the occult, or the mystical, is densely populated with symbols which serve as microscopes through which otherwise hidden truths can be perceived. Those symbols also guard the truths, assuring that they remain special. Hence much of the language of symbols must be enigmatic so as to preserve the veil while penetrating it. This explains, to a great extent, the highly obscure and enigmatic nature of Jarry's symbolism in *Caesar Antichrist.* It is a function of the obscurest language to search after the most remote and undefinable realities. Symbolic language for Jarry has a function that extends greatly beyond the *logos* of the metaphysician. It constitutes an intermediary between the absolute transcendence of God and the finitude of man. It is the word carried beyond the concept that it implies. It is the word as an action or a gesture—the word exerting some creative force rather than searching for its correlative. It is the word creating its correlative.

As in the symbol systems—the tarot, cabalism, heraldry—which fascinated Jarry, Jarry's own science of 'Pataphysics does not regard the act of knowing as the establishment of a rapport between the perceiver as subject and the perceived as object, but the establishment of a rapport that conditions action. Man is not in the process of looking for the truth but of making it. He is, in fact, participating in its becoming. As a result, meditation on symbols is not simply the formation of speculative constructions; it is an effective movement of life.

The desire to explore the mystery of the world of symbols also informed Alfred Jarry's interest in the graphic arts. As an artist, he did his own paintings, drawings, and woodcuts. As an art historian, he co-edited (with Remy de Gourmont) an art journal entitled *l'Ymagier* and later his own *Perhinderion*. The works included in both these journals, generally woodcuts and engravings of a religious nature (including several of Jarry's own works), were treated critically by Jarry in accord with his iconographic bias. The journals were organized by subject, and particular attention was given not to the style, technique, or form of the works, but to what they portrayed and what significance their subjects held. Several of the subjects treated in the journals were transferred directly into the writing of *Caesar Antichrist* (e.g., beasts, the Last Judgment and the Antichrist).

Above all, the mode of presentation that *Caesar Antichrist* utilizes came from Jarry's art criticism. He was interested in visually animating images taken from various works of religious art. The dedication of the play to Saint John of Damascus underlines Jarry's dependence on the symbology of religious imagery. It was Saint John's *Three Discourses on Holy Images* which (1) defended the use of pictures or symbols to represent God, Mary, and the Saints; (2) defended their use without sin or violation of the Church Canon; and (3) urged that they might legitimately be honored, thus causing the use of pictorial images to be accepted for devotional purposes. Not only does Jarry utilize visual images on the stage, but he also has each of the characters (symbolic elements in the stage picture) speak in a poetry that is itself highly imagistic. The more symbolic the physical character is, the greater the use of images in his speech. For example, when a T-shaped bird sitting on a golden cross in the celestial act speaks, it employs images of the tau, the cross, the hammer, and the tree.

> Je suis le Tau, le protecteur des anciens Mages; et même après qu'ils m'ont renié, allant adorer, guidés par l'étoile au regard aimé dont ils obscurcirent de trois grains de poussière la traîne de comète, leur futur ennemi, j'ai combattu pour eux: je me suis fait le maillet qui L'a cloué sur le tronc d'arbre; je me suis fait le tronc branchu où s'est déchiré Son corps; j'ai étendu mes bras pour qu'on y écrasât les Siens; et changeant ma forme immuable pour Le dominer vaincu, j'ai poussé au-dessus de Sa tête mon front où dort le Coq maintenant, le Coq à la queue en croissant.

> I am the tau, protector of the ancient magi. I fought for them even after they denied me and left to adore their future enemy, guided by a star whose comet train was obscured by three grains of dust in their look of love. I made myself the mallet that nailed Him to the tree trunk; I made myself the branched trunk where His body was torn; I spread out my arms so that His might be crushed there; and changing my immutable form to dominate Him vanquished, I grew, my forehead above His head where the cock presently sleeps, the crescent tailed cock.
> (I. ii, trans. Bierman)

Throughout *Caesar Antichrist,* the spoken imagery serves to intensify the visual imagery. In fact, the first, second, and fourth acts are little more than an intense articulation of a symbolic decor. This is true to a lesser extent of the Ubu act, but it can still inform our understanding of *Ubu Roi.*

Heraldry fascinated Jarry for its meeting of symbolic and formal elements. All of the elements of heraldic design have meaning as a function of their position on the shield, their color and their shape, where the various positions are analogous to the parts of the human body and have all of the larger figurative connotations of those parts—the head, heart, legs, arms, navel. Many of the figures or "furniture" on the shield also carry their own symbolic value, particularly natural and chimeric furniture.

Jarry's attempt to incorporate heraldry into the second act

structure of *Caesar Antichrist* was revolutionary. He envisioned the stage as an escutcheon in which each of the characters takes the form of one of the symbolic elements positioned against that field. In effect, they were intended to be both scenery and characters at once. During the act, each scene is a different escutcheon, although it may change only with the positioning of one element. Caesar Antichrist's development is expressed by a progression of emblems advancing toward the moment at the end of the act when he will appear in the real world as Ubu and be capable of acting upon physical phenomena. During the act, the Caesar Antichrist symbols are of the force of generation. Through them, Caesar develops in size and stature until he becomes large and powerful and aware of his Ubuesque nature.

Several of the heraldic elements of the second act of *Caesar Antichrist* were actually transformed into characters in *Ubu Roi,* and our understanding of them can be greatly enhanced by examining their origins. Among them are the three Palotins. The word "Palotin" is one of Jarry's fabrication. It appears in Paul Robert's *Dictionnaire Alphabetique et analogique de la Langue Française* (1962) with the following definition: *"n.m.* (1888 Jarry, *Ubu Roi*) a humorous creation designating the conspirators allied to Ubu who became his courtiers" (V, 80). The word combines *palot* (a rustic), *pâlot* (pale), *palota* (fool), and *palatin* (palatine). As heraldic elements, the Palotins, Pile, Cottice, and Gyron have the following forms:

Pile: The pile (figure 1) consists of three small inverted triangles that point down toward the center of the escutcheon. It is often taken as a symbol of support originally representing the foundations of a bridge that are planted in the mud. When the pile first appears in *Caesar Antichrist,* his color is vert or green. It is a color that symbolizes hope, joy, and "courtly" behavior.

Cottice: The cottice (figure 2) is a diagonal stripe reduced in width from a bendlet. It is also a symbol of support. The cottice appears in *Caesar Antichrist* on an escutcheon containing six azure cottices. Azure is the celestial blue and symbolizes softness of spirit, friendship, and vigilance.

Gyron: The gyron (figure 3), sometimes termed an esquire, is a segment that is cut by a one-quarter sweep of the radius from the center of the escutcheon. As it appears in *Caesar Antichrist,* its color is gules, the color red which indicates courage in combat, valor, and blood spilled for the king.

figure 1   figure 2

In the stream of mutations in *Caesar Antichrist,* the Palotins appear as three birds in the first act, the three heralds that support the Antichrist symbol of the second act, and the satellites to Ubu's meteor-like ascension in the last act. Two passages not found in *Ubu Roi* identify them further. The first stresses their proximity to Ubu, their dependency on his will, and their support. Physically, they are described as having little winglets, large sonorous flat feet, and "at least four earens over which the pole exercises various influences." In the Ubu act, there is another passage decribing them which was excluded from later Ubu plays. This one makes them horrible beasts.

> Nos Palotins sont aussi d'une grande importance, mais point si beaux que quand j'étais roi d'Aragon. Pareils à des écorchés ou au schéma du sang veineux et du sang artériel, la bile financière leur sortait par des trous et rampait en varicocèles d'or ou de cuivre. Ils étaient numérotés aussi et je les menais combattre avec un licou d'où pendaient des plombs funéraires. Les femmes avortaient devant eux heureuses, car les enfants nés leur seraient devenus semblables.

> Our Palotins are also extremely important but not so beautiful as when I was king of Aragon. Like skinless men or with a schema of veinal and arterial bloodways, financial bile oozed from their pores and slithered in gold and copper varicoceles. They were also numbered, and I led them into combat with a halter from which funeral leads were suspended. Women joyfully aborted before them, since children born to them would become like them. (III. xii, trans. Bierman)

This description of the Palotins, which is not found anywhere else in their anthropology, is more appropriate for an Antichrist epic. They correspond to the foul spirits that were born out of the mouth of the Antichrist in the Apocalypse:

> And I saw issuing from the mouth of the dragon and from the mouth of the beast and from the mouth of the false prophet, three foul spirits like frogs; for they are demonic spirits performing signs. (Rev. 16.13-14)

When comparing the heraldic sense of the symbols for which the Palotins are named and the reality of the characters, one cannot avoid the delightful sense of irony that comes from the difference. This is particularly true of the character of Ubu's general, Bordure. The figure called the bordure (figure 4)

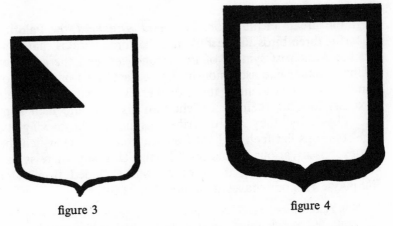

figure 3   figure 4

surrounds the escutcheon. It is a sign of favor or protection usually indicating a recompense given for a service. In the court of King Ubu, Bordure, the favorite, receives an ironic compensation for the services he has rendered when he is imprisoned by Ubu.

Needless to say, an awareness of the heraldic backgrounds of the Ubu entourage is helpful in translating *Ubu Roi*. Otherwise, a translator is tempted to find clever puns that don't exist. Bordure becomes MacNure, while Pile and Cottice becomes Heads and Tails in the Cyril Connolly and Simon Watson Taylor translation (New York: Grove Press, 1969)—a translation which otherwise demonstrates great familiarity with Jarry's work.

Another Ubu element that has its origins in the heraldic act of *Caesar Antichrist* is the physic stick (figure 5). It is born of the heraldic element, the baton, and appears as an independent character leaping about the stage. Its symbolic color is gules, the color of blood. The baton is generally a symbol of bastardy, and within the context of *Caesar Antichrist* takes on additional phallic symbolism. It is constantly being addressed as the uprooted phallus of Siva from Lautréamont's *Maldoror*.

As he develops, Ubu also has his own heraldic forms. He starts out as Caesar Antichrist in the form of a fess in the color carnation, the color of flesh. The fess, or horizontal band, first appears at the top of the escutcheon in the head region and descends to the middle, or the gut. In the center of the carnation fess a black sphere appears which represents both Ubu and the dark sun of the Apocalypse (figure 6). It continues to develop

figure 5   figure 6

until it dominates the stage and black becomes the background color against which the figures work. The significance of these elements emphasizes Ubu's monumental carnality and his roundness (figure 7).

figure 7

It is impossible to consider *Ubu Roi's* position within the four-act structure of *Caesar Antichrist* without outlining the complexity of that structure. At once, the divisions of the acts correspond to the divisions of the cabala, the parts of the soul as defined in Plato's *Republic* along with their various levels of reality, the realms of the literary drug cult of Jarry's time (the "assassins"), the Apocalypse, and the major groupings of the tarot. Taking the cabala as an example, each of the four acts corresponds to one of the symbolic letters that make up the sacred word *Yahweh*; the unpronounced name of God (yod,hé, vav,hé). They share in the cabalistic symbolism of each letter with respect to their mathematical and sexual significances and to their corresponding meanings in the cabalistic book of creation. The three different letters (one repeated) from the ternary or group of three and have a corresponding triangular diagrammatic form (figure 8). These triangles are familiar in Jarry's

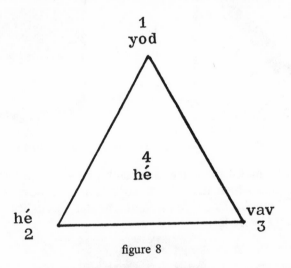

figure 8

drawings to accompany *Caesar Antichrist*. The fourth letter acts as the first element of the following ternary which takes the form of a reversed triangle. When the two are combined, they form a septenary, or group of seven, which has its own transitional element. Jarry uses the triangle and the reversed triangle to represent the Trinity and the reverse Trinity of the Antichrist universe. Together, they form the Star of David, a cabalistic symbol of faith. He saw the interplay of the two realms as continuous.

By a pataphysical principle, everything gives way to its opposite. Day and night, good and evil, Christ and Antichrist, all are but the clutch and release of one pulsating time continuum. In every being, life and death, good and evil exist, and the one gives way to the other as time gives way, in turn, to time.

As indicated above, Alfred Jarry was deeply involved in studies of the Apocalypse, heraldry, and the occult sciences at the time of writing *Caesar Antichrist*, a time which came midway in the period of the formation of his own science of 'Pataphysics. These studies thoroughly inform the structure of *Caesar Antichrist* and the position of *Ubu Roi* within that structure. The following chart illustrates the coordination of structural elements taken from the cabala, the occult sciences, the drug cult, and from Plato.

II

That *Ubu Roi* was intended to mirror the story of Christ seems a ludicrous assertion when we consider the play by itself. Yet this background must have remained in Jarry's mind when he did present the play separately. We find him writing in the program for the play that Ubu is motivated by three things—physics, phynance, and sheit—which are mirror opposites of Christian strivings. Physics is the *"scientia"* of this world as compared to *"sapientia"* or divine wisdom. Phynance is the earthly treasure that bars one from the Kingdom of Heaven, and Ubu's favorite food, sheit, is opposed to manna from Heaven.

It is obvious that *Ubu Roi* stands firmly on its own without the above considerations. Nonetheless, our understanding of Ubu icons is remarkably changed by acquaintance with *Caesar Antichrist* and we are prompted to take an imagistic or symbolic approach which we would otherwise not consider. Seen by itself, *Ubu Roi* does not seem to be a symbolic work, but in the context of *Caesar Antichrist,* such a vision of the play is logical. Above all, we learn that *Ubu Roi* was not just a mindless success by a childish author. On the contrary, Jarry had more serious intentions than readers of *Ubu Roi* alone could imagine. First among these is that Ubu was intended to be the Antichrist on earth—a Nero figure, inaugurator of an age when men rise up in battle against their brothers.

Somewhere in the space between the writing of *Caesar Anti-*

Acts of *César-Antéchrist*	Three inferior worlds of the *Book of Creation*	The three realms of creation	The sacred name Yahweh	Incarnations of Caesar Antichrist
Prologue Act—I	creation	divine world	yod	the golden cross
Heraldic Act—II	formation	astral world	first hé	Caesar Antichrist
Terrestrial Act—III	action	physical world	vav	Ubu
Taurobol Act—IV	transition	transition	second hé	Caesar Antichrist

Acts of *César-Antéchrist*	Sexual and Mathematical	Plato's Soul	Plato's forms	Divisions of the 'Assassins'
Prologue Act—I	+, the golden cross	creative intelligence, mind	pure forms	soul
Heraldic Act—II	-, the fess and the physic stick	spirit, heart	theoretical forms, mathematical	astral body
Terrestrial Act—III	o, androgenous-neuter or the child, Ubu	earthly designs, stomach	material forms	terrestrial body
Taurobol Act—IV	transition	transition	illusion	transition

christ and the presentation of *Ubu Roi* a year later, Jarry's theatre completely reversed itself without changing direction. It seemed to follow that pataphysical process by which a thing becomes its opposite merely by continuing to become itself. For all of the mystical intentions behind the Antichrist Ubu, Jarry's final creation was decidedly earthbound and devoid of symbolic transcendence. The result of that pataphysical shift was a miraculous event in the history of the theatre: the birth of an abstract theatre. As Jarry states in his "Twelve Theatrical Discussions":

> Nous croyons être sûrs d'assister à une naissance du théâtre, car pour la première fois il y a en France . . . un théâtre ABSTRAIT.2

> We believe we are certain to participate in the birth of a theatre, since, for the first time, there exists in France . . . an ABSTRACT theatre.

Nothing since the time of Aristotle has so fully expanded the possibilities of the theatre as the birth that Jarry describes, and nothing has so accurately pointed the way for contemporary *avant-garde* theatre. What follows is a brief biography of that birth.

What Jarry did was to remove from the theatre a limitation that had been set by Aristotle's very first principle and defined his basic aesthetic prejudice toward the theatre. We find *The Poetics* beginning with the following:

> . . . let us begin with the principles which come first. Epic poetry and Tragedy, Comedy also and Dithyrambic poetry, and the music of the flute and of the lyre in most of their forms, are all in their general conception modes of imitation. They differ, however, from one another in three respects—the medium, the objects, the manner or mode of imitation, being in each case distinct. (Trans. S. H. Butcher)

The notion that the object is one of the three elements by which one classifies all theatre (or all art for that matter) puts a decided emphasis on *mimesis* as the essential creative process. Aristotle wastes no energy in underlining his belief that it is "the imitation that makes the poet." The limitation implied by this notion is obvious. Using the object to categorize the theatre sets its boundaries short of any non-objective theatre, and Alfred Jarry was the first consciously to break through this limitation and to establish a non-objective or "ABSTRACT" theatre. Since it was a momentous step, Jarry himself capitalized the word "ABSTRACT."

There are a variety of elements by which we can differentiate the abstract theatre from the theatre of imitation. The most important of these is the plot, which is placed first on Aristotle's rank list of the constituent elements of any play. Starting with Aristotle's contention that "the objects of imitation are men in action," one can see that the primary means of forming that imitation is the construction of the plot—the ordering of the events. It is not the events themselves (or "episodes," to use Aristotle's word) which convey the movement of the play, but rather the syntax of their arrangements. Often very little occurs on stage, but a seemingly static scene can represent great motion if the situation changes greatly from that of former scenes. Since action is what is important, Aristotle puts the emphasis upon plot construction—not on the events themselves, but on their ordering, since for him it is essential that the connective links of the plot be governed by necessity and probability. "The function of the poet [is] to relate what is possible according to the law of probability or necessity," says Aristotle. What he is doing is to locate the essential poetic process in the space between the events that occur on stage. The emphasis is on their causal relationship: the measure of the truth of causality, which Aristotle calls necessity and probability, must be empirical in accordance with his basic leaning toward imitation. Until Jarry, the history of the ancient and modern Western theatre can be charted in terms of the shifting kinds of accepted motivations of stage events. Whether they are political, economic, psychological or whatever, their validity depends on their accord with the human experience of their age.

In his neo-scientific novel, *Exploits and Opinions of Doctor Faustroll, Pataphysician,* Jarry pays homage to the most hermetic of contemporary symbolist writers—to Stéphane Mallarmé, Lautréamont, Maurice Maeterlinck, and the Sâr Joséphin Péladan. He admired their work and the directions that it led. He adopted their interests in mysticism, drug experience, heraldry, and the occult, and he attempted to carry their work to its extreme in *Caesar Antichrist.* Whether intentional or not, the result was a drama that surpassed the extreme limits of symbolism, and Jarry discovered from it that a play can retain its validity even if the sense of the causal links that connect the events is lost. The pataphysical logic of the piece is so obscure that the complex relationship of his symbols to what they symbolize is destroyed. The thin strand attaching the symbols to their realities is severed and they are left alone, devoid of their connecting logic. Yet they can still make a strong impression on the human psyche without any knowledge of what they represent. Without the special understanding that informs the structure of *Caesar Antichrist,* the juxtaposition of its images and actions still has the power that the asyntactical relationship of images has in poetry. Jarry was the first to become aware of the possibilities of a purely abstract theatre whose constituent elements, color, shape, form, sound, and action, could be enjoyed for themselves, and capitalized on that recognition in the writing of such plays as *Par la Taille* and *l'Objet Aimé.*

After *Caesar Antichrist,* Jarry concluded that a complex symbolic drama could only be understood by about five hundred people in the world—a rather small sufficiently informed and creative audience. For the rest, one might just as well abandon plot as it had been traditionally understood. Jarry felt that classical theatre had merely created the illusion of invention anyway by presenting its audience with plots with which they were already familiar from the Homeric legends. In the same way, the *Comédie Française* played for a pre-educated audience by constantly reheating a steady diet of Molière, Racine, and Corneille plays whose plots had originally been borrowed from the Greeks, the Italians, or the Spaniards. So why not reduce plot to some sort of minimum which would be easily understood by anybody? In effect, what Jarry anticipated was a form of drama in which plot would be replaced by situation. Some controlling force or desire, or a strange quality of the environment would provide sufficient permission for the events. Such predominance of situation over plot was to become the norm in works like *Waiting for Godot, Endgame,* the early Ionesco plays, or "happenings." This is also true of *Ubu Roi,* where Jarry's nonexistent Poland is about as strange as the zeroland of *Endgame.*

Just as Jarry was willing to reduce plot out of existence, he was also ready to thin his characters down until they ceased to exist as characters. Again, Jarry was quick to point out the accepted transparency of Molière's comic characters—characters governed by a single motivation or inclination. It was his feeling that any Chinese or Siamese visitor to France would have no problem understanding Molière's miser nor predicting what would happen to him. In the same way, although Père Ubu ranks with Don Quixote, Faust, Gargantua, and Don Juan Tenorio as one of the great archetypal character types of the Western world, there is no particular complexity to him. His motivation is certainly as thin as that of Molière's miser. It is difficult to ask for less. In fact Ubu can be rapidly characterized by just one of his lines:

> J'aurai vite fait fortune, alors je tuerai tout le monde et je m'en irai.

> I will have made my fortune fast, then I'll kill everyone and go away. (*Caesar Antichrist*, III. viii, trans. Bierman)

It is normally believed that this type of hero is more appropriate to comic books than to the stage since he is more of a caricature than a character. What is more amazing is that Jarry did manage to create even less than a caricature in *Caesar Antichrist* where we find that the leading character can be nothing more than a golden cross or a heraldic figure. In effect they are simply symbols or emblems. They have an intended meaning, but no other marks by which we usually identify stage characters. And if you agree that little is left of character at this stage, imagine what happens when the sense of the symbols or emblems presented becomes so obscure that it is lost to them. The situation bears some resemblance to the other abstract arts. Meaning is no longer a useful question.

Imagining a written play so simplified that plot and character are virtually eliminated, Jarry then set out to examine the staging appropriate to such a theatre. Two things were quick to go—actors and scenery. Jarry's directives to Lugné-Poe regarding the original production of *Ubu Roi* made it obvious that what he wanted to do with those fine actors they had borrowed from the *Comédie Française* was to make human marionettes of them. They were to be given masks and padding, and were told to speak in a special monotone voice as if they were talking through the megaphone in a Greek mask. They were asked to minimize their gestures and to avoid mime technique. One imagines Jarry's unusual vision of the ancient Greek actors: masked, under a large headpiece, walking on six-inch blocks of wood, robed and speaking through a megaphone installed in their masks. Seen from a distance, they were puppet figures. For a more intimate theatre, Jarry was ready to substitute something like the little toy flute Ubu gave King Wenceslas for a megaphone, but he nevertheless still insisted on puppets. The intention was to eliminate the art of acting by taking away from the actor any possible articulation of body movement or modulation of voice. What could be more appropriate for the portrayal of characters who were merely emblems of some universal trait or truth?

Of course puppets and marionettes were Jarry's first love in the theatre. From the beginning to the end of his career almost all of his practical theatre experience centered around puppets. Jarry attested to that love in his "Lecture on Puppets" presented in Brussels in 1902:

> Les marionettes sont un petit peuple tout à fait à part chez qui j'ai eu occasion de faire plusiers voyages. Ce furent là des expéditions peu périlleuses qui ne necessitent point le casque d'explorateur ni une nombreuse escorte militaire. Les petite êtres de bois habitaient à Paris, chez mon ami Claude Terrasse, le musicien bien connu, et semblaient prendre grand plaisir à sa musique. Terrasse et moi-même avons été, pendant un ou deux ans, les Gullivers de ces lilliputiens. Nous les gouvernions, comme il convient, au moyen de fils, et Franc-Nohain, chargé d'inventer la devise pour le Théâtre des Pantins, n'a pas eu à en trouver de meilleure que la plus naturelle: en avant, par fil.[3]

> Marionettes are an entirely isolated little people to whose land I've had several occasions to travel. Those were hardly perilous expeditions, necessitating neither an explorer's helmet nor a large military escort. These little wooden beings lived in Paris, in the home of my friend Claude Terrasse, the well-known musician, and seemed to have enjoyed his music. Terrasse and myself have been, for a year or two, the Gullivers for these Lilliputians. We governed them as was fitting, by means of threads, and Franc-Nohain, given the job of inventing a motto for the *Théâtre des Pantins,* found none better than the most natural: "forward by thread." (Trans. Bierman)

Jarry's co-director at the *Théâtre des Pantins,* Franc-Nohain, wrote in praise of the acting skills of marionettes in an article entitled "La mystique des marionettes" (*Nouvelles littéraires,* Feb. 18, 1903, pp. 1-2). Like Jarry, he believed that the marionette theatre compensated for all the mediocrity of the regular stage, and the best the regular theatre could do would be to imitate it:

> Mais surtout on ne manque jamais à proclamer que les marion-
> nettes sont infiniment supérieurs à la plupart des artistes en
> chair et en os, que leur répertoire est pour nous consoler de la
> médiocrité et de la platitude des pièces du théâtre con-
> temporaines.[4]

> But above all, we never miss the chance to proclaim that mar-
> ionettes are infinitely superior to most artists in flesh and bones,
> and their repertoire consoles us for the mediocrity and the plati-
> tude of the contemporary stage.

If real people were to be used on the stage, Jarry preferred that they be considered as personae or performers, not actors. They were to be people performing assigned tasks, not pretending that they were somebody else. But, of course, the best option was simply not to use people on the stage.

Jarry also conspired to do away with scenery. If scenery was to be used, as in the original production of *Ubu Roi,* it should be abstract so that it could not force its representational logic on the audience. But Jarry observed that scenery was usually not consciously noticed by an audience except when it was unveiled at the beginning of an act or when the curtain went up for the first time. He therefore proposed no scenery whatsoever, complemented by the use of placards such as Shakespeare allegedly had used to indicate location. Somewhere on the way to this end comes Jarry's experiment with the symbolic settings of the second act of *Caesar Antichrist:*

> Nous avons essayé des décors *héraldiques;* c'est-à-dire désignant
> d'une teinte unie et uniforme toute une scène ou une acte, les
> personnages passant harmoniques sur ce champ de blason. Cela
> est un peu puéril, la dite teinte s'établissant seule (et plus
> exacte, car il faut tenir compte du daltonisme universel et de
> toute idiosyncrasie) fur un fond qui n'a pas de couleur. On se
> le procure simplement et d'une manière symboliquement exacte
> avec une toile pas peinte ou un envers de décor; chacun péne-
> trant l'*endoit* qu'il veut ou mieux, si l'auteur a su ce qu'il voulut,
> le vrai décor exosmosé sur la scene. L'écriteau apporté selon les
> changements de lieu évite le rappel periodique au non-esprit par
> le changement des décors matériels, que l'on percoit surtout à
> l'instant de leur différence.[5]

> We tried *heraldic* décors, where a single shade is used to repre-
> sent a whole scene or act, with its characters "passant" har-

monically against the heraldic field. This is a bit puerile, as
the said color can only establish itself against a colorless background (but it is also more accurate, as we have to take into
account the general red-green color-blindness, as well as other
idiosyncrasies of perception). A colorless background can be
achieved simply, and in a way which is symbolically accurate by
an unpainted backcloth or the reverse side of a set. Each
spectator can then conjure up for himself the background he
requires, or better still, if the author knew what he was about,
the spectator can imagine that by a process of exosmosis, what
he sees on the stage is the real décor. The placard brought in
to make the change in place prevents his periodically having
recourse to a negative state of mind, because with the conventional sets one only becomes aware of them at the moment
of their change. (*On the Futility of the "Theatrical" in the
Theatre*, trans. Barbara Wright)

The heraldic act of *Caesar Antichrist* therefore is extraordinary
in its implications for staging. There are no actors, only moving
and speaking elements of the scenery; or there is no scenery,
only the visual spectacle of emblematic characters. Jarry did not
completely succeed in eliminating both actors and scenery, but
for him they became one and the same thing. Such results were
not produced again until the time of Oskar Schlemmer's figural
cabinets.

III

What remains? After Jarry starved such basic elements of
the written play as plot and character down to the point where
they are about to vanish, and did the same to such elements of
the staged play as acting and scenery, what is left? The question
is the same one that a person can pose with regard to any abstract art. After its representational elements have been eliminated, what remains? The thing that first informs Jarry's answer
to that question is his feeling about the elements he found himself destroying. Basically, he considered them to be dishonest.
They lied to the audience about *who* the actors are, *where* they
are, *when* the action takes place, and *why* the events come about
and the characters become what the actors pretend they are.
Jarry's taste in the theatre was completely without pretense with
regard to the popular illusions of causality and reality. Not only
did he choose puppet theatre as the purest form of the art, but
he insisted that even such theatre capitalize on its artifice and

avoid the illusion of reality. Marionettes at the *Théâtre des Pantins* flopped about on only two strings to assure that their movements remained artificial, and Jarry insisted that the people governing them should do so in full view of the audience. He meticulously did his best to be honest with his audience and not to involve them in an illusion from which they would have to return at the end of the evening. Leave that for André Antoine's *Théâtre Libre* where audiences went to impress themselves with the depth of a slice of life. Jarry's stage would not present a butcher shop with real sides of beef hanging there and real flies buzzing around them.

When the lies of *who, when, where,* and *why* are erased, one thing remains: *what.* That *what* is the action of the piece. It is what happens. Remember Aristotle's insistence that "life consists in action, and its end is a mode of action." For Aristotle, the action of a play is its very heart. It must be whole, and everything in the play must relate to it as a whole. Jarry reinforced this attitude by creating a drama which is so direct that little or nothing confuses one's vision of exactly what is happening. All of the considerations that qualify the action on the stage have been eliminated, and one is left to contemplate exactly what is there. What is, is all there is: no *who, where, when,* or *why.* The answer to the question "what remains?" is exactly that. *What* remains.

Breaking through the representational limits—limits that had been imposed on the theatre up to the turn of the century—represented a monumental liberation of the possibilities of the art. It was a liberation that was further utilized by dramatists who knew Jarry in his own time such as Henri Rousseau, Guillaume Apollinaire, and F.-T. Marinetti in addition to others such as Tristan Tzara, André Breton, and Antonin Artaud who later acknowledged their debt to Jarry's work. In effect, the entire tradition of the twentieth-century *avant-garde* grew out of Jarry's discovery of an abstract theatre: a discovery that uncovered once again the very essence of action upon which Aristotle had insisted. The reason Jarry ridiculed the rise of the sciences in the nineteenth century was that he felt that we had created a civilization so involved in considerations of *who, where, when,* and particularly *why* that we failed accurately to perceive what we were dealing with. If this distortion of observation to the point where the explanations became more important than the reality of the facts they explained was true of life in its normal diluted form, it was ever more true of the theatre. Jarry learned this lesson with great precision when the complex network of explanations around *Caesar Antichrist* fell away in order to reveal *Ubu Roi,* which remains a perplexing and involving piece.

University of California,
Santa Cruz

NOTES

1 *Caesar Antichrist* (*César-Antéchrist*) was first published in 1895 by the *Mercure de France.* It was subsequently included in the 1949 edition of the *Oeuvres Complètes* (Editions de grand-Chêne, Lausanne) and appeared in the writer's English translation in 1972 (Tucson, Arizona: Omen Press). All of the translated quotations are from the Bierman translation.

2 "Douze Arguments sur le théâtre," in *Tout Ubu* (Paris: Livre de Poche, 1962), pp. 146-47.

3 "Conference sur les Pantins," *Tout Ubu,* p. 493.

4 Franc-Nohain, "La mystique des marionnettes," *Nouvelles littéraires,* Feb. 18, 1903, pp. 1-2.

5 *Tout Ubu,* p. 141.

Anouilh's Little Antigone: Tragedy, Theatricalism, and the Romantic Self

Michael Spingler

The loss of a tragic sense in the theatre is a major concern of many modern dramatists and critics. In his *Antigone,* Jean Anouilh suggests that the reasons for this decline may be located within one of the fundamental developments of modern tragedy, that is, the replacement of action by character as the dramatic mainspring.[1] He sees the predominance of character as a fundamentally romantic development which leads to the emergence of a protagonist whose self-consciousness diminishes the tragic event. Anouilh's disenchantment with romantic posturing is expressed primarily in terms of a theatricalism which implies that tragedy based solely on character is really role-playing and self-dramatization. He does not see the role as a solution to the problem of writing a modern tragedy but as a reflection of the dilemma. In *Antigone,* the self-conscious role is inimical to the tragic spirit.[2]

There are three elements in the play which comprise the design Anouilh uses to dramatize his theme. At the heart of *Antigone* lies a persuasive denial of tragic vision put forward by Creon who, traditionally, should be the partner in the tragic action. In counterpoint to this, we find a highly sentimentalized and romantic rendering of Antigone which makes the play seem to be, at least superficially, a tragedy of character rather than of action. The unifying perspective through which we are invited to judge the conflict caused by a sentimental character replacing the moral structure of a tragic universe is provided by Anouilh's use of the chorus as a distancing device. Anouilh depends primarily upon the chorus to establish the play's essential theatricality.

Anouilh's chorus does not follow the Greek model of dancing

and singing the transcendent vision of the tragedy. It is comprised instead of a single actor, a commentator whose observations invite the audience to assume a detached and critical perspective toward Antigone and her drama. A frame for the play and a creator of distance between it and the spectator, the chorus' presence on the stage recalls the Brechtian admonition not to mistake the staging of the event for the event itself.

This function of the chorus is clear from the first words of the play in which he introduces the characters as actors waiting to play a part: "Voilà. Ces personages vont vous jouer l'histoire d'Antigone."3 The key word here is *jouer*, and the use of *histoire* rather than *tragédie* is also significant. He clarifies Antigone's position within the play by referring to her as a character who has not yet become fully realized: "Elle pense qu'elle va être Antigone toute à l'heure, qu'elle va surgir soudain de la maigre jeune fille noiraude et renfermée que personne ne prenait au sérieux dans la famille et se dresser seule en face du monde, seule en face de Créon, son oncle, qui est le roi. Elle pense qu'elle va mourir, qu'elle est jeune et qu'elle aussi, elle aurait bien aimé vivre" (p. 9). Initially, these words seem to be an introduction to the tragedy which is about to unfold, a preparation of the audience in order that it be familiar with the plot. Yet, if we consider these words more carefully and ask who, precisely, at this very moment, is thinking these thoughts, it becomes apparent that Antigone is an actress thinking about the characteristics and demands of her part just before going on.

This view of Antigone as both actress and character is essential to the play's theme. The chorus repeats it when she is led in by the guards: "Alors, voilà, cela commence. La petite Antigone est prise. La petite Antigone va pouvoir être elle-même pour la première fois" (p. 58). The sense of the importance of the role is very strong here, and the chorus has, in fact, pointed out the connection between Antigone's role and the element of fate within the play: ". . . et il n'y a rien à faire. Elle s'appelle Antigone et il va falloir qu'elle joue son rôle jusqu'au bout" (p. 10). Because of the chorus' insistence upon Antigone's dual nature as both character and player, we see her as tragic actress rather than tragic victim.

The chorus establishes a similar view towards the play itself. Because of his comments, we do not experience tragedy in the play as rhythm and structure but consider it at a distance as an abstract concept and problem. The chorus occasionally interrupts the action in order to explain the proceedings to the audience. His remarks before the confrontation between Antigone and Creon remind one of a public lecture on "The Theory of Tragedy." "Et voilà. Maintenant le ressort est bandé. Cela n'a plus qu'à se dérouler tout seule. C'est cela qui est commode dans la tragédie" (p. 56). The major theme of the chorus' comments is that tragedy is comforting because of its inevitability: ". . . on n'a plus qu'à se laisser faire. On est tranquille. Cela roule tout seule. . . . C'est propre, la tragédie. C'est reposant, c'est sûr . . . Et puis, surtout, c'est reposant, la tragédie, parce qu'on sait qu'il n'y a plus d'espoir . . ." (pp. 57-58). We may be tempted to consider this theory of tragedy an extremely dubious one, which is very possibly the reason for its inclusion in the play. We shall see that the notion that tragedy is restful because it is sure has its appeal for Antigone. Most important is the effect upon the audience of the intrusion, at a critical juncture, of any theory, doubtful or illuminating, which considers tragedy conceptually. A spectator cannot be expected to share in a tragic experience when he is being lectured about it by a man in evening dress.

The effect of the chorus is to create a climate of ambiguity much the same as the one described by Richard Coe concerning the theatre of Genet: "The drama is both true and not true simultaneously—it commands or should command, absolute belief, but only in a context of absolute unbelief; and the absolute belief (or suspension of disbelief) is only valid if it knows itself to exist in a context of unrealities—that is, if it is unceasingly aware of itself as illusion"[4] (p. 214). This self-conscious ambivalence is the essential mode within which the conflict between Antigone and Creon must be assessed. This conflict, as Anouilh presents it, is between a character who rebels against his tragic type-casting and a heroine who represents a romantic decaying of the tragic mold.

The principal set piece of the play in which Antigone faces Creon should contain the essence of the tragic issue. In Anouilh's version, instead of confronting a tragic antagonist who represents an opposing ethical view, Antigone faces a pragmatic and cynical man who refuses to enter into the tragic action with her. Creon's major argument is not that Antigone's act is wrong, merely that it is without significance. Moreover, his intent is not

to justify his own moral position, but to convince Antigone that
there is no longer an ethical base which would give her position
the moral value of tragedy.5 He begins his case by attacking the
idea of tragedy associated with Antigone's father: "Et tuer
votre père et coucher avec votre mère et apprendre cela après,
mot par mot. Quel breuvage, hein, les mots qui vous con-
damnent? Et comme on les boit goulument quand on s'appelle
Oedipe ou Antigone. Et le plus simple après, c'est encore de se
crever les yeux et d'aller mendier avec ses enfants sur les routes"
(p. 73). The direct reference to the events of *Oedipus Rex* is
a device for self-conscious allusion: the character who looks
from a distance at a dramatic tradition from which he springs.
In this sense Creon's words and the chorus' complement each
other. Both suggest an outside or alien view of tragedy and
together they raise the question of the need, or lack of need,
for tragedy in modern theatre.

Whereas the chorus' attitude toward tragedy is ambiguous,
Creon's bias against it is clear. He looks upon Oedipus and his
family as a pack of vain trouble makers, and he is intent upon
banishing the tragedy they carry with them from his realm:
"Thèbes a droit maintenant à un prince sans histoire. . . . J'ai
résolu avec moins d'ambition que ton père de m'employer tout
simplement à rendre l'ordre de ce monde moins absurde, si
c'est possible" (p. 73). Creon, like the chorus, uses the word
histoire to refer to the tragic material of the Oedipus myth. The
king's use of the word has the sense of troublesome and annoy-
ing business, and he makes it clear that he has no intention of
becoming involved in such an affair: "Et si demain un messager
crasseux dévale du fond des montagnes pour m'annoncer qu'il
n'est pas sûr de mon naissance, je le prierai tout simplement
de s'en retourner d'où il vient" (p. 74). Creon is the protagonist
who, when confronted with the tragic revelation, would simply
turn his back on it and act as if nothing had happened. He refuses the tragic moment as being politically inexpedient.

The king's problem is to convince Antigone to refuse tragedy
also. To do this, he attempts to discredit any external ethical
support for the tragic act. He starts by questioning the religious
values which are behind Antigone's deed, maintaining that there
is no reason for Antigone to bury Polynices since the burial
ritual is, in itself, meaningless: "Tu y crois donc vraiment, toi, à
cet enterrement dans les règles? A cette ombre de ton père

condamné à errer toujours si on ne jette pas sur le cadavre un peu de terre avec la formule du pretre? . . . Et tu risques la mort maintenant parce que j'ai refusé à ton frère ce passeport dérisoire, ce bredouillage en série sur sa dépouille, cette panto-mine dont tu aurais été la première à avoir honte et mal si on l'avait jouée. C'est absurde" (pp. 76, 77). There is little that Antigone can reply to Creon's debunking of the burial rituals since she does not believe in them herself. She agrees that it is absurd to invoke them and admits that she has, in fact, thought of stopping the priests if they ever recited their prayers over someone she loved. Both Creon and Antigone reflect here a world in which skepticism weakens the sort of belief necessary to a tragic universe. The issue at the heart of the tragic necessity, Polynices unburied, is considered by both as based on nothing but a shabby hoax.

However, regardless of her attitude towards the burial cere-mony, Antigone's loyalty to her brother remains the major external justification for her act. Polynices is the last prop Creon pulls out from under her. He does so by revealing that her brothers were merely two thugs who plotted to murder their father and who were involved in a struggle with each other which resembled more a gangland war than a political revolt: "Nous avions à faire à deux larrons en foire qui se trompaient l'un l'autre en nous trompant et qui se sont égorgés comme deux petits voyous qu'ils étaient pour un pur règlement de comptes" (p. 95). Creon even claims that the bodies were so disfigured that he couldn't tell them apart, thus being obliged to choose arbitrarily one as the war hero and the other as the traitor. This final detail is certainly Anouilh's most imaginative twist to the classic myth, and, together with Creon's earlier remarks and the chorus' commentary, it completes the discrediting of the tragic universe associated with Antigone and her family.

At this point, any vestige of Greek tragic thought has been erased from the play. Without the moral basis for defying Creon, Antigone has no justification for continuing her tragic revolt. There is nothing for her to do but turn and go up to her room. Until this midpoint, Antigone's stand has been modeled after the Greek example; she defies Creon because of loyalty to Poly-nices. But Creon has very thoroughly discredited her tragic ideals and, now, she does not believe in the universal, ethical basis of tragedy any more than he does. The play must either stop or find a new direction. This new direction is based on Antigone's turning within herself to renew her tragic vocation.

Creon, himself, through a blunder, allows Antigone to find a justification for tragedy based on her sense of self which will replace the discredited moral universe. Like many cynical and ruthless men, the king has a sentimental streak which leads him to make a comparison between Antigone and a Creon of the past: "Je te comprends, j'aurais fait comme toi à vingt ans. C'est pour cela que je buvais tes paroles. J'écoutais du fonds du temps un petit Créon maigre et pâle comme toi et qui ne pensait qu'à tout donner lui aussi" (pp. 97-98). Creon then advises Antigone to be content with the simple things of life in which she may find some happiness. Her reply is one of the most telling of the play: "Quel sera-t-il mon bonheur? Quelle femme heureuse deviendra-t-elle la petite Antigone?" (p. 99) The term "un petit Créon" is a mistake which undoes all the king's previous argument because it causes Antigone to articulate her private sense of being. She responds with a term of her own, "la petite Antigone," which has already been used several times by the chorus. The definite rather than indefinite article suggests that she considers this definition of the self complete, permanent, and not to be compromised by Creon's picture of her future life. Antigone is now able to fill the void created by the disappearance of the tragic universe with an interior world whose major value is her fidelity to her self-conception. In dramatic terms, Antigone is clinging to her role which she sees in danger of being changed by Creon's view of the future. This is the turning point of the play. Antigone must abandon the Greek model and enter into the contemporary theatre of self-consciousness. Her sense of herself as a specific character is the third element in Anouilh's dramatic design. It complements the chorus' distancing commentary and Creon's rejection of a tragic universe, and, therefore, Anouilh establishes the character carefully in the opening scene of the play.

The scene between Antigone and her nurse is an invention of Anouilh and, from the first, it contains troubling inconsistencies with what one expects from tragedy. Its tone and mood are sentimental and domestic, the rough, loving, scold of a nurse contrasted with the sweet and fragile heroine.

Antigone's initial replies to the nurse are the most important indications of her character: "*La nourrice:* D'où viens tu? *Antigone:* De me promener, nourrice. C'était beau. Tout était gris. Maintenant tu ne peux pas savoir, tout est déjà rose, jaune, vert. C'est devenu une carte postale. Il faut te lever plus tôt nourrice si tu veux voir un monde sans couleurs" (p. 14). These words may strike a strange note when one considers that they are spoken just after Antigone's burial of Polynices. The mood is lyrical and elated and seems inconsistent with the gravity of the situation. This is surely the point of the scene. The dialogue between Antigone and her nurse directs the spectator's attention away from Antigone's act and toward the personality and character of the girl herself. Her second reply to the nurse intensifies our impression of her: "Le jardin dormait encore. Je l'ai surpris nourrice. Je l'ai vu sans qu'il s'en doute. C'est beau un jardin qui ne pense pas encore aux hommes" (pp. 14-15). This Antigone will be quite familiar to a French audience. Her replies contain a preciosity which evokes the *poésie de banlieue* one might find in a Prévert scenario. When Antigone says, ". . . je me suis glissée dans la campagne sans qu'elle s'en aperçoive" (p. 15), we are reminded of the arabesques we expect from the lovely and eccentric girls who populate Giraudoux's theatre.

It is essential that we see Antigone in sentimental closeup because what counts finally is not what she does but how we see her and how she sees herself. It is a characteristic of self-conscious theatre that the two perceptions are very much the same. So, Anouilh provides a striking number of sentimental touches in the opening moments of the play. Antigone still uses her baby name for her nurse, "Nounou." The heroine has a little dog named "Douce" whose fate seems to be at least as important to her as the unfolding of the tragic action. Perhaps the best example of the sentimentality which eventually overshadows ethical considerations is the revelation later that Antigone has buried Polynices with the toy shovel with which, as children, they built sand castles at the beach.

These details are extremely important to the play's design. The distance from tragedy established through the Chorus and Creon are all the more effective since Antigone is touching and convincing. One of the play's peculiar tensions is this combination of distance and intimacy; we are asked to judge at a distance a character with whom, in other circumstances, we might sympathize or identify. Having raised the problem of the place of tragedy in modern theatre, Anouilh asks whether a sentimental character can be the equal of a great tragic vision.

Antigone is clearly a type, suggesting a role, not of the Greek tragic heroine, but one defined by the lyricism of her first scene. She is the fresh, delicate ingenue caught up in her own image of youthful purity and sensitivity. She is a romantic who is enamoured of extravagant attitudes and gestures. What Antigone lacks in tragic stature she makes up for in touching character. Compared to her Greek counterpart, she is, indeed, the little Antigone. The very fragility of this role necessitates Antigone's protecting it with her life against the possibility of its corruption in time.

This concentration upon the self is the most important distinction the play suggests between Greek and modern tragedy. Whereas in Sophocles' play, Antigone's burial of Polynices is an act which cannot be undone, we have seen that, in Anouilh's version, that is precisely what happens when Creon undermines the tragic universe. Antigone does not claim that she owes it to a higher good to bury Polynices. In fact, her brother is never mentioned again. The reason for her defiance becomes her devotion to herself.[6] In answer to Creon's question of for whom she has done this deed, she replies, "Pour personne. Pour moi" (p. 78). Creon realizes too late that the only necessity for Antigone's death lies within herself: "Antigone était faite pour être morte. Elle-même ne le savait peut-être pas, mais Polynices n'était qu'un prétexte. Quand elle a dû y renoncer, elle a trouvé autre chose tout de suite. Ce qui importait pour elle c'était de refuser et de mourir" (p. 102). Death becomes the only way that Antigone can dramatize herself in a tragic role.

Antigone attempts to impose upon the world an interior mythology which pits a youth of intransigent purity and innocence against an old age of corrupting compromise. She sees the danger of "la petite Antigone" being transformed with the years into the equivalent of the corrupt and cynical king. So her stand becomes, essentially, a refusal to grow old in order to give her identity the lasting form of the role, removing it from the changing flow of life:[7] "Moi, je veux tout, tout de suite, —et que ce soit entier—ou alors je refuse! Je veux être sûre de tout aujourd'hui et que cela soit aussi beau que quand j'étais petite—ou mourir" (p. 97). Ironically, Antigone's position results from her acceptance of Creon's version of life, and she is

left consequently with an extremely limited choice: either con-
form to the king's cynical view, or say no and die. Her stance
recalls J. L. Styan's observation that sentimental plays often
indulge a romantic impulse to accept or reject life.8

However, it is Anouilh's heroine, not his play, that is romantic. The play puts romantic attitudes in a perspective which
reveals the flaws and pitfalls to which they can be prey. Rebellious postures such as Antigone's are essential to a romantic
affirmation of the self which makes liberty synonymous with
heroism and views heroism as a fundamentally solitary and self-
fulfilling endeavor. When Ismene belatedly rushes in and offers
to die with her sister, Antigone cries, "Ah! non. Pas maintenant.
Pas toi! C'est moi, c'est moi seule. Tu ne te figures pas que tu
vas venir mourir avec moi maintenant. Ce serait trop facile!"
(p. 105) Antigone's infatuation with dying makes her resemble
those modern heroes described by Victor Bromberg as fascinated
by "the poetry of insurrection and the pathos of defeat."9 Her
fall is self-willed, and it reflects a romantic attempt to achieve
tragic stature through attitude and gesture.

But it is not sufficient for Antigone to want to be tragic,
for tragedy cannot be based solely on the self. As Lionel Abel
observes, "We cannot urge the tragic sense on ourselves or on
others. To try to attain it or recommend it is comical and self-
refuting, tragedy being real only when unavoidable. There would
be no such thing as tragedy if a tragic fate could be rationally
chosen."10 This is the fundamental problem explored in *Antigone*. There is a gap between the tragic spirit and the romantic
desire for self-assertion, since tragedy takes place in the world
whereas romantic affirmations such as Antigone's depend primarily upon a consciousness which has become uncertain as to
what the world is.11

Antigone's enduring interest lies in the way it dramatizes
the decline of tragic myth in the labyrinth of modern self-
consciousness. The play itself seems to be earnestly seeking its
own tradition. A discredited tragic universe has been replaced
by sentimental character. The inadequacies and ultimate failure
of this romantic substitute for tragedy are reflected in a theatricalism which questions the authenticity of the heroine. In a
sense, Anouilh, through Creon and the chorus, has hollowed
out the Greek myth, and the play's theatricalism is what is left
when nostalgia for the tragic form's lost power to convey wisdom
remains.

The play's theatricalism intersects with the idea of the impossibility of tragedy, and it is within this matrix that Antigone's fate looks, ultimately, absurd. This is the chorus' sour, final assessment of what has happened. As in all his remarks, he begins with a laconic and sardonic *voilà*: "Et voilà. Sans la petite Antigone, c'est vrai, ils auraient tous été tranquilles. Mais maintenant, c'est fini. Ils sont tout de même tranquilles. Tous ceux qui avaient à mourir sont morts. Ceux qui croyaient une chose, et puis ceux qui croyaient le contraire—même ceux qui ne croyaient rien et qui se sont trouvés pris dans l'histoire sans y rien comprendre. Morts pareils, tous, bien raides, bien inutiles, bien pourris. Et ceux qui vivent encore vont commencer tout doucement à les oublier et à confondre leurs noms. C'est fini. Antigone est calmée maintenant, nous ne saurons jamais de quelle fièvre" (p. 132). The suggestion of waste and futility conveyed by these words is the antithesis of the redemptive possibilities of tragedy.

The anti-tragic sense in *Antigone* is so strong that one is tempted to conclude that Anouilh has written the play to rid himself and his theatre of an exhausted dramatic tradition. His decided preference for the ambiguities of theatricalism over the affirmations of tragedy suggest that *Antigone* has much in common with his *pièces grincantes* and with contemporary dark comedy in general. The play shares with dark comedy the atmosphere of doubt brought on by the uneasy feeling that the myths which have given our civilization spiritual coherence are now without energy. In such plays commonly held affirmations give way to a climate of self-conscious anxiety. A world which Anouilh sees as containing more chance and play than structure and high purpose is epitomized in the card game which, fittingly, brings down the final curtain, suggesting that Antigone and her myth, at least for Anouilh, have finally been laid to rest.

Clark University

NOTES

1 Eric Bentley has described this development in his discussion of "bourgeois tragedy," in *The Playwright as Thinker* (New York: Meridian Books, 1946), pp. 23-47.

2 Anouilh has been criticized for his emphasis on character. John Harvey cites Hubert Gignoux's complaint that the hero's personality is more important than his tragic destiny. Mr. Harvey, however, sees the role as the key to Anouilh's writing

a successful tragedy—*Anouilh, A Study in Theatrics* (New Haven and London: Yale Univ. Press, 1964), pp. 92, 100. My view is that the emphasis on personality is deliberate and that Anouilh uses the role as an anti-tragic element in the play.

3 Jean Anouilh, *Antigone* (Paris: La Table Ronde, 1971), p. 9. Further references to the play will be from this edition.

4 *The Vision of Jean Genet* (New York: Grove Press, 1968), p. 214.

5 Jacques Guicharnaud points out that Creon breaks down Antigone's "Greek" reasoning. He does not, however, discuss the implications of this breakdown in terms of role-playing and theatricalism—*Modern French Theatre from Giraudoux to Genet* (New Haven and London: Yale Univ. Press, 1967), p. 127.

6 It may be argued that Sophocles, also, is a dramatist of character. But, as H. D. F. Kitto observes, he is interested in the way character intertwines with a complex of events—*Greek Tragedy* (Garden City: Doubleday, 1954), p. 157. Anouilh's Antigone is not interested in events; she responds solely to her self-conception.

7 As befits a playwright who spent his formative years with the Pitoëff Company, Anouilh owes more to Chekov and Pirandello than to Sophocles. The influence of Pirandello on French theatre has been treated in Thomas Bishop's *Pirandello and the French Theatre* (New York: New York Univ. Press, 1960).

8 *The Elements of Drama* (Cambridge: Cambridge Univ. Press, 1967), p. 222.

9 *The Intellectual Hero, Studies in the French Novel, 1880-1955* (Chicago and London: Univ. of Chicago Press, 1964), p. 150.

10 "Is There a Tragic Sense of Life?" in *Moderns on Tragedy*, ed. Lionel Abel (Greenwich: Fawcett, 1967), p. 178.

11 *Moderns on Tragedy*, p. 183n. *Antigone* would fit Abel's definition of a metaplay. Abel asks the following significant question: "If Antigone were self-conscious enough to suspect her own motives in burying her brother Polynices, would her story be a tragic one?"—*Metatheatre* (New York: Hill and Wang, 1968), p. 77. Mr. Abel does not mention that Anouilh has devoted an entire play to answering the question.

Brecht's Quarrel with God:
From Anti-Theodicy to Eschatology

Edward M. Berckman

O Lord, how long shall I cry for help,
and thou wilt not hear?

. . .

For the wicked surround the righteous,
so justice goes forth perverted.
Habakkuk 1.2, 4

The most important historical consequence of the disintegration of the Christian theodicy in the consciousness of
Western man has . . . been the inauguration of an age of
revolution. History and human actions in history have
become the dominant instrumentalization by which the
nomization of suffering and evil is to be sought.
Peter Berger, *The Sacred Canopy*

Why is malice well rewarded? Why do punishments await
the good?

. . .

what's to be done?
Change human nature or—the world? Well: which?
Believe in bigger, better gods or—none?
Shen Te, in Brecht, *The Good Woman of Setzuan*

Bertolt Brecht's acknowledgment that the Bible was the
single book which had influenced him most has elicited from
scholars several investigations into the nature of that influence
on his work, particularly his style and use of Biblical sayings.[1]
Less attention has been given to the personal relationship to
Christianity and its God reflected in his writing. In his later years
as a dialectical materialist, Brecht took the position that the only
significant religious questions had to do not with "the inner
essence of religion, the existence of God," but with "the behavior
of religious men, discourse about God."[2] Yet many of his writ-

185

ings suggest that he found the existence and behavior of God a significant question indeed. And scrutiny of his total work reveals a persistent concern with what may be called the theodicy question, illustrated in its Biblical and Brechtian forms by the first and third quotations cited above as epigraphs.

The insights of Biblical scholars and sociologists of religion can help us see this concern as a crucial factor in Brecht's development from a bitter nihilist into a Marxist committed to the struggle and the hope for a changed world of justice and friendliness. The young Brecht responded to the persistence of human misery and injustice with accusations against Christians and their God, who permitted these evils by His indifference or nonexistence. Once Marxism provided Brecht a diagnosis and the promise of an ultimate remedy, he labored to arouse audiences to the same perception and commitment which gave his own life meaning—while continuing to attack religious beliefs and institutions which justified the status quo. Concern with theodicy was therefore a basic element of continuity in the thought of a playwright whose career is usually divided into three, or four, distinct phases.

Most scholars who have considered Brecht's relationship to Christianity agree, at least, on the ambivalent and contradictory nature of his attitude.[3] Reinhold Grimm, modifying his earlier view that Brecht's response to the Christian message was "uncompromisingly rejecting," has proposed that Christianity was "the stumbling block which constantly excited his creative impulse anew." In fact, Grimm believes, "Brecht's contradictory relationship to Christianity forms the hidden ground out of which sprang the poet's turning to Marxism."[4] Norbert Kohlhase devotes a chapter of his book on Brecht and Camus to "Negative and Hidden Theology." He offers the cryptic comment that "Brecht's atheism stands in the middle of faith and draws its strength from it."[5] Like Grimm and Kohlhase, Barbara Allen Woods, in her study of Biblical sayings in Brecht's work, relates his Marxist conversion to his disappointment with regard to Christianity: "Since Brecht sees in Christianity the failure to create conditions favorable to the achievement of its own ideals, he turns against its institutions, and demands a changed society that will carry out the ancient commandment [love thy neighbor] in its new formulation: 'dasz der Mensch dem Menschen ein Helfer ist' [that man be a helper to man]."[6]

These clues, however, have not been followed up systematically to trace the evolution of Brecht's compassionate, antireligious humanitarianism into the eschatological hopes which supported his Marxist commitment. And scholars who have noted in Brecht's work the presence of "the utopian" or the strategy of "a look backward from an imagined Golden Future of justice and friendliness" have not observed the relationship of this future-orientation to his earlier remonstrances against the divine.7 But awareness of the patterns of theodicy and eschatology in the Judaeo-Christian tradition assist us to identify similar elements in the thought-world of Brecht's writing.

The Relation of the Theodicy Question to Eschatology. Max Weber has defined the theodicy question as "the problem of how the extraordinary power of [a transcendent, universal] god may be reconciled with the imperfection of the world that he has created and rules over."8 Talcott Parsons, introducing Weber's study of the sociology of religion, interprets it as the problem of the discrepancy between normative expectations and actual experiences.9 As solution to this problem, Weber described four basic types of theodicy, three of which rest on some sort of eschatological hope. One of these, the principal Biblical theodicy, is the messianic expectation of "a political and social transformation of this world."10

In *The Teachings of Jesus* T. W. Manson expressed the relation of the theodicy question to eschatology as a kind of psychological law: "Whenever a living faith in a righteous, holy and loving God is brought up hard against the facts of human experience, some sort of eschatology must emerge if men are not to deny either their faith or their experience."11 The theologian Jürgen Moltmann finds a similar connection in the literature of late Judaism: "The basic question, from which the apocalyptic images of the future arose, is the theodicy question: When will God's righteousness triumph over this world of evil and pain?" From his Biblical studies Moltmann deduces the generalization, "The theodicy question, born of suffering and pain, negatively mirrors the positive hope for God's future."12

It should be clear from these statements that both eschatology and the theodicy question, both the hope and the protest, are based on the conviction that life ought to be better, that man has been promised—or somehow has a right to—liberation, justice, deliverance from suffering. This conviction, I believe, was central to Brecht's writing and was the controlling factor in his movement to Marxist humanism. Evidence from his works, as I will demonstrate, indicates a process of development something like the following.

One might say that Brecht's faith in a righteous and loving God was, in his youth, "brought up hard against the facts of human experience." The immediate result, it appears, was not the "emerging" of an eschatology but the denial of faith—at least faith in a *righteous* and *loving* God; this faith was replaced by the ambivalent belief/unbelief in a cruel, indifferent and empty Heaven. Yet his concern for what ought to be, his love of life and the world, persisted; finally, he found a this-worldly and "scientific" solution to his theodicy question—Marxism. But Marxism was, at the same time, a faith to replace both Christianity and nihilism, though a faith healthily tempered with doubt and, eventually, tested by disappointment.

In Brecht's first Marxist plays, the *Lehrstücke* (learning-plays) of the late 1920's and early 1930's, his eschatology barely surfaces. In those pre-Nazi years of political and economic crisis a Communist takeover in Germany seemed imminent. Instead of anticipating the society of the future, Brecht was dealing with the immediate problems of serving the revolution.

Eschatological hopes hardly appeared in his plays until the years of exile from Hitler's Germany, when, as he wrote in 1938,

> The goal
> Lay far in the distance,
> Easy to see if for me
> Scarcely attainable.[13]

In the great plays of his exile, particularly *The Good Woman of Setzuan, The Life of Galileo,* and *The Caucasian Chalk Circle,* that goal comes into view and, though not attained (or attained only fleetingly), exercises important dramatic functions.

Brecht himself described one of these functions with the word "*historicize,* that is, to consider people and incidents as historically conditioned and transitory."[14] The perspective from which the stage action is viewed is that of the future, specifically, "another social system's point of view."[15] This historicizing future-perspective is an essential ingredient of Brecht's hope, for it exhibits present behavior as changeable; it affirms the possibility of an alternative outcome to the unhappy or uncertain conclusion within the play.

This imagined future, which is not simply the Marxist class-less society but also that time when "man is a helper to man," functions additionally as a criterion of moral judgment on the present. Finally, the *nature* of this future as envisioned and occasionally enacted on stage acts upon the spectator to moti-vate him toward action which may bring such a time of harmony and justice closer to realization.

Anti-theodicy remains in Brecht's later works but not merely as an outlet for his morally based hostility to religion. It is re-directed to serve his Marxist aim of removing all blinders which prevent recognition of the true cause of human suffering, namely, the capitalist system. God can and will not help or compensate us, either now or later. The "nomization of suffer-ing and evil" must be accomplished by ourselves, in history, through revolution. The elements of eschatological hope in the plays are incentives, carrots, to motivate audiences toward that goal. But the terrible realities of injustice and exploitation, the stick, are also dramatized. My conjecture is that the hopes are ultimately a psychological necessity for the playwright himself and, following Moltmann's principle, are, in a sense, the pro-duct, the personal resolution of the "theodicy question, born of suffering and pain." But, whatever personal significance they may have had for Brecht, their development in his work is what I wish to delineate.

Anti-theodicy in Brecht's Early Works. Born in Augsburg sixteen years before World War I began, of a Protestant father and Roman Catholic mother, Berthold Brecht's adolescent writings already show awareness of the contradictions between conventional piety and the harsh realities of the world, between normative expectations and actual experiences. Reinhold Grimm has convincingly demonstrated this awareness in his essay, "Brecht's Beginnings," which cites numerous schoolboy writ-ings from the years 1913 to 1918.[16] The two works which reveal the discrepancy of the theodicy question most acutely, perhaps, are the poem "A Modern Legend" of 1914 and a one-act play written in 1913, *The Bible.*

With remarkable economy and restraint, the poem states the news that a battle has been won and then describes the reactions on each side to this news. At one end of the world wailing and curses, at the other rejoicing and prayers—each "crashed against the dome of the Heavens." There is no response from the Heavens. At the poem's end quiet descends on both sides. "Only the mothers wept/ Over there—and over here" (pp. 26-27).

The Bible presents the first of many situations in Brecht's drama where the behavior of Christians is contrasted with and judged by the standards of Christianity. As an enemy army approaches, a grandfather reads aloud from the Bible: "Serve thy neighbor, Break bread with the hungry, and have pity on him who suffers." But he himself does not follow these injunctions and is reproached by his grandson with the threat of divine judgment: "Outside, men scream and you hear them not; outside, flames burn and you see them not. Grandfather, when the Day of Judgment arrives, how will you stand?" (p. 34).

There is also apparent condemnation of the grandfather's attitude that "a single soul is worth more than a thousand bodies!" For he counsels his granddaughter to remain at home, chaste, rather than save their besieged city by offering her body as a "human sacrifice" to the enemy. As the attack begins, the girl cries, "Merciful God! Have pity on our poor stricken city." She, however, takes action herself as the appropriate response to her plea. Amid the thunder of cannon she leaves the house. "Then, suddenly, everything is completely still . . ." (pp. 32-33). Her sacrificial act has saved the city.

These two juvenile works include three elements which recur in Brecht's later writing: (1) prayers and pious mouthings of Christians whose passive waiting for God is shown to be totally futile; (2) the complex and cruel reality of man's inhumanity to man which renders traditional Christian virtues ineffective and even dangerous; (3) above it all the Heavens which remain silent, unresponsive to the pathetic appeals from humans.

Students of the poetry Brecht wrote before his conversion to Marxism (about 1926) differ sharply in interpreting the meaning of his response to the emptiness of the Heavens. This poetry is said to be characterized, on the one hand, by nihilist despair and, on the other, by a vitalist love of life.17 This controversy is not pertinent to my thesis except that it is necessary to reject any extreme view, such as Martin Esslin's, which attributes to the pre-Marxist Brecht "a self-destructive attitude of complete moral anarchism." The usefulness of his commitment to Marxism, according to Esslin, was that it "resolved the deep feeling of nihilism and despair that pervaded his early writings, canalized the destructive forces within him, and allowed him to rationalize his poetic impulse by giving it a purpose."[18] Esslin overlooks the positive implications of Brecht's bitterness; for many of these early works contain evidence of an underlying moral passion in their protest against the inhumanity of men and God. What Marxism helped to "canalize" in Brecht was not so much, or not only, destructive forces but constructive impulses as well.

The form as well as the content of Brecht's first book of poems, published in 1927, manifested his quarrel with God. *Die Hauspostille,* later translated as *Manual of Piety,* was printed on thin paper and bound in soft, black leather. In appearance a sequence of devotional poetry, it is, in part, a serious parody ridiculing false religion and bourgeois morality from the standpoint of implied standards of honesty and compassion.

The bitterness of Brecht's disappointment in man's failure to be a helper to man is expressed in one of the ten "Supplications" of the book's "First Lesson," "On the Infanticide Marie Farrar." The poem's central figure is a poor and unattractive housemaid whose attempts at abortion and prayers to the Virgin Mary are equally ineffective. Her traumatic childbirth leads to a fit of murderous rage. The poem concludes with a temperate, restrained request whose irony is more powerful than the harsh condemnations of *The Bible:*

> You who give birth in snow-white childbed sheets
> All you who call your pregnant bellies Blest
> Do not condemn the outcast and the weak
> For if their sin was grave, great was their grief.
> *Therefore, I beg, do not give way to indignation*
> *Each creature needs the help of all creation.*[19]

This is one of several poems in which Brecht expresses sympathy for those rejected by men and by God. Other such outcasts are the drowned girl, whom "God forgot . . . bit by bit" *(Manual of Piety,* p. 215), François Villon, who never received blessings from Heaven (p. 56), and the pious whore Evlyn Roe, who was turned away from both heaven and hell after drowning herself.[20] Other poems, however, portray God as so malicious one would prefer to escape his attention. "Grand Hymn of Thanksgiving," a parody of Neander's seventeenth-century hymn, offers ironic praise of the grass and beasts which "die just as you will" and includes this stanza:

Rejoice that Heaven above us has such a bad memory
And cannot place
Either your name or your face.
No one knows you are still living. (p. 121)

Brecht's case against God and also his ambivalence are most powerfully and succinctly conveyed in "Hymn to God," written in 1919 but not included in *Die Hauspostille*. Here the beauty and radiance seem almost to be aspects of the remoteness and indifference of the deity:

Deep in the dark shadows the hungry are dying.
You—show them bread, and let them die.
You—are enthroned invisible, eternal,
Radiant, and cruel above your eternal plan.

. . .

Many say that you are not—and it were better so.
But how can that not be—that can so deceive?21

It is as if Brecht needed an object for his rage and allowed himself at least a poetic fulfillment of that need. It is similar to the need or wish expressed in Thomas Hardy's "Hap," where the speaker's suffering is accentuated by his reluctant realization that it is randomly meted out to him by "purblind Doomsters." Unlike Hardy, however, Brecht complains of others' sufferings, not his own. This difference and his subsequent evolution into a Marxist suggest that his position is closer to the atheistic humanism of another Victorian, George Eliot. Basil Willey's summary of her conclusions could also apply to Brecht: "Heaven will not help us, so we must help one another; this realization tinges our whole life with anguish, but it is the cross which the new elect must bear."22 The young Brecht felt this anguish but did not take "we must help one another" as a cross to bear. Even as a Marxist he did not preach this principle as a moral imperative. Rather, it became the norm for truly human society, a norm which judged the existing capitalist order, even though helpfulness as such could not be safely indulged until the proletarian revolution had created the conditions in which man might be a helper to man.

Bitter complaints at human suffering and divine *apatheia*, poignant and shocking images of death, decay, and cold beauty— these fill the early poems of Brecht. Some critics have failed to see that anything beyond cynicism and revulsion is thereby expressed. But the humanist moral passion is there, too, and remains in Brecht's work to form the basis on which Marxist activism and hope come to be built. For many years, however, it could only be expressed in attacks on institutions which pretended to righteousness or masked in a blatant hedonism presented as the corollary of disillusionment.

It is the latter attitude we find in the main characters of his first plays—Baal, Kragler of *Drums in the Night,* Edward II. Kragler's remark is typical: "Can you get rid of all the pain and suffering man has taught the Devil? No. You can't get rid of it, but you can drink whiskey."23 Even Brecht's study of and conversion to Marxism did not immediately produce in his plays the implication that an alternative kind of world is possible.

The Threepenny Opera of 1928 demonstrated in numerous ways that "The world is poor, and man is bad"—but so amusingly that it played more than a thousand performances in Berlin, apparently failing to disturb capitalist complacency. The attacks on Christianity, too, were made palatable by a coating of bittersweet, satiric irony. Using a method to be frequently repeated, Brecht associated the Bible or Biblical figures and symbols with those characters whose behavior is the most immoral and despicable.

Jeremiah Peachum is the king of beggars who exploits both his employees and those whom their faked misery moves to generosity. It is Peachum who quotes the Bible and sings a "Morning Anthem" warning of Judgment Day. And Macheath the master thief is, by conspicuous parallels, presented as a Christ-figure. Betrayed on Thursday evening by someone whose name begins with J—the whore Jenny—he makes another disloyal friend weep bitterly by a "fearful gaze," a feat acknowledged to be a "trick from the Bible."24

More important, for this study, is the introduction of a theme which becomes a dominant motif in subsequent plays. As Brecht the Marxist begins to value and advocate an activist, revolutionary approach to human injustice and suffering, he adds another count to his indictment of God and religion (though it has antecedents in his portrayal of the Grandfather in *The Bible*). He exposes religion as a particularly harmful kind of delusion because it keeps men ignorant about the true causes of their troubles and discourages their taking action to help themselves. Behind this attack is the same humanistic concern previously expressed in protestations against divine and human indifference to man's plight.

"Only Men Help"—Not God. It is *Saint Joan of the Stockyards,* written in 1932, which most forcefully dramatizes the case against religion as a distraction from humankind's real troubles. The play depicts the manipulation of meat supplies and prices by a shrewd packer, J. Pierpont Mauler. But its main theme is expressed through the education, or undeceiving, of Joan Dark, a Black Straw Hat (Salvation Army) lass. What she gradually learns is summarized thus: "Only force helps where force rules/ And only men help where men are."25

When Joan observes integrity overcome by hunger, she decides that the alleged "wickedness" of the poor is a result of— and *is*—their poverty. At first she proposes a liberal-reformist answer, which is to "raise moral purchasing-power" (i.e., wages) (p. 126). Then she begins to realize the whole system is at fault, that it is "a seesaw, with two ends that depend/ On one another." Those on top would lose their places if the workers on the bottom rose up (p. 165).

We are shown that religion has blinded Joan Dark (and others) to the true cause of poverty and that it continues to help preserve this exploitative system by telling people their unhappiness "comes down like the rain, and no one knows where from" (p. 140) and by otherwise diverting them from earthly affairs to heavenly. After Joan comes to this understanding, she leaves the Straw Hats but is soon killed. As she is dying, she utters a kind of curse on religious deceivers:

> . . . anyone down here who says there is a God
> When none can be seen
> A God who can be invisible and yet help them
> Should have his head knocked on the pavement
> Until he croaks. (p. 196)

Here again we seem to hear the note of (Brecht's) bitterness against the God who will "show [men] bread, and let them die" —and overtones also, perhaps, of Jesus' violent condemnation of any who cause a child to sin: "it would be better for him to have a great millstone fastened round his neck and to be drowned in the depth of the sea" (*Matthew* 18.6).

Joan, of course, has the name of a saint and undergoes a mocking canonization by the packers, who, with the Black Straw

Hats, shout and sing to keep her dying words from being heard. She is associated with Jesus, both in her moral indignation and in her final inability to rectify the situation. In Scene 7 she drives the packers from the House of God; and in Scene 5 she warns Mauler, in language echoing Jesus' Parable of the Last Judgment, that his deceitful manipulations of the market will be revealed on Judgment Day.

The Mother is another story of a woman's conversion, but it ends on a more positive note. Pelagea Vlassova, the mother, is educated out of her belief in God and into a commitment to Communism. She explains her position during a conversation with two Christian ladies which ends in a ludicrous but significant quarrel—involving not Vlassova but the Christian landlady and her tenant whom she has evicted. When the tenant asks for a Bible to show her landlady the verse about loving your neighbor, the result is a fight in which the Bible is torn to shreds. From the preceding theological discussion and the quarrel itself come two lessons typical of Brecht: "Do not fear death so much, but rather the inadequate life!" and "Your God does me no good if I can't see any signs of Him!"26

At the end of the play, after a militant speech by Vlassova, the theodicy question, in effect, is debated with a housemaid who argues: "Many people say what we want will never happen. We should be content with what we have." Vlassova answers in the tones of a confident Communism whose eschatology is about to be realized:

> Who's to blame where oppression rules? We are.
> Who's responsible where the rule is smashed? We are.
> Those beaten down shall rise up tall!
>
> . . .
>
> The victims of today will be victors of tomorrow
> And Never is changed into Today. (p. 131)

That confidence was misplaced, or premature, for a year after the first performance of *The Mother* Hitler came to power, and Brecht had to flee Germany for a fifteen-year exile. Yet disappointment regarding the immediate future had the paradoxical effect of deepening Brecht's ultimate hope. In the plays written between 1938 and 1945, as Brecht's *Marxist* faith was "brought up hard against the facts of human experience," a more developed eschatology emerged in images and scenes of a hoped-for friendliness, harmony, and justice.

Eschatological Hope in the Later Plays. Unlike Joan Dark and Pelagea Vlassova, the heroines of *Mother Courage* and *The Good Woman of Setzuan* never quite accept the conclusions their experiences should have taught them. Mother Courage's illusion has to do with war and what it costs those who profit from it, not with religion. About the latter subject she is appropriately (for Brecht) cynical. When the Chaplain, who, as we might expect, is corrupt and cowardly, exclaims at a critical point, "We're in God's hands now!" Courage replies, "I hope we're not *that* desperate. . . ."27 But it is precisely the ineffectuality of deity and of traditional virtues to which Shen Te, of *Good Woman,* remains blind. This play was Brecht's most direct attack on religion and religious ethics, his most pointed expression of anti-theodicy. And yet its total effect is not so depressing as that of *Mother Courage;* for here a different kind of world is made visible in the actions and hopes of Shen Te and is thus perceived as an alternative to, and ethical judgment upon, this present world.

On the one hand, Shen Te is seen as a naive idealist for following the three gods' urging to be good while at the same time initiating a capitalist enterprise, her tobacco shop. On the other hand, the sincerity of her efforts to help her neighbors and correct the injustice done to her friend Wang, the tenderness of her love for the unemployed pilot Yang Sun, the intensity of her desire to believe in friendliness—these elicit our sympathy for her and therefore add to the poignance and pathos of her failure "To be good to others and to myself. . . ."28 We are made to feel as well as to see how regrettable is her trust in doing good and in the gods.

These gods refuse to "meddle with economics" or to "admit our commandments to be deadly" (pp. 11, 104). Shen Te is forced to adopt the guise of a "cousin" whose harsh exploitation of employees enables her to survive but nullifies all the helpful actions she had planned. At the end we are impelled to protest, with her, to the gods—"Something must be wrong with your world"—and, with her, to reject their lame assurance—"Just be good and everything will turn out well!" (pp. 103, 105).

This frustrating ending prepares us to make the desired response to the questions posed in the Epilogue: "What's to be done?/ Change human nature or—the world? Well: which?/ Believe in bigger, better gods or—none?" (p. 106). Obviously we need no such gods as these, but we do need a changed world. The kindness and passion for justice of Shen Te, her vision of a productive economy where her pilot-lover "brings to friends in far-off lands/ The friendly mail"—these expressions of Brecht's eschatological hope show us the kind of world we would prefer; they function, therefore, to move us toward world-transforming action.

The eschatological content of *Galileo* is more visible and explicit. "The play," Brecht declared in his "Postscript to the American Production," "shows the dawn of a new age and tries to correct some of the prejudices about the dawn of a new age."29 The disappointment of Galileo's recantation is balanced by dialogue and images depicting what might have been *if* Galileo had kept faith with his own aim of science for the people. These hopes reach a climax in the carnival scene where the crowd is invited to "cast a glance into the future" in which a revolutionary social order will prevail as a consequence of Galileo's scientific revolution.

Brecht's Notes warn against presenting *Galileo* chiefly as an attack on the Catholic Church and insist that the Church of the sixteenth century simply represents Authority, secular as well as spiritual. But the choice of this historical episode as a dramatic subject provided further ammunition in his life-long assault on religion as an obstacle to the pursuit of truth and justice.

In *The Caucasian Chalk Circle,* written in 1944-45, Brecht's eschatological hope comes to full flower. The Prologue presents the only post-revolutionary situation in Brecht's drama, a Soviet village where reason prevails, and the play's happy ending is almost equally rare. The historicizing perspective is most evident here through the actual look backward from the Prologue to "olden times, bloody times," and through the device of a narrator or singer, who is introduced in the Prologue. His interjections in the action function to make us aware of alternate possibilities and to suggest standards of judgment on the predatory rulers of Grusinia.

The action is dominated by two of Brecht's most vivid and appealing characters, Grusha, the simple servant girl who rescues the princely child Michael, and Azdak, the revolutionary-minded village clerk who becomes the rascal-judge. If kindness and justice are, for Brecht, characteristic of the eschatological age, Grusha embodies the former quality, while Azdak makes possible "a brief/ Golden Age that was almost just."30

Azdak's antinomian administration of justice is described in terms that recall Jesus' feeding of the multitude: "To feed the starving people/ He broke the laws like bread" (p. 80). Later he is removed from office by soldiers who "invest" him with a robe and, instead of a crown, a basket. One critic has compared Azdak's fear of death, when the old regime is about to return, with Jesus' reaction in Gethsemane.31 An intended parallel is there, certainly, but if Brecht clothes this bringer of radical justice in images and actions recalling Christ, it is to emphasize the *contrast* between the two. Azdak used his power not just to help the poor but to take bribes and satisfy his lust. He becomes a total coward, obsequiously promising to oblige the Governor's wife. He is *not* a hero; he has no virtues. Brecht's point here is the same one made by his Galileo after recanting: "Unhappy the land that is in need of heroes."32 If injustice is to be overcome, there is no messiah, no hero—human or divine—to do this for us. We ourselves must do it, by overturning the present social order, which is actually disorder, and bringing in the "chaotic" time when "the masters' noses are put to the grindstones" and "the simple folk [are] full of joy" (p. 81).

Brecht and the Bible: Structural Similarities. Paul Tillich has pointed out several aspects of a "structural analogy" between the Marxist and the prophetic Christian interpretations of history. (In the view of both, history moves from a beginning, through a center "where its meaning becomes visible," toward an end that brings its fulfillment after various catastrophic events; and both emphasize historical judgment "as the inescapable consequence of social injustice."33) Frederick Polak links Marx's view of history with Jewish apocalyptic and argues that it functions as a theodicy to explain and justify the present misery of the proletariat.34 These are by no means the only scholars to find similarities between Marxism and Judaeo-Christian faith and eschatology.

The existence of such a relationship or "structural analogy" makes more plausible my contention that the influence of the Bible on the Marxist playwright Brecht goes beyond his style and language to basic elements of his thought-world. In particular, his obsession with the meaning of life and history—in light of the discrepancy between what is and what ought to be—

and the form of his solution to these problems reveal the imprint of the concern with theodicy and the answers of eschatology of the Jewish-Christian tradition.

Like Amos (*Amos* 4. 1-3, 5. 10-12) Brecht pointed to social injustice and the sufferings of the poor as a judgment on the virtuous pretensions of the powerful and comfortable (*Saint Joan,* the early scenes of *Chalk Circle*). Like Jeremiah (12.1) his characters bitterly complain that it is not good persons but evil ones who prosper in the present age (Shen Te, the women of Kurgela in *Puntila*). Like Luke, or Luke's Jesus (*Luke* 2. 51-53), his plays anticipate a future that will reverse the present state of things and bring the mighty low (the ballad-singer and others in *Galileo,* Azdak). Like Isaiah (2.4, 11.6-9) Brecht envisions a time when swords will be beaten into plowshares, there will be harmony in nature, and none shall hurt or destroy (the Prologue of *Chalk Circle*).

It is true that the playwright frequently uses images and sayings from the Bible in order to deny or contradict their validity or meaning in the original context. Nevertheless, their "structural" content can be appropriated and utilized within Brecht's Marxist humanist outlook. Thus, several references to a final judgment may be found in Brecht's works. In some cases these are employed to apply stringent ethical criteria to Christians—or even Jesus himself (in *The Threepenny Novel*). But the *principle* that men are accountable for their actions is taken over by Brecht and operates throughout his work.[35]

More generally, the role of hope and a future-perspective in Brecht's theater is similar to the function of eschatology in the Bible and in Christian thought. "Hopes and anticipations of the future . . . are realistic ways of perceiving the scope of our real possibilities, and as such they set everything in motion and keep it in a state of change."[36] This statement about Christian hope could as well apply to Brecht's technique of historicizing.

The Gospels show the present world tested and judged by the standards of the New Age announced by Jesus, and, similarly, Brecht contrasts the inequities of capitalist society with the vision of a future community of reason, justice, and harmony. And, as the letters of Paul speak of the presence of the Spirit as "first fruits" of the fulfillment to come (*Romans* 8.23), so Brecht's plays include brief moments—e.g., the carnival scene of *Galileo,* Azdak's judgeship—which afford foretastes of that goal remaining "far in the distance" in order to sustain present hope and effort directed toward that goal.

To observe such parallels, if "parallels" is not too strong a word, is in no way to impute to Brecht some hidden allegiance to Christianity. On the contrary, it is clear that he used every occasion to expose what he saw as the falsity of Christian doctrine, the numbing effects of belief in it, and the shortcomings of Christian practice. But this very antipathy may have kept Christianity in the forefront of his attention. In any case, evidence of the impact of certain key issues and thought-forms of Biblical religion, particularly the theodicy question and the answers of eschatology, remains visible in Brecht's work and helps us discern its underlying unity.

Lakeland, Florida

NOTES

1 See, among others, the following: Thomas O. Brandt, "Brecht und die Bibel," *PMLA*, 79 (1964), 171-76; Bernard F. Dukore, "The Averted Crucifixion of Macheath," *Drama Survey*, 4 (Spring 1965), 51-56; Volker Klotz, *Bertolt Brecht: Versuch über das Werk* (Hamburg: Verlag Gehlen, 1967), esp. pp. 46-49, 52, 104-08; Barbara Allen Woods, "A Man of Two Minds," *German Quarterly*, 42 (January 1969), 44-51.

2 *Schriften zum Theater*, II (Frankfurt: Suhrkamp Verlag, 1943), 143-44.

3 An exception is Peter Paul Schwarz in his argument that nihilism provides the thematic unity of Brecht's early poetry. Instead of a continuing ambivalence there, Schwarz detects stages of disillusionment: expressions of "cosmic terror," then rebellion against a fictive, empty transcendence, before the poet's whole-hearted affirmation of nothingness. *Brechts frühe Lyrik, 1914-1922. Nihilism als Werkzusammenhang der frühen Lyrik Brechts* (Bonn: Bouvier Verlag Herbert Grundmann, 1971).

4 *Bertolt Brecht: Die Struktur seines Werkes* (Nürnberg: Verlag Hans Carl, 1965), p. 45, and "Bertolt Brecht," in *Deutsche Dichter der Moderne*, ed. Benno von Wiese (Berlin: Erich Schmidt Verlag, 1965), pp. 509, 511.

5 *Dichtung und politische Moral: Eine Gegenüberstellung von Brecht und Camus* (Munich: Nymphenburger Verlagehandlung, 1965), p. 202.

6 Woods, p. 50.

7 Jost Hermand, "Utopisches bei Brecht," *Brecht-Jahrbuch 1974* (Frankfurt am Main: Suhrkamp Verlag, 1975), pp. 9-33; Darko Suvin, "The Mirror and the Dynamo," *The Drama Review*, 12 (Fall 1967), 57.

8 *The Sociology of Religion*, trans. Ephraim Fischoff (Boston: Beacon Press, 1963), pp. 138-39.

9 Ibid., p. xlvii.

10 Ibid., p. 139.

11 Cambridge: Cambridge University Press, 1951, p. 244.

12 "Resurrection as Hope," *Harvard Theological Review*, 56 (April 1968), 131, 146.

13 "To Posterity," *Selected Poems*, trans. H. R. Hays (New York: Grove Press, 1947), p. 175.

14 From "Über experimentelles Theater," cited in Frederick Ewen, *Bertolt Brecht: His Life, His Art, and His Times* (New York: Citadel Press, 1967), p. 222.

15 *The Messingkauf Dialogues*, trans. John Willett (London: Methuen, 1965), p. 103.

16 *The Drama Review*, 12 (Fall 1967), 22-35.

17 Two representative and opposing views: "The much discussed 'death of God' did not mean an act of liberation for [Brecht] but led to a vacuum which was not again filled until later by the holy teaching of Communism" (Bernhard Blume, "Motive der früher Lyrik Bertolt Brechts [II. Der Himmel der Enttäuschten]," *Monatshefte*, 57 [1965], 275). "Nowhere else in modern literature . . . is there such a clear understanding that what Nietzsche called 'the death of God' does not necessarily lead into despair but, on the contrary, since it eliminates the fear of Hell, can end in sheer jubilation, in a new 'yes' to life." (Hannah Arendt, *Men in Dark Times* [New York: Harcourt, Brace and World, 1968], p. 233).

18 *Brecht: The Man and His Work* (Garden City, N. Y.: Doubleday 1961), pp. 165, 236.

19 *Manual of Piety*, trans. Eric Bentley (New York: Grove Press, 1966), p. 31.

20 "Legende der Dirne Evlyn Roe," *Gedichte*, II (Frankfurt: Suhrkamp Verlag, 1960), 46-48.

21 Translated and cited by Ewen, p. 83; *Gedichte*, II, 39.

22 *Nineteenth Century Studies* (London: Chatto and Windus, 1949), p. 237.

23 Translation from Ewen, p. 99; cf. Frank Jones' translation in *Jungle of Cities and Other Plays* (New York: Grove Press, 1966), p. 146.

24 *The Threepenny Opera*, trans. Desmond I. Vesey and Eric Bentley, *Plays*, I (London: Methuen, 1960), 143.

25 Trans. Frank Jones, *Plays*, II, 197.

26 Trans. Lee Baxandall (New York: Grove Press, 1965), p. 117.

27 *Mother Courage and Her Children*, trans. Eric Bentley (New York: Grove Press, 1962), p. 45. The play also contains a scene reminiscent of the contrast in *The Bible* between the passivity of pious older people and the sacrificial action of a brave young person. I refer, of course, to Kattrin's drumming to warn the people of Halle of imminent attack, while the old peasants can only pray—another illustration of what Brecht perceived as the debilitating effect of religion (pp. 109-10).

28 *The Good Woman of Setzuan*, in *Parables for the Theatre*, trans. Eric Bentley and Maja Apelman (New York: Grove Press, 1948), p. 103.

29 In *Plays*, I, 341.

30 In *Parables for the Theatre*, p. 96.

31 Albrecht Schöne, "Bertolt Brecht, Theatertheorie und dramatisch Dichtung," *Euphorion*, 52 (1958), 295.

32 *The Life of Galileo*, trans. Desmond I. Vesey, *Plays*, I, 320.

33 *The Protestant Era*, trans. James Luther Adams (Chicago: Univ. of Chicago Press, 1948), pp. 254-55.

34 *The Image of the Future*, trans. Elise Boulding, I (New York: Oceana Publications, 1961), 279.

35 A reference to final judgment that itself illustrates this principle occurs in *The Trial of Lucullus*. The Judge of the Dead says to the Roman general: "You must account for your life among men. Whether you have served them or harmed them" (trans. H. R. Hays, *Plays*, I, 202).

36 Jürgen Moltmann, *The Theology of Hope*, trans. James W. Leitch (New York: Harper and Row, 1967), p. 25.

Brecht's Contacts With the Theater of Meyerhold

Vsevolod Meyerhold was born in Russia in 1874, the son of prosperous German parents. His career as a theatrical innovator began in 1905 and ended with his death in prison in 1940. Well before the October Revolution, when Bertolt Brecht, the "Einstein of the new stage form," was still a boy, Meyerhold was known to St. Petersburg audiences as "the man with the new ideas."[1] Some of Meyerhold's ideas closely anticipated the theory and practice of Brecht. Most notable are those stylistic innovations used to destroy the realistic stage convention: film projections and posters which comment on or announce the action; interpolation of dances, jazzband style music, and songs; masks and grotesque costuming; emphasis on stage movement and gesture; the combination of realistic and stylized stage settings; training of the actor to be both self and character onstage, and finally the attempt to obliterate the social and psychological distance between audience and actors. Beyond the fact that Brecht and Meyerhold were influenced by the same revolutionary milieu, they shared these innovations because they believed in a non-illusionistic art which served the people. Moreover, they were attracted to similar elements in the traditional theaters of the Orient and the West. Still, there remains the question of influence, direct or otherwise, of Meyerhold on Brecht. It is the purpose of this study to establish the possible links between the theaters of the two men, saving until later a comparison of their dramatic theory and practice.

First of all there is the general historical circumstance. In the "Golden Twenties" and early thirties Western artists and intellectuals showed considerable interest in the Soviet Union and Bolshevik experiment. Their interest, if not always their political sympathies, was shared by the large number of Russians living abroad, a number which was growing rapidly due to the flood of new emigrés. Already by 1910 there were almost 140,000 Russians in Germany, more than in all the rest of Western Europe, and outside of Russia the largest "Russian" city was Berlin. Carl Zuckmayer has described the cultural atmosphere which he and his friend Brecht enjoyed there in the twenties.

> There were evenings when an unknown young writer like myself could sit at a table with writers and directors of the stamp of Eisenstein and Pudovkin—for they all visited Berlin—and listen worshipfully to their talk. . . . Thus there was the everlasting influence of the Eastern Russian temperament upon Berlin's cultural life, and that influence was more productive, more stimulating, than most of the things that came out of the West at the time. . . . We loved the Russians and felt a kinship with them in our own intellectual and moral aspirations, and in our libertinage.[2]

Before the turn of the century Russians had come to Germany to sit at the feet of German university professors; after 1900, as Zuckmayer suggests, Russians increasingly brought to the West new ideas in the plastic arts, theater, literature, music, and the sciences.

The modern Russian Time of Troubles—First World War, the revolutions of 1917, and Civil War—accelerated the flow of emigrants to Germany. By the end of 1919 approximately 70,000 Russians were living in Berlin and were arriving at a rate of more than 1,000 a month. They tended to settle in the southwestern section of the city, near the Tiergarten, gathering in cafes on Nollendorfplatz and on the Kürfürstendamm to talk politics, philosophy, and art, and to listen to poetry readings. Shklovsky and Bely were among the emigré writers who frequented the Russian cafes where German artists and intellectuals also liked to gather. There were dozens of such cafes, "with balalaikas, and zurnas, with gypsies, pancakes, shashlyks and naturally, the inevitable heartbreak. There was a little theater that put on sketches. Three daily newspapers and five weeklies appeared in Russian."[3]

Interest among Germans for news about the Soviet Union was answered in part by German-Soviet friendship organizations such as the Bund der Freunde der Sowjetunion, which was founded in 1928 and attracted mainly working class people, and the Gesellschaft der Freunde des neuen Russlands. This Society, founded in 1923, drew primarily on middle class artists and the intelligentsia for members, many of whom knew Brecht. The Society published a journal, *Das neue Russland,* and sponsored lectures by visiting Soviet cultural leaders. One of them was Anatoly Lunacharsky, a lover of theater, the first Commissar of Enlightenment (1917-1929), a frequent contributor to *Das neue Russland,* and a friend of both Meyerhold and Brecht. Meyerhold's pupil Sergei Eisenstein spoke on Soviet film; an actor from Tairov's Kamerny Theater lectured on "The New Russian Theatrical Art," and Brecht's friend Sergei Tret'iakov gave a report on "The Socialist Countryside and Its Writers." The Society's section for literature and art presented evenings of Russian music, such as that of Scriabin and Prokofiev, readings of Russian literature, and screenings of Soviet films.[4]

In 1925 a special edition of *Das neue Russland* was devoted to theater (and especially Meyerhold's theater) in the Soviet Union. This special edition evoked additional articles and interviews about Soviet theater in other German journals and newspapers.[5] Among the Meyerhold productions which were reviewed in detail in *Das neue Russland* were *The Magnificent Cuckold, The Earth Rears Up, Trust D. E., The Warrant, The Forest, Teacher Bubus,* and *Roar China!.* All of these plays, as the reviewers pointed out, were extremely important as vehicles for Meyerhold's latest innovations. In 1926 it was reported in the same journal that Meyerhold had visited Society members in Berlin in order to entrust them with the arrangements for his company's forthcoming tour in Germany.[6]

Besides *Das neue Russland,* a wide variety of periodical literature published in Berlin and other German cities regularly reported on Soviet cultural events, including Soviet theater. Some of these reports were quite detailed, such as those done in 1921 by Arthur Holitscher and Max Barthel on the revolutionary mass theatricals which were being produced in Petrograd. From 1924 the German revolutionary workers' press, particularly *Die rote Fahne* and *IAZ* reported frequently on Soviet theater.[7] In 1926 the Berlin journal *Die Weltbühne* published a detailed report on Meyerhold's innovations, praising his revitalization of the techniques of *commedia dell' arte,* with its masks, improvisations, and consciously "theatrical" theater. The article also describes Meyerhold's Eastern-style presentation of

Blok's *The Fairground Booth* with its narrating "author," simply dressed "stage-hands" who openly bring on and remove props, and uncurtained stage. In addition there is a description of Meyerhold's efforts to advance stage decoration into a full-blown art for the theater: "not a painted theater, but a theatricalization of painting."8

In 1928 Brecht's friend and associate Bernhard Reich, who had emigrated to the Soviet Union, published an article which analyzed the strengths and weaknesses of Meyerhold's episodic style, a style which "already embodies the sort of Lunatheater which is Bert Brecht's unrealized dream."9 In the same year the Berlin theatrical journal *Scene* carried an essay on Meyerhold's innovations. The author, Bess Brenck-Kalischer, had just returned from Moscow where she had attended rehearsals at the Meyerhold Theater and had seen productions of *The Forest* and *Roar China!*. Articles such as these and information brought back from Russia by his friends helped Brecht keep up with the Soviet theater.10

The actual production of Russian plays in Berlin had become fairly commonplace since 1906 when Stanislavsky's Moscow Art Theater made its first trip to Germany. From that time until the early thirties Russian and Soviet visiting theatrical companies were warmly received and prompted critical discussion. The first avant-garde Soviet theatrical troupe to visit Germany, the Vakhtangov Theater, performed in Berlin before full houses from the third to ninth of August, 1923. Alexander Tairov's Kamerny Theater also visited Germany late that year, performing in Berlin and other cities. Both the Vakhtangov and Tairov theaters were deeply influenced by Meyerhold's innovations, a fact which is reflected in the report of a Munich journalist who noted that Tairov's actors were "not just actors, but dancers, singers, musicians, acrobats." The impact of this group is suggested by the fact that when a theatrical exhibition was held in Magdeburg (May-June, 1927) to show the historical development of German theater, Moscow's Kamerny Theater was represented (in the otherwise all-German presentation) "as a theater which had exerted a great influence on the development of modern German theater" (Murav'ev, 188-89).

In 1927 German audiences were entertained by a Soviet agitprop group known as Blue Blouse which staged performances directly patterned after the style of Meyerhold's "Theater October." In Berlin the troupe played at Piscator's theater.11 Piscator's dramatic work had much in common with Meyerhold's; the two directors had even begun to develop similar agitprop techniques about the same time, around 1919 and 1920. It is difficult to tell what influence, if any, they had on each other but it is more than likely that both strongly influenced Brecht who in 1927 was a writer in Piscator's company.12

Three years later, in the spring of 1930, Meyerhold himself brought his ensemble to Germany on their first foreign tour. Their first three weeks were spent in Berlin. Brecht evidently saw some of their performances because he defended them against the attacks of conservative critics. He was especially impressed by Tret'iakov's *Roar China!*, one of the most popular and successful productions in the group's repertoire.13 Meyerhold also staged his tradition-shattering version of Gogol's *The Inspector General*. In the six weeks which the Meyerhold Theater spent in Germany, hundreds of reviews and articles (many unfavorable) about its productions appeared in the German press. People were struck by Meyerhold's use of mass scenes in which numbers of ordinary working people took part, as in the performances of *Roar China!* and *Commander of the Second Army*. Doubtless they were also struck by the fact that his actors, in their turn, took part in a workers' May Day demonstration in Cologne—such was Meyerhold's belief that actors be intellectually and politically aware, on the stage or off (Murav'ev, 190).

Kamerny Theater, Vakhtangov Theater, Blue Blouse, and the Meyerhold troupe exemplify the relatively free passage of dramatic art from Russia to the West. Among the willing emissaries were Anna Lacis, Bernhard Reich, Anatoly Lunacharsky, Sergei Tret'iakov, and Sergei Eisenstein. German artists and intellectuals (such as Brecht, Piscator, Toller, Becher, Huppert, and Benjamin) in their turn travelled to the Soviet Union in order to experience for themselves the tenor of art and life in what was heralded as a new and more humane society. Brecht made five trips (1932, 1935, 1936, 1941, and 1955). The meeting of minds which occurred as the result of the reciprocal visits of Soviet and German artists has been celebrated by Hugo Huppert "und wäre die stirn uns versteinert,/ sie trüge tief eingegraben/ in erzprägung/ die rühmlichen namen, die heiligen jahre—."14 These personal contacts were a source of new ideas for Brecht and provided him a vivid access to Meyerhold's innovations.

One of Brecht's most important contacts with Russian theater and Meyerhold was Anna Lacis, a Latvian actress, director, and teacher whose own work owed much to Meyerhold. In 1913 Lacis was a student in St. Petersburg where she saw a number of productions of the Imperial Theaters, then under the directorship of Meyerhold. In her memoir she describes his theatrical experiments. In his production of Sologub's *The Hostages of Life* (1913) "the proscenium was covered with blue material. On the stage were an endless succession of doors, through which the actors entered, exited, appeared, vanished like a many-colored conveyor belt—a symbol of the absurd chaos of life." In Pinero's *Mid-Channel* (1914) the stage set was constructed entirely of cubes, to the great scandal of Petersburg. Even the actors balked at performing. One critic wrote that Meyerhold had turned the academic theater into a "futuristic Hanswurstiade." Lacis also saw some of Meyerhold's early and important innovative work with opera. The director was fascinated by the possible uses of music and dance in every sort of theatrical production. His presentation in 1913 of Strauss' opera *Electra* had also earned him a storm of critical attacks, but some critics viewed this work as progressive music-drama. "We students," wrote Lacis, "were on their side."[15]

Lacis was especially interested in Meyerhold's experiments with the dramatic use of movement and followed this and other aspects of his work in his journal, *The Love of Three Oranges* (1914-16), which chronicled his Studio's activities and had articles on dramatic theory and history. Even when she left the capital for Moscow in 1914 to become a student in Fedor Kommissarzhevky's studio, her links with the Meyerhold Theater continued to be strengthened, for Kommissarzhevsky had worked with "the Master" and in many respects had assimilated his dramatic art.[16] And in 1920 when Meyerhold founded the theatrical movement which he called "Theater October," the goal of which was to combine agitprop drama with new theatrical forms, Lacis became one of its most enthusiastic supporters.

In 1922 Lacis went to Berlin; theater people there asked her about Stanislavsky, Meyerhold, and Tairov (Lacis, 35). The following year she and her husband Bernhard Reich travelled to

Munich where Reich had been appointed *Oberregisseur* at the Munich Kammerspiele. It was there that Lacis and Reich met Brecht who was also a director at the Kammerspiele and had just begun to plan the production of his play *The Life of Edward the Second of England* (written with Lion Feuchtwanger). When Brecht was introduced to Lacis, he questioned her about the Russian theater, the Soviet Union, and Soviet *Kunstpolitik*.[17] He was so impressed with her theatrical knowledge that he offered and she accepted the job of production assistant for *Edward II* and in addition the role of young Edward.

During rehearsals Brecht tried to perfect the dramatic movement of the actors. According to Lacis, "he wanted every gesture to express the whole character: he formed dialogue and verse differently from what the actors were accustomed to. He wanted them to avoid what was vague, foggy, common. That was no doubt the beginning of gestural speech" (Lacis, 37). Lacis does not draw any parallels between Brecht's development of gestural expression and similar work done by Meyerhold. Yet, at the very time when she had been introduced to his theater in 1913, Meyerhold was teaching his students the art of gesture and writing about the "scenario of movement" in his journal, *The Love of Three Oranges*. "Movement," he wrote, "is the most powerful means of theatrical expression."[18]

Lacis met Walter Benjamin in the summer of 1924, and later that year, in Berlin, introduced him to Brecht (Lacis, 49). Benjamin traveled to the Soviet Union in 1925 and 1926 at the invitation of Lacis and Reich. He saw several theatrical productions while there but was most impressed by Meyerhold, whose theater was the only one in Moscow which he thought worthwhile.[19]

The most important Meyerhold production which Reich, Lacis, and Benjamin saw in 1926 was Gogol's *The Inspector General*. It was so unusual and alien to the expectations of its audiences that it provoked a greater outburst of critical and popular controversy than was customary even for Meyerhold's innovations. Russian audiences resented his tampering with a beloved national property. Meyerhold, however, had always asserted the director's right to alter a text for his own purposes; with *The Inspector General* he gave free reign to that prerogative: adding dialogue, characters, and scenes from other of Gogol's works, and rejecting the traditional interpretation of the play as sheer farce, by presenting it as a pessimistic vision of public and private vanity, greed, and hypocrisy. As was his custom, Meyerhold organized a public debate about his staging of the play. Reich, Lacis, and Benjamin attended the discussion and the latter two wrote about it—Lacis many years later but Benjamin shortly after the event. There was more at stake than the question of artistic prerogative, for Meyerhold, despite his fame and influence, was having difficulties with the critics. "Thousands gathered in a great hall. . . . They followed the dispute with every fiber; between speakers they shouted, applauded, screamed, whistled. . . . Among the speakers were Mayakovsky, Meyerhold, Bely," and Lunacharsky (Lacis, 54-55). Lacis saw the debate as a great victory of the pro-Meyerhold forces (the roster had been heavily weighted on the director's behalf). Benjamin was more perceptive; he saw the debate as the beginning of the end for Meyerhold.20

Lacis returned to Germany in the early fall of 1928 as an official consultant of the film department of the Commissariat of Enlightenment to the Soviet trade mission in Berlin, and emissary from the Soviet Proletarian Theater to the German BPRS (Union of Proletarian-Revolutionary Writers). Under the sponsorship of BPRS she gave public lectures on the most notable playwrights and directors then at work in the Soviet Union. She frequently met with "the three Bs"—Brecht, Benjamin, and Becher—and discussed Soviet theater. They often talked about Sergei Tret'iakov, who was a close associate of Meyerhold and became a good friend of Brecht (Lacis, 58).

Tret'iakov was born in Latvia in 1892 and educated in Riga. During the Civil War he first fought with the Whites but later joined the Bolsheviks for whom he became an ardent and hard-working servant, devoting himself both as a government official and as an artist to the construction of a new social order. From the early twenties he was in the thick of the Futurist movement, collaborating with Mayakovsky as editor of and contributor to the Futurist journals *LEF* and *Novyi LEF*. Tret'iakov and Brecht first became acquainted in Germany in the late twenties or early thirties, and soon thereafter became close friends.

> In my friendship with Brecht, I have experienced that feeling of comradely closeness which makes one strong. I translate his work; I accept much of it, I protest much of it, but I follow his

every step with the utmost attention, if you will, with love.
Just such relationships, just such an exchange of letters, I wish
for each of you.

(From a speech by Tret'iakov to the First
All-Union Congress of Soviet Writers, June 1934)21

In a poem mourning Tret'iakov's violent death (he was shot in
1939 in a Siberian concentration camp) Brecht refers to him
as "Mein Lehrer/ Der grosse freundliche."22

Tret'iakov's association with Meyerhold began in 1922.
The former had just returned from the Far East and the other
had just begun to organize his own theater and actor's studio.
Tret'iakov became deeply involved in those enterprises: as
administrator, organizer, and playwright. The two men complemented each other artistically: Tret'iakov, a "master of
dramatic language," and Meyerhold, who at that very time was
formulating his theory of "bio-mechanics" and working on the
problem of including "verbal elements in the exercises of dramatic movement." Together they started a course called "Word-
movement."23

Tret'iakov's work at the Meyerhold Theater was interrupted
in 1924 by a trip to China where he had been invited to lecture
on Russian literature at the University of Peking. His experiences
in China gave him material for the highly successful agitprop
drama *Roar China!*, an exposé of the brutality of colonial government, which opened at the Meyerhold Theater in January,
1926.

Brecht and Tret'iakov probably met for the first time in the
late twenties, or in 1930-31 when Tret'iakov was in Germany
on a lecture tour.24 In 1932, the year Brecht and Slatan Dudow
travelled to Moscow for the première of their film *Kuhle Wampe,*
Tret'iakov was their cicerone.25 During their visit he published
an article on Brecht in *Literaturnaia gazeta* (12 May 1932),
pointing out that Brecht was striving, in his plays, to create
dialectic drama (as Tret'iakov and Meyerhold had tried to do
in the twenties with Tret'iakov's own play, *I Want a Child*). In
another article in 1933 Tret'iakov described the didactic theater
of Brecht in terms that make it practically identical with his
own theatrical philosophy, which he had outlined in 1929, with
its dialectic spiral reaching into the "audience's discussions and
into their non-theatrical activities."26 Again in 1933, during
an informal meeting of writers at the club of the *Literaturnaia*

gazeta, Tret'iakov argued that a play should not only be relevant to current social problems but also offer a social "prognosis" by anticipating the political and social conditions of the future. He gave as an example his own *Roar China!*. He also told the writers that he had translated and reworked three of Brecht's plays "to the extent that they differ fundamentally from the author's originals."

Tret'iakov: The playgoer is not finally satisfied—[with Brecht's problematic theater] this is what troubles Brecht. The playgoer leaves anxious . . .
Usovsky: A perplexed playgoer.
Tret'iakov: No. A thinking playgoer.
Amaglobeles: Isn't the playgoer a thinking one to Sophocles?
Tret'iakov: The problem of the playwright is to lift the playgoer out of his equilibrium so that he will not leave serene, but ready for action.27

Tret'iakov's observation about the "thinking playgoer" complements an anecdote which Walter Benjamin told of Meyerhold:

The Russian producer Meyerhold was recently [1930] asked in Berlin what in his opinion distinguished his actors from those of Western Europe. He replied: 'Two things. First, they think; second, they do not think idealistically but materialistically' . . . The epic actor is oriented towards knowledge, and this knowledge, in turn, determines not only the content but also the *tempi,* pauses and stresses of his whole performance.28

When Brecht visited Russia again, in early April, 1935, he and Helene Weigel stayed in the Tret'iakovs' Moscow apartment. It was there, during a discussion of theatrical matters, that Reich first heard the word *Verfremdung:*

We spoke about a very unusual theatrical performance. . . . I referred to a certain detail of the production and Tret'iakov interjected: 'Yes, that's a *Verfremdung,*' and threw Brecht a conspiratorial glance. Brecht nodded. That was my first acquaintance with the word *Verfremdung.* So I must assume that Brecht got this term from Tret'iakov; I think that Tret'iakov somewhat recast Shkovsky's term *otchuzhdenie,* 'to distance,' 'to alienate.'29

Some critics have proposed that Brecht's concept of the "V-Effect" derives from the theories of Russian Formalism.30 Others object: Soviet and DDR critics (Formalism has been out of favor in the Soviet Union since about 1930) and some Western critics because of insufficient evidence or on linguistic grounds.[31] Jan Knopf says there is no evidence that Brecht met with any Russian Formalist while in Moscow in 1935.[32] This argument ignores the close ties between Futurists and Formalists, a relationship which is clearly shown in Shklovsky's memoir *Mayakovsky and His Circle,* as well as by a reading of any of the numbers of *LEF* and *Novyi LEF,* journals of avant-garde literature and art which were produced by people who called themselves Futurists or Formalists or both, such as Shklovsky, Tret'iakov, Mayakovsky, Brik, and Terentev. In Tret'iakov, Brecht had a friend who was at home with all the ideas and "catch-words" of the Futurist-Formalist movement.

On an April evening in 1935, Brecht was the guest of honor at a Moscow gathering of Russian and German intellectuals and artists, a meeting sponsored by the Organization of Writers of the Soviet Union. Tret'iakov spoke on Brecht's epic theater and on his artistic and political significance. Kirsanov read his translation of Brecht's "Ballad of the Dead Soldier" and actors from Tairov's Kamerny Theater performed excerpts from *The Three-Penny Opera.* Wieland Herzfelde spoke on Brecht's role in German poetry and Lacis gave her views of him as regisseur. The highlight of the evening was Carola Neher's singing of ballads and songs from *The Three-Penny Opera.*[33]

It was during this visit to Moscow that Brecht saw a performance of the Chinese actor Mei Lan-fang and his troupe; Meyerhold also saw the group perform. If Brecht found in the critical theories of Shklovsky certain ideas which complemented or even inspired his own, he saw in the highly stylized art of Mei Lan-fang a demonstration of some of these ideas. In particular Brecht admired the ability of the Chinese actor to separate himself emotionally from his role so that the audience is never tempted to forget that acting and not actual life is occurring on the stage. Brecht described, in language very close to that used by Shklovsky, the Chinese theater's transformation of nature into art: the Chinese "show how actors produce human gestures in their own way, because actors translate everyday language into their own speech." "By means of this art, routine objects are lifted beyond the pale of the obvious" (*GW,* XV, 427-28; XVI, 621). Brecht found the mental attitude demanded of a Chinese theater audience very much to his liking. In order to fully enjoy their national drama the Chinese have to come to the theater mentally armed with a working knowledge of its theatrical rules. Thus the playgoers have their own sort of art (*Zuschaukunst*) which they bring to the play. Moreover, this art is not limited to a select group of intellectuals but is the accomplishment of an entire people. In the Moscow performance of Mei Lan-fang, Brecht saw personified his ideal of a non-illusionistic drama which attracted a mass audience of ordinary people who neither wished nor expected to be hypnotized by the actors.

Brecht may also have been influenced by Mei Lan-fang's enactment of female roles. In writing about these characterizations Brecht ironically informed the reader that Mei was nonetheless a "thoroughly manly man . . . indeed even a banker" (*GW*, XV, 427). Mei had a repertoire of conventional female types: the good-hearted matron, the aged woman, the loose housemaid. One of the more unusual types (which made the greatest impression on Eisenstein) was that of the woman warrior. In this role, he accomplished a sort of double alienation by impersonating a woman who impersonates a man. It may be that Mei's performance, together with Tret'iakov's interest in and experience of Chinese culture (as reflected in his play *Roar China!* and in his 1930 novel *Den Shi-hua*) provided Brecht with certain ideas which bore fruit in *The Good Person of Sezuan* for which he created a male-female central character.

At a discussion and analysis of the performances of the Chinese company, an event which took place April 14 at the Moscow chapter of VOKS (the All-Union Society for Cultural Relations with Foreign Countries, in which Tret'iakov was a high official and which sponsored Brecht's visit to the Soviet Union in 1935 as well as Mei's 1935 Russian tour),[34] Meyerhold spoke on various aspects of Mei's art, in particular on the use of gesture and rhythmical movement. He was so impressed by the performance of the Chinese troupe that he dedicated his next production (Griboedov's *Woe to Wit,* which opened in Leningrad in September, 1935) to Mei. Meyerhold explained that his latest adaptation was influenced in large measure by "the unforgettable Mei Lan-fang" and that as the result of Mei's performance his version of *Woe to Wit* contained "features from the theatrical folklore of the Chinese troupe."[35]

In 1923 Tret'iakov wrote an essay in which he listed what he felt were Meyerhold's most important contributions to the theater: the transformation of the traditional stage into an agitprop theater, of the "academic" actor into a socially active organizer of the masses, of the audience from a chance gathering into a "firmly established collective, which interacts with the play, the transfer of attention from the purely narrative aspects of the play to the methods of its construction, [and] the invention of the best methods for the organization of a group into a co-operating collective."36 These accomplishments represented revolutionary changes in theatrical goals. But they are only a part of the innovative approaches to theater which Tret'iakov learned from Meyerhold and perhaps transmitted to Brecht. Such revolutionary changes in the arts and easy transmission of ideas was made possible in the 1920s partly because the official head of Soviet culture was Anatoly Vasilievich Lunacharsky (1875-1933). He also represents a link between Brecht and the Soviet theater.

The Commissar for Enlightenment was a man of vast culture and creative energy. He appeared to his contemporaries as "a man in a 'smoking jacket,' pointed graying goatee, inquisitive, intently scrutinizing, narrowed eyes" (Kopelev, 209). His approach to art was generally tolerant and eclectic; he never advocated or practiced the forceful suppression of politically unpopular ideas or art forms. Late in 1917 he invited 120 leading Russian artists to a conference to consider the problem of organizing the arts under state control. Meyerhold's decision to attend (only five accepted the invitation) "amounted to a hazardous act of faith," which he affirmed the next year by joining the Bolshevik Party (Braun, 160). Soon after the arts conference Lunacharsky appointed Meyerhold deputy chief in Petrograd, and then, in 1919, chief of the Theatrical Department of the Commissariat of Enlightenment. The two men remained on a good personal footing despite sharp ideological differences which were occasioned by Meyerhold's attacks on traditional art forms.

Though he disapproved of Meyerhold's "leftist" excesses, Lunacharsky generally praised his theatrical genius. Moreover, he was convinced that Meyerhold was evolving a politically mature, socially useful, innovative, and uniquely Soviet contribution to the theater. He further believed that Meyerhold's use of music, dance, masks, circus devices, etc., was helping to extend the horizons of realism in the theater. For the Commissar's idea of "realism" was not a narrow concept bound to certain conventions of nineteenth-century art. Rather, he held a view of realism similar to Brecht's in that he welcomed the use of any device or style which could promote an awareness of the world as it is and as it may become. He seemed to regard Meyerhold as a living embodiment of the principle that better forms will inevitably emerge if opposing ideas are given the opportunity to develop and conflict. To those who condemned Meyerhold's production of *The Inspector General*, Lunacharsky wrote, "of course, there will continue to be arguments about *The Inspector General*. So what?! Let's argue!"37

Lunacharskaia-Rozenel' recounts a meeting between her husband and Brecht in 1928 at the Schiffbauerdamm Theater, during a performance of *The Three-Penny Opera* (they had previously met at gatherings of a Soviet-German friendship society). After the performance the Lunacharskys were invited to join Brecht and various members of the cast along with Kurt Weill and several of Brecht's other friends and associates. Lunacharskaia recalls that the Germans pressed her husband for information on the latest plays being produced in the Soviet Union. They already knew *Teacher Bubus* (by A. Faiko) and *The Warrant* (by N. Erdman), both of which had been staged by Meyerhold in 1925. They asked Lunacharsky to recommend other Soviet plays, but instead he recommended that the theater of Brecht be introduced to Russia; and he promised to speak to the directors Tairov and Radlov about producing *The Three-Penny Opera* in Moscow and Leningrad. In fact, Lunacharsky was eager to have the play staged in the Soviet Union. He envisioned an adaptation based on Brecht which would use elements from Gay's *Beggar's Opera*, from Brecht's original adaptation of Gay, from the text of the 1928 production, plus further alterations which would tailor the play for Soviet audiences. When the first Soviet version did appear in 1930, under Tairov's direction, "purely as entertainment drama," it disappointed both Lunacharsky and Brecht.38

In his 1928 review of the Berlin production of *The Three-Penny Opera*, Lunacharsky remarked on the striking similarities between the devices used by Brecht and similar devices employed by the Soviet theatrical organization TRAM (Theater of Working Youth):

> Of course, the parallels are purely coincidental. The production of the *Opera* is extremely realistic . . . but just as in TRAM

> (which is also realistic) music suddenly bursts over the stage, people dance or sing . . .
>
> TRAM realism loves to suddenly shift into an interlude, to an imitation of film, to Expressionist fantasy. These elements are present in the Berlin production of *The Three-Penny Opera,* in a lesser degree perhaps, but in a very sophisticated style.
>
> *(O teatre,* II, 368-69)

Perhaps the resemblances between the two styles were not purely coincidental, given the contacts between Brecht and the Soviet theater. In her history of the German revolutionary theater, Anna Lacis emphasizes the impact of TRAM and other Soviet acting groups, all of which derived their style and purpose from Meyerhold's pioneering "Theater October." Although Lacis (in 1935) denied the direct influence of Meyerhold on either Piscator or Brecht, she pointed out that the Soviet Blue Blouse troupes made such a forceful appearance in Germany that "a 'Blue Blouse' manner of acting became widely established" there, on the avant-garde stage. TRAM's contribution to German theater, according to Lacis, came specifically in the areas of "original reworkings" of plays and the "report" genre.39

Early in 1933 the Lunacharskys were again in Berlin and were invited to a party at Brecht's apartment. At this gathering the increasingly ominous political situation in Germany was discussed. Someone suggested that emigration was the only practical answer. Lunacharsky, citing his own example as an Old Bolshevik, urged his German friends to keep fighting, to remain at the ideological barricades, whether in Germany or abroad (Lunacharskaia-Rozenel', 162). Lunacharsky died of a heart attack later that year in the south of France; at least he escaped the purges.

When Brecht visited Moscow in 1936, in connection with his editorship of *Das Wort,* he met with Lunacharsky's widow and reminisced about his friendship with her husband, savoring the memory of his prophecy of a "Brecht Theater" organized along the lines of Soviet ensemble theaters.40 But by 1936, things which the Commissar had once encouraged, artistic experimentation and the free flow of ideas, were almost at an end in Germany and Russia. Brecht himself was in exile (since 1933). Though still at the ideological barricades, he was unable to get his plays produced in any major theater.

His Russian friends had already begun to disappear. That

Brecht was aware of the danger is indicated by his poem, written in 1937, "Advice to Tret'iakov, to Be Healthy."

> Schwimmen zum Vergnügen im See. Das Wasser
> Das dich ersäufen könnte
> Trägt dich.
> Das du schwimmend zerteilst, hinter dir
> Tritt es wieder zusammen.
>
> (*Gedichte*, V, 93)

Tret'iakov was arrested in 1938, convicted by a People's Tribunal of spying for Japan, and shot to death in a Siberian prison camp the following year. Meyerhold was arrested in 1939 and died, perhaps under torture, in 1940. Shortly after his arrest Meyerhold's wife was murdered, quite possibly by the police.

Brecht visited the Soviet Union again in 1941, on his way to the United States. Of all the friends and acquaintances he had made there only Reich greeted him when he passed through Mocow. Brecht knew that Lacis had been arrested and imprisoned and promised Reich he would use his influence with a Soviet diplomat to intercede on her behalf.[41] But she remained in prison ten years and Reich also was eventually imprisoned. Thus ended "die heilige Jahre."

The Soviet critic Lev Kopelev has noted that Brecht's visits to Moscow in the 1930s were "abundant with encounters and observations which for a long time after influenced Brecht and grew in his consciousness" (Kopelev, 236). These encounters were the culmination of several years of contact with the innovations of Soviet art of the early twentieth century. News about Soviet avant-garde theater, of which Meyerhold was the acknowledged master, was of special interest to Brecht. There were various links between Brecht and Meyerhold: published reviews and reports, and personal contacts with Soviet friends, with Russian emigrés, and with German friends who had emigrated to or visited the Soviet Union. Lacis, Reich, Benjamin, and Lunacharsky were among those who shared Brecht's artistic and political interests and had seen and admired Meyerhold's work. Tret'iakov, of course, had been close to both Brecht and Meyerhold. Even the greatest artists owe much to their times and to concepts which their predecessors have developed. It does not detract from Brecht's achievements to suppose that he incorporated into his work some of the original accomplishments of Meyerhold, thus keeping alive the ideas of the Russian director even after the man himself had been destroyed and his work suppressed.

Denton, Texas

NOTES

1 Stella Arbenina, *Through Terror to Freedom* (London: Hutchinson, [c. 1929]), p. 70.

2 Carl Zuckmayer, *A Part of Myself. Portrait of an Epoch,* trans. Richard and Clara Winston (New York: Harcourt, 1970), p. 233.

3 Ilya Ehrenburg, *Men, Years, Life,* Vol. III: *Truce: 1921-33,* trans. T. Shebunina and Y. Kapp (London: MacGibbon, 1936), p. 18; Robert C. Williams, *Culture in Exile. Russian Emigres in Germany, 1881-1941* (Ithaca, N. Y.: Cornell Univ. Press, 1972), pp. 14-20, 28-29, 131-33; Zuckmayer, p. 233.

4 Iu. P. Murav'ev, "Sovetsko-germanskie sviazi v oblasti literatury i iskusstva v gody Veimarskoi respubliki," in *Slaviano-germanskie kul'turnye sviazi in otnosheniia,* gen. ed. V. D. Koroliuk (Moscow: "Nauka," 1969), pp. 180-81, 187; subsequent references to this article are in the text.

5 Joachim Fiebach, "Beziehungen zwischen dem sowjetischen und dem prole-tarisch-revolutionären Theater der Weimarer Republik," in *Deutschland-Sowjetunion,* ed. Heinz Sanke (Berlin: Humboldt-Universität, 1966), p. 425; Henri Guilbeaux, "Meyerhold et les tendences du théâtre contemporain," *Les humbles,* XV, no. 5/6 (May-June 1930), 22; Erhard Pachaly, et al., "Die kulturelle Beziehungen zwischen Deutschland und der Sowjetunion," in Alfred Anderle, et al., eds., *Die grosse sozia-listische Oktoberrevolution und Deutschland,* I (Berlin: Dietz, 1967), 450.

6 Detailed descriptions of Meyerhold's work appeared in *Das neue Russland* from 1924 through 1926. After 1926 there was no further mention of him in that journal.

7 Fiebach, "Beziehungen," p. 425.

8 Oscar Blum, "Russische Theaterköpfe. II: Meyerhold," *Die Weltbühne* (Berlin, 22 June 1926), 265. Meyerhold used similar Oriental devices in his production of Blok's *Unknown Woman.* The plays were performed as a double bill in 1914.

9 Bernhard Reich, "Meyerholds neue Inszenierung," *Die literarische Welt,* IV, no. 18 (1928), 7.

10 Guilbeaux, 22-23; Nataliia Lunacharskaia-Rozenel,' *Pamiat' serdtsa* (Moscow: "Iskusstvo," 1962), 156; subsequent reference to this book is in the text.

11 The Blue Blouse guest appearance in 1927 in Piscator's theater was an event which "gave a strong impulse to the development of political theater in Germany. The troupe brought actual news about construction in the Soviet Union, as well as reviews, musical dramas, and oratory. They played without stage settings in an artistic-rhythmic style which derived from Meyerhold," see Eva Kreilisheim, *Brecht und die Sowjetu-nion* (unpublished Ph.D. dissertation, U. of Vienna, 1970), p. 12. According to Kreilisheim (12-13) after the performance of the Blue Blouse troupe, several agit-prop troupes sprang up in Germany. Their productions were characterized by short episodes, lack of a strong connecting plot, and baldly stereotyped characters.

12 Piscator denied that Meyerhold influenced him but saw Brecht as having been influenced by both his own and Meyerhold's style; see Herbert Knust, "Piscator and Brecht: Affinity and Alienation," in Siegfried Mews and Herbert Knust, eds., *Essays on Brecht. Theater and Politics* (Chapel Hill: Univ. of North Carolina Press, 1974),

pp. 64-65; see also Guilbeaux, pp. 20-22. Regarding the influence of Meyerhold on the theaters of Vakhtangov and Tairov, see Boris Alpers, *Teatr sotsial'noi maski* (Moscow: Gos. izd. khudozhestvennoi lit., 1931), pp. 112-13, 116.

13 Bertolt Brecht, *Gesammelte Werke* (Frankfurt am Main: Suhrkamp, 1968), XVI, 62; subsequent references to this edition are in the text *(GW,* Vol., page).

14 Hugo Huppert, "Das Taubenhaus," *Neue deutsche Literatur,* 20 (Dec. 1972), 6-34.

15 My information on the life and work of Anna Lacis is drawn from her memoir, *Revolutionär im Beruf, Berichte über proletarisches Theater, über Meyerhold, Brecht, Benjamin und Piscator,* ed. Hildegard Brenner (Munich: Rogner, 1971); subsequent references to this work appear in the text.

16 Alpers, *Teatr sotsial'noi maski,* pp. 116-17.

17 Bernhard Reich, *Im Wettlauf mit der Zeit, Erinnerungen aus Fünf Jahrzehnten deutscher Theatergeschichte* (Berlin: Henschelverlag, 1970), p. 239, or see his *Vena Berlin Moskva Berlin,* p. 127.

18 Vsevolod Meyerhold, in *Liubov k tryom apelsinam,* no. 4/5 (1914), quoted in Edward Braun, ed. and trans., *Meyerhold on Theatre* (New York: Hill and Wang, 1969), p. 147; subsequent references to Braun's work are in the text.

19 Walter Benjamin, *Briefe,* I, ed. Gershom Scholem and T. W. Adorno (Frankfurt, 1966), 440; Lacis, *Revolutionär,* pp. 42, 54.

20 Walter Benjamin, "Der Regisseur Meyerhold—in Moskau erledigt?," *Die literarische Welt,* III, no. 6 (11 Feb. 1927), 3.

21 *Pervyi vsesoiuzny s'ezd sovetskikh pisatelei* (1934), p. 345; quoted in anon., "Bertolt Brecht und die sowjetische Kunst und Literatur," *Geschichte der russischen Sowjetliteratur 1917-1941* (Berlin: Akademie-Verlag, 1973), p. 611.

22 Brecht, *Gedichte,* V. (Frankfurt a. M.: Suhrkamp, 1964), 139.

23 Aleksandr V. Fevral'skii, "S. M. Tret'iakov v teatre Meierkhol'da," in Sergei Tret'iakov, *Slyshish' Moskva?!,* ed. G. Mokrusheva (Moscow: "Iskusstvo," 1966), pp. 188-89.

24 "Bertolt Brecht und die sowjetische Kunst und Literatur," pp. 610-11, claims that Tret'iakov's 1934 essay, "Vvodnyi etiud," to *B. Brekht, epicheskie dramy* (Moscow, 1934), pp. 3-22, gives evidence of an acquaintanceship dating back to the twenties. Anna Lacis *(Revolutionär,* p. 58) recalls that in Berlin in 1928 Brecht asked her about Tret'iakov.

25 According to an article written by Tret'iakov the visit of Brecht and Dudow was sponsored by the (Soviet) Journal-Newspaper Society and the two planned to stay one week, "Bert Brekht," *Literaturnaia gazeta* (12 May 1932).

26 Tret'iakov, "Dramaturg-didakt. O pese B. Brekhta Mat'," *Internatsional'naia literatura,* no. 2 (1933), 116-18; Tret'iakov, "Chto pishut dramaturgi—S. M. Tret'iakov," *Rabis,* no. 11 (Moscow 1929), 7, quoted in Fevral'skii, "S. M. Tret'iakov," pp. 203-04.

27 Anon., *International Literature,* no. 2 (Moscow 1933), p. 141.

28 Walter Benjamin, *Understanding Brecht,* trans. A. Bostock (London: NLB, 1973), pp. 10-11.

29 Reich, *Wettlauf,* pp. 371-72; Shklovsky agrees that his concept of *ostranenie* (which, in his writings was shown to have political as well as literary uses) was transmitted to Brecht by way of Tret'iakov; see Marjorie Hoover, "Brecht's Soviet Connection: Tretiakov," *Brecht Heute,* III (Frankfurt a. M.: Athenäum, 1973), 45.

30 John Willett, *The Theatre of Bertolt Brecht. A Study from Eight Aspects*, 2nd ed. (New York: New Directions, 1960), p. 179; Willett's argument is based on the fact that "conception and catch-work alike only enter [Brecht's] work after his first [second] visit to Moscow in 1935."

31 The linguistic argument is that Shklovsky's *priem ostranenie* does not really translate into *Verfremdungseffekt*, but into *Seltsammachen*, etc. On the other hand, Brecht may not have been particularly concerned about precise translation.

32 Jan Knopf, *Bertolt Brecht; ein kritischer Forschungsbericht. Fragwürdiges in der Brecht-Forschung* (Frankfurt a. M.: Athenäum, 1974), pp. 15-20.

33 "Bert Brekht v Moskve," *Pravda*, no. 112 (23 April 1935), 4.

34 Lev Kopelev, *Brekht* (Moscow: "Molodaia gvardiia," 1966), pp. 204, 233; subsequent references to this book appear in the text (author, page); A. C. Scott, *Mei Lan-fang, Leader of the Pear Garden* (Hong Kong: Hong Kong Univ. Press, 1959), p. 117.

35 Vsevolod E. Meierkhol'd, *Stat'i, pis'ma, rechi, besedy*, II, *1917-1939* (Moscow: "Iskusstvo," 1968), 322, 563.

36 "Vsevolod Meierkhol'd," *LEF*, no. 2 (April-May 1923), 169.

37 Lunacharsky, "Eshche o teatre Meierkhol'da" (1926), *Sobranie sochinenii*, III (Moscow: "Khudozhestvennaia literatura," 1964), 301, 303, 362.

38 Lunacharsky, "Na tri grosha" (1928), *O teatre i dramaturgii*, II (Moscow: "Iskusstvo," 1958), 369, subsequent reference to this book is in text; Dora Angres, *Die Beziehungen Lunačarskijs zur deutschen Literatur* (Berlin: Akademie-Verlag, 1970), p. 194.

39 Anna Lacis, *Revoliutsionnyi teatr Germannii*, trans. from German mss. by N. Barkhash (Moscow 1935), p. 250; many of the German workers' theater troupes travelled to Moscow and Leningrad to learn the playwriting and acting style of TRAM, see Fiebach, "Beziehungen," 430.

40 Lunacharskaia-Rozenel', *Pamiat' serdtsa*, p. 164. Angres feels that in certain respects Lunacharskaia's rosy picture of the relationship between Brecht and her late husband is not to be trusted. In particular Angres disputes those passages which "give the impression that Lunacharsky recognized Brecht's significance, and predicted a great future for him" (Angres, *Die Beziehungen*, 195). Angres believes that such an impression is not compatible with the fact that Lunacharsky, a wondrously prolific writer, had almost nothing to say about Brecht in print. Lunacharsky's first mention of Brecht in writing occurred with his 1928 review of *The Three-Penny Opera* and then he wrote of Brecht only once more, just in passing, in 1932, in an article on "The Twilight of the Bourgeois Theater" *(Sob. soch.*, VI, 494). "Either he knew no other works of [Brecht], or—and this is much more likely—Brecht's skeptical non-illusion concerning the expressionistic rhetoric of redemption as it is somewhat exaggeratedly manifested in the figure of Kragler, contradicted his esthetic views so strongly, that he did not understand Brecht's intentions and probably even viewed them as an attack on avantgardism in literature. He disregarded the philosophical discussions in Brecht's work. In a conversation with [Dora Angres], A. I. Deich revealed that Lunacharsky thought Brecht's writing was affected [gekünstelt] . . . in any case . . . the picture which Lunacharskaia-Rozenel' presents, must, in essential points, be rejected as incorrect" (Angres, *Die Beziehungen*, p. 196).

41 Klaus Völker, *Brecht-Chronik. Daten zu Leben und Werk* (Munich: Carl Hanser, 1971), p. 86; Reich, *Wettlauf*, p. 376.

Defeated Sexuality in the Plays and Novels of Samuel Beckett

Kristin Morrison

"I summoned up my remaining strength and said, Abort, abort. . . ."[1] This cry of the reluctant father in the short novel *First Love* suggests an element which is prevalent throughout Samuel Beckett's work: concern with the physical details of reproduction, its success or lack of success, and specifically the impotence, sterility, and decay of the sexual organs, repulsive copulation and the destruction of progeny. The earlier novels abound with scenes of grotesque and defeated sexual activity (e.g., Watt's laborious and futile fondling of Mrs. Gorman[2]) but in the plays such lengthy scenes are usually replaced by a single word, phrase, or allusion, often oblique and obscure but as important in its context as are the more elaborate fictional passages in theirs. It is these varied and elusive sexual references in the plays which I will discuss, showing them to be not random and incidental details, but rather, as in the fiction, significant metaphors for the misery of human life itself.

Throughout Beckett's career, the fiction with its greater explicitness has provided an important context for words and phrases which appear in the plays. In the increasing condensation which has marked his later work, there is no diminution of sexual references, but their meaning is not always immediately apparent. It is thus very helpful to keep the earlier novels in mind while looking at the later plays. *The Unnamable* (1949) provides a representative and particularly repulsive reference to copulation: "the two cunts . . . the one for ever accursed that ejected me into this world and the other, infundibuliform, in which, pumping my likes, I tried to take my revenge."[3] This passage provides the most explicit statement of motive for the hatred which permeates the story of "Mahood's" return home, where he stamps "underfoot the unrecognizable remains of [his] family, here a face, there a stomach. . . ." Birth—and the sexuality that leads to it—is the great enemy. The only triumph over this enemy is death, a death which *precedes* birth, an annihilation which *precedes* existence, as the narrator makes clear later in this novel when he states, "I'm looking for my mother to kill her, I should have thought of that a bit earlier, before being born" (p. 391).

Copious references of this kind in the fiction alert the reader to the importance of similar, but quite elliptical, references in the plays: that very important "panhysterectomy" in *Embers,* Minnie's menopause in *All That Fall,* the negligent fathers in *Endgame,* Winnie's sexless non-existent legs and breasts in *Happy Days.* These references present a striking coherence from novel to novel, from play to play: over and over again abortion or some kind of sterilization is presented as the term of human existence.[4]

The radio drama *Embers* (1959) provides a useful place to begin this discussion of defeated sexuality because as an early play it is relatively detailed and explicit, and the sexual references (though brief and for the most part unobtrusive) fit together quite neatly. Because the play is directed entirely to the ear and not to the eye, words and their interrelationships have even more importance than they do in a stage play where gestures affect meaning: when Holloway states, "I have a pan-hysterectomy at nine,"[5] his listeners cannot miss the word and find themselves wondering what a panhysterectomy has to do with the action, the meaning of this play. The answer is, everything.

The main voice in *Embers* is that of Henry, a lonely, tormented man who speaks to himself and conjures up the voices of others in order to cover the sound of the sea, which he constantly hears and hates. The dramatic situation is thus a kind of monologue; and although there is another voice heard at length, that of Anna, his wife, it is clear her voice exists "in" his mind; she is not physically present there on the beach with him (stage directions indicate his movements make noise on the shingles, hers do not). These imaginary conversations include his father (who now will not answer him, will not "appear") and some brief anecdotes concerning his daughter, Addie, with her Music Master and with her Riding Master. Interspersed with these voices are the sounds of galloping hooves and clashing stones summoned by Henry to "drown out" the sucking sound of the sea (heard constantly throughout the play, sometimes softer, sometimes louder). In addition to creating these imaginary sounds and voices, Henry also tells himself a story about an old man named Bolton and a doctor named Holloway. These, then, are the pieces of the structure of the drama: fragments of narrative, snatches of sound, memories worked into imaginary conversations, various characters who relate to Henry in terms of his feelings about them. Among these relationships the most important is that of Henry (as son) to his father and mother, and Henry (as father) to his daughter; of lesser importance is the relationship of Henry (as husband) to his wife. Less clear (but tantalizingly important) is the relationship between Bolton and Holloway and their joint relation to Henry. What ties all these elements together are a few references to methods of preventing or destroying the results of copulation: sterilization and abortion.

The first reference to abortion comes a third of the way through the play. Henry has just been speaking about his own hatred of the sea, his attempts to get away from it, his father's love of the sea and apparent suicide by drowning; he has digressed at length on his Bolton-Holloway story then switches back suddenly to memories of his father:

> Father! *(Pause.)* You wouldn't know me now, you'd be sorry you ever had me, but you were that already, a washout, that's the last I heard from you, a washout. *(Pause. Imitating father's voice.)* "Are you coming for a dip?" "No." "Come on, come on." "No." Glare, stump to door, turn, glare. "A washout, that's all you are, a washout!" *(Violent slam of door. Pause.)* Again! *(Slam. Pause.)* Slam life shut like that! *(Pause.)* Washout. *(Pause.)* Wish to Christ she had. (pp. 101f)

In this flow of memory with its psychological rather than logical organization, the phrase "Wish to Christ she had" is elliptical but explicable: wish to Christ she had washed (me) out. This man who feels so keenly his father's disappointment, shares his father's sorrow that he was ever born: he should have been aborted (or perhaps prevented by douche). This wish is Henry's own ineffectual equivalent of his father's suicide. But Henry's wish for death, to have been washed from the womb and never to have lived, extends not only to his own relationship with his

parents but also to his relationship with his child. Immediately
after the line "Wish to Christ she had. *(Pause.)*" the monologue
continues with memories about his wife and daughter:

> Never met Ada, did you, or did you, I can't remember, no
> matter, no one'd know her now. *(Pause.)* What turned her
> against me do you think, the child I suppose, horrid little crea-
> ture, wish to God we'd never had her. . . . (p. 102)

He, as father, duplicates his own father's disappointment; he,
too, would prefer a child never to have been born; both important women in his life, mother and wife, should have aborted
rather than delivered: "better off dead, better off dead" (p. 103).

Even the copulation which led to these unfortunate births
is described with words which suggest a certain displeasure in
the act: "It took us a long time to have her. *(Pause.)* Years we
kept hammering away at it" (p. 114). In Henry's mind copulation is associated with the sea—"Where we did it at last for
the first time" (p. 113)—and the sea is the antithesis of life.
(The clashing sounds of stones and horses' hooves he describes
as preferable to the sound of the sea: "That's life! . . . Not this
. . . *(pause)* . . . sucking!" pp. 112f.)

The fact that reproduction—its act and its result—is connected with death, not life, is further indicated by the Bolton-
Holloway story. Bolton is, according to Henry's story, "an old
man in great trouble" (p. 98) who has called his doctor on a
cold wintry night and begged a special service, something the
doctor has repeatedly refused despite Bolton's desperate pleas.
The most that Holloway is willing to do for Bolton is give him
an injection. Nothing more explicit is stated, but the details of
the scene—the deteriorated old man, his tearful pleas, the
candle "guttering all over the place" (p. 120), the cold embers—
all suggest that Bolton is begging to be put out of his misery,
to be given something more permanent than a standard pain-
killing injection. This association with voluntary death is reinforced by the fact that Henry has resumed his story at this point
immediately after reflecting on his father's suicide and his
speculation that Ada may have witnessed it (pp. 118f); the
story seems, in fact, to be an escape from that memory, a more
acceptable distraction, or perhaps a disguised way of thinking
about his father's death (both Bolton and his father have "eyes
drowned," p. 121).

In his impatience to get away, to avoid any involvement in

Bolton's death, Holloway indicates he has other work to do: "If it's an injection you want, Bolton, let down your trousers and I'll give you one. I have a panhysterectomy at nine" (p. 119). After all the colloquial vagueness and imprecision of Henry's language—"washout," "hammering away," "did it"—and his reliance on imagery and mystery in the Bolton-Holloway story, this sudden intrusion of a technical term is startling: the audience notices "panhysterectomy" and is meant to notice it. Somehow the play deals with radical sterilization—not only with frustrated copulation, abortion, and suicide, but with the destruction of the possibility of any existence at all, the utimate state of pre-annihilation for those "better off dead."

But, of course, Beckett's technical terms, allusions, erudite references are not explicated by an audience while the play is in process; they have their effect almost unconsciously. So, too, with this single technical term; "panhysterectomy" is spoken and the play moves swiftly on. The final lines of the play, however, achieve their impact through whatever meaning "panhysterectomy" has managed to register with the audience. Henry moves toward the sea, continuing his monologue, looking at his appointment book:

> This evening . . . (Pause.) Nothing this evening. (Pause.) To-morrow . . . tomorrow . . . plumber at nine, then nothing. (Pause. Puzzled.) Plumber at nine? (Pause.) Ah yes, the waste. (Pause.) Words. (Pause.) Saturday . . . nothing. Sunday . . . Sunday . . . nothing all day. (Pause.) Nothing, all day nothing. (Pause.) All day all night nothing. (Pause.) Not a sound. (p. 121)

"Plumber at nine" echoes "panhysterectomy at nine," and both plumber and doctor deal with the "waste." As is so often the case, Beckett turns a simple ordinary word into a complex pun: the waste is the drain through which the washing out occurs (whether of sink or womb), but it also refers to that which is drained off, that which is discarded because it is waste, refuse; even further, the word "waste" serves as a commentary, "the waste" meaning "such loss, what a pity!" When all is drained, when all is discarded, when all is lost, nothing remains. And this, in fact, is Henry's ideal state: "All day all night nothing. Not a sound." Parents, wives, children, all those causes and effects of reproduction, all that pervasive sucking sea is a torment for him: being a father, a lover, a child are equally intolerable. He prefers imaginary relationships, conjured sounds rather than actual ones. He wants a panhysterectomy for his life.

This concern with impaired reproductive powers is found in other early plays. In *All That Fall* (radio drama first broadcast in 1957), Mrs. Rooney, "a lady in her seventies," laments the loss of "little Minnie" (her daughter, it seems, who died long ago) and chooses to speculate about Minnie's menopause: "In her forties now she'd be, I don't know, fifty, girding up her lovely little loins, getting ready for the change. . . ."[6] As she continues her laborious progress to the train station to meet her blind husband, Mrs. Rooney continually inquires about the wives, daughters, mothers of those she meets (there is an occasional father mentioned, but women relatives predominate); she receives answers such as Mr. Tyler's reply that his daughter is "Fair, fair. They removed everything, you know, the whole . . . er . . . bag of tricks. Now I am grandchildless" (p. 38). Even some of the animals heard along the way are described as sexually impaired: the play opens with references to Christie's hinny and later Mrs. Rooney speculates whether hinnies can procreate. (There are also sounds of maternity, a wooly little lamb and its mother, and references to a "true" donkey, all of which serves to emphasize the sterility of the hinny.)

The natural barrenness of women after menopause or hysterectomy is accompanied, in this play as it is in *Embers*, by suggestions of man's hatred for children. Mr. Tyler curses the "wet Saturday afternoon" of his own conception (p. 39) and Mr. Rooney raises the question, "Did you ever wish to kill a child?" (p. 74). In the context of the children's howling and jeering (pp. 74, 79), this is a question any adult might ask, but there is some indication Mr. Rooney may have acted on his impulse. He pretends not to know why the train has been delayed; he tries to prevent Jerry from telling Mrs. Rooney that "a little child fell out of the carriage, On to the line, Ma'am. *(Pause.)* Under the wheels, Ma'am" (pp. 90f). These final words provide an unusually shocking climax to the play, not only as ironic contrast to the lines from Scripture which Mrs. Rooney had sardonically quoted earlier—"The Lord upholdeth all that fall and raiseth up all those that be bowed down" (p. 88)—but also as an implied revelation about Mr. Rooney. What was he doing with the ball Jerry said he left behind on the train; had he used it to lure the child; had he taken it away from the child; did he push the child?

In this play, too, birth and death are closely related, not only by the metaphors of impaired sexuality and child murder but by even more explicit statements. Mrs. Rooney recalls the "mind doctor" whom she consulted—"hoping he might shed a little light on my lifelong preoccupation with horses' buttocks" (p. 83)—and from whom she heard the "story of a little girl, very strange and unhappy in her ways, and how he treated her unsuccessfully over a period of years and was finally obliged to give up the case. He could find nothing wrong with her, he said. The only thing wrong with her as far as he could see was that she was dying. And she did in fact die, shortly after he washed his hands of her" (p. 83). What has haunted Mrs. Rooney about this story is the Doctor's comment "as if he had had a revelation. The trouble with her was she had never been really born!" (p. 84). Rarely is Beckett as direct and obvious as he is in these early plays: "The only thing wrong with her as far as he could see was that she was dying" is a clear statement about "the human condition," as timeless as any *memento mori* of medieval devotion; "The trouble with her was she had never been really born" capsulates the state of every Beckettian character, whose partial life is a living death. Mrs. Rooney's concern with forms of sterility and frustrated procreation and Mr. Rooney's desires to "nip some young doom in the bud" (p. 74) fit into the larger context of the fact that all living beings must die and thus their lives are never fully alive because of this shadow of death. This fact, in turn, has its larger, "cosmic" context in the premise of a benevolent God who watches over all life protectively, a premise Mr. and Mrs. Rooney find laughable. Thus they, too, are "all alone in that great empty house" (p. 87) of their world, "destroyed [as Mrs. Rooney says of herself] with sorrow and pining and gentility and church-going and fat and rheumatism and childlessness" (p. 37). They are not themselves children of a heavenly father nor are they parents of a solacing child: "It's like the sparrows, than many of which we are of more value, they weren't sparrows at all" (p. 86). This play, too, ends with Henry's comforting and tormenting "nothing."

In *Endgame* (1957), a long one-act for the stage, there is no mention of abortion, hysterectomy, sterilization, or similar impairment; instead, the play, like the fictional piece *First Love,* emphasizes the fear that procreation will succeed and an ancillary disgust with the consequent burden of life. Clov, for example, says he has been trying "to be off," to die, ever since he was "whelped";7 Hamm calls his father "accursed progenitor" (p. 9) and later asks angrily why Nagg engendered him (p. 49). Both Hamm and Clov are grotesquely concerned lest further procreation occur: they want to kill the flea so that humanity won't start all over again (p. 33); and at the end of the play they worry that the small boy on the horizon is "a potential procreator" (p. 78).

This desire to "end"—not only Hamm's individual existence but that of all living things—is not merely an expression of generalized *Angst* but has more specific connection with the parent-child relationships in the play: a missing, negligent father stands at the center of Hamm's experience of loss and constitutes a mutilation of his life equivalent to the physical excisions mentioned in *Embers* and *All That Fall.* The importance of the absent father is established throughout the play by the contrast between the story Hamm tells and his own actual relationship with his father. Hamm's "chronicle" deals with a wasted world in which there are, apparently, only a few people still alive. A man comes crawling out of the devastation to beg food for his dying son; Hamm tries to persuade this man to abandon his son, then to enter Hamm's service (where, presumably, there will be food and shelter); in both versions of the story (pp. 52-54, 59-60) the man asks instead to bring his son with him to share these benefits. This refusal of father to abandon son haunts Hamm; it is one of the last things he talks about before achieving his own end:

> You don't want to abandon him? You want him to bloom while you are withering? Be there to solace your last million last moments?
> *(Pause.)*
> He doesn't realize, all he knows is hunger, and cold, and death to crown it all. But you! You ought to know what the earth is like, nowadays. Oh I put him before his responsibilities! (p. 83)

Hamm's "beneficent" argument tries to establish that it would be better for the child to die since life in the world is miserable, but his terms "bloom" and "withering" betray the real envy age has of youth. As a deteriorating adult, Hamm resents the vigor and potential of childhood. But even more he resents and envies the devotion of this father to this son because it represents a loving care Hamm himself never experienced yet still yearns for. In an attempt to establish his independence, Hamm boasts not having had a father (p. 38), but later in the play he acknowledges Nagg and even tells him the story of devoted father and needy son (pp. 48ff). At the end of this narration Hamm insists they pray: Nagg begins, "Our Father, which art" but after several intervening lines Hamm comments, "The bastard! He doesn't exist!" (p. 55). And, indeed, for Hamm a powerful and loving father never has existed, and that is why his life appears a wasteland which no amount of fantasy can alter.

Nagg's memories indicate the extent of Hamm's paternal deprivation: "Whom did you call when you were a tiny boy, and were frightened, in the dark? Your mother? No. Me. We let you cry. Then we moved you out of earshot, so that we might sleep in peace" (p. 56). Nagg goes on to criticize the way Hamm treats him now when their roles of dependency are reversed: "I was asleep, as happy as a king, and you woke me up to have me listen to you. It wasn't indispensable, you didn't really need to have me listen to you" (p. 56). But, of course, that is exactly what Hamm needs. He has never gotten over being a frightened child in the dark, with Nagg his "only hope." So now, when he wants to feel powerful, he plays the role of tyrant father, withholding comfort from all his "sons" (dependent Nagg, adopted Clov, suppliant beggars and dogs). And when he wants to end, to die, he simply imagines that frightening double role, the weak child neglected by his powerful father, the aged father neglected by his adult son (p. 69). Hamm calls to them both, father and son, and they do not answer. Thus he is once more, at the end of his life, "a solitary child" afraid, in the dark (p. 70), the dark which is death. By terminating himself, Hamm kills both the negligent father (whom he hates and has become) and the helpless child (whom he once was and now resents). Here, too, as in *Embers,* both parent and child are "better off dead." The play ends as it began, with Hamm's reference to the "old stancher," a final ironic play on words: the primary loyalty of blood relationships is destroyed; parents and children have cut each other out of their lives. Only the rag that binds the wound remains.

In *Happy Days* (1961), one of Beckett's few full-length dramas, physical action is almost entirely absent; and as a result the single strenuous bodily movement which finally occurs constitutes a release of tension, a welcome climax in an otherwise rigid and stifling day. Appropriately enough, this climactic event is a parody of sexual intercourse and as such serves to connect elements in the play which otherwise seem to be unrelated. Here, too, as in *Embers, All That Fall,* and *Endgame,* Beckett is concerned with impaired sexuality. Yes, it is certainly true that—as Hugh Kenner has commented—*Happy Days* presents "an emptiness filled by indomitable energy"[8] and that in some general way the play has to do with a perhaps futile attempt to find, or make, meaning in an absurd world; but more than that, the play deals quite specifically with sexual disability, its cause and its result.

The principal image of sexual disability is Winnie's physical immobilization. For the whole of Act I she is "imbedded up to above her waist" in earth, which she calls that "old extinguisher."[9] That it is sexuality which has been extinguished is indicated by the anecdote about Mr. and Mrs. Shower, by her comments on the dirty postcard, and by her repeated references to hog setae. As she chatters to herself she recounts the remarks made by the last people to see her, Mr. and Mrs. Shower: "What's the idea? he says—stuck up to her diddies in the bleeding ground—coarse fellow—What does it mean? he says— What's it meant to mean?" (p. 43). This question finds the beginning of an answer in his further suggestion: "Why doesn't he get her out? he says—referring to you [Willie] my dear— What good is she to him like that?—What good is he to her like that?—and so on—usual tosh." When this "coarse fellow" asserts that he would dig her out even with his bare hands, Winnie assumes the couple are man and wife. This connection indicates that what is lost by Winnie's burial is not merely physical mobility (for that, a friend or relative might dig one out), but access to sexual organs: Winnie is no good, as a wife, to Willie, nor is Willie any good as a husband while she is buried up to her waist; a real man, a coarse fellow, would dig her out even with his bare hands.

That Willie leaves her where she is because of his own sexual disability is suggested by the incident of the postcard and the hog setae. Throughout the first part of Act I Winnie has, with great comic difficulty, been struggling to read the words inscribed on her hairbrush; her eventual triumph—"fully guaranteed genuine pure hog's setae"—occurs while Willie relishes a postcard which Winnie judges to be "genuine pure filth" (p. 19). She rejects the pornographic picture and returns to her intellectual pursuits, wondering for the rest of the act about the meaning of the word "hog" (and not, as one might expect, about the presumably more obscure word "setae"). A climax for these apparently unrelated details occurs at the end of Act I when Willie finally speaks to her, announcing the definition of "hog" to be "castrated male swine" (p. 47); thus the one thing he chooses to say makes explicit yet another image of sexual impairment. Whether from some actual physical incapacity of his own or simply from Winnie's rejection of "filth," Willie, too, is associated with sexual deprivation.

Winnie remains buried, refusing to notice her loss. The mechanism of denial by which she copes with sexual deprivation is indicated by a remark she makes in Act I: "And should one day the earth cover my breasts, then I shall never have seen my breasts, no one ever have seen my breasts" (p. 38). Thus because they cannot now be seen, her nether regions have in effect never existed. When in Act II the earth indeed covers her breasts as she stands buried up to her neck, all her sexuality is lost except for fantasy and memory, all her physical fire extinguished.

As is usual in Beckett's drama, fantasy and memory (anecdotes and stories the characters recount) are crucial elements in establishing the coherence of the play as a whole. In addition to the anecdote about Mr. and Mrs. Shower (or Cooker, Winnie isn't sure of the name) who comment on her useless buried state, Winnie also enlivens her daily monologue with a series of literary allusions, with memories of her first love, her first kiss, her courtship by Willie, but most important, with her story, "when all else fails" (p. 54). The literary allusions serve as ironic counterpoint to Winnie's reliance on language as a substitute for "life" and her determined optimism in the presence of ultimate disaster (her comic pleasure in quotations containing the word "woe"; her eager association with the blighted loves of Ophelia and Juliet). The various memories also serve a similar ironic function. Most revealing, however, is the story Winnie tells herself, which, like the Holloway-Bolton story in

Embers, serves to focus the various sexual references in the play on death, not life, establishing once again Beckett's repeated emphasis on impaired reproductivity. The story concerns a little girl, Milly, who gets up early and begins to undress her doll (Milly, it would seem, herself sleeps naked since one of Winnie's corrections in her narrative involves backtracking to add that Milly "slipped on her nightgown," p. 55). As Winnie gets to the description of undressing the doll, with its associations of surreptitiousness and wickedness ("crept under the table," "scolding her") she mentions a mouse and for some reason begins to feel uneasy, leaving the narrative and calling on Willie for attention. He, as usual, ignores her, so she begins a long digression, including reference to sadness after song (less explicable to her than sadness after intimate sexual intercourse, which she takes for granted), and another reference to Mr. Shower and her own buried legs; then, after it becomes apparent Willie is not going to reply to her repeated call for help, she suddenly plunges back into her narrative at the point where she had abandoned it, describes the mouse running up Mildred's thigh, imitates her piercing screams, and lists all the family members who came running to see "what on earth could possibly be the matter." But they arrive "Too late. *(Pause.)* Too late" (p. 59). The story itself is innocent enough, quite general in its description of a childhood terror; what makes it seem fraught with special meaning is its association with the various sexual references in the digression and the concern with nakedness and surreptitiousness in the narrative itself. Whatever "up her little thigh" means to Winnie (whose legs are fully protected), it is clear that something terrible has happened, something irrevocable. Winnie's only solace after this ritualistic reliving of an intense and climactic moment, is to comment that "it can't be long now, until the bell for sleep. *(Pause.)* Then you may close your eyes, then you *must* close your eyes—and keep them closed. *(Pause.)* Why say that again?" (p. 59). Why, indeed, except that a return to buried sleep is the only refuge from the dangers to which little Milly's thigh so fatally awoke. Sexual disability is safer than sexual activity.

In real life, outside her story, Winnie has avoided sexual activity by immobility and by choosing a man who she knows will fail. This fact, and its association of sexuality with death, is most explicit in the final, culminating scene. Immediately after Winnie ends her narrative and begins a coda of miscellaneous memories, Willie finally emerges from behind the mound and begins to advance toward her on all fours. After so much visual tedium, this physical action shocks the audience: something, at last, is about to "happen." According to Beckett's stage directions, Willie is "dressed to kill" (p. 61): dressed up in "top hat, morning coat, striped trousers, etc." but also ready for physical violence. After taunting him ("Reminds me of the day you came whining for my hand") and encouraging him ("Come on dear"), Winnie asks an important question: "Is it a kiss you're after, Willie . . . or is it something else?" (p. 63). The "something else" is, of course, that "revolver conspicuous to her right on mound" (p. 49). Is it murder or love he is after? The question is never answered because Willie does not complete his climb; the play ends with a tableau of the two of them looking at each other. What is important dramatically is not the actual answer but the charge of emotion this potential violence (either murderous or erotic) gives to the climax of the play. Once again Willie has come courting, once again he approaches her mound, her *mons veneris;* in surprised excitement she gleefully urges him to "put a bit of jizz"[10] into his efforts, but now, as in the past, he fails: "There was a time when I could have given you a hand. *(Pause.)* And then a time before that again when I did give you a hand. *(Pause.)* You were always in dire need of a hand, Willie" (p. 63). Her psychological/sexual put-down sends him slithering "back to foot of mound," and once again sexuality is rendered impotent and grotesque, the man grovelling, the woman buried. Winnie's fear of the mouse running up her thigh and Willie's lack of "jizz" constitute mutual sexual disability which results in that barren mound in which Winnie lives, rigid and extinguished, a state even more fatal than the death, the revolver Willie cannot reach.

Although Beckett's later plays have gotten progressively briefer and more elusive, even they contain specific references to impaired sexuality or to birth as a particularly damaging and disgusting event.[11] In *Theatre II* there are the "five or six miscarriages which clouded . . . the early days of our union" and the resultant avoidance of "anything remotely resembling the work of love" (pp. 86f) and later in that same piece the anecdote of the man who accidentally shot off his own genitals (p. 98). *Radio I* concludes with elliptical reference to difficult

birth: "a confinement? . . . *(long pause)* . . . two confinements?
. . . *(long pause)* . . . one what? . . . what? . . . breech? . . .
what? . . ." (p. 112). *Radio II* contains repeated reference to
Caesarean delivery, but in this piece the pregnant person is a
man who feels he carries his brother inside him, his twin: "Have
yourself opened, Maud would say, opened up, it's nothing, I'll
give him suck if he's still alive . . ." (p. 121). Another character
interprets and justifies this bizarre situation of the pregnant
male: "No, no, such things happen, such things happen. Nature,
you know . . . *(Faint laugh.)* Fortunately. A world without
monsters, just imagine! *(Pause for imagining.)*" (p. 123). The
most disgusting image of birth in Beckett's later plays occurs
in *That Time* when the central male character talks to himself
about various stages in his life and remembers his most important turning point as his birth itself: "that time curled up
worm in slime when they lugged you out and wiped you off and
straightened you up . . ." (pp. 31f). Here, however, birth has
not led to personal identity; in this same passage the character
berates himself: "for God's sake did you ever say I to yourself
in your life . . ." (p. 31). The question is a crucial one because
it connects the failure of life with the failure of birth (as Beckett
had earlier done in Mrs. Rooney's story of the little girl who
"had never been really born" and, in fact, as he has been doing
in all his work since *Proust* [1931], where it is suggested that
gravesheets ought to serve as swaddling-clothes12).

   In *That Time* the question is answered only implicitly, but
in a related play, *Not I,* Beckett shows dramatically what happens to a person who never says "I" to himself or herself, and
he makes clear that such failure is a function of impaired or
deficient birth, of the child's coming "out . . . into this world . . .
before its time . . . " (p. 14). In this short monologue a seventy-
year-old woman, who has probably had a stroke but whose
brain and mouth continue to function, remembers her loveless
life. The significant stage direction for this female character is
her "vehement refusal to relinquish third person" (p. 14). As
she repetitively recounts her miserable existence, abandoned by
her parents, reared in an orphanage, cynical of benevolence,
haunted by guilt, silent and shamed by her few attempts to
communicate—a woman utterly bereft—it is apparent to the
audience that hers is a life deserving tears; yet she boasts of not
crying since birth. As she struggles to understand her life, to

find what it is in her present unchecked flow of language that she must tell, it is clear that her real tragedy is her own refusal to say "I," that is, her insistence on keeping herself remote, not letting herself feel, seeing herself as "she": "tiny little thing . . . out before its time . . . godforsaken hole . . . no love" (p. 22). Who is this, calling for attention and release, who is this whose only cry was a birth cry and who has not allowed herself further expression since emerging from that godforsaken hole, the womb of her damaging mother: "who? . . . no! . . . she! . . . SHE! . . ." And so the evasion continues, "Not I," the ultimate assertion of self-annihilation.

In the play *That Time* love is described as something "just made up," a contrivance to keep the shroud of death away (p. 31), but there, too, as in so many other plays, the real remedy for the damage of birth is "never having been" (p. 33). Similar ideas are advanced in Beckett's later fictional pieces. In *The Lost Ones,* for example, sexuality is shown as merely a futile attempt at "making unmakable love."[13] It is significant that the only extended description of human interaction in this fairly recent "story" involves grotesque attempts at copulation; the event occurs in a passage describing "the effect of this climate" upon the skin:

> This desiccation of the envelope robs nudity of much of its charm as pink turns grey and transforms into a rustling of nettles the natural succulence of flesh against flesh. The mucous membrane itself is affected which would not greatly matter were it not for its hampering effect on the work of love. But even from this point of view no great harm is done so rare is erection in the cylinder. It does occur none the less followed by more or less happy penetration in the nearest tube. Even man and wife may sometimes be seen in virtue of the law of probabilities to come together again in this way without their knowledge. The spectacle then is one to be remembered of frenzies prolonged in pain and hopelessness long beyond what even the most gifted lovers can achieve in camera. For male or female all are acutely aware how rare the occasion is and how unlikely to recur. But here too the desisting and deathly still in attitudes verging at times on the obscene whenever the vibrations cease and for as long as this crisis lasts. Stranger still at such times all the questing eyes that suddenly go still and fix their stare on the void or on some old abomination as for instance other eyes and then the long looks exchanged by those fain to look away. Irregular intervals of such length separate these lulls that for forgetters the likes of these each is the first.

Whence invariably the same vivacity of reaction as to the end
of a world and the same brief amaze when the twofold storm
resumes and they start to search again neither glad nor even
sorry. (pp. 53-55)

The very length of this passage is significant in showing how
even in his later highly-condensed fiction Beckett's reference to
grotesque and futile sexual activity is described much more
elaborately than in the plays. But the meaning is the same. In
the Dantean hell of *The Lost Ones,* the way out to "the sun
and other stars" (p. 18) is only available "prior to never having
been" (p. 19)—yet another of those neat temporal impossibili-
ties that so abound in Beckett's work. Here, in recent fiction,
as well as in the recent plays, death *before* life provides the only
effective deliverance from pain. And here, too, the metaphor
that best expresses this pain and its futility is grotesque, impaired
sexuality with its occasional unhappy result of damaging birth.

Character after character in Beckett's plays and fiction finds
himself or herself pursued through life by the terrible cry of
birth, and—like the reluctant father in *First Love*—feels "all
that matters is that it should cease."[14] But unfortunately that
cry persists; the slime of birth clings. The only real solution is
"panhysterectomy," forestalling the cry, defeating sexuality altogether by removing beforehand those reproductive organs
which one embarrassed character has called "the whole . . . er
. . . bag of tricks." And if that fails, then "abort, abort."

Boston College

NOTES

1 Samuel Beckett, *First Love and Other Shorts* (New York: Grove Press, 1974),
p. 34.

2 Samuel Beckett, *Watt* (New York: Grove Press, 1959), pp. 139-42.

3 Samuel Beckett, *Molloy, Malone Dies, The Unnamable* (New York: Grove
Press, 1965), p. 323.

4 See also the many abortion references throughout the trilogy identified in the
previous note, especially that in *Molloy,* p. 18.

5 Samuel Beckett, *Krapp's Last Tape and Other Dramatic Pieces* (New York:
Grove Press, 1960), p. 119.

6 Ibid., p. 42.

7 Samuel Beckett, *Endgame* (New York: Grove Press, 1958), p. 14.

8 *A Reader's Guide to Samuel Beckett* (New York: Farrar, Straus, and Giroux, 1973), p. 152.

9 Samuel Beckett, *Happy Days* (New York: Grove Press, 1961), p. 37.

10 As well as meaning "vigor; speed; animation; excitement" (as in the sentence "put a little jism into it"); "jism" also has the taboo meaning, semen. See Harold Wentworth and Stuart Berg Flexner, *Dictionary of American Slang* (New York: Thomas Y. Crowell, 1960), p. 292.

11 Samuel Beckett, *Ends and Odds* (New York: Grove Press, 1976); all quotations in the next two paragraphs are from this volume.

12 Samuel Beckett, *Proust* (New York: Grove Press, 1957), p. 8.

13 Samuel Beckett, *The Lost Ones* (New York: Grove Press, 1972), p. 37.

14 Beckett, *First Love*, p. 36.

Krapp's Last Tape and Critical Theory

SueEllen Campbell

If "literary theory is a literary genre . . . interrelated with other genres in terms of parts and methods, and . . . analyzable with them as a member of a group, movement, or period,"[1] then we ought to be able to discover in a fictional work relations with theory contemporary to it. My argument is that we can; my example is Beckett's *Krapp's Last Tape*. Krapp—author, editor and actor—is a sort of literary Jack-of-all-trades; his tapes and taping are paradigmatic literary products and processes. Consequently, the play's complexities—its elaborate layering and mixing of genres, time-frames, and points-of-view—offer abundant material for such an analysis. Looking carefully at the play, we will find thematic and structural parallels to several major issues addressed by twentieth-century critical theory: the nature of genres, the characteristics of literary and non-literary language, the importance of history in interpretation, and the role of readers and critics as creators of a work's meaning through interpretation and evaluation.

I

As a play, *Krapp's Last Tape* shares the basic formal ambiguity of all dramas: it is at once a text to be read and reread and a guide for live performance. While to a theater-goer this duality might not seem important, a reader of this text constantly realizes the contrasts between performance and text and their interdependence. Indeed, the reader's awareness of a potential performance partially constitutes the text's meaning; if we are to make any sense of the play, we must read with especially active visual imaginations. Stage directions comprise almost a third of the text—explicit directions which prescribe even the length in seconds of some of Krapp's silences. Many of these are naively descriptive: rather than directing Krapp to drink a bottle of beer in the dark, the text describes the noises we would hear—corks popping, liquids pouring, glass clattering—were we watching a performance. Not only must we imagine Krapp's appearance, surroundings, and movements as we might Lear's or Hamlet's, but we must also imagine ourselves watching an actual performance in which perception depends equally on sight and sound.

As in other modern plays (Ionesco's *The Chairs,* for example), the non-linguistic stage activity in *Krapp's Last Tape* is substantive: Krapp's nearsighted fumbling with drawers, tapes, and bananas, his ramblings and pauses, and his alcoholic forays into the darkness surrounding his brightly lit desk comprise the largest part of the performance and flesh out the play's linguistic skeleton. Thus, while reading, we rely on imagination for the visual and auditory stimulation the text cannot provide; we always realize that our experience necessarily differs from that of a performance's audience. While we can envision Krapp slipping on a banana peel, we know that the joke is essentially a sight-gag: watching the play we would laugh; reading it we only imagine laughing. And while we tend to forget Krapp's comically grotesque appearance as we read the words he speaks and hears, we could not, watching, ignore the juxtaposition of his extreme physical decrepitude with the intellectual vitality displayed by his tapes. *Krapp's Last Tape* emphasizes the visualizing that is a normal part of the reading process; the contrast between reading and watching becomes part of our conscious experience of the text.

As we recognize that our experience of *Krapp's Last Tape* mediates between read text and imagined performance, we begin also to recognize the play's exploration and exploitation of other generic ambiguities. If, for instance, we were to consider it from the perspective of Georg Lukács' idiosyncratic but suggestive 1916 genre definitions, we should have to call Beckett's play a novel or a lyric. Making his distinctions on the basis of a work's ontological concerns, Lukács explains that in drama and epic there is "nothing of the passage of time, they allow of no qualitative difference between the experiencing of past and present; time has no power of transformation, it neither intensifies nor diminishes the meaning of anything."[2] Rather, "only in the novel and in certain epic forms resembling the novel does memory occur as a creative force affecting the object and transforming it"(127). That these statements do not describe this play about the effects of time and memory on personality not only illustrates the limitations of Lukács' genre distinctions but also suggests the formal and generic ambiguities in *Krapp's Last Tape*. For the play is multi-generic; elements of other literary forms are woven into its traditional dramatic structure.

When we realize that a performance would ease the task of separating the words of the taped Krapp from those of the taping Krapp, we become aware of the peculiar fact that the play has both one and many characters. Both monologue and dialogue, it fulfills our traditional dramatic expectations only in part. Again Lukács illuminates the situation: "But a paradox attaches to loneliness in drama. Loneliness is the very essence of tragedy . . . yet the dramatic form of expression—the dia-logue—presupposes, if it is to be many-voiced, truly dialogical, dramatic, a high degree of communion among these solitaries. The language of the absolutely lonely man is lyrical, i.e. mono-logical . . . Such loneliness is not simply the intoxication of a soul gripped by destiny and so made song; it is also the torment of a creature condemned to solitude and devoured by a long-ing for community"(45). The interplay between monologue and dialogue, or, in Lukács' terms, lyric and drama, not only parallels structurally the thematic concern with Krapp's changes in personality and perspective, but also both creates and em-bodies the play's peculiarly intense loneliness. We see Krapp at the end of a life-long effort to transcend his own solitude through communication, to establish some kind of community, even if only with his own changing self; but his aloneness has remained absolute, and even his dialogue with his tapes remains irremediably one-sided. Following Lukács, we might even call *Krapp's Last Tape* the quintessential tragedy, for by using two voices that are in many respects indistinguishable, Beckett re-tains the dramatic form without sacrificing the tragic and lyric force of monologue.

Yet to call this play tragic is to ignore its evident comic aspects. Finally, whether we call it a tragedy or a comedy will depend primarily upon our *interpretation* of Krapp's activity as success or failure. The question is this: has Krapp wanted to find patterns of stability in his life; or, rather, has he wanted to find meaning in change itself? If we believe that his long separ-ating of the grains of his experience from the husks has been

motivated by his desire to transcend mutability, then we will
see his perennial dissatisfaction with his past efforts and final
abandoning of his last tape as evidence of failure. His tapes
have not succeeded in preserving meaning through change; the
only patterns we can discern are the absurdly trivial ones of
bananas, liquor, a penchant for women's eyes. From this perspective, the identity that the tapes preserve is unalterably a
collection of discrete descriptions. As Gaston Bachelard writes
in a completely different context, "In the theater of the past
that is constituted by memory, the stage setting maintains the
characters in their dominant rôles. At times we think we know
ourselves in time, when all we know is a sequence of fixations
in the spaces of the being's stability—a being who does not
want to melt away, and who, even in the past, when he sets out
in search of things past, wants time to 'suspend' its flight."[3]

On the other hand, if we believe that underlying Krapp's
endeavors has been the awareness that change is the very essence
of experience, then we will see his tapes as an exploration of
the effects of time and a gradual acceptance of impermanence.
From this perspective, Krapp learns *not* to wish for "time to
'suspend' its flight"; instead, he comes to accept the uncertainty
of flux. The inexplicable endurance of his experience on the
punt, his "farewell to love," is an unexpected triumph: the
wonder is not that so little remains to Krapp, but that anything
remains. Our choice between these alternative interpretations—
or our refusal to make a choice—will inform our sense of the
play as tragic or comic as much as our generic labelling will
influence our interpretation. Again, the ambiguities (and arbitrariness) of these generic categories parallel the play's ambiguities of meaning.

Perhaps the most interesting aspect of the problem of genre
in *Krapp's Last Tape*, like this interplay between the tragic and
the comic, is as much thematic as structural. For Krapp's tapes
constitute an autobiography of sorts, and his situation reflects
the special questions raised by the relationship of this to other
literary forms. Autobiography notoriously traps those who would
distinguish literary from nonliterary language because of its
complicated mingling of fact and fiction. In this play, the difficulty increases with the biography's own dramatic fictionality.
Like many other modern works, this play exploits the possibility of layering genres, of emphasizing the artist's manipula-

tive power by exponentially increasing a work's fictionality.

While we may sense that Krapp has in places deliberately manipulated his language for aesthetic effect, we find that we cannot give rigorous evidence to support our impression. When he describes on tape his night on the jetty (". . . unshatterable association until my dissolution of storm and night with the light of the understanding and the fire"4) or the ball symbolizing his mother's death ("In the end I held it out to him and he took it in his mouth, gently, gently. A small, old, black, hard, solid rubber ball"[20]), he seems to depart from ordinary vocabulary and syntax; we may even interpret his later impatience with these passages as a rejection of their purple rhetoric. But we must also recognize that not all of the language on the earlier tapes is equally decorative or metaphoric, that even on his last tape are semantic and syntactic excesses ("Everything there, everything on this old muckball, all the light and dark and famine and feasting of . . . the ages!" [24], and that Krapp apparently has a habit of playing with words which is indistinguishable from the playing on the tapes. Of the few things he says in the play that are not to be taped, at least two bear witness to an unmotivated love of words: he "relishes" "vidua-bird" and "revels" in "spool," calling his moment of linguistic delight the "happiest moment of the past half million" (13, 18, 25). And the crowning complication, of course, is that from *our* perspective, all of Krapp's statements, taped or untaped, are identically literary insofar as they are all part of the play. Just as Gide experiments in *The Counterfeiters* with Chinese boxes of fact and fiction—real and imagined journals, real and imagined novels, real and imagined autobiographical elements in those novels—so too Beckett layers fact and fiction, drama and autobiography, history and imaginative narrative, literary and ordinary language.

But the autobiographical nature of the tapes does more than reveal the qualities of the play's language; it also determines its structure. As Francis Hart points out, "the relation between the autobiographer and his personal, historical subject . . . has several elements," all of which influence narrative and dramatic form:

> To seek the personal focus of an autobiographical truth is to inquire what kind of "I" is selected, how far the selected "I" is an inductive invention and how far an intentional creation,

and whether one single or one multiple "I" persists throughout the work. Moreover, the autobiographer's relation to the
pastness or historicity of his selected "I" involves his sense and
manipulation of the problem of continuity and discontinuity of
identity and perspective. Again, perspective implies access, and
the autobiographer's limited and erratic access to the past and
present of that ambiguous "I" implies the problem of the form
and authority of personal memory.[5]

Evidence of Beckett's concern with these problems abounds.
The device of annual tapes itself attempts to regularize or ob-
jectify memory: Krapp says, for example, "This I fancy is what
I have chiefly to record this evening, against the day when my
work will be done and perhaps no place left in my memory,
warm or cold for the miracle that . . . for the fire that set it
alight"(20-21). And his regular reviewing of his earlier tapes
questions the "I" he has been presenting, the truth of his recorded memories and judgments, and his continuity or discontinuity with this autobiographical figure. Thus he comments,
"hard to believe I was ever as bad as that"(24), and detects a
"false ring" in his earlier "Sneers at what he calls his youth and
thanks to God that it's over"(17).

Structurally, these autobiographical problems motivate the
play's temporal patterns. As Hart says, "every autobiography
necessarily moves on 'two temporal planes' juxtaposed, narrative past and dramatic present"(226); *Krapp's Last Tape,*
characteristically, exploits this necessity and operates on as many
as five explicit levels of time. The primary pattern of relationships is one of embedding, complicated by the facts that each
level is simultaneously narrative and dramatic, and that each
relates with the others both by historical influence and by the
alternating focus of the play. At the center of the pattern is
Krapp's past, recorded on two tapes, one from his late twenties
and one from his thirty-ninth birthday. The former is summarized and criticized on the latter, which dominates the language
of the play; much of Krapp's activity consists of listening to this
tape and remembering the events it records. Moreover, because
he has made a tape on every birthday for many years, these two
levels imply over forty other past times: we assume the existence of other tapes similar to those we hear.

The third level, of course, is Krapp's present, his sixty-ninth
birthday. Although this time occupies less of the spoken dialogue
than do the two old tapes, it is emphasized in the stage direc-

tions and in performance by the silent action, which establishes a distinct kind of reality for the present. The past is circumscribed entirely by language—the words on the tape—but the present is defined by the slow, tedious, meaningless motions and mutterings of the old man. Furthermore, Krapp at sixty-nine controls our knowledge of the two enclosed times: by editing the tape as he plays it, he limits the information we receive. This power is most obvious in his refusal to listen to the full account of his "memorable" experience on the jetty; here, his seemingly arbitrary cutting of the narrative allows us to hear only fragments of what we are led to expect to be an important passage. Thus this third layer controls as well as encloses the first two. But it is also, though less conspicuously, controlled by them, insofar as Krapp at sixty-nine is influenced by his past. Just as he moves on stage between light and dark, so the dialogue and the audience's attention move between Krapp and his tapes, and so, too, Krapp's thoughts characteristically move between his present existence and his memories. In a sense, his listening to the birthday tapes only exemplifies his continual reminiscing. He goes to church, for instance, because he went when he was a child; and, as he goes to sleep, he amuses himself with memories of his happier days. The words in which he speaks of this activity make especially clear its importance: "Be again, be again. . . . Once wasn't enough for you"(26-27). Krapp does not just remember; he re-lives his past.

Less apparent than Krapp's past and present times is the fourth temporal layer: the sense of future implied by the stage direction setting the play during "a late evening in the future." This direction, first, frustrates our expectations by reversing the usual setting of plays in the past. We expect only works which are identifiably fantastic—science fiction, for instance—to occur in the future; here, though, the relative realism of the situation forces us to search for either a technological explanation (i.e., when the play was written, the tape recorder had not existed for the necessary forty years) or a symbolic one. Second, the direction extends the tape sequence into the future. Despite our knowledge that the number of tapes is finite and our impression that the current tape will end the series, the future setting, like the implied existence of other past tapes, suggests that the notion of annual tapes expands beyond its actual bounds.

Finally, the direction tends to divorce Krapp's time from ours: his present is in the audience's future, and so we are not allowed to assume any firm temporal relationship with the play. Because we cannot completely adjust ourselves to this situation, we become more aware of the arbitrariness, and the importance, of time divisions. Or perhaps the direction simply marks Beckett's awareness that he was writing for performances and readings in the future—both his own and that of each reader until the last. For it is our own time—that of the performance or reading—which is the play's fifth and most inclusive time-layer: just as Krapp at sixty-nine listens to the story of Krapp at thirty-nine, who listens to a still earlier recording, so the audience experiences and comprehends the play, the record of all these fictional times.

II

The function of the temporal structure in the play becomes clear when we recognize that it parallels the relationship between synchronic and diachronic orderings.[6] Insofar as each tape represents a one-year "slice of time," comprising Krapp's impressions of his life on the day of the recording and a few instants of the year which has just ended, it summarizes a year from the perspective of a moment, ordering time synchronically. (One year is synchronic relative to a lifetime; a moment is synchronic relative to a year.) Krapp's characteristic collapsing of important experiences into epiphany-like "grains" of time suitable for such a synchronic organization is evidenced by his frequent use of the significantly indeterminate time-word, "moments," rather than other words (like "minutes") suggesting a more specific duration. But this characteristic is not simply a formal strategy; more importantly, it signifies Krapp's desire to *reduce* experience to a few moments of meaning by separating the "grain" from the "husks," determining "those things worth having when all the dust has . . . settled"(14-15). Even his impatience with some of his taped epiphanies does not reject the search for lasting, momentary significance; it is still the timeless moment of his "farewell to love" which continues to stir his imagination. In this respect, Krapp's approach to his own experience is itself synchronic: each moment of significance exists without reference to past or future.

On the other hand, because each tape records a year and

the whole series records his entire adult life, Krapp's tapes also attempt to order time and experience diachronically, to record and examine the processes of change and the effects of past on present. While he may wish to isolate moments of significance, he nevertheless (and simultaneously) knows that one cannot disregard the importance of the past; consequently, each tape in some way incorporates its predecessors and marks the continuities of his life. He draws the energy to begin each tape from an earlier one, explaining, "These old P.M.s are gruesome, but I often find them . . . a help before embarking on a new . . . retrospect"(16). And each tape reevaluates his past from his new perspective, indicating his willingness to acknowledge the changes in outlook which come with time. Furthermore, as we have seen, each tape tries to create a dialogue with his earlier and later selves. Clearly, the audience for which Krapp records is his future self; he wants to replace the discontinuities of faulty memory with a more reliable diachronic description of his experiences.

We might say, then, that *Krapp's Last Tape* deals with the intersections of Krapp's synchronic and diachronic life-descriptions. What this implies for the play can be made clear by comparison with the function of the same structure in modern critical theory, where it appears consistently, if in different forms (most frequently, of course, in the works of theorists influenced by the Formalist and Structuralist adoption of linguistic schema). Because it too deals directly with problems of historical interpretation and evaluation, Hans Robert Jauss's formulation of the relation between synchrony and diachrony is perhaps the most illuminating theoretical parallel to Beckett's play. In an essay entitled "Literary History as a Challenge to Literary Theory," Jauss argues that interpretation of literature must be concerned with its "historical character," which "appears exactly at the intersection of the diachronic and synchronic approaches."[7] In this context diachronic means (in Jakobson's phrase) a series of successive synchronic descriptions.[8] Jauss proceeds by considering the critical reception of a work both when it first appears and later as its status has begun to alter with changes in the literary taste of the society. He is interested in the changing interpretations of literary works, and posits that no one reading is the correct one; rather, each interpretation displays a different meaning of the work. "A literary work," he

says, "is like an orchestration which strikes ever new chords
among its readers and which frees the text from the substance
of the words and makes it meaningful for the time: 'words
which must, at the same time that they speak to him, create an
interlocutor capable of listening' "(14). Each new reading of a
text alters our understanding of that text; each new reading
adds to our knowledge of the ways in which we read and interpret. Interpretation must, then, mediate between the past and
the present—between old ways of understanding a work and
its present meanings. "The tradition of art presupposes a dialogue between the present and the past, according to which a
past work cannot answer and speak to us until a present observer has posed the question which retrieves it from its retirement" (Jauss, 27). "Understanding," Jauss says, "is always the
process of fusion of such horizons which seem to exist inde-
pendently"(24).

The pattern Jauss describes is the same as that of Krapp's
tapes; and Krapp's responses to his earlier tapes parallel Jauss's
approach to literary criticism. That Krapp's attitude towards his
memoirs is in part that of a reader or audience is apparent, for
instance, in his repeated playings of the story of the punt: once
would suffice if the only purpose of listening were to remind
him of past incidents or to give him something about which to
comment on his new tape, but Krapp listens to the "farewell to
love" even after he has abandoned his current recording. Listening to his old tapes, he judges their value as narrative (their
"aesthetic" value) as well as their truth as history. Similarly, as
he summarizes his reactions on the new tapes, and as he edits
the tapes he plays, he judges his old statements just as a critic
judges the work he or she is reading or rereading. In Jauss's
terms, each listening is a rereading of the text, and Krapp's
response constitutes the work's critical reception at the time of
the new tape. As we have seen, Krapp's texts are explicitly a
dialogue between the past and the present. His lack of interest
in some sections, thus, results from their failure to "create an
interlocutor capable of listening," and these sections cease to
be a part of the canon available to the audience. Only Krapp's
interest in reexamining the tape of his thirty-ninth birthday
allows us to consider it at all, and we must see the contents of
that tape from the past which interest him as answers to a question which he asks in the present.

Jauss's framework also suggests a way to deal with the failure of two of the important moments on Krapp's earlier tape. "When understanding . . . is thought of as 'becoming part of a self-sufficient tradition in which the past and the present are continuously in mutual mediation,' " Jauss explains, "the 'productive moment which lies in understanding' must be short-changed. This productive function of progressive understanding, which necessarily also includes the criticizing and even forgetting of tradition, forms the basis of the aesthetics of reception"(27). Krapp's moments in the park at his mother's death and in the storm on the jetty are such moments of understanding; his continual reevaluation of experience necessarily involves forgetting and criticizing some things which he once considered important. In this light, Krapp's rejection of these youthful epiphanies is not a failure, but a necessary part of intelligent interpretation: his willingness to ignore the things which now seem of limited value indicates his openness to new understanding.

The value which Jauss sees in his approach to criticism is this: "Once the substantial conception of a self-continuing literary tradition has been replaced by a functional explanation of the process relationship of production and reception, it must be possible to see behind the transformation of literary forms and content that change of positions in a literary system of the interpretation of reality which makes the change of horizons in the process of aesthetic experience intelligible"(34). The effect of my reading of *Krapp's Last Tape* is similar: if we consider the important aspect of the play to be the assumptions and changes in assumptions which lie behind Krapp's changes in personality, then we are freed from the puzzles which arise from an interpretation more concerned with Krapp's immediate experience.

The contradiction between the last words of his thirty-ninth birthday tape and his new tape, for instance, ceases to be problematic. At thirty-nine, he says, "Perhaps my best years are gone. When there was a chance of happiness. But I wouldn't want them back"(28); when he is sixty-nine, he closes, "Be again, be again. . . . All that old misery. . . . Once wasn't enough for you. . . . Lie down across her"(26-27). These lines indicate the change in Krapp's attitude toward his past: he can now accept what he thinks is valuable in his past as an important part of his present. He begins to record his new tape with the same approach he has taken in the past—by criticizing the faults in his earlier personality and attitudes—but he realizes that he no longer wants to judge in the same way. "Everything there, everything on this old muckball, all the light and dark and famine and feasting of . . . the ages! (In a shout.) Yes! (Pause.) Let that go! . . . Ah well, maybe he was right. (Pause.) Maybe he was right"(24).

Similarly, at the end of the play—"Krapp motionless staring before him. The tape runs on in silence"—we see his implicit acceptance of his past. This final attitude echoes the moment in the punt, which may be seen as a symbolic illustration of the experience in which time is closest to standing still: "We lay there without moving. But under us all moved, and moved us, gently, up and down, and from side to side"(27). Time itself never stops, but its effect on our lives may be suspended: the water under the boat continues to move gently, and the tape continues to run, but Krapp is still and silent.

In this sense, then, for Krapp as well as for theorists like Jauss, meaning resides at the intersection of change and stability, diachrony and synchrony. This recognition illuminates the play for us. It also underlines Krapp's role as a paradigmatic audience and critic. As we realize the nature of his interpretive and evaluative activities, we understand the final and most significant connection between Krapp's layers of time and the audience's. The structure of organization we see in Krapp's tapes does not stop with the play itself; it extends into many other areas of our intellectual lives. We must ask, finally, not simply whether there are parallels between literature and theory; we must also explore the nature of these parallels. Is the relationship one of culturally shared issues and structures? If literary works somehow embody problems or aspects of human existence, then perhaps literary theory (with its strong connections with other humanistic disciplines) tries to deal intellectually with the same problems, either as they are suggested by immediate experience or as they appear in the literature on which theory is based. From this perspective, it comes as no surprise to find that many literary theorists in fact define their own activities with the same paradigm that Krapp's tapes display, as a continuing but not necessarily progressive evaluation and reevaluation of an always changing body of data. What was thirty years ago a workable and apparently accurate interpretation of experience—for all readers and critics as well as for Krapp—we must now modify in the light of our new knowledge and awareness. Like Krapp, we too are looking for an organizational structure adequate to our understanding of change.

University of Virginia

NOTES

1 Ralph Cohen, "Literary Theory as a Genre," *Centrum*, 3, No. 1 (1975), 45.

2 *The Theory of the Novel*, trans. Anna Bostock (Cambridge, Mass.: MIT Press, 1971), p. 126.

3 Gaston Bachelard, *The Poetics of Space*, trans. Maria Jolas (Boston: Beacon Press, 1969), p. 8.

4 Samuel Beckett, *Krapp's Last Tape and Other Dramatic Pieces* (New York: Grove Press, 1960), p. 21.

5 "Notes for an Anatomy of Modern Autobiography," in *New Directions in Literary History*, ed. Ralph Cohen (Baltimore: Johns Hopkins Univ. Press, 1974), p. 228.

6 I use these terms as names for two ways of organizing or looking at historical developments. They are heuristic devices rather than mutually exclusive categories.

7 "Literary History as a Challenge to Literary Theory," in *New Directions in Literary History*, p. 33.

8 Roman Jakobson, "Linguistics and Poetics," in *The Structuralists From Marx to Lévi-Strauss*, ed. Richard and Fernande DeGeorge (New York: Doubleday, 1972), p. 88.

Genet's *The Blacks* and *The Screens:*
Dialectic of Refusal and
Revolutionary Consciousness

W. F. Sohlich

Genet's first three plays are dramatizations of his personal adventures. *Deathwatch* and *The Maids* permit only the staging of an abbreviated version of the scandalous chronicle of his life because their form is neo-classical. *The Balcony,* which is a chronicle, presents the significant stations of his journey completely. The anti-heroes of all three plays pursue essentially the same adventure and make similar moral choices. So much so that Joseph Campbell's description of the epic quest, when turned upside down, might serve as a workable definition of the action of the plays. The anti-hero ventures forth from the order of the bourgeois state into the underworld of pariahs and felons. Fabulous forces are there encountered and a decisive defeat is won. The anti-hero comes back from his mysterious adventure with the power to avenge himself on the bourgeois state and the society of reprobates whom he rejects because they rejected him.[1]

Lefranc *(Deathwatch)* excludes himself from the order of the bourgeois state by committing a petty theft for which he is sent to prison. By rejecting a moral order founded on the imperative of work and inviolable property rights, he enters into the wondrous world of criminals. He will ultimately refuse their world as well by murdering the cowardly Maurice. His odious deed neither impresses the criminals nor the guard, and as a result he fails to define himself as the avenger he wanted to be for others. Humiliated and despised, he merely succeeds in making his solitude incommunicable. Solange and Claire *(The Maids)* follow the quest to completion. They are nameless housemaids who must endure the moral condemnation of their employer for performing what is considered demeaning work according to the moral code of the bourgeoisie.2 They perform their rites of double separation from their masters and from their nameless condition as servants-objects by choosing a life of crime. The attempted betrayal of Monsieur fails; but when Solange kills Claire who plays the role of Madame, the ritualistic murder of Madame and the real murder of Claire abolish both terms of the manichean master-slave system. The maids are initiated into the annals of crime as murderess and victim, and society is compelled to recognize them as Mlle. Solange Lemercier and Mlle. Claire Lemercier during the ensuing trial and conviction. With *The Balcony* Genet finally succeeds in giving shape to his passage from the moral solitude of the social outcast to the moral solitude of the damned poet. The quest is staged by means of three surrogate figures: the tramp, the beggar, and the slave. The acts which each of these characters performs pertain to a single adventure in the course of which the anti-hero separates himself from the bourgeois state, causes a workers' revolution to fail by betraying it, and returns from his mysterious adventure as the avenging poet.

The pattern of exclusion which the action of these plays traces clearly gives evidence of an anarchistic but non-revolutionary consciousness.3 For the exclusion from one system of values is inevitably doubled by a rejection either of its underside or, in *The Balcony,* of its opposite. In each case the anti-hero practices his solemn rites of auto-excommunication from social systems which are dominated by the imperative of production and where the moral perception of the other is sustained by ideologies which exclude those who commit crimes against property, those who perform menial labor, or those who do not work at all. While the anti-hero crosses the frontiers of the bourgeois and the workers' state, he consistently refuses solidarity with the heterogenous groups of disenfranchised citizens, whether they are criminals, servants, workers, or slaves.

If one can speak of a change in Genet's social awareness on the evidence of the first three plays, it is to be found in his understanding of himself as an artist in relation to society. The plays transpose his passage from the solitude of the socially undesirable to the solitude of the damned poet who is aware of his alienation and engages in symbolic expressions of revenge against his former torturers. One might think that the intense labor of self-definition of the alien would finally sustain an ideology for political action which might effect a transformation of the political systems which Genet felt made him a pariah. In fact, his pre-occupation with the politics of third world peoples in *The Blacks* and *The Screens* bears witness to his search for political alternatives; however, absolute refusal and revolutionary consciousness coincide only in *The Blacks,* while with *The Screens* Genet proposes his definitive refusal of history.

The action of *The Blacks* may be described by using an infinitive phrase: to make communication between blacks and whites impossible. Three interrelated secondary patterns give dramatic form to the play which is performed by an all black cast. The first is the ritualistic murder of a white girl before a court of justice composed of white colonial authority figures. The ritual is performed in order to affirm the black man's hatred for the whites and to force these to condemn the blacks. The second intermediate pattern dramatizes the love relationships between Village and Virtue, Village and his white victim, and between Diouf and white people. The third intermediate pattern is roughly parallel to the first since it describes the commission of a crime, the trial, and the punishment. The event is built into the play by means of the messenger Newport News. It takes place off-stage and is a political rather than a sacramental event. The determination of the relationships between these patterns constitutes the play's message.

The ritualistic murder of the white girl separates the blacks irremediably from the community of white colonials and from the system of moral and esthetic values by which the white masters define their social relation to the indigenous blacks. Frantz Fanon described eloquently how this system, created by the white conqueror, produces the concept of negro as an absolute negation of white, i.e., as a negation of value: "The colonizer is not content with declaring that values have deserted, or better, have never inhabited the world of the colonized. The indigenous person is declared impervious to ethics, absence of value, but also negation of values. In this sense he is absolute evil."[4] In the first instance it is color which defines the colonial world as a system of opposites, not economic relationships; and black actors, savages in the eyes of the whites, terrorize a cultured white audience—preferably French bourgeois who know their classics—with a savage caricature of this system.5 Negroes who are predestined to be guilty by virtue of their color reenact an odious crime because they choose to merit their condemnation; and since the white man made them savages, they negrify themselves to earn the demeaning label.

The ritual is acted out before a court of white authority figures which consists of a queen, a judge, a governor, a missionary, and a valet—played, of course, by blacks. The situation produces a discourse of absolute separation from which whites are excluded but which they must witness as a passive audience. Since the blacks create themselves as stereotypes in the image in which the whites imprisoned them—as killers, animals, prolific studs, and spontaneous exotic creatures—and return the favor by stereotyping the whites in the mold which these cast for themselves—benevolent masters and culture heroes—the dialogue becomes a series of meta-communications between false selves. The blacks did not only kill, but they did it after their fashion, savagely, as Archibald insists. Since any corpse would do for the nightly performances provided it was white, Village and Mr. Herod Adventure killed an old drunken and defenseless tramp. While Genet's characters frequently break whatever tenuous bonds they have with society by committing particularly heinous murders, their gestures are usually individual acts of rebellion. The murder committed by Village and Adventure, however, is a political act because the group requires a white corpse to assist them in their rites of negrification. Thus Snow refuses to approve their deed unless they acted for the purpose of merging with the humiliation of the group: "If I were sure that Village bumped off the woman in order to heighten the fact that he is a scarred, smelly, thicklipped, snub-nosed Negro, an eater and guzzler of Whites and all other colors, a drooling, sweating, belching, spitting, coughing, farting goat-fucker, a licker of white boots, a good-for-nothing, sick, oozing oil and sweat, limp and submissive, if I were sure he killed her in order to merge with the night. . . ."6 Murder and ritualistic murder are in themselves meaningless unless the perpetrator chooses by his act to refuse the label of negro and become a terrorizing nigger.

The exchange of the image of nigger for that of negro pertains to the dialectic of cultural revolution. Designed to terrorize the whites, the rites of negrification also incite and maintain a group feeling of rage among the blacks and thus recreate the affective conditions for revolutionary action.7 This rage is not inborn but rather initially cast upon the black man by the manichean ethics of his white masters. If he chooses to sustain it in daily rites, it is because he wants to be reminded of his humiliation, of his malediction, the negro-object which he is compelled to live. Archibald: "Be careful and choose only reasons for hatred. Keep magnifying our savageness. Be careful not to seem a wild beast. If you do, you'll tempt their desire without gaining esteem" (26). If he wishes to gain *their* esteem the black man must attempt to create an image which he himself can respect. But given his status as a negro in the social context of colonial rule where the color of his skin initially reveals to him the indelible proof of his inferiority, his personal choice is severely limited to the exaggeration and distortion of the moral and esthetic codes forced upon him. As Fanon puts it, his consciousness has to lose itself in the night of the absolute, his only condition to attain to consciousness of self.8 Viewed as a psychological problem, he must journey to the limits of humiliation, shame, and hatred before he can rise like a phoenix from his ashes. Snow says, "I've been burning for so long, burning with such ardent hatred, that I am a heap of ashes" (17). In the context of the play, this descent into hell is transitory, the root of its own destruction. It yields the vision of a society without races and the knowledge that the reification of the black man is, in the last instance, deeply rooted in economic structures, in the division between capital and labor, and in the struggle between the haves and the have-nots. Felicity: "To my rescue Negroes, all of you! . . . Tribes covered with gold and mud, rise up from my body, emerge . . . Negroes of the docks, of the factories, of the dives, Negroes of the Ford plant, Negroes of General Motors, and you too, Negroes who braid rushes to encage crickets and roses, enter and remain standing" (76). Felicity's incantation summons the hatred of Africa and of the downtrodden of the earth in order to assist Village reenact the murder of the white girl with appropriate vengeance. What makes it an important moment of the revolutionary dialectic is the shift of meaning of the concept negro from *savage* to *exploited*.

The ritualistic murder and the love relations are ultimately functions of revolutionary activities which presumably happen off-stage. In this sense both patterns are strategic ploys designed to divert a white audience from knowing what is going on until

the traitor has been executed and a new revolutionary leader
has been named. But they also stage the human drama which
preceded the revolution and justifies it, and while doing so they
demystify the relationships between colonizer and colonized
with the displacement of the terms white-negro from cultural
superstructures to economic infrastructures. Thus the blacks
who play white culture heroes demystify the idea of white
cultural supremacy. While simulating a rearguard action on the
field of culture against the lyrical terrorism of the blacks, they
manage to unmask white culture heroes as insidious exploiters.
For instance, while Village insists that he be allowed to say his
lines more spontaneously than Archibald wishes, the Governor
requests the latest market quotations on African rubber and
gold which the Queen's valet shouts out (18-19). He up-dates
quotations on coffee and gold while Village struggles to express
his ambivalent feelings of love and hatred for his white victim
during the murder ritual. In each case, the connotation of the
concept *white* shifts abruptly from civilized masters to ruthless
exploiters.

During an intensely moving scene when Village and Virtue
attempt to create a love relationship on the premise that black
is beautiful, the Queen falls asleep and dreams of Celtic remains
and the stained-glass windows of Chartres (43). During the
same scene, Virtue steals the Queen's voice by attributing to
herself the esthetic qualities of a white woman. The frightened
Queen summons to her defense the ludicrous memorabilia of a
defunct classical humanism which ignores economic relations
as determinants of cultural superstructures: "To my rescue,
angel of the flaming sword, virgins of the Parthenon, stained-
glass of Chartres, Lord Byron, Chopin, French cooking, Aristotelian principle, the Unknown Soldier, Tyrolean songs, heroic
couplets . . ." (47). The lyrical massacre of white culture heroes
coupled with the negrification of blacks constitute a ritualistic
murder-suicide, a double negation by which the blacks proclaim
their agony, debunk the moral and esthetic parameters of
colonial life, and accede to a revolutionary consciousness.

The intermediate pattern of love relations discloses the
revolutionary vision as coexistent with its own contradiction.
Unlike moral and esthetic categories, hate and love are not
emotional equivalencies of social and political apartheid. Rather,
the need of black persons to love and their inability to do so

under the gaze of the whites constitutes their private pain which makes the abolition of colonialism the absolute condition of love. Diouf's failure doubles the human failings of colonialism. He would like the ceremony to be more anodyne. Negroes should insist on their beauty rather than on their savageness and thereby sever whatever tenuous bonds they have with the whites. After years of living the inferiority which the colons projected on him, he has finally succumbed to what Bobo calls the temptation of the whites. Diouf comments: "The kindness of the white settled upon my head, as it did upon yours. Though it settled there lightly, it was unbearable. Their intelligence settled upon my right shoulder, and a whole flock of virtues on my left. And at times, when I opened my hands, I would find their charity nestling there . . ." (33).

As much as anyone else Diouf is a prisoner of the attitudes, beliefs, and prejudices which determine the limits of colonial life for the colons and indigenous alike. But he is too old and too exhausted to sustain the uncompromising hatred for the others. The poison of charity and paternalistic kindliness has effectively neutralized his sense of outrage. An eternally grateful nigger, he wishes only to reassure the whites and gain their approval with a spectacle of beautiful black Africa. His hopes are illusory because black beauty and whatever love and respect that beauty may elicit from the whites are human givens of post-revolutionary relationships.

The life of the blacks in the colonies is historically overdetermined toward an emotional stasis between love and hatred by the class *habitus,* the attitudes, dispositions, and prejudices of the dominant class. Whether he is treated charitably or becomes the object of a moral and esthetic condemnation, the black person is compelled to live the humiliation of the negro. Village recreates this humiliation with the ritualistic murder so that the group of blacks may sink collectively into abjection as the very condition of hatred—i.e., of freely chosen social and political exclusion. He lives the emotional paralysis of the black/negro and he lives it doubly, in his relation toward his white victim and in relation toward the black/negress Virtue: "When I beheld you, suddenly—for perhaps a second—I had the strength to reject everything that wasn't you, and to laugh at the illusion. But my shoulders are very frail. I was unable to bear the weight of the world's condemnation. And I began to hate you when everything about you would have kindled my love and when love would have made men's contempt unbearable, and their contempt would have made my love unbearable" (36).

It may perhaps not be entirely facetious to state axiomatically that love is a human phenomenon and not a racial one. But this need is socially inhibited by the modalities in which black/white relations are being thought. As a result, even the relations among blacks become problematic because they cannot be lived outside the colonial context where the contempt of the dominant whites for the blacks is the key structural component of the affective life of the dominated group. The fact that Virtue, in real life a prostitute who prefers to dominate her white customers sexually, cannot think of herself as beautiful (worthy of love) except by stealing the *Queen's* voice, by assimilating the *habitus* of the dominant class, is merely another disclosure of the hold which ideological superstructures have over the emotional life of blacks.

The ceremony is designed to break this hold by summoning and sustaining the hatred of blacks for whites. Yet Village's role reveals the extent to which the white class *habitus* determines him even in the commission of the crime. Village the negro is on trial before the blacks because his comrades suspect that his crime was not a revolutionary act but the ultimate gesture of his humiliated and frustrated desire. Snow says: "You were talking of sweet love. From far off, from Ubangi or Tanganyika, a tremendous love came here to die. Negro, you were in love. Like a sergeant in the marines . . ." (49). This perception is accurate only as an expression of the revolutionary group consciousness. But Village's relation to Marie, like his relation to Virtue, contains the contradictions of his existence as a person-object. It is being thought and felt by a colonial negro who is struggling to become a revolutionary.

In fact, the entire intermediate pattern of love relations derives dramatic tension from the clash between the revolutionary vision of the group and the personal agony of Village who attempts to free himself from the white class *habitus*. He will approach the Mask (Diouf-playing-Marie) at one point as the avenging African savage consistent with the expectations of the group. "In my eye I trotted out a big parade of warriors, diseases, alligators, amazons, straw huts, cataracts, hunts, cotton, even leprosy and even a hundred thousand youngsters who died in the dust . . ." (65). Yet moments later he falters and addresses Virtue instead of the Mask in the language of the whites: "The limpidity of your blue eyes, that tear gleaming at the corner, your heavenly bosom . . ." (65). Village is a negro who cannot love a negress unless he can constitute the relations as a value—and in the colonial context that means making her white. On the same premise he cannot wholly hate Marie since he has been conditioned by the moral and esthetic norms of the whites. As a result he changes the revolutionary purpose of the ceremony when he speaks lovingly to the Mask: "The gentlest of your movements delineate you so exquisitely that when I'm on your shoulder I feel that you've been borne by the wind" (68). An instant later he slides back into the role of the revolutionary who, guided by his comrades, interprets his murder as an act of vengeance for the humiliation his race has suffered: "It's no longer a Negro trailing at your skirt; it's a marketful of slaves, all sticking out their tongues. Just because you've kindly given me a drink of rum you think . . . eh, you bitch. Pull me toward your lace. . . . Underneath you're surely wearing some sort of black petticoat that's silkier than my gaze . . ." (74). Obviously Village does not free himself entirely from the colonial attitudes which conditioned him since his crime is tainted by desire. His complex role gives shape to the personal drama of the Negro-in-the-process-of-becoming-black. Emotionally paralyzed in love-hatred relations, existing in the agonizing ambivalence of his longing for social inclusion and the reality of his exclusion, the drama of his love relations points toward the abolition of colonialism as the absolute social condition of love and to revolution as the time for choosing hatred.

The trial and self-indictment of blacks playing savage before a fake white court and the trial of the negro in Village amplify the colonial experience of negroes who are in ontological checkmate but who are becoming aware of the ideology and the economic conditions which caused it. The strained relationship between the group consciousness (Archibald, Bobo, Felicity, Snow) which attains to the vision of revolution during the rites of symbolic murder and the passion of Village who struggles to attain it, produces the human reality and lived contradictions of a disenfranchised group becoming aware of the nature of its alienation. To the extent to which their liberation is poetic (and poetic discourse discloses what is most intensely personal), the lyricism of hatred and of impossible love does not appear to break with the ideology of *Deathwatch, The Maids,* and *The Balcony*. But instead of transforming a personal history into art, a quest which the anti-heroes of the first three plays pursue with varying degrees of success, *The Blacks* stages the transformation into art of the existence of an entire class which is socially deprived.

Surely, however, the more important change is in dramatic structure. Within the framework of the fiction the play itself is a dramatic function of revolutionary activities which take place in the real world. A black revolutionary has succumbed to the temptation of the whites and betrayed his comrades, receives a fair trial, and is expeditiously executed. In itself this pattern suggests rather forcefully that the contradictions of revolutionary praxis, the militancy of hatred, and the betrayals which attest to the human failings of those who are compelled to think their lives in the mode of the moral code of the whites are not merely the terms of a lyrical dialectic but the very real human drama of an oppressed group making revolution. In fact, since the function of the play is tactical (to keep a white audience spellbound while the revolution is in progress), art becomes a function of revolutionary praxis. When Archibald concludes the exacerbating clownerie by proclaiming that the time has not yet come to present noble matters on stage, he is merely saying that what is noble for blacks is, of necessity, a given of the postrevolutionary situation. As long as the colonial system exists the black must be an object for himself and for others; as long as the revolution lasts he must alienate himself in hatred.

Archibald was in no position to say what noble matters await liberated third world people. *The Screens,* which stages the successful Algerian revolution against French colonial rule, could do precisely that but remains singularly mute on the subject. The Algerians can hardly be blamed for this reticence because it is Genet who backtracks. But why? I imagine Genet's consternation when he was faced with the responsibility of having created that nameless traitor of *The Blacks;* I can imagine Genet agonizing over his fate. For instead of continuing or intensifying the revolutionary thrust of *The Blacks, The Screens* communicates a message of total social disengagement. Three dramatic patterns give shape to the action: 1. the rites of passage of Said assisted by his mother and by Leila; 2. the

revolt of the Arabs against their colonial masters; 3. the perception of purpose and suffering which the dead adversaries bring
to the struggle of the living.

"If a Frenchman robs me, that Frenchman's a thief, but if
an Arab robs me, he hasn't changed. He's an Arab who has
robbed me, and nothing more."9 Sir Harold, colonial landowner
complete with cork helmet, whip, and riding boots, formulates
the prejudices of the white man tersely: all Arabs are alike.
Just as hard work, moral purpose, fine rose gardens, and the
exquisite language of Mallarmé are the undisputed signs of
superiority of white culture heroes and of the civilization they
force on the indigenous people, laziness, the sloth of brothels,
nettles, and illiteracy shape the abject image of inferiority of
the Arab. Said, condemned like all Arabs to live this malediction, does not join his compatriots in the revolutionary struggle
but pursues instead the singular adventures of the twice rejected
outcast. What else could he do? Subsisting by doing odd jobs
for whites in exchange for hand-me-downs and trinkets, forced
to marry the ugliest woman of the region because he is too poor
to afford another, Said is compelled to live the isolation of the
despised *bicot*. The whites will not have him because he is an
Arab, and the Arabs exclude him contemptuously because he
is illegitimate and poor. Shamed and humiliated by both groups,
he chooses to travel the road of shame and humiliation without
returning. He steals from Arabs, compells the Cadi to find him
guilty, goes to prison and eventually betrays the revolutionary
cause. When he is finally forced to choose between the revolution and the image he has become for others, he responds with
devastating sweetness: "To the old gal, to the soldiers, to all of
you, I say shit" (XVII, 197). Shot by the Arab combatants
as a traitor, he simply fades into oblivion. Said refuses the call
of the anti-heroes who emerge from their mysterious adventures
in order to avenge themselves on the society which rejected
them. Unlike the maids whose heinous deed guaranteed them
immortality in the annals of crime, unlike the poet whose song
condemns his oppressors to the death house of the brothel, Said's
journey into abjection is a one-way trip into oblivion.

The meaning which Said gives to his life—a meaning which
denies the colonial reality of repression and the pertinence of
revolutionary commitment—does not fully disclose the social
implications of his choice. Situated in a defined socio-political

context, his acts must assume social and political connotations for others which are not necessarily related to his private intentions. In fact, his absolute refusal participates in the revolutionary dialectic as the absolute negation of value which the Arab is for the white man and which the revolution must negate in order to constitute itself as a human value. The initial proposition is clear: the color *white* signifies value and the Arab negation of value or evil. In choosing to live this proposition to the logical nihilation of himself, Said the *bicot* makes the revolutionaries conscious of the image which they must live during the struggle in order to sustain their hatred of the adversary, but which they must reject in victory in order to found their existence on freely chosen values. Said's quest holds precisely this double meaning for others. If stealing from the whites or the Arabs does not modify him in the eyes of the whites, stealing from the Arabs alters their perception of him and of themselves. Sir Harold is intelligent enough to understand that this knowledge will be the undoing of his interests: "if our three lascars recognized the fact that one of their fellows is a thief, they hesitated a long time before telling me. . . . Oh, oh! . . . it's because there's something in the air. . . . And that Said, whose reputation keeps swelling!" (X, 75-76).10 Said's immorality makes the Arabs aware of their own moral values because to condemn theft as immoral they must look upon property as a value, and if they do that they must recognize that the white property owner is a thief.

In the revolutionary camp the social excommunication of members of the unholy triad—the Mother, Said, and Leila—always triggers a feeling of group solidarity and purpose; conversely, their inclusion, especially by the revolutionary women Kadidja and Ommu, is accorded only to the extent to which the immorality of the outcasts serves as emblem of evil, of the delirium and the wrath which sustains the destructive period of armed revolutionary combat. Scenes VI and VIII dramatize the expulsion of the Mother—by extension of Said and Leila—from the revolutionary camp. Public opinion in the spokesperson of Kadidja denies the Mother the right to mourn the revolutionary hero Si Slimane during the funeral rites. She is reviled and driven off because she raised a brood of thieves. Rites consecrated to the memory of heroic deeds and to the legacy of hope which Si Slimane passed on to the Arab community strengthen the militant will of the community to the degree to which this community also assails and proscribes those among them whose opprobrious adventures spread hopelessness and defeatism.

Nor does the monstrous pride which sustains the purpose of the moral outcasts meet with the approval of the dead Si Slimane. Not that he rejects them in the name of class or race solidarity. Dying in *The Screens* is a continuing process of disengagement from the world theater of illusion so that neither the delirious hatred of the Mother nor the revolutionary passion of the architects of the legend of Si Slimane could compel his allegiance. He refuses to honor the Mother's request to participate in the funeral rites because her pursuit of an individual destiny, reactionary from the perspective of the revolution, condemns her to live the idea of personal worth *(à rebours,* to be sure) which the detachment of the dead unmasks as pious self-deception. Si Slimane's metaphysical view of events illustrates that it will ultimately not be possible to decode the revolutionary message of the play as a militant appeal for action since the political patterns are contextually dependent on the metaphor of the World-as-a-Stage.

In the stunningly structured Scene XII, Kadidja organizes the revolution by provoking an open break with the colonialists and by giving moral purpose to the struggle. At the foot of a long six-panel screen, an Arab dignitary of the colonal administration tries desperately to hold a group of restless Arabs in check in the name of public order. On the tops of the screens appear the symbols of colonial economic, military, and moral authority, among them a banker, a general, an academician, and a little girl in communion dress charitably feeding the birds of the deserts while the Arabs are starving. The political message of the scene is transmitted by juxtaposing the sharply parodied values of white culture heroes with Kadidja's resolute defiance. Just as the revolutionaries of 1789 donned the dress and language of ancient Romans in order to cloak their economic and political ambitions in the time-honored mantle of nobility, the colonialists see themselves acting out a glorious chapter of history on the African stage. The general speaks of vast conquests of Sahara lands and the future renown of the conquering armies, a soldier of the virile beauty of tanned legionaries, and the academician of civilization radiating from the splendor of Chartres and of the conversion of young delectable Mohammedans to the joys of Péguy and the delight of inverted sexual relations with French culture heroes.

The Arabs reply to this charade with a shot that kills the little girl in the communion dress while she is doling out holy bread to the underprivileged desert birds. When Sir Harold makes a final effort to paralyze the revolt by condemning the Arabs to the moral inferiority of trembling and stinking jackals, Kadidja breaks openly with the colonialists: "and I say that your force is powerless against our hatred" (XII, 96). Although she is killed immediately, she cannot be silenced: "Said, Leila, my loved ones! You, too, in the evening related the day's evil to each other. You realized that in evil lay your only hope. Evil, wonderful evil, you who remain when all goes to pot, miraculous evil, you're going to help us" (XII, 97). Kadidja formulates an ideology for action which is appropriate for the early revolutionary phase. She opposes contempt with hatred and the eternal moral superiority of the colonialists with the logic of anarchism and the immorality of destruction. In this specific context the lives of the members of the unholy family serve the revolution as models of the value of individual acts of destruction. Indeed, all those who committed individual acts of violence dedicate their deeds to the revolution on orders from Kadidja. Kaddur bequeaths two slain soldiers, M'Barek three disembowled cows, Lahoussine the rape of a white girl, Amer a bank robbery, etc. The mother insists in vain on the uniqueness of her and her family's adventure which consisted of robbing the revolutionaries while they were fighting the colonial army. Kadidja assimilates their betrayal to the moral purpose of the revolution by casting her out of the village with the advice to continue her life of crime: "Continue, and do well what you have to do" (XII, 104). Thus the sovereign rites of refusal of the anti-heroes are transformed into signs of heroic personal sacrifice during the anarchistic period of the birth of the revolution.

The organized struggle against colonial rule precipitates a scandal in the whorehouse. Soldiers find a welcome respite from the slaughter on the front in the arms of enraged prostitutes, and the women of the village look kindly on the usually much abused harlots. To be a whore is to refuse the world—at least in Genet's fictional world. It is to choose to die as a person and become what one does for a living. But in war different moral laws prevail, as a soldier explains to Ommu: *"We're burning with anger too, but our anger is slower. We have to carry the machine gun and set it up. Have to feed it. Have to watch the horizon. A rebellion takes place, but our rebellion is weightier. You can dance all around us and sing, but we have to protect your dances, your waltzes, and your insults"* (XIV, 136). Discipline and organized combat must follow the delirium of spontaneous uprisings. Formerly the place of immorality, the bordello supported as pure negativity the moral structure of the community. The war has changed that because whores are now the necessary relaxation of weary warriors and betrayal the detestable immorality, the negativity of martial ethics. Thus the changing political situation once again creates a different group consciousness which in turn determines the socio-political significance of private acts. The whores who were seeking to transform their lives into legends are enlisted against their will in the cause of the revolution. Conversely, Said, together with his wife and mother, are being mustered out.

The reasons for this expulsion are not exclusively political. Soldiers who put their life on the line for a cause must have a positive self-image. The Soldier insists: "One fights less well in rags. (With sudden venom.) And one fights less well when one has an ugly mug and is less attractive to women. (In a fury.) And if men are to envy our death, then our way of going out to die must make them envious!" (XIV, 137). It would be a contradiction in terms to ask soldiers to perform heroic deeds under the banner of abjection to which Kadidja and Ommu had raised Said's solitary adventure. No self-respecting knight ever rode into battle with the image of an odious pariah emblazoned on his shield. Of course, the moral purpose of the outcast, which is to descend into the hell of the morally damned, participates by its very negativity in the dialectic of revolution, but with the grimly ironic twist that the meaning which Said, Leila, and the Mother attribute to their acts is tragically dissociated from the meaning these acts assume in changing political situations. This irony does not merely pertain to the destiny of the unholy triad but is inherent in the structure of human relations where others constantly encroach on the self in matters of personal choice. What Said is for himself he is not for Kadidja and Ommu, and what he is for them he is not for the combatants. Ultimately, he skirts the danger of losing his real self and begins to live for others, as Leila notices astutely: "Said, I understand your leaving me. . . . You're expected at the turning of a greater destiny, and you knew it. You were getting conceited, unbearable. Conceited as a schoolteacher" (XV, 156). The last thing Said wanted was to be a teacher. Sergeant Gadget shares Said's alienation because he sees himself as a beautiful maiden, is cruelty personified for his comrades in arms, and France will honor him as one of her fallen patriots. While the combatants fight for a new social order, Ommu charges that they go to war in order to create a beautiful image of themselves.

The point is that not even revolutionaries may lay claim to historical authenticity because the new order—we are not given to understand just what it will be—inevitably creates a new moral code with the result that the forms of alienation change while the sickness remains. In the wake of the success of the revolution, the brothel once again assumes the burden of evil and will sustain as pure negativity the new moral order. Meanwhile the Cadi, formerly a judge, plays the role of the condemned who sets forth on his journey of absolute refusal in imitation of Said.

Genet seems to be implying that history is other people; that while each moment of the historical dialectic creates a different topology of human interactions, personal choice— what one decides to do within the limits of a given situation— will always conflict violently with the meaning others attribute to it. Viewed as a problem of dramatic form, he needs the transcendent space of the dead to communicate his idea of history and to signal his refusal of it. This is accomplished in the final three scenes where significant historical events—the defeat of the legionaries, the assassination of Said—assume the meaning of a wholly equivocal *Maskenspiel* because they are being played before the assembly of the dead whose truth discloses the illusory nature of history. When Kadidja arrives among them, she still wants to be the organizer of resistance which she was for others. But political concerns do not pertain to the terrible wisdom of the dead:

> *Kadidja:* But then, if we're among ourselves, do we
> on the fight? We can still help those up above?
> *Si Slimane:* Help them become what we wanted to
> become when we were up there?

Kadidja: Yes.
They all burst out in very soft laughter.
Brahim: That would mean trying to die less. And one
must die more and more. (XV, 145)

Among the dead no one can pretend what he is not; but if
he ceases to be what he is not, he is nothing. Their truth is
inapplicable because dying is viewed as a journey of infinite
regression during which the initiate passes through multiple
screens of self-concealment and concealment from others, shed-
ding in the process such self-definitions as Mohammedan/
Christian, Arab/white, revolutionary/legionary, anti-hero, evil/
good, etc., only to discover, like Mallarmé's clown, that stripped
of his masks he is nothing. It is not without a touch of savage
irony that Si Slimane, the hero of the Arab revolt, should be
the bearer of this supreme wisdom. Furthest removed from
history because he has been dead the longest, his voice falters
as he reaches the threshold of silence, then fades away in
convulsive laughter. In the context of this perception of ontological checkmate each event is reduced to a pseudo-event, each
human drama to a pseudo-drama, and every attempt to communicate either entraps speaker and listener alike in a series of
meta-communications or must lead to silence. Said's journey
into oblivion describes his refusal to play the game. Since Ommu
offers him life only on condition that he live it for others, as a
symbol of negativity in the Arab's quest for selfhood, he prefers
to die and begin, or rather continue, his journey of infinite
regression.

Economically dependent on the French bourgeoisie for
whom he wrote plays only to signal his absolute refusal of their
world, Genet has, with the exception of *The Blacks,* consistently
refused to think his exclusion in the ideological mode of Marxism. The characters of his plays are engaged in intense strategic
maneuvers of self-definition in order to extricate themselves from
ontological encirclement by others. Their pathos resides in their
failure to break the vicious circle of meta-communications, for
there appears to be no escape from the practice of applying
demeaning labels to those who are in revolt against the pre-
vailing moral code. Either they are compelled to exchange one
label for another (servants/murderess—victim; tramp—beggar
—slave/damned poet) or they must confront the void as do
Lefranc and Said. *The Blacks* is a revolutionary play since it

ascribes the alienation of a *group* to economics and relegates art to a function of revolutionary praxis. *The Screens,* however, reverts to the problematic of the earlier plays since it pinpoints alienation as being inherent in human interactions and not in class distinctions.

Genet perceives praxis as an expression of class *habitus* as do the Marxists. Alienation, however, is not for that reason the necessary condition of the oppression of workers by the bourgeoisie but the inevitable by-product of the phenomenon of social life. Clearly, Genet demonstrates sympathy for social reprobates and oppressed groups, and that sympathy acquires the rigor of a revolutionary vision with *The Blacks.* Yet his obsession with the individual, his project of transforming biography into art, and, in *The Screens,* the hypostatization of a political problematic indicate that he thinks his exclusion from the dominant class in the ideology of that class. In this sense, Genet's drama is the drama of a writer who felt himself *morally* disenfranchised by the dominant class but not economically. Surely, Genet's scepticism toward political solutions is not entirely misplaced. The history of revolutions, the most recent experiences at home and in Indochina, are sobering reminders that no political ideology has a monopoly on terror. Monolithic minotaurs, they all seem to need victims to "stabilize" whatever old order they proclaim to defend or whatever new order they propose.

University of Oregon

NOTES

1 *The Hero with a Thousand Faces* (1949; rpt. Princeton, 1972), p. 30: "A hero ventures forth from the world of common day into the region of supernatural wonder: fabulous forces are there encountered and a decisive victory is won: the hero comes back from his mysterious adventure with the power to bestow boons on his fellow men."

2 The onus which the bourgeoisie has cast upon the worker has a long history and prevails even today. See esp. Régine Pernoud, *Histoire de la bourgeoisie en France* (Paris, 1960-62), 2 vols.

3 For a more detailed analysis of the first three plays see W. F. Sohlich, "Genet's Drama: Rites of Passage of the Anti-Hero: From Alienated Existence to Artistic Alienation," *Modern Language Notes,* 89 (1974), 641-53. The position taken here and maintained in this study conflicts with Lucien Goldmann's contention that *Deathwatch* is homologous to middle-class consciousness, *The Maids, The Balcony,* and *The Blacks* to anarchism, and *The Screens* to socialist revolutionary thinking. See his "The Theater of Genet: A Sociological Study," *The Drama Review,* 12 (1968), 51-61.

4 *Les damnés de la terre* (Paris, 1970), p. 10: "Il ne suffit pas au colon d'affirmer que les valeurs ont deserté, ou mieux n'ont jamais habité, le monde colonisé. L'indigène est déclaré imperméable à l'éthique, absence de valeurs, mais aussi négation des valeurs. Il est, osons l'avouer, l'ennemi des valeurs. En ce sens, il est le mal absolu."

5 A sociological study of Genet's public still needs to be undertaken. Sartre (*Saint Genet* [New York, 1971], pp. 584-99), who enjoins us to read Genet with a sense of outrage, in other words like a hypothetical bourgeois, leads us into ontological checkmate since he asks us to be what we are not in order to know what Genet is. Goldmann seems more persuasive when he contends that Genet expresses the disillusionment of left-wing European intellectuals with Marxism and capitalism. Neither critic, however, has actually done field research to establish just who the public is.

6 *The Blacks*, trans. Bernard Frechtman (New York, 1960), p. 27. Subsequent references will appear in text. All translations were checked against original texts: *Les Nègres*, ed. Arbalètes (Paris, 1958) and *Les Paravents*, ed. Arbalètes (Paris, 1961).

7 "If your rage was a long one, I'd urge you on. Slice him up, I'd advise you. But what's the use if you *don't* slice him up because you can feel your tail between your legs?"—Bertolt Brecht, *Mother Courage*, trans. Eric Bentley (1966; rpt. New York, 1966), p. 67. Sustained rage is the stuff revolutions are made of, Mother Courage tells the Young Soldier, whose angry outburst against his unjust commander lacks the continuity to be effective.

8 *Black Skin, White Masks*, trans. Charles L. Markmann (New York, 1967), pp. 133-34.

9 *The Screens*, trans. Bernard Frechtman (New York, 1962), Scene X, p. 75.

10 "—si nos trois lascars ont reconnu qu'un des leurs est un voleur, ils ont hésité longtemps avant de le dire. . . . oh, oh! . . . c'est qu'il y a quelque chose dans l'air . . . (*Les Paravents*, p. 99). Frechtman incorrectly translates the conditional *si* as *although*, then incorrectly makes the subordinate clause dependent on the parenthetical *they waited a long time before telling me*.

Dance to a Cut-Throat Temper:
Harold Pinter's Poetry as an Index to
Intended Audience Response

Christopher C. Hudgins

By the time Harold Pinter wrote his first play, *The Room* (1957), he had completed several hundred poems.[1] Although an extensive analysis of the published verse would be interesting in its own right, perhaps more importantly, a brief examination sheds light on the intended audience response to the mature plays. Most critics concur that Pinter depicts human relationships as based in patterns of dominance and subservience, or aggressive vs. escapist behavior, but few discuss the motivations for such behavior or intended response to Pinter's richly ambiguous portrayals. Like the poems, the mature plays depict wonderfully particularized situations involving memorably idiosyncratic characters, yet at the same time both situation and character evoke metaphorical associations. The poems not only clarify those associations, but also emphasize that intended response to the plays entails the recognition that the characters' refusal fully to confront the fact of death motivates much of their behavior. Such refusal accentuates a radical insecurity that necessitates aggressive or escapist responses.[2] Recognition of such a concatenation, the poetry emphasizes, is in turn intended to lead to positive changes in audience behavior.

The importance of "death-consciousness" in the poetry necessitates a reconsideration of Pinter as absurd dramatist, especially in light of the pervasive references to death throughout the canon. Though not fashionable, such a reconsideration is particularly important now, both because of the presence of such step-children of the absurd as *Gin Game* on Broadway and *The End* in the movie theaters and because understanding of the absurd continues to be erroneously rooted in Martin Esslin's seminal *Theatre of the Absurd* rather than in Camus' *Myth of Sisyphus*. Camus' idea of the absurd, as opposed to the existentialism with which it is often confused, can help us understand much of contemporary theater, for his work effectively summarizes or conceptualizes a modern milieu, a popular *zeitgeist* reflected in a significant proportion of contemporary literature, largely written, after all, by writers formed by the modern period. Especially significant in this context, though generally ignored, is Camus' aesthetic, his ideas on audience response to absurdist literature. Such a reconsideration should not "pigeonhole" dramatists or plays, but can aid in contextualizing those plays, allowing fuller understanding of a broad range of issues.

Although Esslin emphasizes the "poetic" form of the earlier absurdist plays at the expense of the absurdist theme, which he mistakenly understands as "healing," Camus emphasizes theme, or audience response, more centrally, clearly including realistic forms within his definition of absurdist literature.[3] For Camus, there is no cure for, no "healing" of the human condition, which largely because of mortality is absurd. Though most try to escape such a recognition, in the broadest sense, human activity is useless, purposeless, because death makes it impossible to fulfill human aspirations to the eternal. The *contradiction* between such human aspirations and the limitations imposed on them, their presence together, *is* the absurd. In turn, "the absurd has meaning only in so far as it is not agreed to."[4] In other words, men and women should act "as if" meaningless action has significance even in the knowledge that death makes such activity purposeless in relation to any universal or eternal scale. Humanity must constantly struggle to maintain consciousness, to confront that condition; a limited happiness, revolt, passion and freedom are the potential results. Camus defines "revolt" as "the certainty of a crushing fate without the resignation that ought to accompany it" (p. 40). "Freedom" results from the consciousness of death and the consequent negation of meaning, of purpose, and of future, which maximizes the importance of choice and present (pp. 43-44); such freedom should produce "passion," which "urges toward the greatest quantity of experiences," as opposed to any emphasis on the quality of experience or on any future-oriented experience, both made meaningless by death. From this strangely optimistic perspective, the alternative to consciousness and its potential consequent is literal or meta-phorical suicide, the refusal of consciousness of one's condition. Unlike the existentialists, however, whom he sees as eventually deifying that which they first find oppressive, i.e. human ex-perience, Camus suggests that such consciousness is still not "healing," that such a perspective is still not "certain," or even significant. Humanity is constantly tempted away from such a perspective, and it must constantly be re-examined.

Despite the possibility of absurd joy in the present through the recognition of death from this philosophical perspective, Camus asserts that great art is without lessons, that great artists are "convinced of the uselessness of any principle of explanation and sure of the educative message of perceptible experience. They consider the work of art both an end and a beginning. It is the outcome of an often unexpressed philosophy, its illustra-tion and its consumation. But it is complete only through the implications of that philosophy" (p. 75). Further, the work of art should not arouse hope or create illusions, and the artist should be aware of its gratuitousness; its only importance "lies in the ordeal it demands of a man and the opportunity it pro-vides him of overcoming his phantoms and approaching a little closer to his naked reality." Art, for Camus, is the most effective way of disciplining the will to maintain "awareness," which is "the staggering evidence of man's sole dignity: the dogged revolt against his condition" (p. 85). The early work of the absurd artist, though, frequently tries "to give the whole experience in the lace-paper of an explanatory literature;" when the absurd artist produces a mature work it "is but a piece cut out of ex-perience, a facet of the diamond in which the inner lustre is epitomized without being limited. In the first case there is . . . pretension to the eternal. In the second a fecund work because of a whole implied experience, the wealth of which is suspcted" (p. 73). Though often imaginatively, even chaotically complex, Pinter's poetry is the equivalent of Camus' "explanatory litera-ture," the early work that more specifically, if less brilliantly, reflects the philosophy without the implications of which the fecund work is incomplete. Such similarity of theme, of basic intent, in no way implies that the mature works are not pro-foundly different in other respects, but they are rooted in a particular but pervasive vision of an age and its aesthetic which Camus summarizes well.

Pinter's mature work *is* both "an end and a beginning"—it is an end for the artist, a type of revolt, and potentially a beginning for the audience in terms of the ordeal, the struggle it requires. The response Pinter intends entails an "intellectual identification." This paradoxical term emphasizes the necessity for a balanced, holistic response to Pinter's plays. He has commented that by calling everything a symbol, by intellectually distancing his work, "it is easy to put up a pretty efficient smokescreen on the part of the critics or the audience against recognition, against an active and willing participation"; he adds that "a character, become symbol, can be talked about but need not be lived with."5 To live with a Pinter character, though, requires first an objective or distanced response, and then a recognition of self in the characters on stage. Metaphors or symbols are present, but point toward the intended recognition. Initially the audience is distanced from or appalled by the seeming strangeness of the situation on stage; only gradually does it notice the similarity between the dramatic action and its own life. Though difficult, members of the audience should identify with the seemingly strange Pinter character, often "negative examples" like Stanley, Davies, Ted, should recognize the absurdity of their own lives through such identification, and "revolt" from their own similar behavior. Such revolt, dependent on an emotional identification, is initiated, however, by a questioning, intellectual objectivity.6

In this context, more thematically explicit than the plays, Pinter's poems provide evidence with which we can read the "indexes" of intended audience response to the ambiguous plays with some assurance. There are three types of thematic emphases in the poetry which broadly correspond to Camus' schema for the recognition of the absurd. Most similar to the mature dramas, poems of the first type objectively "contemplate" the mechanical, that is habitual and unthinking, nature of much human activity, the purposelessness of that activity, and death. Poems of the second type depict recognition of the absurd and/or "rage," the equivalent of Camus' "revolt." Finally, in several poems Pinter depicts the potential results of such revolt, which correspond to Camus' "freedom" and "passion." Camus concludes that "The present and the succession of presents before a constantly conscious soul is the ideal of the absurd man" (pp. 46-47). Pinter asks his readers, and later his audience, to maintain just such an absurdist perspective, to avoid the constantly tempting but ignoble retreat toward despair or any "existential leap" or other form of exaltation.

"The Islands of Aran Seen from the Moher Cliffs" (1951) is the single poem that most clearly embodies a progression through all three types of thematic emphases.7 From a vantage point on Moher's Cliffs, dark "like coalvaults," the poet's persona comtemplates the islands' high, rocky headland. The object of his contemplation is similarly black, like a whale, but unable to move. Aran's black "mourning" clothes simultaneously personify the islands and emphasize that their painful isolation springs both from the separating sea and from the fact of death. Continuing personification suggests that human experience, like Aran's, entails a bleak isolation in a hostile, relentless world, a pounding sea devoid of mercy. On the Atlantic side, its cliffs are constantly exposed to terrible pounding, "thumped to losses/ By its season's neighbour." The sea makes Aran a widower, destroying his "legs," implying that there is no escape, no possibility of human relatedness.8 Other lines also suggest constant pain: the island is "Distended" and must "hump," or strain, against the sea which surrounds it. Even the sun, usually benevolent in connotation, here has destructive teeth. And Aran's unavoidable pain is completely "without gain," like that of Sisyphus.

The persona's contemplation of Aran's grim reality finally suggests that the islands embody revolt. The three islands "Make tough bargain with the cuff/ And statement of the sea"; straining, the island "Stares out the waves," connoting a confrontation, a refusal to yield to the elements, to look away from the brutal "statement" of human experience. Such a confrontation, or revolt in the face of "the certainty of a crushing fate," suggests a type of nobility. At the poem's conclusion, the persona sees Aran, "pebbled/ In the fussing Atlantic"; he regards Aran as paradoxically triumphant, as bound but free. The pounding waves can slowly beat the stones into smaller pieces, but they cannot destroy those cliffs immediately. Aran's tough bargain with the sea reduces the previously hostile, potent Atlantic to the "fussing Atlantic," petty and ineffectual. In sum, the persona realizes that "revolt" can produce a limited victory, if a tough bargain is made and if, in the full realization that no retreat is possible, no retreat is attempted. The poem pictures a type of "tragic gaiety," "Gaiety transfiguring all that dread."9

Prefiguring Pinter's mature dramatic technique, two poems unflinchingly contemplate the human condition with little statement on recognition or revolt, requiring the reader to draw his or her own conclusions. The titles of both "Rural Idyll" (1950) and "European Revels" (1950) establish expectations of a joyful description but immediately dash those expectations, foreshadowing the ironic titles of the plays.. The "idyll" depicts the hopeless, absurd condition of a woman of indeterminate age living in the country. The first stanza details her day's labor and two of her futile attempts at escape, dancing and reading. She grinds "the crossing plat of a pig, stabs/ The day's navel and begins her labours."10 *She* is not aware of the hostility of the day or of the absurdity of her life; this is the poet's knowledge, for she is "blinded" by "A hay's dance and a stub of lighted carrion," her reading candle. Pinter's use of the pervasive sight imagery is typical. Unlike Aran, she does not "stare out the waves"—she is blinded by futile efforts at escape from a vague threat. Even the *stub* of lighted carrion will soon burn out, eliminating the flickering vision it affords. "Carrion" suggests both that the motivation for such escape is a fear of death and that the escape itself is death-like.

The second and third stanzas question the implications of such a reality. The poet first asks "What in her life's centred dilemma,/. . . shall give help/ To the heart's masquerading searcher?" Her search for love is another form of escape. In masquerade, disguising its true goal, her heart blindly seeks a lover for solace. But the lover answers, "The web the well of her lover cries," that the help she seeks will "never be found." The search is hopeless because the lover is as empty and masquerading as she is, and because she seeks security, control, not love. The web, like that associated with Mark in *The Dwarfs*, suggests entrapment or control as a substitute for any viable conception of relationship; "well" is somewhat confusing in this context, but certainly carries associations of emptiness and dank entrapment along with potentially positive connotations. That the poem is largely negative about the relationship with the lover, though, is emphasized by the first line of the third stanza: "Who holds the nap of pity?" Directed to the reader, in context the line both questions the reader's superiority and evokes a strangely mixed response of pity and condemnation of this

woman, who escapes her "life's centred dilemma" through empty
dances, empty lovers, and finally through reading a book in the
dark corner of her room with the "Rind of her stúnned thumb
and untouch of a kiss," ignoring "a broken sea's calling." These
lines suggest a complete retreat from reality. Even the thumb is
"stúnned" and her kisses are "untouches"—they embody no real
sensation or communication. She escapes the call for confrontation with experience, which the broken sea represents here as
well as in "The Islands of Aran." Since free will exists in Pinter's
world, this is a type of suicide. The woman is metaphorically
dead because she has chosen not to live fully, or consciously.

"European Revels" again describes the absurd and details
another form of escape, one which creates the illusion of purposeful movement.11 "Zendalover, the old Serbian claptrap,"
flees from the one moment when she was "self-begetting," a
moment during which she "From adoration strangled her
brother." Metaphorically, if ambiguously, the fratricide suggests
that she envied what she saw as her brother's power and "destroyed" him through her resulting aggression and control.
Ironically, though "self-begetting" has existential associations,
such action is revealed as both death-dealing and ineffectual in
the sense that it produces no "cure" for the absurd. Now bored
with her "dead" brother, Zendalover escapes into revels in
Europe. But all of the men she goes to become artificial and
burdensome, "plasterlads . . . wasted in heart and breath,/
Summerheavy on her blood's altar." They, too, pursue their
particular revels as escape, exhausting themselves; they become
"Dribbling loonies" who "jug Slav Kinches,/ Rip through their
maidenheads,/ Slum and stem the waxing blood." This concluding image applies both to the reveling men and to Zendalover
and the other women in the poem. The escapist revels only check
waxing blood, painful initiatory experience, momentarily. The
blood reference, while obviously sexual in connotation, also joins
with the images of old dribbling men to reinforce the absurdity
of such activity because of aging and death. Thus, neither idyllic
attempts at escape in the room's corner nor frenzied activity
can permanently avoid the implications of the absurd.12 We are
meant to recognize the variants of both motifs in our lives, and
both echo throughout the canon, most obviously in the contrasting negative examples of Davies and Mick in *The Caretaker*.

Four of the poems explicitly describe either a recognition of absurdity or the absurdist rage or revolt which may follow such recognition. Again emphasizing the centrality of death to Pinter's thematic statement, "The Midget" (1950, *Poems,* p. 2) depicts one of the few absurd heroes in the canon.13 The poem paraphrases the absurdist insight that living men are actually as good as dead because death comes so quickly, so unexpectedly: "[I] saw the voyagers stand stiff,/ Deathsure, stiff and coffined," all in a "still place." But the persona also recognizes the midget on the crest, in the ringing wind, a marked contrast to the motionless voyagers who have allowed the fear of death, the fear of confrontation with the wind, to force them to retreat early to their coffins. Their stiff formal attire represents, in much the way Stanley's does in *The Birthday Party,* a refusal to confront experience. They are more "dead" than the midget, who has the courage to stand in the night wind and face the "silent beast," death, that lurks beneath it. Like the pounding sea in "The Islands of Aran," the wind image suggests hostile experience, and the midget's confrontation with that wind suggests the possibility of the absurd man's living "on the peak," in full recognition of the absurd but without the resignation which usually accompanies such consciousness. Pinter's choice of the midget for his hero echoes Camus' emphasis that even such courage is utterly insignificant. The midget, then, reflects Pinter's vision of human stature, of human insignificance, as do the dwarfs in a more pejorative context.

A later poem, "The Error of Alarm" (1956, *Poems,* p. 15) describes an interesting variant of the "coffined voyager," clarifying the complex relationship between sexuality, especially sexual fears and insecurities, and the absurd in the Pinter canon while detailing another type of suicide. The poem begins, *"A woman speaks:"* thinking about intercourse, she describes a pulse in the dark which she could not stop and which results in "The error of alarm." These are subtle reactions; she cannot summon a witness to the "bargain," the implicit agreement between herself and her lover or husband. The necessity for such a bargain is rooted in the man's fear, his uncertainty about women and sexuality in general:

> If his substance tautens
> I am the loss of his blood.
> If my thighs approve him
> I am the sum of his dread.

For the man, the woman is the embodiment of all that threatens his identity, his control. She is describing the male's fear of the female's controlling him by getting more pleasure from the experience than he does. She recognizes that any such feminine threat necessitates an aggressive, controlling response on the man's part.

In the third stanza, the woman summarizes her lover's idea of a good "bargain." He wants the woman to "cajole" him, to coax him with false words, to flatter him, and he wants her mouth to "alay him," to put his fears to rest. Only then will she be "his proper bride." The woman yields to his desire. As a result, she "die[s] the dear ritual/ And he is my bier." The male's fear of the mysterious female becomes a metaphor for humanity's fear of confronting experience or reality. Resultant attempts at control "kill" both male and female. The "error" or "fault of alarm," then, lies in the female's yielding despite her recognition of the "killing," masculine conception of her identity as merely that through which to solidify his own. She should not be "alarmed" at this absurd situation between the sexes, submitting to his control out of her own fear, but should confront it, and should refuse to "die." Pinter's labeling this woman's behavior erroneous supports a particular reading of Ruth's refusal of the same "error" in *The Homecoming* and of several other female responses in the canon.14 At the same time, the poem suggests that there are various responses available after such recognition, including renunciation of self, or "death."

"New Year in the Midlands" (1950, *Poems,* p. 1) more explicitly describes the absurd revolt or rage which can follow such recognition. Although its title ironically creates the expectation of celebration, on another level, like the plays, the poem embodies a "straight" celebration of the absurd. Here, the persona, an actor "between the boards," is again trapped, this time in an inn of questionable reputation where the landlady sings "O Celestial Light" while swinging her wooden leg, the conjunction emphasizing the futility of such trust in the divine in a clearly flawed universe. He feels himself "Straddled, exile always in one Whitbread Ale town,/ Or such." Aware of his own isolation, he describes the sailors buying prostitutes to "calm the coin of a day's fever" and suggests that he himself, "your spluttered guide," attempts to escape his own "fever" through such "bargains." Such "cures" are clearly hopeless, ineffectual. Neverthe-

less, in the last lines, separated from the rest of the poem by a
long hyphen, the reader's "guide" *tells* his audience:

> — Watch
> How luminous hands
> Unpin the town's genitals —
> Young men and old
> With the beetle glance,
> The crawing brass whores, the clamping
> Red shirted boy, ragefull, thudding his cage.

Like so much of Pinter's work, the lines are at once particular and evocatively metaphoric. On one level, as the "Or such"
phrase suggests, this is a world view; it makes no difference
whether it is one town or another. All the patrons of the yellow
pub celebrate the arrival of the New Year, but nothing will
change, nothing will be new; the same absurdity will prevail
during the coming year, both here and elsewhere. The persona
displays sympathy for all of these people: the sailor boys "rocked
to sleep," the landlady swinging her fake leg and singing the
hymn, the thin homosexual in the raincoat. His message is to
watch *all* of this, including him, like the others, fresh from the
whore's arms, as in Genet a broad symbol of illusion, "brass"
masquerading as gold. The red-shirted boy, "ragefull, thudding
his cage," is the persona's objective vision of himself. He, like
the rest, participates in the absurd reality; the difference is that
he is aware, that he can warn or cajole his audience and himself
to "Watch"; such awareness initiates the thudding of the cage.
Unlike Ted's resigned, "objective" vision in *The Homecoming,*
the red-shirted boy's rage, his refusal to be resigned, represents
the first step toward absurd, passionate freedom.

The other "rage" poem, "Jig" (1952, *Poems,* p. 7) makes
a similar thematic statement. Here, the persona watches "my
portholed women/ Fall on the murdered deck"; such contemplation causes him to "rage in my iron cabin." Like the cage in
"New Year in the Midlands," the iron cabin images the absurd
hopelessness of the human condition, not an escape from a
murderous reality. Pinter's persona watches the women through
the cabin window, in other words from his irreversible isolation.
They are "portholed," too, however, by the blows, sexual and
otherwise, which fell them; it is this death, whether literal or
metaphoric, this letting in of the hostile light, which causes the
rage. "Portholed" also differentiates the fallen women from the

"starboard women," who do not fall, but who, "Spun by the metal breeze,/ Dance to a cut-throat temper." The persona clearly admires these women and their choice; like the midget, they can stand, even dance, in the "ringing air" of experience, which is hard, like metal, and ultimately death-dealing, like a sword. His only advice to them is to dance "faster," to experience more, or, as Camus would have it, to maximize the quantity of their experience. This dance differs from the escapist dance in "Rural Idyll," for it is dancing in awareness of that metal breeze. Again, there is a sympathy for the portholed women, but it is alloyed with a condemnation similar to that reserved for characters like Meg in *The Birthday Party* and Rose in *The Room*.

The image of men and women on a ship broadens to represent all men and women in the last verse, which emphatically links the deck and the dance to the absurd:

> Women and men together,
> All in a seaquick temper,
> Tick the cabin clock.

This vision or recognition of constant aggression is important because that cabin clock is ticking; repressed, literal death produces the "seaquick temper," but confronted it allows an absurd joy in the dance. The ticking cabin clock is one of the first of several "tick" images carrying similar implications, for instance the tick that disturbs Pete in *The Dwarfs* and the one that keeps Lenny awake in *The Homecoming*. Although the persona here must occasionally escape such a devastating vision of time—he "skip[s] to drydock" when he can no longer weather the sea— he struggles to avoid such escape; at the poem's conclusion he resumes his rageful awareness of humanity and the ticking clock.

Three poems specifically delineate the positive results, the passionate if limited freedom, such painful confrontation can produce. "I Shall Tear Off My Terrible Cap" (1951, *Poems,* p. 4) describes the absurd, the persona's confrontation with it, and finally his determination to act in spite of that dreadful reality. Here, the so-called Pinter "menace" results in the persona's being hung in a strait jacket under a hostile sun; threatening experience restricts his movement, a parallel to the coffin image in "The Midget," and many versions of Pinter's "rooms." At first, his actions and thoughts occur in a timeless void, in "a hostile pause in a no man's time," because he attempts to deny time, to ignore death. As a result, he sees only "onelegged dreams" and "walking brains," a life not fully lived or integrated, not whole. Eventually, however, the persona tells those around him that only the very few can understand "The miles I gabble," and his "dances of dunce and devil," for "Only the deaf can hear and the blind understand," and "only the dumb can speak." "Deaf," "dumb," and "blind" suggest that such awareness as the persona hints at is an almost ineffable attitude. Yet he attempts to speak it:

> Time shall drop his spit in my cup,
> With this vicious cut he shall close my trap
> And gob me up in a drunkard's lap.
> All spirits shall haunt me and all devils drink me;
> O, despite their dark drugs and the digs that they rib me,
> I'll tear off my terrible cap.

The lines suggest that the awareness of time, and finally of death that will "close my trap," frees man from his straitjacket in the "hostile pause in a no man's time," and allows him to act. The cap which the persona tears off is the dunce's cap, which most people accept, fearful of time's implications and threats. Such inversion permeates this poem, which accounts for the atypical use of blindness. The "normal" vision of reality is actually insane, and blind. Once the dunce cap of this normal perspective is removed, the straitjacket is loosened and freedom and passionate action are possible. Such a realization clarifies many of Pinter's later works, especially *The Dwarfs, The Birthday Party,* and *The Caretaker.* The "cures" in all of these plays are far worse than the mental "illnesses" they supplant.

"Book of Mirrors" (1951, *Poems,* p. 5) portrays the benefits to be gained through such refusal of "cures." The poem begins "My book is crammed with the dead/ Youths of years." The line refers to the persona's own and various "Youths," that is to his constantly shifting personality, and to the fact that he now recognizes death. He describes the "Fabulous," unbelievable image he had of himself as favored by chance, by the winds; he has seen himself as able to guide his life with precision. All this, the persona thought:

> Till crowed lips I kissed,
> Supped with a blood of snapping birds,
> In a doom and ring of belladonna to sleep.

The lines suggest a beneficent recognizance of death. The persona kisses the old, dying lips, and he makes his meal, gets his nourishment from snapping birds, his hostile experience; he goes to sleep in the arms of a poison flower, again, paradoxically beautiful and deadly.

The succeeding lines emphasize that such recognition of death, of the strange "doubleness" of human experience, allows a type of freedom, of passion. Aware of death, the persona continues, "Spruced, I welcomed their boneating smiles,/ Till I grew bound and easy with ills." Despite such limitation, he is able to pursue "a hundred grails," acknowledging that such action is meaningless, for it will not change his "bound" condition, but also aware of his freedom to choose such action. His ills "prop the mad brideworld up," and with infinite sympathy he concludes:

> May they breathe sweet; the shapes
> That ounced my glad weight
> With ripe and century fingers,
> That locked the skeleton years
> With a gained grief.

The persona blesses both the awareness of death which brought him such knowledge and his experiences, even the grievous ones, because the "ouncing" of his weight is a "gained grief"; the pain is a part of his experience and thus intensely important.15

One of Pinter's most evocative and confusing poems, "One a Story, Two a Death" (1951) again lauds such awareness of death.16 The title suggests the simple but devastating idea that of any two people, one will always die first. The poem's first section objectively describes a young boy "scorched" by a woman's death in "an ebon mirrorless age." The boy cannot face himself and his reality, an age that apparently offers only blackness, revealing nothing about the self; like Stanley, he tries to refuse the mirror. The woman's death evokes both grief and a desire to plunge an arrow in the corpse's eye. Threatened by awareness, the boy wishes to "kill" that which threatens to control him, death itself. Such aggressive behavior is self-destructive. The boy suddenly becomes "I" and continues:

> Ten thousand years marbled
> When I wept on her corpse,
> Gnawed my lips on her coffin.
> Not anytime now, not anytime.

The "gnawed lips" image emphasizes that the refusal to confront death must eventually be self-consuming. Because death is inevitable, refusal of confrontation makes the eventual encounter much worse. An awesome confrontation, however, *can* produce a new perspective. The first section of the poem ends as, with no time now, the persona contemplates laughing dancers, flinging "their furs in the urn" while "his great breaking hands/ Choke some petal in my throat." Much as in Whitman's "When Lilacs Last in the Dooryard Bloom'd," in context, death begins to force on the boy an awareness of the absurd, a recognition of the extremely limited time men and women live. Such recognition makes quantitative experience important *because* there is not "anytime" left. The word reflects the two visions of time in the Pinter canon, the attempt to deny time's passage in the hope of denying death, on the one hand, and the recognition of the extremely limited time we live on the other.

The poem's second section clarifies the image of the "Breaking hands," which belong to "The giant negro [who] tones in ether his flute," beckoning the boy to a Styx-like black lake. The vision occurs while the persona lies with the corpse like "a young narcissus/ Couched on her breasts," weeping in a corner dimly lit by a moonbeam. The image of narcissus lying on a corpse comments on the escapist, self-centered and aggressive, "killing" nature of love emphasized in the plays but also suggests that the boy is so upset about this woman's death because it reminds him of his own—and so he retreats into a corner. However, an absurd awareness of the implications of death struggles to the surface; the boy accepts the Negro, the rejected if powerful and wise outsider, and is able to see in the lake black caverns which imprison the poets below. He decides now, like the giant Negro, to blow through his pipe, to force the awareness of death on the poets, and on his audience, and thus to:

> . . . release them, all mordant and tender,
> Anemone necklaced,
> And bring from her tears,
> Smothered in sunning.

In effect, the stanza describes the purpose of absurd artistic creation, the evocation through a contemplation of death of "tragic gaiety."

In the third section, the poet's persona describes the freedom, his own "release," gleaned from such painful awareness and the limited happiness that results. Clouds of bees drop singing to the dead woman's lips, and on those lips, "in his cape walks the negro/ Growing flowers on his groin," simultaneously threatening, potent and beautiful. The flaming crocuses of the first section are destroyed by death, but the potentially painful bees make them grow again. Because of the persona's awareness of death, a strange sense of happiness with the fleeting present returns to him. Now the boy weeps, for he realizes that he is the dead woman's brother, that he, too, will die. In context, however, the boy weeps "tears,/ Smothered in sunning," again paradoxically reflecting both grief and joy. As the poem concludes, the persona is "drugged" by the "night thighs" of the giant Negro where now grow the flowers. Again depending on inversion, this strangely threatening yet beneficent drug, the recognition of death and life together in absurd conflict, unlike the denigrated anesthesia of escape, can provide a legitimate, if limited sense of happiness. Essentially this poem embodies a recognition of doubleness, too, a regenerative, powerful merging of darkness and light. The boy only regrets that he has known too late the darkness that painfully reasserts itself in the final lines, pouring acid into his brain, again tempting him toward despair. Significantly, the insight that the giant Negro has given the boy emerges from the depths of his own personality. As in *The Room,* the giant Negro represents, on one hand, the subconscious, particularly the artistic instinct, threatening sexuality and the repressed knowledge of death, and on the other literal death, from Norman O. Brown's perspective the motivation for our repressing much of our experience and for aggressive behavior. The poem's statement reveals much about the metaphorical associations of mysterious, darkly threatening figures in the mature work.

Finally, "You in the Night" (1952, *Poems,* p. 9) directly addresses the reader and didactically asks him to confront the absurd and to profit from such confrontation. The 'you" in the title emphasizes that Pinter intends his audience, in its own "night," to identify with other "trapped" characters. He tells his reader that he or she "should hear/ The thunder and the walking air," "shall bear/ Where mastering weathers are." He suggests that much of human experience, both in the night and under the deliberate sun, is painful. Again, the wind, the "walking air," and the pounding waves, the "mastering weathers," reflect that painful experience. Typically, Pinter's theme centers upon the idea that his readers, and later his audience, should

confront their reality and that such confrontation, in the full
knowledge of hopelessness, is beneficial. The awareness of the
absurd, of the fact that "honoured hope/ Shall fail upon the
slate," *itself* "break[s] the winter down/ That clamours at your
feet." "Enamouring altars," or religious escapes, are tempting,
as is any type of exaltation, but the poet nevertheless urges
"You'll tread the tightrope." The thought echoes Camus' conclusions. Even the awareness of death, of ultimate hopelessness,
and the freedom and passion for the present that such awareness can produce, should not be looked upon as certain or as
saving. Since struggle gives life its legitimacy, men and women
must be aware of temptations toward exaltation as well as
toward despair, and must walk the absurd tightrope between
the two.

Here Pinter instructs his reader that this is what he or she
should do. Later, he presents absurd situations in the theater,
confident in "the educative message of perceptible experience,"
requiring the audience to struggle to draw its own conclusions.
A close reading of the poetry provides substantial evidence for
an absurdist thematic reading of Pinter's elusive, poetic "sub-
text" in the plays. Although space prohibits any discussion of
examples beyond the scope of the broad references above to
attitudes toward women, escape, confrontation and death, Pinter's recurrent use in the plays of motifs and image patterns initiated in his more openly didactic poems points to the similarity
of the audience response he intends to evoke. Apparently confusing details, almost subliminal in effect, in the plays—the
cures Goldberg and McCann offer Stanley in *The Birthday
Party,* Gus' pleasure at the black and white pattern in the crock-
ery in *The Dumb Waiter,* the strange sequence of opening and
closing windows and curtains in *The Basement* and *The Caretaker,* images of rain, wind and sun in various plays, Ruth's
walk in the night air in *The Homecoming,* the reference to
Deeley's and Kate's house in the country as far from the crashing ocean, and references to vision throughout the canon—all
emerge more forcefully as significant, concrete indexes of intended response from this perspective.

Clearly the poems are the work of an intelligent, talented,
but very young man struggling to enunciate his vision of the
human condition without sentimentality. When so explicitly
stated as in "You in the Night," "The Islands of Aran," or "The

Midget," Pinter's absurdist theme does seem limiting or explanatory. Although this broad theme remains constant, played with interesting variations in the later work, Pinter's brilliantly maturing mastery of form and his rejection of even the subtle didacticism of the poems produces richly evocative plays. Nonetheless, our understanding of these later works is impoverished without reference to that "often unexpressed philosophy," the theme, whether we term it absurdist, neo-romantic, or Laingian. The poetry helps us recognize ourselves in Pinter's plays in the context of that theme, an intended positive response to negative examples through a broadening of identification, which can lead to revolt or change.

University of Nevada, Las Vegas

NOTES

1 Harold Pinter, "Writing for Myself," *Twentieth Century*, Feb. 1961, p. 173.

2 Critics who do attempt to explain motivation for such behavior typically rely on Freudian or Jungian conceptions, figures with essentially 19th-century sensibilities. The poetry makes clear that Alfred Adler's conception of the will to power, R. D. Laing's more radical vision of the "divided self," and Norman O. Brown's dictum that the root of insecurity lies in the individual's failure to acknowledge death more accurately frame Pinter's world. See, for example, Alfred Adler, *Understanding Human Nature*, trans. Walter Beran Woolfe (Garden City: Garden City Publishing, 1927); R. D. Laing, *The Divided Self: A Study of Sanity and Madness* (London: Tavistock, 1960); Norman O. Brown, *Life Against Death: The Psychoanalytic Meaning of History* (Middletown, Conn.: Wesleyan Univ. Press, 1959). In "The Paranoid Community in Pinter's *The Birthday Party*," *Educational Theatre Journal*, 30, No. 2 (1978), E. T. Kirby suggests that a psychopathological approach rooted in the work of Karl Jaspers, Ludwig Binswanger, and Eugène Minkowski is the *only* way to view Pinter's world. While too reductionistic, his suggestion that we consider Pinter's characters from a phenomenological or existential psychological perspective as exhibiting paranoid behavior is a fruitful one, although he limits his discussion of the motivation of such paranoia to a vague "projected hostility and infantile fears" regarding a future blocked by a terrifying, destructive event.

3 In *The Theatre of the Absurd*, rev. ed. (Garden City: Doubleday, 1969), p. 5, Esslin sees the theme of absurdist theater as "the sense of metaphysical anguish at the absurdity of the human condition." Largely basing his definition of absurdity on *The Myth of Sisyphus*, he nevertheless concludes that a confrontation with the absurd heals (p. 362) and that "there is no contradiction between recognizing the limitations of man's ability to comprehend all of reality in a single system of values and recognizing the mysterious and ineffable oneness, beyond all rational comprehension, that, once experienced, gives serenity of mind and the strength to endure the human condition" (p. 376). Camus would regard this statement as an existential rationalization, as an *acceptance*, similar to that he ascribes to Chestov, Kierkegaard, and Jaspers, whom he clearly understands as abandoning absurdist thinking. Indeed, in *The Peopled Wound: The Work of Harold Pinter* (Garden City: Doubleday, 1970), p. 27, Esslin describes Pinter as an existentialist playwright, though at least partly because Pinter no longer writes within what Esslin understands to be the form of the absurdist theater. Not all critics follow Esslin, of course. For example, in "Between Absurdity and the Playwright," *Educational Theatre Journal*, 15 (1963), 224-35,

William J. Oliver correctly observes that subject matter, not craft, distinguishes absurdist playwrights of all ages. His suggestion that absurd playwrights should show the positive advantages of absurd living and should simplify their work to make it more readily available to audiences, however, I think is unfortunate, and certainly not consistent with Camus' vison of absurdist literature with which we are primarily concerned here.

4 Albert Camus, *The Myth of Sisyphus and Other Essays*, trans. Justin O'Brien (New York: Vintage, 1955), p. 24. I have used the English translation as more readily available to a wider audience; further references to this edition will be indicated parenthetically in the text.

5 Harold Pinter, "Writing for the Theatre," *Evergreen Review*, 8 (1964), 80. Orig. a speech to National Student Drama Festival at Bristol published as "Pinter Between the Lines," *Sunday Times Magazine*, 4 March 1962, pp. 25ff.

6 Much simplified here, the audience response theories of Walter J. Ong and of Hans Robert Jauss elucidate such a dynamic of intended audience response. Ong maintains that the author provides the audience with clues, indexes which inform it of the role which the author wishes it to play ("The Writer's Audience is Always a Fiction," *PMLA*, 90 [1975], 9-21). Calling for a receptional aesthetic, Jauss suggests that many contemporary artists place their audiences in the position of "an uninitiated third person, who in the face of a still meaningless reality must himself find the question which will enable him to discover the perception of the world and the interpersonal problem to which the work's answer is directed" ("Literary History as a Challenge to Literary Theory," trans. Elizabeth Benzinger, *New Literary History*, 2 [1970-71], 37). Jauss further argues that the audience is often intended to identify with the world portrayed, but that such identification depends on the willingness of the spectator to broaden the basis of his identification. In other words, the audience can refuse recognition. The fifth mode of Jauss' receptional aesthetic, "ironic identification," most aptly describes Pinter's typical technique, which attempts to undermine purely aesthetic, objective responses and force communication of an idea in violation of the norm. Such communication requires identification with an "abnormal" figure, resulting in a positive thematic statement through the use of negative example. The alternative response is "aesthetically deficient" and simply derides the figure as comic or sees in the play only "Shocking novelty, unpalatable alienation, and irritating obscurity" ("Levels of Identification of Hero and Audience," trans. Benjamin and Helga Bennett, *New Literary History*, 5 [1973-74], 289, 310-11, 316). Though both Ong and Jauss deal primarily with reader response, their broad conclusions apply to theatrical audiences as well.

7 Harold Pinter, "The Islands of Aran," in *Poems*, ed. Alan Clodd (London: Enitharmon, 1968), p. 6. All further references to this edition will be indicated parenthetically in the text. A second edition, with several additional poems, was published in 1971. Most of the poems in both editions originally appeared in *Poetry London* between 1949 and 1958; all but one of the poems discussed here, the 1956 "Error of Alarm," appeared between 1950 and 1952, that is when Pinter was between twenty and twenty-three years old.

8 In addition to the islands' legs, the persona comments on a "head" at Connemara, a rocky projection lying across the Bay. Irish tradition suggests that Galway Bay was once a lake and that the three islands are remnants of a strip of land formerly ringing that lake, connecting Moher and Connemara; the destroyed legs and the separated head perhaps refer to this tradition. It is also common for the islands to be parched in the sun while showers deluge the neighboring hills—hence the "sun's teeth" image. See Daphne D. C. Pockiss Mould, *The Aran Islands* (Newton Abbott: David and Charles, 1972), pp. 12, 16. Lucky's absurdist speech in Samuel Beckett's *Waiting for Godot* (New York: Grove, 1954), p. 29, includes several references to "the skull the skull the skull the skull in Connemara," which again suggest that the poem is influenced by local tradition and is centrally concerned with death.

9 In *Mac* (London: Emanuel Wax for Pendragon Press, 1968), p. 15, Pinter

describes Anew McMaster's acting by referring to lines from Yeats' "Lapis Lazuli": "They know that Hamlet and Lear are gay;/ Gaiety transfiguring all that dread."

10 Harold Pinter, "Rural Idyll," *Poetry London*, Nov. 1950, pp. 8-9. Published under "Harold Pinta."

11 Harold Pinter, "European Revels," *Poetry London*, Nov. 1950, p. 9. Published under "Harold Pinta."

12 Although "European Revels" and "Rural Idyll" implicitly depict a world view, "Chandaliers and Shadows" (1950, *Poems*, p. 3) explicitly pictures the world, mountains, pastures, and kingdoms, as absurd, berates various ineffectual attempts to escape confrontation with such a world, and depicts a brief revolt initiated by a vision of death.

13 Despite Louis G. Gordan's assertion that absurdist works must be about absurdist heroes in *Strategems to Uncover Nakedness: The Dramas of Harold Pinter* (Columbia, Mo.: Univ. of Missouri Press, 1969), pp. 9-10, Ruby Cohn is certainly correct in her earlier judgment that the central figure in absurdist works need not be a hero (see "Four Stages of the Absurdist Hero," *Drama Survey*, 4 [1965], 195-208).

14 Interestingly, "Stranger" (1953, *Poems*, p. 11) depicts a male figure recognizing the absurdity of his possessive behavior, again using the bargain image; this persona describes his fear of "dying" if the female betrays him. The poem is cast in the form of a legal indictment in which the male condemns the woman's betrayal as eventuating her widowhood, as metaphorically killing him. After twenty-six lines of indictment, the poem breaks off in mid-sentence and concludes: "—/ No case."

15 Almost as romantic, "The Anaesthetist's Pin" (1952, *Poems*, p. 8) conveys this same idea, condemning any anesthesia, any attempt to "amputate" a problem area, as a limitation of experience; the poem implies that any semblance of communcation, of breaking out of isolation, is dependent on the willingness painfully to confront one's experience.

16 Harold Pinter, "One a Story, Two a Death," *Poetry London*, 22 (Summer 1952), 22-24. Published under "Harold Pinta."

Time and Memory
in Pinter's Proust Screenplay

Enoch Brater

Those of us who have watched Pinter develop a personal style dramatizing the effects Time works on the shape of Memory are not at all surprised by his attraction to Proust's *À la Recherche du Temps Perdu* as raw material for cinematic adaptation. What is surprising, however, is his admission that he had read only *Du Côté de Chez Swann,* the first volume of the work, before he embarked on this project.[1] For Pinter's theater has long been engaged in what we might be tempted to call a Proustian fascination with recapturing the past. On stage Pinter's characters habitually struggle to recreate a past which they say they can remember—a past which exists on stage in that hazy realm somewhere between imagination and reality. "That imagining," the playwright has said with particular reference to *Old Times,* "is as true as real."[2] How Pinter came to write the Proust screenplay and how he reworked Proust's grand design into a bold cinematic reduction offer us a new study in literary relationship, for the adaptation through condensation has important implications as it bears on Pinter's work as a whole.

Let us for a moment situate the Proust screenplay in its proper place in the Pinter canon. Early in 1972 Nicole Stephane, who owned the film rights to *À la Recherche du Temps Perdu,* asked Joseph Losey if he would like to work on a film version of the book. Losey then asked Pinter if he was interested.[3] They had already worked together on three films: *The Servant, The Accident,* and *The Go-Between.* The planning stage, however, actually began some months before that. Late in 1971 Pinter told Mel Gussow of the *New York Times* that he was thinking in terms of this project, though at the time he was still reluctant to discuss the venture in the public forum of an interview. He admitted only that the new adaptation would be "a film which

is going to be the most difficult task I've ever had in my life—
and one which is almost impossible. I'm pretty frightened, but
I'm also excited."4 Pinter spent three months in 1972 reading
Proust and taking hundreds of notes. That summer he made
several trips to Illiers, Cabourg, and Paris, steeping himself "in
the Proustian locations." He finished a draft of the screenplay
in November and a complete final revision in early 1973.
"Working on À la Recherche du Temps Perdu," says Pinter,
"was the best working year of my life."5 What we should be
careful to notice about this chronology is that Pinter worked on
the Proust screenplay after Old Times and before No Man's
Land, the two plays which deal most definitively with the
changes Time works on Memory.

In adapting Proust to the screen Pinter makes us see an
À la Recherche du Temps Perdu which bears his own personal
stamp. Quickly dismissing the notion of producing a film centered around only one or two novels of Proust's seven-volume
network, Pinter was determined "to distill the whole work, to
incorporate the major themes of the book into an integrated
whole."6 Joseph Losey and Barbara Bray, an authority on
Proust who was for many years script editor for B.B.C. Radio,
supported Pinter's decision, agreeing that this would make a
far more comprehensive cinematic statement. The choice was a
crucial one, for what results from it is the experience of seeing
Proust through Pinter's eyes. Unlike the architecture of the
novel where the narrator builds sustained, stable constructs of
memory in generous selections of prose, the screenplay evokes
sharp, momentary images encapsulating Proustian duration. We
move quickly from scene to scene as the past, dissected and
fractured, suddenly moves before us in a vast panorama of
concise visual segments. Broken up as it is into short pieces, the
past is not so much recaptured as it is recycled in a style more
Pinteresque than Proustian. In place of long sections of verbal
rotundity, the result of the novelist's preoccupation with making
something concrete and enduring from the flux of the past,
Pinter scales down Proustian memory into the size of a fragment.
Scenes from the past have lost their fullness: they become as
fleeting as the images passing swiftly before our eyes. One might
argue that once the choice is made to do the whole of Proust
rather than a part, the screenwriter, having few choices, is
obliged to give us small sections of the original experience.

Pinter, however, not only welcomes this limitation, but makes it the principle upon which the entire film is organized. We move rapidly from frame to frame, from moment to moment. The carefully chiselled inter-relatedness of Proust's world, the slow process of revelation which gradually unfolds for Proust's readers, has been rapidly accelerated. But the result here should not be mistaken for Proust. In the screenplay memory no longer makes of the past that beautiful and secure tapestry it once was. In place of the original's wholeness, we now have Pinter's predictable fragmentation and instability.

This tone of insecurity has been further amplified by Pinter's departure from the novel's tight historical sequence. Pinter focuses, instead, on a past whose moments have been synchronized by an elaborate principle of historical simultaneity. "All of the years of the novel," as Stanley Kauffmann observed, "are assumed to exist simultaneously, and the film moves in and out of them as it needs to."7 But the frequent changes are by no means immediately clear. The confusion each time a cut is made is important: it forces us to re-orient ourselves in relation to a past recorded on a reel furiously on the run. As in *The Go-Between*, this peculiar past "is a foreign country. They do things differently there."8 Pinter has changed Proust's past by making it mysterious, unfamiliar, and threatening. A cut is made and as the camera eye suddenly opens on the next scene we aren't at all sure exactly where we are. The absence of certainty, the initial problem of validation, has been cleverly designed for its cinematic effect of calculated disruption. It is Pinter's authentic signature on *temps perdu* and *temps retrouvé*.

Pinter has been careful to note that "the architecture of the film should be based on two main and contrasting principles: one, a movement, chiefly narrative, toward disillusion, and the other, more intermittent, toward revelation, rising to where time that was lost is found, and fixed forever in art."9 In the novel Proust designed a pattern of images to make his reader perceive the inter-connectiveness of his fictional world. We remember, in particular, the madeleine, the refrain from a Vinteuil sonata, the sound of a spoon hitting a china teacup, the lady in pink, and Vermeer's painting. After Pinter completed the screenplay he was impressed by how much of Proust's style was compatible with the technical possibilities inherent in film. In 1974 he read Paul Goodman's essay on "The Proustian Camera Eye."10 The

piece was written in 1935, but Pinter was able to find it reprinted in an anthology called *American Film Criticism,* edited
by Stanley Kauffmann and Bruce Henstell. Pinter was struck
by the affinity Goodman found between Proustian narration and
cinematic values—the same thing he had recently discovered
while working on the adaptation. The essential images Proust
used to give symmetry to the novel were cinematic ones: the
visual and the aural. Proust made us see the past and made us
hear the voices of the past. He gave Time, what Beckett called
in his essay on Proust that "double-headed monster of damna-
tion and salvation,"11 an authentic fictional form.

In translating Proust to the screen, Pinter exercises a highly
disciplined pattern of selection. Not all of Proust's images have
been used. Too many would confuse the viewer by upsetting the
sense of unity they are called upon to impart in the constricted
time span of screening a movie. Purists may scoff, but in the
screenplay there are no madeleines. This was the only caveat
Losey made on the writing of the Proust screenplay, that there
should be no madeleines. Losey convinced Pinter that this image
would be far too superficial if incorporated into a film based on
Proust's work. It was the one image people knew from *À la
Recherche de Temps Perdu* even if they had never bothered to
read it.12 In place of madeleines Pinter therefore chose a far
more striking visual metaphor: the yellow screen. The choice is
an excellent one, for as the camera draws back we only gradually recognize this screen as a minute part of Vermeer's *View
of Delft.* In the screenplay the camera returns again and again
to render a momentary glimpse of the same yellow screen. Like
Swann, our eyes remain "fixed" on a thing we do not know.13
Pinter accomplishes pictorially what Proust accomplishes verbally: the wonder of a fragment which only slowly reveals itself
as a small part of a far more comprehensive canvas.

With sounds, too, Pinter has been similarly discreet. Here
the adaptation features the Vinteuil sonata and the sound of a
spoon hitting a china teacup, but both are not nearly so striking
as the visual frames which accompany them. The sonata is
played before an audience grotesque, ugly, philistine, and bored.
Only Swann and Marcel appreciate its poignancy. The camera
discovers heavily-made-up faces in a series of harsh close-ups.
At first glance these faces appear to be young. But as the camera
lingers on the group, we see that these individuals are decaying

and disfigured, desperately trying to cling to their youth in a grotesque visual parody of the narrator's attempt to recapture the past. The sonata plays on as cinematic time moves on. Two subsequent close-ups juxtapose a yawn on an anonymous powdered face with Swann's pained facial expression. Pinter's point has been made in a typical "line with no words in it at all."[14] The cinematic eye concisely records those nuances Proust captures so graphically in the words of his novel. The clink of a silver spoon on a china teacup can be similarly chilling. Swann, arriving late for a chamber recital, sits alone, cold, isolated, and finally disillusioned. The sonata plays on in a distant room. Marcel will suffer the same fate as he endures the same sounds later on.

One of Proust's very special talents is the way in which he makes us hear his people speak from the pages of his fiction. Charlus, Cambremer, Saint-Loup, Madame Verdurin, and of course the unforgettable Françoise, are some of the greatest talkers in all of literature. Proust has recaptured their way of speaking far more exactly than any line he has them say. Here Pinter has made a concession to the medium in which he is working. He substitutes how Proust's people *look* for how Proust's people *sound*. The dimension is Time and its "poisonous ingenuity,"[15] so the adaptation features characters who literally age before our eyes. But in this screenplay Time is as often backward as it is forward. Saying very little but implying very much, each *look,* punctuated by Pinter's characteristic silence or pause, tells us everything we need to know. Revelation and disillusion have been rendered visually through cinematic time rather than verbally through fiction. This is Pinter's Proust after all.

Pinter's special interpretation of Proust therefore highlights two very individual visions of the way Time works to shape Memory. A variation of a theme by Proust, the screenplay not only adapts *À la Recherche du Temps Perdu* into a different medium, but fulfills our expectations of the original way memory is made to work in plays like *Old Times* and *No Man's Land*. Pinter's characters are still struggling to recapture the past, but that past has now become fractured, unstable, and ultimately hazy. Gone is the security Proust was still able to find in the temple of his art. No Marcel appears on the boards to direct the show with definitive narrative authority. The screenplay, however, does offer us the cinematic analogue for Pinter's own recent experimentation with the games Time plays with Memory on his stage. *Betrayal*, produced at the National Theatre in London in 1978, confronts us with a naturalistic plot of sexual, social, and psychological hypocrisies whose chronology has been deliberately reversed.16 We move counterclockwise: the play closes in 1968 and opens in 1977. "Nice sometimes to think back, isn't it?" is the interrogative flourish in Pinter's Proustian transfiguration of adultery in *Betrayal*. The Proust screenplay is another such journey into the formal mistiness of the past, but the road Pinter takes in getting there continues, as always, to be ridden with implicating detours.

University of Michigan

NOTES

1 Harold Pinter, *The Proust Screenplay* (New York, 1977), p. ix.

2 Mel Gussow, "A Conversation (Pause) with Harold Pinter," *New York Times Magazine*, 5 December 1971, sec. 6, p. 43.

3 *The Proust Screenplay*, p. ix.

4 Gussow, p. 133.

5 *The Proust Screenplay*, p. x.

6 Ibid., p. ix.

7 Stanley Kauffmann, "*À la Recherche du Temps Perdu: The Proust Screenplay* by Harold Pinter," *The New Republic*, 24 and 31 December 1977, p. 23.

8 Harold Pinter, *Five Screenplays* (London: Methuen, 1971), p. 287.

9 *The Proust Screenplay*, p. ix.

10 Kauffmann, p. 22.

11 Samuel Beckett, *Proust* (London, 1931), p. 1.

12 For this information I am indebted to Professor Peter Bien of Dartmouth College. Professor Bien obtained this information from Losey during the semester the director taught a course at Dartmouth.

13 Marcel Proust, *Swann's Way*, trans. C. K. Scott Moncrieff (New York, 1928), p. 281.

14 Martin Esslin, *Pinter: A Study of His Plays* (London, 1973), p. 124. Esslin quotes from Pinter's unpublished novel, *The Dwarfs*: "But tell me this. What do they do when they come to a line with no words in it at all?"

15 Beckett, p. 4.

16 See Russell Davies, "Pinter Land," *The New York Review of Books*, 25 January 1979, p. 24.

The Sound of a Poet Singing Loudly:
A Look at *Elegy for Young Lovers*

Marc A. Roth

When W. H. Auden wrote to Igor Stravinsky to accept the offer to write the libretto for *The Rake's Progress,* he closed his letter with an unusually unguarded expression of joy: "I need hardly add that the chance of working with you is the greatest honour of my life."[1] Auden's remark, besides praising Stravinsky, reveals the reverence which characterized his view of operatic collaboration. Auden saw opera as the remaining verbal art form which employed the "High Style," and could offer a modern poet the chance to sing loudly.[2] His fondness for musical theatre grew as he answered requests for new libretti and translations. One could say that opera became a serious business for Auden, since he boasted that the commissions given to him and his collaborator Chester Kallman paid quite well. During his later years opera came to occupy a significant place in his criticism and public lectures. In the series entitled *Secondary Worlds* given as the T. S. Eliot Memorial Lectures in 1967, Auden devoted his most comprehensive talk to the world of opera. The following year, Auden was invited to deliver the prestigious opening address at the Salzburg Festival. His speech, entitled "Worten und Noten," dealt with the relationships between language and music, and standing before the Salzburg audience Auden said that "opera is now to me the most fascinating of art-forms."[3]

The critical neglect of the bulk of Auden's operatic collaborations is curious, especially given the poet's own devotion to the genre. With the exception of a few scholars (e.g., Monroe Spears, John Blair, and Ulrich Weisstein), the majority of Auden's critics have avoided giving serious consideration to his works written in collaboration for the musical theatre. Moreover, the absence of an edition of Auden's collected libretti further testifies to the lack of attention given to this aspect of his poetic canon. Through the efforts of Stravinsky's assistant, Robert Craft, the exchange of letters between composer and poet over *The Rake's Progress* was documented and appeared in Stravinsky's *Memories and Commentaries* (1960). The opera itself has received extensive commentary in musical circles, and has been described by Joseph Kerman as one of the major operas of the twentieth century which "show most triumphantly the continuing life of *dramma per musica* in our time."[4] Auden's next ventures as a librettist were with the German composer Hans Werner Henze. Auden and Kallman wrote the texts for *Elegy for Young Lovers* which was produced in 1961, and *The Bassairds,* an operatic adaptation of *The Bacchae* commissioned for the 1966 Salzburg Festival. These works have received their appropriate notoriety in the musical world, but have suffered from an unexplainable and systematic neglect by Auden's literary critics. For example, in the tribute to Auden compiled after his death by his literary executors and Stephen Spender, there was no article by or about Henze, nor was there any commentary about *Elegy for Young Lovers* or *The Bassairds.* Robert Craft, however, did contribute an entertaining update of Auden's relationship with Stravinsky during and after the writing of *The Rake's Progress.*[5] Especially in the case of *Elegy for Young Lovers,* the critics have avoided commenting upon a unique international collaboration which in the last two decades has become a highly significant work in the contemporary musical theatre.

Elegy for Young Lovers was first performed in a German translation of the English libretto at the Schwetzingen Festival on May 20, 1961. It was the third in a series of new operas commissioned for this festival by the South German Radio (Suddeutsche Rundfunk). The opera received subsequent performances in German at Zurich before being heard in its original English version at the Glyndebourne Festival on July 19, 1961. Successful productions of the German version took place at the Munich Festival of 1961, the Berlin Festival of 1962, and the Holland Festival of 1967. All of the above-mentioned German performances were staged by the composer and featured Dietrich Fischer-Dieskau in the lead role of Gregor Mittenhofer. Since its English premiere at Glyndebourne, *Elegy for Young Lovers* has yet to be produced as part of the regular season at a major opera house in England or the United States, though it was included as a production of the San Francisco Spring Opera in April, 1978. The American premiere, which Henze conducted himself, took place at the Juilliard School of Music on April 29, 1965. Conrad Osborne, reviewing the performance for *High Fidelity/Musical America,* commented that *Elegy for Young Lovers* "seems to me far and away the most important new opera to be introduced in New York in many years; I would rank it with *Peter Grimes* and *The Rake's Progress* as the most important since World War II."6 In his review of the same premiere for *Opera,* Martin Berheimer commented upon the circumstances of the performance: "the locale for this important event was—predictably, I am afraid, not the Metropolitan Opera House, or even its counterparts in Chicago or San Francisco."7 *Elegie für Junge Liebende* has become a part of the regular repertory at Munich and Berlin, and it has been performed in Italian and French. Yet in spite of its German success and apparent international appeal, impressarios in the English speaking world are unwilling to take a chance on *Elegy for Young Lovers* in its original form.

The merits of *Elegy for Young Lovers* as a German opera were initially reinforced by the English and American reviewers who witnessed performances in both languages and usually preferred the German version. Arthur Jacobs, for example, in his review of the Glyndebourne performance found that some of the English sounded awkward and suggested that the German text was superior because "fitted to the notes [it] has a more natural stress."8 Martin Berheimer's comments on the American premiere indicated a similar preference for the more natural sound of the German version: "What in German translation had seemed natural was awkward, obvious, and precious in the English original."9 These observations reflect some of the difficulties faced by a composer working with an operatic text in a foreign language. In addition, the German version was produced under optimum performance conditions: the composer wrote the roles with specific German singers in mind, and he also staged the opera himself. A German production of Henze's opera might seem more natural because of the subject matter itself: *Elegy for Young Lovers,* an opera about the crimes of an artist, is especially German. German speaking audiences, nourished on authors such as Goethe, E. T. A. Hofmann, Grill-

parzer, Mann, and other developers of the *Künstlerroman,*
would be inclined to view *Elegy for Young Lovers* as a version
of the favorite German fictional genre written for the musical
theatre.

The central figure of the opera, Gregor Mittenhofer, is a
meglomaniacal, turn-of-the-century Austrian poet who murders
as he creates. Compared to the possessed Romantic artist such
as E. T. A. Hofmann's Cardillac who must murder in order to
create, Mittenhofer is a far more distasteful figure because he
kills with cynicism, style, and indifference. The opera takes place
at a *Gasthaus* in the Alps where Mittenhofer and his entourage
make annual visits so that the poet can receive inspiration from
the visions of a mad widow, Hilda Mack (soprano *leggiero*),
whose husband disappeared on the slopes forty years ago. The
respected poet's travelling companions include: his mistress,
Elizabeth Zimmer (soprano), who is young enough to be his
daughter; his physician, Wilhelm Reischmann (bass), who ad-
ministers daily injections of "tonic" to insure his master's performance; and Mittenhofer's patroness and secretary, Countess
Carolina von Kirchstetten (contralto), who pays for all of the
above necessities and keeps the master's affairs in order. The
surname of the Countess is an "in-house" joke since it is also
the name of the Austrian village where Auden lived for many
years. Much of the text of *Elegy for Young Lovers* was written
there. Dr. Reischmann's son Toni (lyric tenor), who is also
Mittenhofer's godson, arrives for a visit, and he and the poet's
mistress fall in love. A complicated tug-of-war over Elizabeth
ensues: Mittenhofer of course wants to keep her, Frau Mack
wants to take Elizabeth away on holiday, and Toni wants to
marry her. Mittenhofer decides that Elizabeth should be allowed
to choose her own salvation, which he knows will be with his
younger rival. The poet, however, will use this event as raw
material since he needs a poem to read at his sixtieth birthday
party. Mittenhofer then reads a part of his new poem which he
calls "The Young Lovers." As a conciliatory gesture he asks the
lovers to climb the mountain and bring back a sprig of edelweiss
which he claims that he needs for inspiration. After they have
gone Mittenhofer tells Carolina that he will try to finish his
"Elegy" in time for his birthday celebration. As she questions
him about the new title, an alpine guide enters to warn them
that a storm is brewing, and asks if they know of anyone on the

mountain who needs to be rescued. Looking his patroness squarely in the eye, the respected poet very coldly and deliberately says: "Nobody that I know of." Carolina desperately tries to preserve herself in the face of what she has just witnessed. In the final scene we see the couple, who now recognize that their love was an illusion, preparing themselves for death. The opera concludes with an epilogue: at his birthday celebration Mittenhofer solemnly dedicates his "Elegy for Young Lovers" to the memory of Toni and Elizabeth and prepares to read it, but instead of the poet's voice we hear the collective voices of the others in the opera—all of whom contributed to the writing of the poem.

In "The World of Opera," Auden describes *Elegy for Young Lovers* as a statement about the myth of the "artistic genius" created by the European Romantics.[10] The artist in Auden's example is a destroyer, fanatically devoted to his work, and he needs a group of will-less but well-meaning people to treat him like a spoiled child so that he might produce. The late nineteenth century bore many species of the artistic genius: composers, actors and actresses, the prima donna, and a few well-to-do authors who could afford to assimilate the self-indulgent daily ritual of wealthy performing artists such as Bernhardt or Booth. Interestingly, Auden notes that the first central figure for his opera was to be an actor—an elderly artist whose lifelong dream was to play the leading role in Byron's *Manfred*. This idea, however, would not work because, Auden said, "we had no myth."[11] The great actor was then transformed into a great poet who would ruthlessly sacrifice everyone around him in order to create his masterpiece. Although Auden tries to argue that his choice of a poet for his central figure was based upon the dramatic requirements of his scenario, his argument is not terribly convincing. Certainly an opera about the myth of the *fin-de-siècle* artist could have been based upon any one of many types, especially performing artists and composers. But for reasons which he wisely chose not to spell out, a highly praised and respectable poet helped to create a devastating portrait of a "mythical" fellow creature.

Auden noted that a guiding light during the preparation of the text of *Elegy for Young Lovers* was Ibsen, and his well-made drama about a destructive artist set in an alpine *Gasthaus* certainly recalls *When We Dead Awaken*. An important aspect

of the well-made construction of *Elegy for Young Lovers* can
be seen through the manner of the introduction of the characters. Each person is first seen contributing to the daily ritual of
the eccentric poet who stands at the center of the work. Carolina,
for example, who is the poet's patroness and his *chef d'affaires,*
is first seen complaining about a recent review. Reischmann, the
poet's physician, busies himself with the necessary tonics. We
quickly learn that "the master's day" consists of composing,
interrupted at regular intervals by feedings and injections. Suddenly, however, a surprising event occurs which breaks this
secure routine: an alpine guide announces that the body of Frau
Mack's husband has been found. In one moment Mittenhofer's
ritualistic world has been undone. Frau Mack will no longer
have her visions and the poet will have to look elsewhere for
his inspiration. Mittenhofer solves his problem by turning to a
set of available young lovers and creating the conditions for
their elegy.

A virtue of the text is that it requires Henze's music for the
completion of its dramatic ideas. The opera is divided into
labelled sections which create the musical and dramatic units.
An example of this effective symbiotic construction occurs in
the portion of the second act entitled "The Young Lovers." The
poet's mistress has caused a crisis by openly declaring her love for
Dr. Reischmann's son Toni. Yet she intends to remain with the
aging poet, and explains to her young lover that "there are some
women, perhaps, / Who can feel only what a wife should / For
an older man."[12] Toni is about to barge into the master's study,
but Mittenhofer has already been disturbed by the noise and
appears on his landing. The poet restores order by generously
offering the young couple their freedom. Although his decision
seems peculiar, Mittenhofer enjoys playing the forgiving father:

> Have you forgotten Toni's my son, too?
> He's fallen in love. I can't see why
> That needs forgiving.
>
> *to Elizabeth again*
>
>   Or why, dear
> Child, if you love my son, knowing how near
> My heart he is, you are still shy—
>   And cannot say
>   Yes, no, or which one,
> And have done. (37)

His forgiving style seems intended to rival King Marke's pardon of Tristan and Isolde. As Elizabeth struggles to make her choice, the mood is suddenly destroyed by the unceremonious ringing of a cow bell which heralds the entrance of Frau Mack accompanied by the same guide who brought the news concerning the recovery of her husband's corpse. The former visionary is now pleasantly drunk, and freely insults the poet and his creative process:

> Put that in a sonnet,
> Ducky, it tops the old rot that you used to
> Steal from me once, but I better had warned you—
> This time I get ten percent or I sue! (40)

Despite her condition, Hilda has entered with a serious purpose in mind: she has come to claim Elizabeth. Amidst the chaos of the moment Hilda comforts Elizabeth with a drink and advises her to reject both Toni and Mittenhofer. "Leave here with me on holiday; / We need it" (40). In a truly operatic moment, Elizabeth rises to announce her decision to marry Toni. Everyone, with the exception of Toni of course, protests the decision, but Mittenhofer calms his retinue by blessing the pair of young lovers. He then asks them to listen to an excerpt of the new poem he has been working on entitled "The Young Lovers":

> Out of Eden, bringing Eden
> With them, the young lovers come
> Hand in hand to the cold lands.
> The snow falls. There is no welcome.
> Their singleness reproaches our mingled
> Isolations, their love our songless
> Ice-altars; we refuse the rose
> Of Heaven's children. Nevertheless
> One who dare break the barrier . . .
> His own . . . who only will turn, will move to
> Reach for and bless their happiness,
> Shall heedlessly enter Eden too.
> They bring us a gift from afar:
> A fragile, and eternal flower. (41-42)

The presentation of this poem, however, is uniquely musical. The first line is preceded by an *arpeggio* in F minor played on the harp which establishes the tone and tempo of the verse as Mittenhofer begins to recite. At the fifth measure, however, Elizabeth joins the poet by repeating his phrase "hand in hand." She sings the phrase using the same intervals as the poet, but a full tone higher and in a soprano register which is an octave above Mittenhofer's baritone. After her opening phrase she contributes to the poem on her own as Mittenhofer continues to recite. The other characters join the ensemble in the same fashion by taking their cue from a phrase of the poet and then continuing to compose on their own; ultimately Mittenhofer's poem becomes a sextet. It is significant that each contributor takes his cue from the poet and not from anyone else. Toni, for example, who joins the ensemble after Elizabeth and Hilda, does not begin with a phrase uttered by his beloved, but he repeats Mittenhofer's line "their love." Each character is similarly struck by specific words of Mittenhofer's verse which evoke an emotional response. Hilda Mack, for example, enters the poem by repeating Mittenhofer's phrase "the snow": an appropriate beginning for the former visionary who was imprisoned by the snowstorm which buried her husband. As Frau Mack contributes to the poem, she recovers the *coloratura* of her former visions which has not been heard since her liberation by the discovery of her husband's body. Thus the musical arrangement of the sextet conveys important dramatic ideas, and through their contributions each character becomes a part of Mittenhofer's poem. Following the sextet, the stage is cleared by an exchange of farewells, and Mittenhofer, now alone, curses his entourage: "BAH! What a bunch! . . . Why don't they all die!" (45-46) Auden comments in his postscript to the text that since Mittenhofer is morally responsible for the destruction of three people, the opera will only be effective dramatically if the audience believes that Mittenhofer has produced a great poem (63). The strength of the poem, Auden claims, lies in the music of the sextet: "the very beautiful music which Henze has written for [the sextet] will convince any audience . . . that the poem is going to be a very good one."13

The unusual musical idea which governs this section, however, must wait until the end of the opera to be completed. By that time, the contributors to the ensemble will have been sacrificed (some literally) to the poet's elegy. In the epilogue to the opera, Mittenhofer presents his new poem "Elegy for Young Lovers" to his adoring public. As he opens his manuscript and prepares to recite, a harp and flute begin to play a trill, but at the end of the second measure the harp repeats the *arpeggio* which began the reading of the first excerpt of "The Young

Lovers." Each time the harp repeats this *arpeggio* we hear another character's voice join the ensemble and become part of Mittenhofer's elegy. Now, however, the poem is purely musical for Mittenhofer, nor do the other characters sing any words—we only hear the sound of their voices. Auden argued that an opera, through its combination of verbal and musical media, could present a poet writing poetry, while a drama which tried to do the same thing would inevitably fail. To illustrate his point, Auden compared Mittenhofer to Marchbanks:

> All that Shaw can do with Marchbanks, the poet in *Candida*, is endow him with the artistic temperament. . . . Even had Shaw been a great poet himself, he only could have written Shavian poetry, not a different but equally great kind of poetry which the audience would believe had been written by Marchbanks. But in opera . . . it might be possible to portray a poet convincingly because poetry and music are different kinds of language. If . . . the poetry of our hero could be represented by music, the audience would, if the music were good enough, be convinced that his poetry was good, although the music was not written by him but by Henze.[14]

In this remark Auden denies himself appropriate credit, for if audiences are convinced that Mittenhofer's poetry is good, it is due to the synthesis of language and music achieved through the collaboration of poet and composer. A great compliment on this account was paid to Auden in the comment of a German reviewer after the Schwetzingen premiere: "Even more than the libretti of Hugo von Hofmannsthal, to whom the opera is dedicated, this text fulfills its objective as a vehicle for musical form."[15]

There are many questions about Auden's collaboration with Hans Werner Henze which will probably remain unanswered until the correspondence between the two men is published. The partnership between a well-established and conservative English poet and an angry young German composer is rather unusual at first sight. One can, for example, more easily comprehend the collaboration of Auden and Stravinsky: two major figures closely allied in their respective battles against the avant-garde, who joined forces aggressively to reinvoke tradition. Henze and Auden, however, stood much farther apart in their respective artistic missions and temperaments. In addition to being Auden's junior by almost twenty years, Henze has been a very outspoken and troubled artist whose political commitments and musical tendencies have endured many extreme shifts. Following World War II Henze studied dodecaphonic technique with Wolfgang Fortner and René Liebowitz, and he quickly became allied with other composers of the Darmstadt school such as Stockhausen and Boulez. But in 1953 Henze decided that he could no longer remain a part of the German economic miracle and its music, which he called "a new, subtle, noiseless fascism."16 Like other German artists before him, Henze made his "Italienische Reise." He first lived on the island of Ischia, which is where he probably first met Auden who rented a summer house there until 1957. Finally Henze settled in Naples and, comfortably retrenched, he succumbed to Italian influences: he began to see himself as a new composer of old operas. He was accordingly damned by the avant-garde for writing singable works for the musical theatre. Between 1955 and 1966 Henze composed five full-length operas, the fourth and fifth of these in collaboration with Auden and Kallman. In 1967 he came under the influence of the German radical student leader Rudi Dutschke, who had sought refuge from an assassination attempt at Henze's Italian villa.17 The composer now rejected the bourgeois opera house and all it represented. Between 1967 and 1973, while *Elegy for Young Lovers* and *The Bassairds* received lavish productions in European opera houses, Henze made three trips to Cuba and composed the following works: an oratorio dedicated to Che Guevarra, a "recital for four musicians" based on the autobiography of a runaway Cuban slave, and a "vaudeville-opera" for television called *La Cubana*—the story of an aging dance-hall queen caught in a revolution.18

While Henze tried to gear his musical compositions to a new found political commitment, Auden delivered lectures in which he expressed the fear that art was being undermined by politics. Auden had long ceased to believe in the efficacy of political action, and in his final T. S. Eliot Memorial Lecture of 1967 he argued that art should be politically impotent:

> . . . in certain historical epochs, like the Romantic age, literary artists have been accorded a public status which tempted them to think of themselves more highly than they ought to think. Today, they are in danger of not taking their art seriously enough. Their reaction to their diminished status may take two forms. They may, in a futile attempt to recover social import-ance, attempt to become propagandists for some good cause, to be as the current jargon has it, *engagé*. The world about us

> is, as it always has been, full of gross evils and appalling misery,
> but it is a fatal delusion and shocking overestimation of the
> importance of the artist in the world, to suppose that by making
> works of art, we can do anything to eradicate the one or alle-
> viate the other. . . . The utmost an artist can hope to do for his
> contemporary readers is, as Dr. Johnson said, to enable them a
> little better to enjoy life or a little better to ensure it.19

Henze, however, long before his association with Rudi Dutschke,
had viewed his art within a political context. In essays written
during the late 1950's and early 1960's ("Nach dem Krieg,"
"Künstler als Aussenseiter"), Henze espoused opinions which
Auden would have considered as "a shocking overestimation of
the artist in the world." Perhaps when some of the letters between composer and librettist are published we might find some
lively debates on the subject of art and politics.

Yet despite their political, generational, and cultural differences, Auden provided Henze with a much needed resource.
The text of *Elegy for Young Lovers* was an original drama for
the musical theatre, and before this composition all of Henze's
operas had been adaptations of already existing works. His first
opera, *Boulevard Solitude* (1950), was a reworking of Prevost's
Manon Lescaut in modern dress. *König Hirsch* (1956), which
Henze calls his "Italian opera," was an adaptation of Carlo
Gozzi's *Il Re Cervo (The King Stag)*. Henze, at the suggestion
of Luchino Visconti, next wrote an operatic adaptation of
Kleist's *Der Prinz von Homburg* (1960). Nonetheless, it would
seem unusual that a German composer who had written operas
to three texts in his own language would now turn to an English
poet as his collaborator for his next work. Moreover, since his
new opera had been commissioned by Süddeutsche Rundfunk
for the Schwetzingen Festspiele, Henze knew that it would be
performed in German translation before having its premiere in
the original version. Thus *Elegy for Young Lovers* was intended
from its inception to be a German opera—a curious fact given
Auden's views about opera translation. In an essay coauthored
with Kallman, "Translating Opera Libretti," which appears in
The Dyer's Hand and Other Essays (New York: Vintage,
1968), Auden argues that while it is perfectly all right to translate opera for television, performances in opera houses should
still be done in the original language (484). Additional commentary in this essay focuses upon the specific difficulties of
reconciling the very different rhythms of German and English:

Now it so happens that in English, on account of its vowels and
its many monosyllablic words, there are fewer syllables which
sing well and are intelligible when spread over several notes
than there are in . . . German. English is, intrinsically a more
staccato tongue. (490)

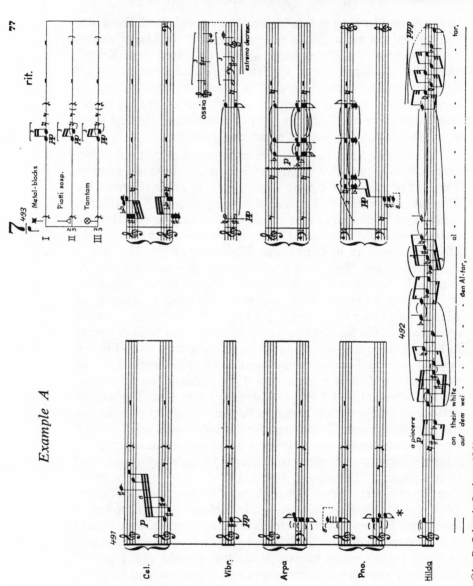

Example A

Using an example from his translation of *Die Zauberflöte,* Auden shows how a quatrain of iambic German verse set to a tune in 6/8 time had to be rendered in English as an anapestic quatrain in order to give one syllable to every note of music as Mozart intended. Although Auden has been an accomplished translator of German poetry and opera into English, he did not attempt to render his own libretto into German. The German version of *Elegy for Young Lovers* was done by two translators, Ludwig Landgraf and Werner Schachteli, in collaboration with the composer.

The preference for the German version by the English and American reviewers notwithstanding, one can find some important instances where the verbal and musical relationships have been changed because of the German translation. A good example of this problem can be found in an excerpt from Hilda Mack's lengthy first act vision (Example A). Her English phrase "on their white altar" can easily be translated into the same number of German words without any distortion in meaning. But as Auden has pointed out, syllables are more prominent than words in musical translation, and clearly the monosyllabic "white" and the duosyllabic "weissen" cannot be sung in the same way. The extra syllable and prominent "s" sound in "weissen" create a different musical shape for the entire German line. In some instances Henze was forced to adjust the music in order to accommodate the translation. For example, Mittenhofer's important admonishment to Reischmann "Bless them, you will" becomes in the German translation, "Gib deinen segen, du wirst es tun." The rhythm and dramatic effect of the line in German are noticeably different because the four English monosyllables, which sound very emphatic, have lost some of their impact through the German transmutation into seven words with nine syllables. The composer had to adjust the score accordingly (Example B). The emphatic quality of "Bless them" is reinforced by each word taking a quarter note, but the additional series of eighth notes added to the score in order to accommodate the German translation diffuses the effect of the English original. A similar change occurs in the second half of the phrase which has been adjusted so that the German words would have one note per syllable. If one version sounds more "natural" in performance, this would most likely be a reflection of a particular singer's skill. Nevertheless, the relationship between words

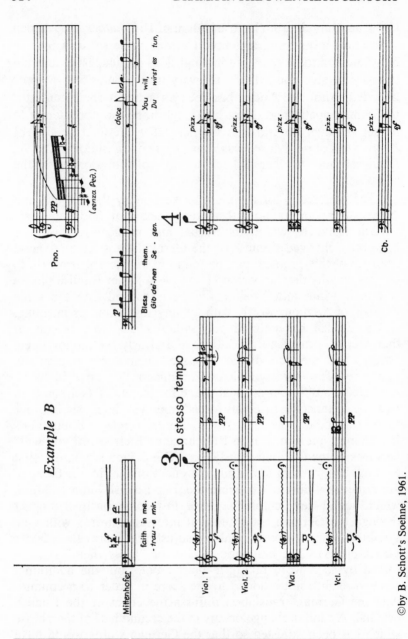

and notes in the original version produces a dramatic effect
which is changed by translation.

Perhaps Henze's choice of English librettists for a German opera can be clarified by looking at his musical rather than his literary goals. According to Henze's biographer, Klaus Geitel, the composer told Auden that he wished to move away from the loosely structured harmonic idiom in which he had written since coming to Italy, and to write a modern opera in "the old style" which would force him to compose in a "more severe and structural form."[20] Given these musical goals Auden was an appropriate choice for Henze because of the poet's work with Stravinsky on *The Rake's Progress*—an opera described by Auden as "the Mozart kind, with set numbers, orchestral recitative and recitative *secco,* and an orchestra of modest Mozartian size."[21] Auden's collaboration with Stravinsky had prepared him to write a libretto for another composer who viewed opera as an essentially musical form. Henze's musical leanings at the time that he composed *Elegy for Young Lovers* were decidedly anti-Wagnerian, and many of his ideas can be seen as extensions of Stravinsky's arguments as set forth in the *Poetics of Music* (1939). Stravinsky disliked the Wagnerian music drama enough to call it "pathological"; it was based, he said, on an essentially unmusical idea of the "synthesis of the arts":

> I hold that this system, far from having raised the level of musical culture, has never ceased to undermine it and finally to debase it in the most paradoxical fashion. In the past one went to the opera for the diversion offered by facile musical works. Later on one returned to it in order to yawn at dramas in which music, arbitrarily paralyzed by constraints foreign to its own laws, could not help tiring out the most attentive audience in spite of the great talent displayed by Wagner.[22]

Although his tone is less volatile, Henze's ideas about the necessity of preserving the musical integrity of opera are essentially the same as Stravinsky's. When asked in an interview about his view of opera, Henze's response was that the artform ought to remain musical:

> I write operas because they are a musical form like quartets and symphonies, with of course different conventions; but all the effects of the stage—movement, scenery, lighting and so on— are but an additional dimension to explain and illuminate the music. You might say that the stage is the open eye of the score. When I choose a plot for an opera, I don't think about what it will be like as a "show," but of certain musical ideas I want to express in a visual form—the music as it were overflowing into forms that are visual.[23]

Henze believed that the salvation of the musical theatre lay in a return to Italian models, and here again he expanded a Stravinskian principle found in the *Poetics of Music*. Like Stravinsky, Henze did not advocate a superficial imitation of Italian models: he sought instead to restore formal musical values as the basis of opera. Although the music in *Elegy for Young Lovers* is often dramatic and symbolically expressive, the opera is separated into arias, recitatives, ensembles, and set pieces. To insist that his opera is not *durchkomponiert*, the composer has gone so far as to describe *Elegy for Young Lovers* as a "number opera."24

Henze's attempt to combine tradition with innovation in *Elegy for Young Lovers* has created a certain amount of confusion, especially for those who admire the composer and want to describe his rather unique synthesis. While his discreditors can attack Henze for not taking a firm position in the battleground of modern music, Henze's more favorable critics often disagree over the essential character of his musical structure. For example, H. L. Stuckenschmidt, who has written extensively on Henze and contemporary German music, argued that the entire score of *Elegy for Young Lovers* is marked by "a dedication to a twelve tone series and its relevant harmonics."25 Arthur Jacobs, who reviewed the Glyndebourne production, was impressed, however, by Henze's ability to write real melodies, and he suggested that tonality was the most prominent characteristic of the score.26 One of Henze's goals, which might account for some of the critical confusion, is to place an old convention in a new musical context. Thus Hilda Mack, his mad widow in *Elegy for Young Lovers*, has *coloratura* visions accompanied by a single flute—a convention derived from Donizetti's best known heroine. Yet the representation of madness through Henze's treatment of the voice is unique. The visions are characterized by freely shifting intervals; the madness is atonal and produces great dramatic effect. The critical debates notwithstanding, Henze's mixture of jazz, *opera buffo*, serialism, and traditional melody often provides the basis for very effective musical drama. The composer's determined eclecticism allies him with Auden, whose lengthy career was characterized by the attempt to create a synthesis from many diverse elements.

One of Auden's more provocative statements about opera is that the libretto is nothing but "a private letter to the composer which is useful insofar as it stimulates the composer to write beautiful music."27 Consistent with the spirit of this remark, Auden kept a low profile as a librettist. Publicly he made only clinical or descriptive statements about his collaborations with Stravinsky and Henze. His composers, on the other hand, have given Auden more credit than he either demanded or expected. Stravinsky, who did not bestow his praise freely, said of Auden in his *Memories and Commentaries* that "few people have taught me as much" (148). Henze has not only praised Auden, but also described how large a role the poet and his works played in the collaborative process:

> Besides my intensive daily work on [*Elegy for Young Lovers*] I read widely from Auden's collected works (which I can now claim to know really well), so as to penetrate fully into his world and imagination and thereby to achieve the greatest possible harmony between libretto and score. I do not know how far I have succeeded, but I do know that I have rarely composed to any text with so much enjoyment, emotion, excitement, and pure pleasure.28

Henze's *Essays,* published in 1964, contain many quotations from Auden's works. A good example of Henze's intellectual debt to Auden occurs in the essay "Über Elegie für Junge Liebende," which includes a lengthy excerpt from *The Age of Anxiety*.29 Concerning the team of Auden and Kallman, Henze has commented that they are "ideal librettists." Kallman is praised for his practical knowledge of the stage, and Auden is most often singled out for his understanding of the subtle but important difference between a drama and a libretto. In addition, Henze has often gone to rather elaborate lengths to emphasize that the process of creating *Elegy for Young Lovers* was truly collaborative:

> Auden and Kallman gave me commentaries, notes and suggestions with each scene, which always applied to the music, even to its tempos and rhythms, and provided valuable help for a foreigner faced with the very difficult problems of the English language. Readers of the libretto will notice how precisely, and yet how musically, the characters develop during the opera. Often it was only after composing a number that I noticed that I had followed the same scenic construction as the authors, and that the development of the characters and their music was often exactly the same as in the text.30

Henze's congenial working relationship with Auden and Kallman appears to have overcome the unusual circumstances of their

DRAMA IN THE TWENTIETH CENTURY

collaboration, and perhaps explains why the same team joined forces on a second venture, *The Bassairds,* which like its predecessor was performed in German translation before having its premiere in the original version. In the second opera Auden took a more active role in the formation of his private letter to the composer. After suggesting the subject of a music drama based on *The Bacchae,* Auden asked Henze to first "make his peace with Wagner."[31] Although he did not seek to change his composer's musical orientation to opera, the poet was able to enlarge its scope for the purpose of their second collaboration.

One area in which Henze does not stand in conflict with Wagner is in the matter of the participation of the composer in the theatrical production of his operas. At Bayreuth Wagner chose to produce rather than conduct, and Henze also has seemed content to leave the musical rendering of his operas in the hands of a qualified colleague. He designed and directed *Elegy for Young Lovers,* and while it might appear that he is dabbling in areas in which he is not trained, he aggressively defends his active theatrical participation. He argues that his musical ideas must be visually realized in order for his operas to be effective theatre, and he finds that most theatre people who stage opera are unequipped to do this:

> The trouble with productions today is that operas are not realized from the meaning of the score, but in terms of the stage only. It is really essential for producers to be musicians as well as producers so that their conceptions do not run contrary to the music.[32]

In this Henze agrees with the late Walter Felsenstein, the artistic director of the *Komische Oper* in East Berlin for over twenty-five years who was perhaps the most respected man of the theatre in contemporary opera. In an address in 1971 at the International Theatre Institute in London on the training of stage directors for the music theatre, Felsenstein argued that "superb musicianship and theoretical knowledge of music" must be part of the essential equipment of the operatic stage director, and he feared that the "overemphasis on staging" endangered the survival of music theatre.[33] Yet the success of Henze's own productions of *Elegy for Young Lovers* has been the most persuasive argument in favor of his views on the staging of his opera. Henze geared the musical and dramaturgical shape of *Elegy for Young Lovers* to the physical characteristics of the German court theatres which commissioned the initial performances of the opera. Most reviewers, their opinion of the music or the performance notwithstanding, have commented that the opera is especially well suited for performances in small theatres. In 1962, however, Henze faced a new production challenge when he brought *Elegy for Young Lovers* to the Berlin Festival and had to redesign and restage his opera to meet the demands of a large theatre. He found that his chamber opera could produce a stunning effect in a large house, even with a small orchestra and only six singers. When the successful Berlin production was seen at the Holland Festival in 1967, the reviewers praised the composer for the effective staging of his own work:

> [Henze] had designed his own sets and costumes, and so the work had an almost unique sense of unity. The atmosphere of that bleak, haunted-like alpine hotel was conveyed by the precisely-observed lounge (with its suggestion of *art nouveau*) within a more abstract backcloth to represent the mountains.
> . . . The production had that "ghostlike reality" described by H. L. Stuckenschmidt reviewing this Berlin production when it was first staged. The whole tale seems to be taking place in a vacuum—almost as if it was a product of Mittenhofer's imagination.[34]

Although other designers and directors have been praised for their productions of *Elegy for Young Lovers,* none has yet rivaled the atmosphere or intensity produced by Henze's own staging. For example, the Glyndebourne production designed by Lili di Nobili and directed by Günther Rennert was praised for its "splendidly imagined inn . . . showing the domestic paraphernalia in realistic, well displayed detail."[35] Yet the "ghostlike" atmosphere of Henze's own productions was missing—a quality which seems to come from the composer's attention to scenic symbolism. Reviewing the Berlin production, Stuckenschmidt noted that Henze's setting "creates a picture in the youthful style of Beardsley or Gustav Klitsch . . . [with] big mauve flowers outside the hotel room and Japanese ornaments near the grandfather clock."[36] Comparable scenic effects were not to be found in other productions, nor were the reviewers inclined to discuss the scenery and staging in such detail. The composer clearly brought imaginative scenic and directorial elements to his work which have not been seen in other productions. Henze is not a dabbler who enjoys playing at theatre, nor does he take a nineteenth-century dictatorial stance about the

sanctity of his own works. Henze commented in an interview
with the *Journal of the Deutsche Oper,* Berlin, that he would
prefer to remain at home and leave the production to someone
else: since he composes with scenic ideas in mind, however, he
views the production of his operas as the final realization of his
music.37

Following his successful productions of *Elegy for Young
Lovers* and the well-received premiers of *The Bassairds* in 1966
and of *Der Junge Lord* in 1968, Henze abandoned the world of
opera both as composer and director. Recently, however, he has
returned to the operatic world he rejected in the late 1960's.
One of the first indications of his return was an essay he wrote
in 1975 entitled "Der Künstler als bürgerlicher Held," which
reinterpreted the musical and dramatic significance of *Elegy for
Young Lovers.*38 He then collaborated with the English dramatist Edward Bond on a work entitled "We Come to the River."
When asked why he returned to the musical theatre, Henze responded: "the theatre was and is my domain—I must always
return to the theatre. My music . . . is understood as drama."39
Henze's return to the musical theatre has been reciprocated by
an increasing interest in his work. In honor of his fiftieth birthday in 1976 Henze was asked to direct a new production of
Elegy for Young Lovers in Bonn, and in the same year a Henze
Festival was established at Montepulciano in Tuscany. Perhaps
the most significant accolade, however, was the new production
of *Der Junge Lord,* mounted for the 1978 Wiener Festwochen.
Since the Vienna Festival is usually devoted to extravagant
productions of Mozart and Strauss, the selection of an opera by
a non-Austrian contemporary composer for its featured work is
a commendable achievement.

When the history of opera in the latter half of the twentieth
century is written, perhaps Henze will be remembered as one of
the composers who continued the tradition of *dramma per
musica* in our time. For the present moment, Henze appears to
be the most significant German operatic composer since Alban
Berg. Had circumstances been different, Auden might have been
Henze's Hofmannsthal, for their dedication of *Elegy for Young
Lovers* to the Austrian poet-librettist indicated that they saw
themselves as the possible inheritors of the Strauss-Hofmannsthal
legacy. Although Auden came to opera late in life, and the
number of his coauthored works for the musical theatre was not

great, he nonetheless made a substantial contribution to the world of opera. He shared in the making of some of the most significant contemporary operatic works, and he greatly aided the revival of English language opera. Most importantly, however, Auden's work as librettist and translator shows that opera is a living international theatrical artform which can offer a major twentieth-century poet the chance to sing loudly.

University of California, Berkeley

NOTES

1 Igor Stravinsky and Robert Craft, *Memories and Commentaries* (New York: Doubleday, 1960), p. 145.

2 Wystan Hugh Auden, *Worte und Noten: Rede zur Eröffnung der Salzburger Festspiele 1968* (Salzburg, 1968), p. 37.

3 Ibid., p. 23.

4 Joseph Kerman, *Opera as Drama* (New York: Random House, 1956), p. 247.

5 Robert Craft, "The Poet and the Rake," *W. H. Auden: A Tribute,* ed. Stephen Spender (New York: Macmillan, 1975), pp 149-55.

6 Conrad Osborne, "Henze's 'Elegy for Young Lovers'," *High Fidelity/Musical America,* 15, No. 7 (July 1965), 95.

7 Martin Bernheimer, "Opera Workshop Henze," *Opera,* 16 (1965), 572.

8 Arthur Jacobs, "Elegy for Young Lovers," *Opera,* Special Festival Number (Autumn 1961), p. 30.

9 Bernheimer, p. 573.

10 "The World of Opera," *Secondary Worlds* (London: Faber and Faber, 1968), p. 102.

11 Ibid., p. 102.

12 W. H. Auden and Chester Kallman, *Elegy for Young Lovers* (Mainz: Schott, 1961), p. 36. All subsequent references to this edition will be indicated in parentheses in the text of my paper. The permission of the publishers, who allowed the inclusion of musical examples in this paper, is gratefully acknowledged.

13 "The World of Opera," p. 107.

14 Ibid., p. 103.

15 H. L. Stuckenschmidt, "The German Premiere," *Opera,* 12 (1961), 435.

16 John Rockwell, "The Search for Hans Werner Henze," *Opera News,* 37 (31 March 1973), 11.

17 Ibid., p. 12.

18 Ibid., p. 14.

19 Auden, "Words and the Word," *Secondary Worlds,"* p. 140.

20 Klaus Geitel, *Hans Werner Henze* (Berlin: Rembrandt Verlag, 1968), p. 108.

21 "The World of Opera," p. 98.

22 Igor Stravinsky, *Poetics of Music in the Form of Six Lessons*, trans. Arthur Knodel and Ingolf Dahl (Cambridge: Harvard Univ. Press, 1970), p. 79.

23 "Henze's New Opera," *Opera*, 17 (1966), 608.

24 Henze, "Meine Musik und dem Theater," *"Österreichische Musikzeitschrift*, No. 8 (August 1966), 371.

25 Stuckenschmidt, "The German Premiere," p. 436.

26 Jacobs, "Elegy for Young Lovers," p. 29.

27 "Notes on Music and Opera," *The Dyer's Hand* (New York: Random House, 1962), p. 473.

28 "On Writing Elegy for Young Lovers," *Opera* 12 (1961), 433.

29 Henze, *Musik und Politik: Schriften und Gespräche, 1955-1975* (München: DTV, 1976), p. 79.

30 "On Writing Elegy for Young Lovers," p. 436.

31 "Henze's New Opera," *Opera*, 17 (1966), 609.

32 Ibid., p. 608.

33 *The Music Theater of Walter Felsenstein: Collected Writings*, trans. and ed. Peter Paul Fuchs (New York: Norton, 1975), p. 43.

34 Allyn Blyth, "Three Twentieth Century Works at the 1967 Festival," *Opera*, Annual Festival Issue (Autumn 1967), p. 92.

35 Jacobs, "Elegy for Young Lovers," pp. 30-31.

36 Stuckenschmidt, "Festival 'Elegy'," *Opera*, 13 (1962), 804.

37 Henze, "Komponist und Regisseur: Gespräch mit Horst Georges," *Musik und Politik*, pp. 82-83.

38 *Musik und Politik*, pp. 231-39.

39 Henze, "We Come to the River," *Musik und Politik*, p. 251 (translation mine).

Edward Bond's *Lear*

Leslie Smith

Imagine, if you will, a mixture of the plays of Brecht and Strindberg, Brecht's social and political purposiveness allied to Strindberg's tormented vision of man's self-destructiveness, and you will get some idea of the double vision that informs Edward Bond's dramatic world. It is a world in which a sombre sense of man's inhumanity to man co-exists with hopefulness and a strong socio-political awareness. Bond has a great playwright's ability to express this double vision in dramatic images, in dialogue and action that have extraordinary force and power. In the earlier plays of contemporary working-class life, *The Pope's Wedding* and *Saved,* the tension between perverse, destructive energies and constructive ones was expressed in naturalistic terms: in *Saved,* the gang stoning the baby in a South London park, Len mending the chair in his girl-friend's house. In later plays, Bond experiments with surrealism and the grotesque: the tug of war between rival armies on Beachy Head in *Early Morning,* the Balmoral Picnic in Heaven in the same play, in which Queen Victoria, her ministers and her subjects, governors and governed alike, devour each other; and Florence Nightingale hides the head of her loved one in her voluminous skirts. The later plays in general make more use of fable and fantasy and are set in places and periods remote from present day England: Japan in the seventeenth, eighteenth, and nineteenth centuries *(Narrow Road to the Deep North),* Shakespeare's England *(Bingo),* a Victorian fantasy world *(Early Morning),* a Britain that is a timeless mix of the primitive and the contemporary *(Lear).* But there is a clear line of development between the earlier, more naturalistic plays, and the later ones. "I think quite often," Bond has said, "one feels the need to see something at a bit of a distance just to see its relationship to oneself better."[1] Fable and fantasy are ways of exploring, not of escaping from, contemporary reality: "I can't think that *Early Morning* is set in a limbo in a way that *Saved*

isn't. In order to express reality, the simplest and best and most
direct way isn't necessarily to say, well, the time is now six
fifteen and it's the third of March. . . . The plays I am told are
based on social realism very ofen seem to me the wildest fairy
stories . . ." (TQ, 8). I would suggest, in fact, that in Bond's
Lear (1972) there is a coming together of the matter-of-fact
realism of the earlier plays, and the mythical, fantasy elements
of *Early Morning* and *Narrow Road to the Deep North*. It is
the culmination of Bond's work up to 1972. And it has particular interest for a modern audience because of the relationship
in which it stands to Shakespeare's great original.

When T. S. Eliot sought to create a distinctive poetic drama
between 1934 and 1958, he felt the overpowering necessity of
escaping from the shadow of Shakespeare, whose genius had
queered the pitch for subsequent poetic dramatists. But Eliot's
efforts were doomed to failure. Putting his poetry on too thin
a diet, he often rendered it indistinguishable from prose; rejecting Shakespeare, he tried for a mixture of classical myth and
drawing room comedy that never quite gelled. Bond suffers from
no such inhibitions. His poetry of the theatre is not dependent
on verse: it functions through the concrete action and the physical images of the drama. "What I begin from," he has said, "is
a series of small visual images . . . when I write, the rhythm—
the whole concentration of the writing—requires action. Finally
somebody has to get up and do something" (TQ, 6). And because he is secure in his own technique and moves confidently
in the medium of drama as Eliot never did, Bond has always
felt free to respond to and use aspects of Shakespeare's dramatic
world in his own plays.

It was indeed a performance by Wolfit of Shakespeare's
Macbeth that gave him his first impulse to become a writer:

> My education really consisted of one evening, which was or-
> ganised by the school (Crouch End Secondary Modern). They
> took us along to a play at the old Bedford Theatre in Camden
> Town. We saw Donald Wolfit in *Macbeth,* and for the very
> first time in my life—I remember this quite distinctly—I met
> somebody who was actually talking about my problems. . . . I
> *knew* all these people, they were there in the street or in the
> newspapers—this in fact was my world. And also out of the
> play I got a feeling of resolution—that there were certain stand-
> ards. My reactions were absolutely naive, but I knew that if one
> could maintain these standards they could work in social situa-
> tions and produce certain results. So that after seeing that play

> I could say, well, yes, now I know what I have to do, what it
> means to be alive. . . . And also what came across from Wolfit's
> performance—and that play suited him very well—was a sense
> of dignity about people. . . . And so I got from that play a sense
> of human dignity—of the value of human beings. (TQ, 5-6)

Bond's subsequent career as a dramatist can be seen as stemming
from that first realisation of the power of the theatre and its
potential for enlarging our sensibilities.

But his approach to Shakespeare was never merely rever-
ential. Bond has pondered deeply the question of the artist's
relationship to society. To be an artist, a dedicated "being apart,"
is not enough; for Bond the artist is a man among men, and he
must be a functioning part of the moral structure of society. In
Narrow Road to the Deep North, the play that preceded *Lear,*
Bond had written a bitter Brechtian parable about the seventeenth-century Japanese poet, Basho, who in his personal pursuit
of wisdom and enlightenment, passes by opportunities to help
his fellow citizens and, in so doing, brings terrible suffering
upon his country. "What particularly incensed me about Basho,"
writes Bond, "was that everybody says oh, what a marvellous
poet. But I really am only talking about his actions."[2] And in
the play that follows *Lear, Bingo* (1973), Bond audaciously
turns an equally disenchanted eye on Shakespeare in retirement
at Stratford. We know that at the time of Shakespeare's retirement, the livelihood of farm-labourers and small-holders was
being threatened by the wealthier landowners, with their policy
of enclosing common land. We know further, as Bond puts it,
that "a large part of [Shakespeare's] income came from rents [or
tithes] paid on common fields at Welcombe near Stratford. Some
important landowners wanted to enclose these fields and there
was a risk that the enclosure would affect Shakespeare's rents
. . . [Shakespeare] sided with the landowners." Bond is keenly
interested in the resulting paradox, between the art and the life.
For art, he affirms, "is always sane."

> It always insists on the truth, and tries to express the justice and
> order that are necessary to sanity, but are usually destroyed by
> society. All imagination is political. It has the urgency of pas-
> sion, the force of appetite, the self-authenticity of pain or hap-
> piness. . . . Shakespeare's plays show this need for sanity, and
> its political expression, justice. But how did he live? His be-
> haviour as a property owner made him closer to Goneril than
> Lear. He supported and benefitted from the Goneril society,

with its prisons, workhouses, whipping, starvation, mutilation,
pulpit-hysteria, and all the rest of it.[3]

To some extent Bond resolves the paradox in his play by having
Shakespeare expiate the moral neutrality into which he has re-
treated, by committing suicide. But Bond is a more complex
playwright than his prefatory statements sometimes indicate.
(He is in this respect comparable with Shaw.) He may have
intended a sardonic portrait of a great artist failing as a human
being and pronouncing his own self-condemnation in suicide.
But what in fact comes over as the strong feeling of the play is
the pain and bewilderment of a man who understands more
profoundly and sees further than his fellow citizens, and is—
perhaps precisely because of that vision—somehow powerless
to act. Not least of the ironies of this fascinating play is that
Shakespeare, the great word-magician, is for large parts of the
action left speechless, stunned into silence by the confusion and
violence he sees around him. Consumed by the suffering he
witnesses, and wandering, the worse for drink, in the snowbound
Stratford landscape past a gallows tree from which a corpse is
hanging, Shakespeare becomes his own tormented Lear, adrift
among the elements, with only a mad old gardener for companion. And when he does speak it is to affirm that writer's
responsibility to his society that is central to Bond's own vision:

> Every writer writes in other men's blood. . . . Even when I sat
> at my table, when I put on my clothes, I was a hangman's
> assistant, a gaoler's errand boy. If children go in rags, we make
> the wind. If the table's empty we blight the harvest. If the roof
> leaks we send the storm. God made the elements but we inflict
> them on each other.

Bond, far from distancing himself critically from Shakespeare,
seems here to identify with him.

When Bond conceived the idea of doing his own version of
King Lear, he did so with a very real sense of its disturbing
power as a play: "I can only say that Lear was standing in my
path and I had to get him out of the way. I couldn't get beyond
him to do other things that I also wanted, so I had to come to
terms with him" (TQ, 8). But he also approached the play in
a questioning and sceptical spirit directed particularly at traditional responses to it:

> I very much object to the worshipping of that play by the aca-
> demic theatre . . . because it is a totally dishonest experience.

"Oh, yes, you know, this marvellous man suffering, and all the rest of it." I think that at the time it would have been a completely, totally different experience to see Lear reacting in the Tudor set up. . . . Now, I think it's an invitation to be artistically lazy, to say, "Oh, how . . . sensitive we are and this marvellous artistic experience we're having, understanding this play," and all the rest of it. . . . He's a Renaissance figure and he doesn't impinge on our society as much as he should. So that I would like to rewrite the play to try and make it more relevant. (G, 24)

One can develop Bond's point a little by saying that what an audience gets from a traditional production of the play is the sense of a man ennobled by suffering, who initially brings that suffering upon himself. Lear's progress through the play is a kind of purgatorial pilgrimage in which his arrogance, moral blindness and inhumanity are stripped away, and a fundamental humanity is left. The deaths of Cordelia and Lear are cathartic in the extreme, arousing deep pity and fear in the audience, the more so since they come so quickly upon the almost paradisal awakening into new life that the old king experiences in the brief reunion with his daughter. Goneril and Regan, in a traditional production, are types of ultimate evil and total inhumanity. In the world of the play that evil is finally expelled, but at a terrible cost in human suffering. In the subdued final passages of the play there is a sense of order in the kingdom reasserting itself. If perhaps any lines can be quoted as central to this traditional view, which Bond rejects, they might be the lines of Sophoclean resignation spoken by Edgar: "Men must endure/ Their going hence, even as their coming hither./ Ripeness is all." But, if Bond rejects the traditional view certain directors take of the play, I do not think Peter Brook's very untraditional and contemporary view of the play, in his production for the RSC, with Paul Scofield as Lear, would altogether have satisfied him. For this production, the bitter despair of Gloucester, "As flies to wanton boys, are we to the gods;/ They kill us for their sport," was more the keynote. Brook, influenced to some extent by Jan Kott's essay on *Lear* in *Shakespeare Our Contemporary,* saw Shakespeare's play in terms of Beckett's *End Game.* The scenes on Dover Cliff between the mad Lear and the blind Gloucester seemed to echo some of the exchanges between Hamm and Clov in Beckett's play: man's existential despair in a world of minimal meaning. Brook refused

to distance his audience in any way from the action. He wished
to involve them totally, as with a play of contemporary life.

To this end, Scofield's Lear was no absolute monarch, set
apart by Divine Right; instead he was an impossibly difficult,
unpredictable and choleric old man, whose knights were indeed
as turbulent and bad-mannered as his daughters alleged: an
elderly relative who would be an embarrassment in any household. Goneril and Regan, in this production, were no types of
absolute evil: unpleasant and vicious certainly, but with some
justification, given Lear's behaviour. Brook made us feel the
kinship between the father and the evil daughters. He human-
ised and scaled down the situation, removing from it some of
the awesome, ritualistic, larger-than-life quality that a traditional
production can give us. One of the small, but significant touches
in Brook's production, symptomatic of his handling of the play,
occurred with the scene of Gloucester's blinding. The sadistic
violence of Cornwall and Regan is visited on the helpless old
man, whose eyes are gouged out on stage in full view of the
audience. At the end of the scene, two of the servants are left
on stage with the blind and bleeding Gloucester. In the script,
they express concern and sympathy, horror at what has
happened.

> If she live long
> And in the end, meet the old course of death,
> Women will all turn monsters.
>
> • • •
>
> Go thou, I'll fetch some flax and whites of eggs,
> To apply to his bleeding face. Now heaven help him.

Shakespeare places the horrific deed in a context of normal and
kindly human behaviour, and to some extent guides our response
to it, through these comments. Peter Brook cut the servants' brief
conversation at the end of the scene, and brought the house
lights up for the interval as the blinded Gloucester attempted to
grope his way off stage, bumped into furniture, was jostled by
indifferent servants—all this while some members of the audience, encouraged by the house lights, were already on their way
to the bar. Brook was most certainly not inviting our mockery
of a blind old man, or adding an extra sadistic turn of the screw
to the cruelty of the scene. What he was doing was to give us a
powerful image of our potentially dangerous indifference to violence and cruelty. He brought this home to us directly, by

bringing up the house lights as the scene ended, enabling a majority of the audience to see a minority of their fellows hurrying off at once to the bar, showing an indifference to Gloucester's fate similar to that evidenced among the servants on stage.

Brook evidently felt that the expressed indignation of the servants in the original script too easily let the audience off the hook, allowing them to feel that condemnation had been expressed, guilt apportioned. He wished to bring the uncomfortable facts more directly home to us. How would we respond, undistanced by the historical perspective and moral framework that may come between us and the play? Brook returns to this problem of violence and our reaction to it in a section of his book *The Empty Space,* which could almost be a comment on his own staging of the blinding scene, and which I quote because his views are very relevant to Bond's use of violence in the theatre. In real life, he asserts, the shocking atrocity stories, or the photograph of the napalmed child,

> are the roughest of experiences—but they open the spectator's eyes to the need for an action which in the event they somehow sap. It is as though the fact of experiencing a need vividly quickens the need and quenches it in the same breath. What then can be done? I know of one acid test in the theatre. And it is literally an acid test. When a performance is over, what remains? Fun can be forgotten, but powerful emotion also disappears and good arguments lose their thread. When emotion and argument are harnessed to a wish from the audience to see more clearly into itself—then something in the mind burns. The event scorches on to the memory an outline, a taste, a trace, a smell, a picture. It is the play's central image that remains, its silhouette, and if the elements are highly blended, this silhouette will be its meaning, this shape will be the essence of what it has to say. When years later I think of a striking theatrical experience I find a kernel engraved in my memory: two tramps under a tree, an old woman dragging a cart, a sergeant dancing, three people on a sofa in hell—or occasionally a trace deeper than any imagery. I haven't a hope of remembering the meanings precisely, but from the kernel I can reconstruct a set of meanings. Then a purpose will have been served. A few hours could amend my thinking for life. This is almost, but not quite impossible to achieve.[4]

Perhaps, of the two kinds of *Lear* production I have been describing, Bond would prefer Peter Brook's untraditional and contemporary view of the play. Brook's views on the problem of violence and how the theatre may deal with it are close to his own. He is equally concerned to see the relevance of the play to our own age. Yet as a dramatist bent on writing his own version of *Lear,* the Beckett-like existential despair of Brook's version serves his purpose no better than the Sophoclean resignation of traditional Lears.

Bond's is a more radical, a more revolutionary concept of art: "Art has to be the equivalent of hooliganism in the streets. It has to be disruptive and questioning, also at the same time to give a rational explanation of the circumstances in which it is occurring" (G, 5). His Preface to *Lear* describes the moralised aggression of our social and political institutions, "as if an animal was locked in a cage—and then fed with the key. It shakes the bars but can never get out." Yet the description of our "diseased culture," our "institutionalised and legitimised tyranny," is given less from a Marxist than a Blakean humanist-anarchist viewpoint. Bond has a healthy disrespect for power-politics, whether of the left or right: "It is so easy to subordinate justice to power . . . when this happens power takes on the dynamics and dialectics of aggression, and then nothing is really changed. Marx did not know about this problem, and Lenin discovered it when it was too late." He has no wish to put forward a blueprint of the future: "If your plan of the future is too rigid you start to coerce people to fit into it. We do not need a plan of the future. We need a method of change." If his art is to have a function, it is to contribute "to a general consciousness of the sort of dangers that society is now in." So, if he sometimes prompts comparison with Brecht, it is not because he is overtly didactic as Brecht can be, but because of a purposiveness in his drama, an impulse towards "a method of change," and because, like Brecht, he is too good a dramatist not to give full value to irony, complexity, and ambiguity in his plays. What he has said of Brecht he could have said of himself: "His naivety covers painful knowledge."

Bond's *Lear* has a three-act structure, which Bond characterises thus: "Act I shows a world dominated by myth. Act II shows the clash between myth and reality, between superstitious men and the autonomous world. Act III shows a resolution of this in the world we prove real by dying in it." In discussing the play I will try to suggest how the Shakespearean original functions as stimulus and point of departure for Bond's contemporary version.

In Act I of Bond's play, Lear does not abandon his authority as in Shakespeare's play. Bond wishes to get away from the Renaissance concept of a betrayal of kingly responsibility which releases powers of evil and anarchy in the land, and instead to focus on an old man, an authority figure, overtaken by revolutionary violence, who becomes as a child again, and learns, ultimately at the cost of his own life, the true nature of his society (which could be our own) and of the folly of its power structure. So, says Bond, "I begin at the Revolution."[5] Lear's great enterprise in Bond's play, his lifetime's work, has been the building of a great wall, to keep his enemies out and his allies in. The play begins and ends with the killing of a man working on the wall. It is one of the great central images of oppression and confinement in the play, and it brilliantly evokes both an ancient landscape and a modern one: we think at one and the same time of the Berlin wall and the Cold War; and of the massive earthworks near Bond's home called Devil's Dyke and Fleam Dyke thrown up by the East Anglians after the departure of the Romans to protect themselves from marauders. Lear, on the tour of inspection that starts the play, could be any contemporary field marshal or bellicose politician claiming to defend the peace by preparing for war, and calling self-imprisonment freedom:

> I started this wall when I was young. I stopped my enemies in the field, but there were always more of them. How could we ever be free? So I built this wall to keep our enemies out. My people will live behind this wall when I'm dead. You may be governed by fools but you'll always live in peace. My wall will make you free.

The dramatic irony of the scene is given an additional savage twist as Lear, in the same breath as he proclaims his love for his people, shoots one of the workers, wrongly suspected of sabotage.

With a number of swift, bold strokes, and using various forms of theatrical foreshortening and simplification, Bond gives us, in the remainder of Act I, the revolution that overthrows Lear, the irresponsible cruelty and violence it brings with it, Lear's madness, and the temporary pastoral refuge he secures with only a "fool" (the gravedigger's boy) and a "wild man" (his tortured general, Warrington) for company. The Shakespearean echoes are strong and insistent: Goneril and Regan, renamed Bodice and Fontanelle, exist in a kind of parodic rela-

tion to their formidable and venomous prototypes. They are, for
Bond, figures of black farce, figures out of Jarry's *Ubu Roi,*
childishly indulging their cruelties and sexual appetites. They
initiate the revolution by contracting marriages with Lear's
enemies, the Dukes of North and Cornwall, and then complain
in bitter asides to the audience of their husbands' sexual incom-
petence. "When he gets on top of me," says Fontanelle, "I'm so
angry I have to count to ten. That's long enough. Then I wait
till he's asleep and work myself off. I'm not making do with that
for long." "Virility," says Bodice, "It'd be easier to get blood
out of a stone, and far more probable. I've bribed a major on
his staff to shoot him in the battle." Bond's variation on the
blinding of Gloucester has Warrington subjected, like a puppet
figure in an evil Punch and Judy show, to every kind of monstrous cruelty. His tongue already cut out, he is methodically
beaten up, while Bodice calmly knits and Fontanelle jumps up
and down with perverse, infantile glee:

> *Fontanelle*:   Christ, why did I cut his tongue out? I want to
> hear him scream . . . smash his hands; . . . kill
> his feet! . . . kill him inside! Make him dead!
> Father, Father! I want to sit on his lungs!
>
> *Bodice* (knits):   Plain, pearl, plain. She was just the same at
> school.

We have to remember that Bond's purpose in Act I is to
create a world dominated by myth. These caricature figures
belong well enough to this mythical world, albeit that world has
its contemporary reference, and we can glimpse something of
twentieth-century cruelties and obscenities in the distorting mirror of farce and grand guignol. The horrible fun that Bond gets
from these grotesque figures also serves some very useful dramatic purposes. Bond knows many in the audience will be
familiar with the *Lear* original. He wants in Act I to confront
directly and in caricature form the extremities of cruelty and
violence in *King Lear,* and, as it were, to exorcise some Shakespearean ghosts. In so doing he prepares the ground for his own
exploration of violence and oppression in Acts II and III. And
it is not only a matter of the *King Lear* original. Bond has written: "I write about violence as naturally as Jane Austen wrote
about manners. Violence shapes and obsesses our society, and
if we do not stop being violent we have no future. People who
do not want writers to write about violence want to stop them

writing about us and our time. . . ."6 For such a writer it is very important to create the right context for the subject. In introducing the theme on a farcical level before returning to it at a deeper and more serious level, Bond prepares the audience psychologically. He does the same thing in *Early Morning,* where the theme of cannibalism is first introduced farcically— Len and Joyce stand trial for eating a man while queuing outside the Kilburn Empire to see a film called "Policeman in Black Nylons"—and cannibalism then becomes more and more the central image for men devouring and destroying each other. It is of course a technique that goes as far back in British drama as the medieval miracle plays, where in the Towneley *Secunda Pastorum* the farcical sheep-stealing and mock nativity precede and strengthen the serious and real nativity.

Lear, overthrown by his daughters, seeks refuge with the Gravedigger's boy, who is a pig-farmer, and his wife, Cordelia (not, as in Shakespeare, one of Lear's daughters). Both are figures of crucial importance in the later action of the play. Suffice here to note that the gravedigger's boy, like Shakespeare's fool, criticises the king, but offers him counsel and friendship; and that echoes of Shakespeare's storm scenes on the heath are never far away. There is Lear's constant obsession with filial ingratitude: "Have you any daughters?" he asks the boy. "No." "Then I'll come. No daughters! Where he lives the rain can't be wet or the wind cold, and the holes cry out when you're going to tread in them." There is the macabre animal imagery that runs through Lear's speeches: "My daughters empty their prisons and feed the men to the dead in their graveyards. The wolf crawls away in terror and hides with the rats. Hup, Prince! Hup, Rebel! Do tricks for human flesh! When the dead have eaten they go home to their pits and sleep." And there is the presence of a Mad Tom figure in the crazed and tortured figure of Warrington hiding in the well. At the same time the house of the gravedigger's boy is a real, if temporary pastoral refuge for Lear; no thunder, lightning, and tempestuous rain show us disorder in the universe, reflecting disorder in the body politic. Here is no great chain of being in the Elizabethan manner. Bond's world is a world without God or the gods. And it is at the end of Act I, when the brief pastoral dream turns to nightmare, that Bond's strong individual presence asserts itself and the very different direction of his play begins to become clear. The pillaging soldiers hunting for the escaped king arrive on the scene. They capture Lear, slaughter the pigs, kill the boy, and rape his wife. The violence here is not in any way caricatured. It is grimly matter-of-fact. And Bond drives home the cruelty most powerfully by two very striking dramatic effects. One is an auditory effect: the off-stage squealing of the pigs as they are slaughtered, a sound which is to return, quite spine-chillingly, near the end of the play. The second is an extraordinary and most powerfully contrived visual effect on the death of the gravedigger's boy. His wife's washing is on the line, and, as he is shot, he clutches at one of the sheets which folds round him. The stage direction reads: "For a second he stands in silence with the white sheet draped round him. Only his head is seen. It is pushed back in shock and his eyes and mouth are open. He stands rigid. Suddenly a huge red stain spreads on the sheet." This is not simply a shock effect. Although it does, undeniably, shock. It is a strange, fantastic image of a living man turning into a ghost before our eyes, preparing the way for the continuing presence of the boy as a ghost accompanying Lear for much of Acts II and III, rather as the skeleton of Arthur's Siamese twin George is fixed to him for much of *Early Morning*. The red stain is a fine image of the creeping and spreading violence consuming the world of the play: and in the strange paradox it also suggests of a bleeding ghost, it evokes a kind of death-in-life, a feeling of something sinister and unhealthy which we shall increasingly come to associate with the ghost of the gravedigger's boy.

In Act II Bond opens up his own contemporary world of dream and nightmare, of purgatorial suffering, through which Lear must pass to achieve sanity and understanding. In a succession of strange and haunting scenes he creates a dramatic poetry of action, speech, and image no less powerful than some of Shakespeare's scenes.

Thus, Lear, put on trial, refuses to recognise either his daughter Bodice or his own reflection in a mirror that is handed to him:

How ugly that voice is! That's not my daughter's voice. It sounds like chains on a prison wall. And she walks like something struggling in a sack (Lear glances down briefly at the mirror). No, that's not the king. . . . This is a little cage of bars with an animal in it. No, no, that's not the king! Who shut that animal in that cage? Let it out. Have you seen its face

behind the bars? There's a poor animal with blood on its head
and tears running down its face.

Bond may be recalling the abdication scene in *Richard II* where
Richard calls for a mirror and eventually shatters it; if so the
echo is apt, for Lear demonstrates a similar self-pity and self-
dramatisation here. But Bond's vivid imagery and terse command of colloquial idiom is very much his own; and the image
of man as a caged animal reverberates beyond the immediate
context, and is as central to the meaning of Bond's play as the
imagery of storm and tempest is to *Lear*. It relates to the governed as much as the governors, people and rulers alike, imprisoned within a social and political structure that does not
answer to their real needs.

The trial is followed by a succession of prison scenes, quite
extraordinary in their blend of realism and fantasy, the timeless
and the contemporary, pathos and terror. In the first of these
scenes (scene 2), it is a little as if Bond had taken the speech
of Lear to Cordelia as point of departure for his own dramatic
invention:

> Come, let's away to prison;
> We two alone will sing like birds i'the cage.
> When thou dost ask me blessing, I'll kneel down
> And ask of thee forgiveness.

The modern soldiers acting as prison orderlies bring Lear to his
cell. He is just another number to be ticked off the list; it's a job
they prefer to front-line duty. Then, as it might be in *Macbeth*
or *Hamlet,* "The ghost of the gravedigger's boy appears. His skin
and clothes are faded. There's old dry blood on them." Lear's
appalled sense of the world's cruelty and destructiveness
strangely now impels him to reach out towards his evil daughters.
"What I wanted Lear to do," says Bond, "was to recognise that
they *were* his daughters—they had been formed by his activity,
they were children of his state, and he was totally responsible
for them" (TQ, 8). The gravedigger's boy, as in some strange
folk ballad, whistles up the ghostly presences of Bodice and
Fontanelle as the children they once were. The scene of mutual
comfort and tenderness that results as Lear cradles the heads of
his daughters in his lap and strokes their hair is in no way
mawkish. It is important dramatically in a number of ways. It
shows Lear reaching out beyond his immediate anguish to a
vision of a world that might be:

> We won't chain ourselves to the dead, or send our children to
> school in the graveyard. The torturers and ministers and priests
> will lose their office. And we'll pass each other in the street
> without shuddering at what we've done to each other. . . . The
> animal will step out of its cage, and lie in the fields, and run by
> the river, and groom itself in the sun, and sleep in its hole from
> night to morning.

Here is a dramatic poetry not dependent on verse which captures something of the same restorative peace as is found in
Shakespeare's "We two alone will sing like birds i'the cage." It
is important too in humanising the daughters after the grand
guignol horror of the earlier scenes. But, above all, it establishes,
in the re-enacted terror of Lear's daughters as little children, the
responsibility of environment and family for shaping or mishap-
ing its sons and daughters. Bond invents a striking and effective
piece of stage business for this. Bodice, as a child, struggles
frantically to get into the dress of her dead mother, and comes
to Lear for his approval. "Take it off!" says Lear. Bodice refuses.
And Lear replies: "Yes, or you will always wear it! (He pulls
her to him) Bodice! My poor child, you might as well have worn
her shroud." Nothing could better suggest the child's development, distorted or misshaped by parental pressures, and Lear's
tardy realisation of his responsibility in this direction. We are
brought back to "everyday" reality from this strange dream
world, with its visual suggestion of Blake's engraving of *Job and
His Daughters,* by the soldier's cell-inspection routine and by the
old orderly coming to fetch Lear's untouched food. The orderly,
like the porter in *Macbeth,* lists all those lost souls including
himself who have been consigned to oblivion in this place of
suffering and death:

> I come in 'ere thousands a years back, 'undreds a thousands.
> I don't know what I come in for. I forgot. I 'eard so many
> tell what they come in for it's all mixed up in me 'ead. I've
> 'eard every crime in the book confessed t' me. Must be a record.
> Don't know which was mine now. Murder? Robbery? Violence?
> I'd like to know. Just t'put me mind t'rest. Satisfy me con-
> science. But no-one knows now. It's all gone. Long ago. The
> records is lost. 'Undreds a years back.

This is, if you like, Shakespearean in its down-to-earth comic
relief; but it also evokes a very contemporary, Kafka-esque
world, of the KGB, the midnight knock on the door; the unspec-
ified crime for which you are put away for ever. The scene ends
with the ghost's frightened plea to remain with Lear:

Ghost: Let me stay with you Lear. . . . Look at my hands,
they're like an old man's. They're withered, I'm young
but my stomach's shrivelled up, and the hairs turned
white. Look, my arms! Feel how thin I am. Are you
afraid to touch me. . . .

Lear: . . . Yes, yes. Poor boy. Lie down by me. Here, I'll
hold you. We'll help each other. Cry while I sleep,
and I'll cry and watch you while you sleep. We'll take
turns. The sound of the human voice will comfort us.

There are echoes here of Shakespeare's Lear and the fool on the
heath:

Lear: Poor fool and knave. I have one part in my heart
That's sorry yet for thee

• • •

In boy, go first. Your houseless poverty
Nay get thee in. I'll pray and then I'll sleep.

Lear's human concern for the boy in the Bond scene is moving;
but there is also a sense that Lear, in embracing the ghost, is
nursing his own grief too much, and withdrawing into an unreal
world. Particularly is this so, as the ghost himself is a strange,
equivocal figure who is already wasting away and clinging
parasite-like to the living Lear. When he whispers ingratiatingly,
"Let me stay with you Lear. . . . Are you afraid to touch me?"
there is already the suggestion, which is to become stronger, of
the ghost representing something in Lear (as George does for
Arthur in *Early Morning*), which has to die before Lear can
find his true strength. After two brief scenes, set in the rival army
camps, of revolution and counter-revolution (Cordelia is now
leading the "freedom-fighter" forces of counter-revolution), the
counter-revolutionaries carry the day; and Bond returns us, for
the conclusion of the Act, to the prison and the caged animals
within it. A chain of prisoners moves along a country road,
with heavy gunfire in the distance. Lear is one of the chain gang,
and to it the defeated Fontanelle, in her turn, is manacled.
Bond's great gift for vivid theatrical metaphor, for images that
act out the meaning of the play, is here again in evidence: one
of the central themes of the play—the vicious circle of violence
and oppression, in which governors and governed, tyrants and
victims end up chained to each other, is simply and memorably
expressed. Then, back in the prison, Bond brings the act to its
audacious climax. Katharine Worth has said that often with
Bond "it is in the most grotesque areas of the play that his

technique is seen at its most boldly inventive, and—strange
paradox—the mystery of human feeling is given most delicate
expression."7 The paintings of Francis Bacon, or the Goya engravings of the *Disasters of War,* might provide comparable
examples in the world of art. In Shakespeare's original we have
the mad Lear crying out in the hovel: "Then let them anatomise
Regan, see what breeds about her heart. Is there any cause in
nature that makes these hard hearts?" Bond, as it were, accepts
the challenge of that despairing question, and uses the idea literally. Fontanelle is executed, and the prison officer conducts an
autopsy in cool scientific fashion. He "anatomises" Fontanelle,
and Lear, tormented by his sense of the cruelty of mankind,
looks on to "see what breeds about her heart."

Lear:	So much blood and bits and pieces packed in with all that care. Where is the . . . Where? . . . Where is the beast? The blood is as still as a lake. . . . Where? Where? . . .
4th Prisoner:	What's the man asking?
Lear:	She sleeps inside like a lion and a lamb and a child. The things are so beautiful. I am aston- ished. I have never seen anything so beautiful. If I had known she was so beautiful . . . how I would have loved her . . . Did I make this— and destroy it? . . . I knew nothing, saw nothing, learned nothing! Fool! Fool! Worse than I knew. (He puts his hands into Fontanelle and brings them out with organs and viscera. The soldiers react awkwardly and ineffectually). Look at my dead daughter! . . . I killed her! Her blood is on my hands! Destroyer! Murderer! And now I must begin again. I must walk through my life, step after step, I must walk in weariness and bitterness, I must become a child, hungry and stripped and shivering in blood. I must open my eyes and see!

Harry Andrews, who played Lear in Bill Gaskill's production at
the Royal Court, was worried about whether this scene would
produce the wrong reactions in the audience; and Gaskill told
him: "The author has made a big gesture. If it doesn't work, it
doesn't work, but you have to have the courage to play it."8 In
the event, the scene did work, and very powerfully, as Katharine
Worth testifies: "[It] could so easily have been either ludicrous
or overpoweringly offensive. But it worked. There was no laughter of the wrong kind. . . . We were too deep in feeling, too

affected by the solemn and complex movements of events."9 Lear, then, at this moment, finds his answer to the question posed in Shakespeare's play. There is no cause in *nature,* that makes these hard hearts. The speech, with its Blakean and Biblical overtones (c.f. "Dare he laugh his work to see? Dare he who made the lamb make thee?"—*The Tyger;* "the wolf shall dwell with the lamb . . . and the calf and the young lion together; and a little child shall lead them "—*Isaiah* 2) expresses Lear's astonished reverence for the mystery and beauty of creation and for the natural innocence of man, uncorrupted by environment. The cause is in man, not nature. And Lear takes upon himself a total, almost Christ-like responsibility for man's destructiveness: " I must become a child . . . I must open my eyes and see. . . ."

Ironically, but aptly enough, it is at this moment, in the crowning act of violence in Act II, that he is blinded. The blinding continues the use of Shakespeare's text for Bond's own purposes. As in Shakespeare, it is a dramatic metaphor for insight. "I stumbled when I saw," says the blinded Gloucester: that Lear is blinded immediately after the revelation he experiences at the autopsy suggests how much that he has needed to learn he has now learnt. What he will choose to do with this wisdom will be the theme of Act III. The blinding also continues and extends the image of power imprisoning and hurting those who wield it. For Lear's "crown" in this scene, which "turns him into a king again," is in fact the square, box-like device fitted over his head to extract his eyes. It is a kind of savage, theatrical conceit, in which Bond forces together the idea of power and the idea of a cruel blindness, a self-imprisonment associated with authority. And it also continues the deliberate and very effective use of anachronisms—the mixing of contemporary and historic detail—in the play. Bond, in a postcard to Gaskill during the rehearsals of the production, spoke of the need to preserve this mixture: "The anachronisms are for the horrible moments in a dream when you know it's a dream but can't help being afraid. The anachronisms must increase, and not lessen the seriousness. . . . They are like desperate facts."10 So here this latest scientific gadget which hygienically "decants" the eyes into a "soothing solution of formaldehyde crystals" and sprays the sockets with an aerosol reminds us of modern torture techniques and pseudo-scientific concentration camp experiments practised on victims of the Nazi terror.

The final act of Bond's play differs in three crucial respects from Shakespeare's. For Bond's Lear, ripeness is not all; and though he is tempted towards an "easeful death" by the grave-digger's boy and his own moments of despair, he finds the courage to resist this mood, to realise that, far from enduring his "going hence" even as his "coming hither," he still has work to do. This Lear's death is a heroic death that comes about as a result of a political act—a small and seemingly ineffectual act, but none the less one of great symbolic importance. Pathos and pity, overpoweringly present in Shakespeare's last act, are associated, in Bond's last act, with the increasingly spectral and parasitical figure of the gravedigger's boy and are seen as debilitating and harmful emotions. Finally, instead of a reconciliation with Cordelia, there is a confrontation between her, as the new head of a people's government, and the old autocratic ruler, in which Lear decisively rejects her.

Consider first the gravedigger's boy. "I can stay with you now you need me," murmurs the ghost insidiously when Lear has been blinded; and his sinister presence remains with Lear for much of Act III encouraging him to despairing and destructive acts: "Get rid of the lot of them, then we'll be safe. . . . Let me poison the well. . . ." At the same time, the ghost is a figure of genuine pathos, wasting away, frightened of dying a second time, haunting the scenes of his happy early life. The beauty of that pastoral existence that Lear briefly glimpsed has its persuasive appeal, and the ghost is there to remind him of it. Through the gravedigger's boy, he has seen a vision of a golden age which his own political activities have helped to destroy. But, as Bond puts it, "he has also to recognise that its loss is irrevocable . . . there are great dangers in romanticising." And so, "it's very important for Lear that he should get rid of this other figure; he has to disown something of himself, this instinctive thing he calls the Gravedigger's boy. . . . Some things are dead—but they die with difficulty" (TQ, 8). That difficult death Bond accomplishes in another striking "coup de théâtre," which eerily brings the wheel full circle, linking past to present. At the moment Lear formulates his plan of action and rejects Cordelia, there is heard off-stage "the distant squealing of angry pigs, further off than at the end of Act One, scene seven." "The ghost stumbles in. It is covered with blood. The pig squeals slowly die out." The ghost, gored and trampled by the pigs, makes a final, anguished appeal to Lear: "Help me! Help me! . . . Lear! Hold me!" But Lear can say nothing but: "No, too late! It's far too late! . . . You were killed long ago! . . . Die, for your own sake, die." As the boy drops dead at Lear's feet, the pig squealing finally stops. And Lear's brief and moving valediction is full of the imagery of light, of clear vision, and of an understanding that goes beyond grief:

> I see my life, a black tree by a pool. The branches are covered with tears. The tears are shining with light. The wind blows the tears in the sky. And my tears fall down on me.

Cordelia, in Shakespeare's play, aroused a strong and hostile reaction in Bond: "One of the very important things in the play was to re-define the relationship between Cordelia and Lear. I don't want to make this seem easy or slick, but Cordelia in Shakespeare's play is an absolute menace. I mean she's a very dangerous type of person . . ." (TQ, 8). Bond's Cordelia is, of course, not one of Lear's daughters. But, like Shakespeare's Cordelia, she is an idealist; she puts her ideals (in Bond's play, political ones) above human needs (condemning a would-be recruit to death because "we can't trust a man unless he hates," and prepared to have Lear killed if he will not cease from preaching to the disaffected); and, just as Cordelia in Shakespeare's play is perhaps most like Lear in a certain uncompromising forthrightness, reckless of consequences, so Bond's Cordelia becomes most like the Lear of Act I. She insists, as he once did, that building the wall is an essential part of the power game; she has the same conviction that she is the saviour of her people. And though Bond is careful to give her respectable liberal arguments in Scene 3, as befits her more enlightened government, those arguments, as Lear recognises, perpetuate violence and the suppression of truth:

> You sacrifice truth to destroy lies, and you sacrifice life to destroy death. . . . Your Law always does more harm than crime, and your morality is a form of violence.

This confrontation with Cordelia is for Lear the crucial turning point. We have seen him in the early scenes of Act III as a Tiresias-like figure, an elderly blind sage, preaching in parables to the crowds who come to hear him. But it is a form of withdrawal from the world that he is practising. No leadership is offered, no action suggested: there is simply the detached wisdom of a man at the end of his life, waiting for death. But now Lear knows that this phase of resignation, of ripe wisdom, is over. He has a journey to go on, and an act to perform. In a brief ending, but one splendidly dramatic in its gathering together of the play's meaning into a final symbolic action, Lear sets to work with bare hands and a shovel to tear down the wall that it has been his life's work to build, the wall that Cordelia wishes to perpetuate. The wall has from the beginning imposed its dark shadow over the action. But Bond reserves its actual physical presence for the last scene. When it looms up, filling the stage, it is a moment of great dramatic effect. And the struggle of the frail old man to demolish it is the inevitable climactic moment towards which everything in the play has been leading. It is a heroic gesture. It is also a tragic gesture, for it costs Lear his life. He is shot by one of the junior officers in charge of operations. But it is not a futile gesture. Bond, in a final stage-direction that reveals his understanding of how dramatic action can sometimes speak louder than words, specifies that, as the workers on the wall move away from the body, at their officer's command, "one of them looks back." In that looking back with its suggestion that the lesson of Lear's death will not be forgotten, lies a frail but real and important hope for the future.

Thus Bond completes a play which, I would argue, does not suffer by comparison with Shakespeare's great original. In the romantic and post-romantic period, critics and writers placed too much stress on the artist's originality. Latterly we have been more willing to concede the artist's right to use another man's themes and subjects as the springboard for his own invention. A writer's originality is often best seen in his individual variation on a traditional theme. One must, of course, discriminate. Nahum Tate, when he decided to "improve" Shakespeare for Restoration taste by giving Lear a happy ending and arranging a marriage between Cordelia and Edgar, merely showed how deep his incomprehension of the original was. By contrast, Bond sets up in his play a real, creative dialogue with the original, out of which comes a theatrical experience of impressive power, a *Lear* as seen by one of the most original and versatile dramatists of our time.

The Polytechnic of North London

NOTES

1 Edward Bond, as quoted by Roger Hudson, Catherine Itzin, and Simon Trussler, in "Drama and the Dialectics of Violence," *Theatre Quarterly,* 2 (January-March 1972), 8. Hereafter, *TQ.*

2 Irving Wardle, "A Discussion with Edward Bond," *Gambit,* 5, No. 17 (1970), 9. Hereafter, *G.*

3 Edward Bond, Preface to *Bingo* (London: Eyre Methuen, 1972), p. ix.

4 Peter Brook, *The Empty Space* (New York: Pelican, 1973), p. 152.

5 Edward Bond, "An Interview with Tony Coult," *Plays and Players* (December 1975), p. 13.

6 Edward Bond, Preface to *Lear* (New York: Hill and Wang, 1972), p. v.

7 Katharine Worth, *Revolutions in Modern British Drama* (London: G. Bell, 1972), p. 183.

8 Gregory Dark, "Production Casebook, No. 5: Edward Bond's *Lear* at the Royal Court," *Theatre Quarterly,* 2 (January-March 1972), 28.

9 Worth, *Revolutions in Modern British Drama,* p. 180.

10 Dark, "Production Casebook, No. 5," p. 22.

Verse Drama: A Reconsideration

William G. McCollom

In 1963, E. Martin Browne published a lecture with the title *Verse in the Modern English Theatre. The Times Literary Supplement* responded with the question: What verse?[1] By that year the work of Eliot and Fry had nearly been completed, and the Angry Young Men had seized popular and critical attention. In the United States, the theater was as angry as in England but less articulate.

The declining visibility of verse drama in this century raises the question whether the verse medium can again attract large numbers of playgoers. About thirty years ago John Gielgud played to enthusiastic audiences of *The Lady's Not For Burning.* A spectator reported that a woman seated directly behind him exclaimed with delight after every witticism from Christopher Fry. Such a response, for better or worse, is not likely to be soon repeated. On February 16, 1980, *The New York Times* in its Theatre Directory recorded some sixty current productions in New York. Of these, only one, listed as Yeats' *Cuchulain,* was evidently a poetic drama of the twentieth century. Similarly, Block and Shedd's large anthology, *Masters of Modern Drama* (1962), printed only one poetic play in English, Yeats' *At the Hawk's Well,* one of his less dramatic plays. Paddy Chayevsky was represented, but not Eliot or one of the many other poets in English who have written plays in verse.

Many reasons contribute to this change of taste—the coming of television and the related decline in demand for excellent or even educated speech, the increasingly high risks of theatrical production, the defensive reaction of the poet to the money-changer, the sense that verse drama belongs to a distant and irrecoverable past, the supposition that iambic pentameter fails to suit our speech patterns, the movement of poets from metered verse to prose rhythms, and their tendency to prefer verse or even prose dialogue to drama. In addition, verse drama has been met with criticism ranging from indifference to savagery. An author of a recent book on the subject finds the genre of slight value. A classical scholar treats with scorn a dramatic poet's return to a myth found in Euripides. Kenneth Tynan ridicules what may be Eliot's best play.2 All this suggests that verse drama, along with medieval allegory, Elizabethan tragedy, and Augustan wit, may soon become a historical phenomenon, whatever the achievement of individual plays.

In a time when the philosophy of criticism veers toward the conclusion that critical conclusions are impossible,3 few would claim certainty for critical judgments on that most protean of forms, drama. When estimating a playwright, one is interpreting and judging the words on the page but also their potential for theatrical success. Yet predicting success on the stage is notoriously difficult, and success in the theater has misled critics into wildly excessive praise. Moreover, failure in the theater or failure to reach production may prove nothing. Georg Büchner died in his early thirties and was unknown as a playwright for half a century, but he is now recognized as an astonishingly gifted forerunner of significant modern drama. The multiple bases of dramatic criticism and the whirligig of time, place, and subjectivity are a permanent warning against critical hybris.

In spite of these cautions, I believe that twentieth-century verse drama has been underrated and that much of it deserves the second chance that Büchner received. At any rate we have reached a point when a re-examination of the persisting qualities of this dramatic mode seems called for as a preliminary to any attempt to reassess its place in this century.

Though much great drama is in prose, it is obvious that the towering achievements have been poetic drama written in verse. Visions of human reality that are at once vivid, profound, and comprehensive are poetic visions or, what is more to the point, are poetry. But since the Renaissance, such insight has less and less often been confined to verse. In a brief essay suggesting that verse is no longer necessary in drama, John Wain wrote that *"Waiting for Godot* is the play of recent times that best deserves to be called a poem, and it is in prose."4 Although he did not take the time to explain, presumably he was saying that the play is vivid, profound, and universal. But when one says that Clifford Odets is the "poet of the Jewish middle class," one means something much less honorific than Mr. Wain's statement. If we say that the hero's opening speech in *Caesar and Cleopatra* is poetry, we are referring to something closer to poetic drama in verse, since the language is striking in imagery and rhythm as well as conveying a sense of the mysterious connection between genius and nature. Describing a drama as a poem can mean a variety of things.

To call it a verse drama is to make a more limited and a more descriptive statement. If he has a good ear, a verse dramatist can share something of the great tradition, but his play may have far less to do with Webster or Marston—or *Everyman*—than has *Waiting for Godot*. I shall confine my attention mainly to verse drama and drama containing verse, partially because they are more easily identifiable than is modern drama that is felt to be poetic. But obviously, poetic and verse drama overlap. Though much of the latter is without value, this kind of writing has continued to attract important poets—Yeats, Eliot, Frost, Stevens, MacLeish, Jeffers, Auden, Cummings, Nemerov, and Lowell among them. The contemporary Trinidadian poet, Derek Walcott, has written some splendid dramas in verse.

Wain's provocative statement may help to map the terrain shared by poetry and verse. The play by Beckett has the profound originality of form we associate with fine poetry. It expresses with total concentration a point of view that has for many years strongly influenced the thinking of modern intellectuals. In its austere way it displays a shrewd sense of the stage without using the "poetry of the theater"; how else could a work so devoid of action attract even small audiences? Yet the play is generally anti-poetic. When a character begins to sound eloquent, the current is switched to bathos. One is constantly aware that the writer can be poetic as well as "poetic" if he wants to be, but in fact the work stages a great refusal of eloquence. The chief reminiscence of poetry comes from the lips of a madman. Other allusions might be called ambivalent rejections of poetry. Vladimir says, "Thinking is not the worst," and then, after a diversion, "What is terrible is to have thought"[5] —a twisted rewrite of Edgar's "the worst is not/ So long as we can say 'This is the worst'" (*King Lear,* IV.i.27-28). There is Vladimir's half-remembered biblical quotation: "Hope deferred

maketh the something sick, who said that?" (Prov. 13.12). Or
Estragon studies the moon:

> VLADIMIR: What are you doing?
> ESTRAGON: Pale for weariness.
> VLADIMIR: Eh?
> ESTRAGON: Of climbing heaven and gazing on the likes of us.
>   (p. 34a)

The lines affectionately insult Shelley, as if to say: the tradition
is false, but what else is there? Beckett knows very well what
he is rejecting, but the question remains: how much poetry can
you reject while writing poetry?

Not all is rejected, as one clearly sees when a conversation
intended to stave off despair turns into a poem re-introducing
it. At first we have what seems to be a conversational game
about the virtues of conversation:

> ESTRAGON: It's so we won't think.
> VLADIMIR: We have that excuse.
> ESTRAGON: It's so we won't hear.
> VLADIMIR: We have our reasons.   (p. 40a)

These lines open the first of four sections arranged in the overall pattern AABA. Without conscious intent Vladimir and
Estragon begin "thinking" about what they would forget:

> ESTRAGON: All the dead voices.
> VLADIMIR: They make a noise like wings.
> ESTRAGON: Like leaves.
> VLADIMIR: Like sand.
> ESTRAGON: Like leaves.

So long as the elegy continues, it keeps the pain under control.
But when silence follows, the suffering redoubles. On such
pages, form and feeling collaborate to produce poetry. At other
moments, the absence of poetry is like the solid nothingness of
the existentialists, for the text is big with what is unstated. More
often, Beckett prefers to hold poetry at arm's length.

Poetic prose may approach verse, especially in a period
when the latter is heavily influenced by prose rhythms. Odets'
Awake and Sing! is poetic partially because of an abundance of
jolting images like "What this country needs is a good five-cent
earthquake" and partially because of the imagination with which
the Utopian theme is worked out: the Berger family are struggling burghers who must stop acting like *bergers,* for life isn't

as pictured on the wall calendar. But an important reason for
the poetic quality of the play is the vigorously rhythmical language, as in Ralph's opening speech, here reproduced as verse:

> Where's advancement down the place?
> Work like crazy! Think they'd see it?
> You'd drop dead first,

where the first two lines are trochaic and the contrasting third
line is spondaic—thrusting protest followed by heavy bitterness.
The play is written in predominantly prose rhythms occasionally
accented by sentences as measured as most contemporary poetry:

> You made a cushion—sleep! . . .
> A lover I kept—Mr. Gigolo. . . .
> Where you going, Little Red Ridinghood?
> Nobody knows, Peter Rabbit. . . .
> I swear to God I'm one week old![6]

The speakers are close to passionate verse, which, according to
Yeats, comes from the speaker's effort to restrain violence or
madness.

   The natural speech required for realistic drama in English will occasionally fall into iambic lines, which Aristotle
thought the most natural arrangement; more often (I believe)
into anapaests;[7] and still more often into the Greek paeon,
especially the fourth paeon (xxx/), or into an extended version
of this foot (xxxx/), with the trochaic and the dactylic providing contrast, especially for outbursts of emotion. After recording and listening to a wide variety of speakers interviewed
on television during late seventies, I observed that many or
most seldom speak metrically. Lord Carrington, questioned on
Rhodesia, spoke carefully but haltingly and irregularly.[8] A
farmer in the Vale of Belvoir, asked why he didn't seek a
livelihood elsewhere, alternated metrical speech and free
rhythms. I italicize the metrical sections of his answer: *"Well,
that's the question we're often asked. But of course if we went
somewhere else,* assuming we could find 500 million tons of
coal somewhere else, *which is not very easy,* we'd have exactly
the same problems." The first sentence is iambic; the other
italicized sections are anapaests. The statement was made
firmly, with one pause for breath, and with clearly marked
accents, but it was not until the second or third hearing that I
was fully conscious of the meter. The point is of interest in

connection with the speaking of blank verse, which will seldom get five clear accents a line.

Among those recorded, two women, Lillian Carter and Patricia Davidson, were surprisingly similar in their speech rhythms. Each used fairly short segments consisting of roughly equal numbers of equivalent beats, with an accent in the middle or near the end of the segment. A characteristic "line" in Mrs. Carter's statement consisted of two segments, with a pause made or felt between the two, as here: "I wanted him to come out of it." In pitch the segments would look something like this:

$$\frown \quad \frown$$

But Mrs. Carter interrupted these with iambic clauses (e.g., "I couldn't see how Bert should go"). When asked to describe her prayer for Bert Lance, this was her reply:

> What did I pray?
> I wanted him to come out of it.
> I couldn't see how Bert should go,
>   (could stay [sic] after so much slanderous stuff
>   had been said about him).
> But I prayed that he would come out of it
> As good a man as he went in.
> I wanted him to be vindicated.
> I wanted it [sic] vindicated.
> I wanted him to stay in,
> But I knew it was impossible.

Patricia Davidson, a Catholic leader who spoke for a united Ireland, opposed the peace movement led by Betty Williams:

> It will only be a recipe
> For further strife
> In another ten years. . . .
> It will only be a temp'ary measure,
> Whereas what we're looking for
> Is the British to withdraw,
> The communities to get together,
> And a lasting and permanent peace
> Based on freedom.

Neither passage is strictly metrical for long, but especially when heard, both display a clear pattern of syllables, with strong accents, and a tendency toward short, equal segments.

Both women sounded "natural," though Patricia Davidson had probably used some of these phrases before. For our purpose the point is that these clearly shaped rhythms are close to the way people normally talk and thus tend to justify, if that is necessary, definitely patterned speech in the drama of our time.9

The opposition to verse drama in the twentieth century stems mainly from the disasters of nineteenth-century drama in this mode, and undoubtedly the old failures have been followed by new ones. But if nothing succeeds like success, nothing in the theater fails like failure. As a result, plays that failed for a variety of reasons have been damned because the authors wrote in the metrical patterns associated with Elizabethan drama. Byron's plays are too long, too melodramatic, at times too imitative, and too much to undramatic lyricism. In other words they are nineteenth-century plays. But the verse itself can be fully dramatic. If one turns from the *longueurs* of his *Werner* or *Sardanapalus* to the first act of *Cain,* one is struck hard by the efficiency and suppleness of the blank verse line. The power of the best speeches is both local and integral, for they carry the revolt of Byron's projection, Cain, and of Lucifer, the super-natural projection of the villain-hero—much as Jimmy Porter's words resonate with the anger of John Osborne. Cain's brood-ing has the immediacy necessary to strong dramatic writing:

                              I see
          The gates of what they call their Paradise
          Guarded by fiery-sworded cherubim,
          Which shut them out, and me: I look
          Around a world where I seem nothing, with
          Thoughts which arise within me, as if they
          Could master all things. . . . (I.168-75)

To condemn such writing because it uses the verse form of Elizabethan drama would be sheer prejudice. The controlled intensity of the lines prevents the flow of feeling from spilling into rant, yet voices the emotional drive. One could compare early Jacobean dramatic verse, written at a time when the metronomic line of 1590 had loosened and before the penta-meter trailed off into prose. But such a comparison might confirm the opinion of those who hold that the nineteenth-century dramatic line is doomed by imitativeness. Byron's first four lines are regular, but there are variations, exemplified by the trochee at the beginning of line 3, of which a competent actor would take advantage. The next two lines are freer and increase the sense of a real (not realistic) speaker. The tone moves from the measured irony of "what they call" to the melancholy captured in the delayed stress of "where I seem nothing." At the end of the last full line, "they" is a sigh of defeat. The passage is highly successful verse drama.

Admittedly the writing often fails to reach this level. There are sections where description stops the play or where Byron deliberately sacrifices dramatic movement to the theological exchanges between the two chief speakers. But when he chose to do so, the poet could write for an audience. The weaknesses in the play are not attributable to the verse form he selected.

The controlled intensity of good blank verse in the drama has continued to manifest itself, if intermittently.[10] To show that the form can adapt itself to modern life while retaining its character, I shall quote from a very recent play, William Alfred's *Holy Saturday* (1979), produced in 1980 and forming a part of a longer work. As in his earlier play, *Hogan's Goat,* which ran a year and a half at the American Place Theatre, Alfred has employed blank verse for Irish-American speakers of the earlier part of this century. Here a young woman and her son visit her uncle, Jo-Jo, from whom she has long been estranged. He tells how his wife, now in an institution, rose in the night from her bed, began dressing, and later woke him as she rocked in a chair:

> Gert's rocking in a rocker:
> She's got her summer things on, white, all white,
> White dress, white shoes and stockings, even white bloomers
> (She's got her knees spread rocking, I can see them).
> What's this, I say, your first Holy Communion?
> I think she's kidding, see; she's always kidding.
> She looks at me, but she don't say a word.
> She keeps on rocking. Ah, come on, I says.
> Her nose is running, it's so cold in here.
> Shine your shoes, she says, the cops is coming.
> What for, I says. She looks like she busted something,
> And then she says, Because I don't know my name. . . .[11]

In *Hogan's Goat* the most successful verse was probably the tough talk given to an old-time political boss. Once again Alfred demonstrates that the pentameter line can come naturally from the mouth of an uneducated speaker. Avoiding the literary diction for which Maxwell Anderson was slated when he put the Sacco-Vanzetti case into verse (*Winterset,* 1935), Alfred combines great simplicity of language with a basically regular movement supported by rhetorical repetition and diversified by occasional spondees as well as by the delaying anapaest at the climax of the revelation. It would be easy to say that slangy realism arranged iambically does not constitute poetry, but although no one would propose this passage as great writing, the vision of the mad wife, dressed for summer and rocking with knees spread, works with the rocking movement of the words to create an eerie effect. The actor, of course, may decide to ignore the meter, as American actors tend to do in Shakespeare's plays, but such a decision would sacrifice a significant contribution to the whole.

Blank verse, is, of course, only one of the many different patterns found in the verse drama of this century. Experimentation paralleling that in non-dramatic verse has resulted in lines of radically uneven length or with a variety of feet or based on pure stress, as in some older kinds of English poetry.12 Sometimes the line is built solely on rhetorical repetition, as in this speaker's ironic address to blacks:

> How much white you up to? How much you done took on?
> How much white you pinin for? How white you wanna be?
> (Howard Sackler, *The Great White Hope*, I.vi)

Sometimes the printing seems intended mainly to alert the actor to the importance of rhythm in the play.

Helen in Egypt (1958), by John Heath-Stubbs, illustrates all or most of these irregularities. Writing at a time when the vogue in England for religious drama had recently ended, the playwright wanted to introduce an element of ritual, including ritual rebirth, without any suggestion of a church ceremony. He believed that "verse permits a fluidity of syntax which is nearer to the movement of thought and emotion, and can be nearer to the cadence of natural speech, than any but the most masterly dramatic prose."13 He printed the entire play in verse, but despite his talents as a poet, he is often writing prose poetry, as in these lines:

> IDAS [*bitterly*]
> > The gods guarded over Troy.
> > The divine Poseidon with his own hands
> > Built up her shining battlements. Yes, my grandfather
> > Used to tell me that when I was a child.
> > The Palladium, the image of Pallas Athene,
> > That had fallen down from the sky, stood in our city temple.
> > The town could never be taken, while that remained
> > > with us.   (p. 60)

The lines here range from seven to fourteen syllables. The stresses vary from three to six. Anapaests are nearly as common as iambs; not until the last line is there a clearly iambic movement. There is no reason to ask that the syllables be arranged differently, but should the passage be presented as verse? The question becomes more insistent here:

> The sufferings of that woman have made the face you see there.
> You remember who you are, now, and why you came here. (p. 70)

On the other hand, Heath-Stubbs can write clearly perceptible verse based on pure stress:

> Here we are, stuck on this desert island,
> Provisions and water almost gone.
> And the ship barely seaworthy. And what do we find here?—
> A coven of Egyptian witches, and that fat porpoise. (p. 71)

Although the passage can be scanned in various ways, it can certainly be heard as a series of four-stress lines expressing the irritated Thersites. Finally, there are a good many speeches written in a rather free but recognizable blank verse. Here the Phantom of Helen speaks to a young Trojan admirer:

> I call the gods to witness, Idas, I did not mean
> Ill to your people, the ruin of your city.
> I call the gods to witness! It was they,
> Working through me, laid tinder to the torch
> Incinerated Ilion's pinnacles.
> But you cannot forgive me. (p. 87)

Lines 3-5 are almost perfectly regular, an unusual sequence in the play and one that the dramatist apparently feared to extend.

Dramatic verse is never, of course, purely technical. If we compare a line by Alfred:

> She keeps on rocking. Ah, come on, I says,

with one by Heath-Stubbs:

> I call the gods to witness, Idas, I did not mean . . .

or with one of his finest lines:

> Chirping dry-voiced like crickets in the sun,

we notice that the accents in Alfred are stronger than in the

English poet. The difference is connected with the presentation of the characters. They are more vigorous, and sometimes melodramatically so, in Alfred. In the English play, only the minor character, Thersites, speaks with much force. Though *Helen in Egypt* is polished and entertaining, it has not entirely escaped the gentility that *The Times Literary Supplement* identified in 1963 as the nemesis of modern verse drama.

Any defense of verse drama in our time must take account of the method alternating prose and verse. After 1935 Eliot decided against the plan, arguing that it makes audiences too conscious of the medium. (This would certainly be true of the prose commentary suddenly introduced near the end of *Murder in the Cathedral*.) He thought that the mixture of verse and prose succeeded in the Renaissance but that whereas the Elizabethans could easily shift from one to the other since both were familiar, verse today suffers under the hardship of unfamiliarity and has to be quietly infused through the entire work.[14] Believing otherwise, Brecht often interrupted prose passages with verse in order to reduce illusion, of which he was suspicious, or to change the perspective of the audience. In England Auden and Isherwood's plays embraced prose, blank verse, rhyme, music hall turns, and choral poetry. Twenty years later John Arden appropriated all these patterns and added others.

His creative élan has shown that contemporary drama can indeed shift its ground successfully. Though sometimes sacrificing consistency or credible characterization, he can jolt the audience but also achieve subtle effects by juxtaposing realistic prose and a remarkable repertory of blank verse, doggerel, ballads, and music hall singing. And if a chief value of theater is theatricality and its "existential" overtones,[15] oscillating language can stimulate multiconsciousness in ways mastered by dramatists as different as Shakespeare and Pirandello, both intensely aware of life as a kind of theater. Some of the best moments in Arden's *Happy Haven* create just such stimulation.

Arden's *The Workhouse Donkey: A Vulgar Melodrama* (1964) is a play about political life in Yorkshire. Predominantly satiric, the dramatic action becomes a test case for the author's methods. Though seldom or never moving here, Arden demonstrates an impressive grasp of his subject and continuous vivacity. Though using much song and verse, he calls his work a "play with a musical accompaniment" and a "melodrama" rather than a musical play. I shall list some of the many moments when his basically realistic prose is superseded by imaginative doggerel, blank verse, song and dance, or free verse, the result being sometimes bewildering but always stimulating and often didactic in a manner suggesting the *Lehrstücke* of Brecht.

1. The play begins by telling us, in free verse spoken by Dr. Wellington Blomax, that Yorkshire's moral standards are not London's, for

> From the beginning to the end,
> Each man is bound to act
> According to his nature
> And the nature of his land.16

Blomax will turn out to be a modern equivalent of the medieval Vice, but here, his measured prose seems serious enough (though suspiciously witty) in its deterministic view of man. Near the end of the play Blomax will return to his role as *raisonneur* and playwright's surrogate—this just before he reveals to the audience on stage the widespread corruption in his town. Consistency in character is less important to Arden than dramatic force scene by scene. If a character must alter his style to fit a new context, this will happen. The shift may at times be psychologically justifiable, since each man is in part his relation to another; it may be didactic; but it may be most involving when it forces the audience to speculate about the relation between a character, his listener onstage, his author, and his listener in the theater.

2. Feng, a stiff but well-intentioned man, has been assigned to Yorkshire as Chief Constable of the town. After a passage in prose, he and a leading citizen, Sweetman, fall into blank verse composed in literal language. This is Feng:

> I do not know you, sir.
> I do not know the people. And I must test
> The rigid statutes and the statutes only.   (p. 27)

Sweetman's verse flows easily without calling attention to itself, but Feng's lines add rigidity to an already awkward man. Here and at other moments the verse form is a stage direction telling the actor to move slightly away from the realistic basis of the scene. The pentameter usefully serves as artistic heightening of character.

3. The irrepressible Butterthwaite, long the town boss, now and again breaks into song and dance. The interludes fit his

character very well, but when Wiper, a dull policeman, enters a madam's garden and sings "The lady's walls are large and high" (p. 83), the performance can be justified only because this is the sort of thing people do in *The Workhouse Donkey*.

4. Act II, Scene vi begins with sardonic doggerel from the Borough Councillors. Then Mayor Boocock, a simple, kind-hearted man, enters the sequence.

> *Hardnutt.*
> It sounds to me like balaclava Bugles,
> This day some clown has blundered.
> *Boocock.*
> We all know Charlie Butterthwaite,
> And know him without turpitude,
> Nine times he's held the rank of Mayor,
> And now the people's gratitude.
> With all the battles he has fought
> In all his loyal rectitude
> If he should be in trouble
> We should grant him our support.   (p. 92)

Here the form is right for the Councillors, but it will be difficult for the actor playing Boocock to manage the style, unless he decides to "camp" or to suggest that the slow-witted Boocock is caught up unawares in a rhythm imposed by the previous speakers.

5. A long blank-verse soliloquy by Sweetman is particularly successful. The language is cool and ironic—appropriate for Sweetman, who is intelligent and polished, though no more honest than his political opponents. I select a section of the speech:

> The election lights on Butterthwaite—not once
> But three times three, or nine times nine, I fear.
> No national trend, nor local, gives me hope
> Of an improvement. Yet Butterthwaite must fall
> And fall so low that not the whole ineptitude
> And hopelessness of Tory forecasts can
> Reverse his long-delayed catastrophe.
> He has himself prepared his own trap-door
> And greased his easy hinge.   (p. 74)

The verse falls from the tongue as easily as prose. The lines move between what is actually measured prose ("No national trend," etc.) and poetry quoted and imitated ironically for the pleasure of those with a certain knowledge of literary history. As a whole the speech has few images, but those that occur

are effective. The hypallage in the last line of the extract slides
into place with admirable grace. A competent actor could not
fail to make an impression in this soliloquy.

Arden's decision to use verse of varying kinds was probably
the right choice for our time; what is lost in consistency is
gained in vitality. What is more important, the samples of verse
I have chosen from Arden and others have shown that theore-
tically there is no reason for playwrights to abandon verse
drama. In *Present Laughter* Noel Coward is amusing at the
expense of an untalented young playwright who has written a
play "half in verse." The trouble, though, is not with verse but
with most of those who use it.

Good dramatic verse did not cease at the end of the seventeenth century. Instead of citing Yeats and Eliot, I have taken
my few illustrations from lesser figures. But since the argument
has relied mainly on scattered passages, it seems appropriate to
treat somewhat more fully and as a whole at least one play.

Despite the distinction of its author, Howard Nemerov's
Cain (1959) is not widely known. Like much of his non-dramatic work, the play is in blank verse, and like his "Runes," also
written in the fifties, it stresses the unity of sentience and
"things," speaking also of "The other self, the sacred Cain of
blood" ("Runes," XIII).

Like Byron, Nemerov presents Cain sympathetically, but
unlike Byron, he moves from near burlesque in the opening
pages to a tragic close. Paralleling if not justifying the shift in
tone, the pentameter line is at first loosely, then more firmly
constructed.

At the opening, neither Adam and Eve nor their sons
understand the Fall. Adam and Abel are fatuous. Eve is more
intelligent but timid; Cain is sensitive and modest. His sacrifices
are insulted by the carnivorous Abel, whom God clearly favors,
but though suffering from his position, Cain represses his anger.
All of this prepares for the revelation of God's nature. Voicing
guilt-feeling and bewilderment as he is alone, Cain asks God
to punish him. When he appears, he points out that through sin
Cain can alter the world:

> Things are as they are
> Until you decide to change them,
> But do not be surprised if afterward
> Things are as they are again.[17]

Acting on this suggestion and almost without reflection, Cain murders Abel. Returning, God "casually" asks if Cain is satisfied with his action. Cain can say little except "It was my will I did." Kneeling, he pleads, "Lord God! You spoke, and I did not know" (p. 136). God declares that the murderer must leave his parents:

> I send you away, Cain. You are one
> Of my holy ones, discoverer of limits. . . . (p. 136)

Cain has inaugurated a world of power, with all that means for good and evil. Now he is coming to see that even when exercising will, man is nevertheless necessitated.

Learning of the fratricide, Adam at first wants to kill the murderer, then accepts the horror as beyond his understanding. Despite his mother's pleas, Cain goes into exile, marked on his brow and rejecting God. Alone, Adam and Eve realize that they must begin again.

Nemerov has chosen a great theme and handled it impressively. Although the play is brief—about five hundred lines—it accomplishes the maturation of an intelligent man who acts by his own will but without understanding, only to learn that his decisions are but part of a grim pattern. The tragedy is in this realization combined with a continuing integrity. At the end Cain feels "an enormous power that I do not want" (p. 140), but in the midst of his now total pessimism, he reveals a growing dignity that partially frees him from the fate of being always the self he has been. His final words do not signal utter defeat:

> Father,
> I'd bless you if I could, but I suspect
> That God believes in you.
> And now farewell,
> If that is possible; try not to remember me. (p. 142)

One sign of his development is that he is now speaking a very good line of verse. The style is the new man.

Cain becomes one of God's "holy ones" in somewhat the sense in which Oedipus becomes sacred. Essentially innocent murderers who suffer for their crimes, they test the nature of the world they inhabit. Oedipus becomes a tutelary spirit of Athens. The Cain of this play has no such future, but he will wield the power that is both admired and hated.

The point is made in a speech which develops Nemerov's

theme and his picture of the Lord. At the same time, it illustrates
the strength of the poet's dramatic line. Although some have
suggested that by the twentieth century blank verse had been
"used up" by non-dramatic poetry, God's speech should help to
refute the notion. After the lines on Cain as "discoverer of
limits," the speech continues:

> Your name is the name of one of the ways,
> And you must bear it. You must bear
> The everlasting fear no one can stop,
> The everlasting life you do not want,
> The smell of blood forever on your hand.
> You are the discoverer of power, and you
> Shall be honored among men that curse you,
> And honored even in the moment of the curse.
> From your discovery shall proceed
> Great cities of men, and well defended,
> And these men, your descendants, shall make
> Weapons of war, and instruments of music,
> Being drawn thereto by the nature of power;
> But they will not be happy, and they will not know
> Peace or any release from fear. (p. 136)

The speech varies between regular blank verse and a looser
line of three or four stresses, including anapaests that increase
the conversational tone already called for in a stage direction.
But in the moments carrying the heaviest rhetorical force, the
verse is iambic, as in lines 2-5. The alternation of strict and
more relaxed verse helps to create both a credible and a disturbing picture of a human reality we recognize very well. Blank
verse throughout might have been less credible. Too much
relaxation would have been lacking in gravity.

In this play God at first appears to be a Satanic divinity,
and his cozy announcement that he was the serpent in Eden
does not improve his standing with us. But there are two quali-
fications to be made. If we read the Lord as "real," or if the
actor plays him so, the disturbing force of the lines attaches
not only to our own recognitions but to the consciousness of
the speaker. It is easy to imagine that God himself is troubled
by the tragedy for which he is responsible. Even this divinity
is conceivably moved by "The smell of blood forever on your
hand." But if we read the Lord as primarily a spokesman for
the way things are, even when they change, the question of
whether we "like" him loses importance. Nemerov is fundamentally concerned with the central question in tragedy: can

man escape necessity, and if he can, must his choices place him once more in the grasp of what he would avoid? In *Cain,* necessity is omnipresent, but part of this necessity is man's freedom. Though Cain must be himself, he has chosen himself. Speaking of Eve, he says: "I see now,/ Having chosen myself, what her choice must have been." Man's freedom is no release from his suffering, but it is worth having, and it makes his own worth possible.

At the conclusion, when both sons are gone, Eve sees further into the mystery than does Adam, but even he, shocked into greater intelligence, sees himself and Eve "Doing as we would, and doing as we must" (p. 143). He is beginning to understand paradox, as did the Augustine quoted by Nemerov at the beginning of his "Runes": *moriebar vitaliter.*

Excellent metrical verse, like tragedy and like the life of man itself, is an interplay of freedom and necessity. Verse that is mechanically regular not only fails to approach natural speech but crushes any illusion of life. On the other hand, a good poet can create a line that gives voice to the direction issuing from human will. Nemerov is among the contemporary poets who have brought such creativity to the drama.

Case Western Reserve University

NOTES

1 "On Stage Verse," *TLS,* 5 July 1963, p. 493.

2 Arnold Hinchliffe, *Modern Verse Drama* (London: Methuen, 1977); Dudley Fitts, "The Hellenism of Robinson Jeffers," *Kenyon Review,* 8 (1946), 678-83; Kenneth Tynan, *Curtains* (New York: Atheneum, 1961).

3 See, for example, the remarks of J. Hillis Miller, speaking of the irreducible ambiguity of language: "The uncanny antithetical relation exists not only between pairs of words in this system, host and parasite, host and guest, but within each word in itself. It restores itself in each polar opposite when that opposite is separated out, and it subverts or nullifies the apparently unequivocal relation of polarity which seems the conceptual scheme appropriate for thinking through the system" ("The Critic as Host," *Critical Inquiry,* 3 [1976-77], 443). This kind of argument has been contested by an appeal to the writer's intention as judged by context, but the context of stage drama includes the intentions of author, producer, director, actor, set designer, etc. To the ambiguity of words are added those of facial expression, sound, movement, color, and light.

4 "Why Write Verse Drama?" *London Magazine,* 7, No. 2 (Feb. 1960), 62.

5 *Waiting for Godot* (New York: Grove, 1954), p. 41a.

6 *Six Plays of Clifford Odets* (New York: Modern Library, n.d.), pp. 41, 94, 95, 100, 101.

7 On the contrary, G. S. Fraser believes that iambs are more characteristic of our natural speech than are anapaests (*Meter, Rhyme, and Free Verse* [London: Methuen, 1970], pp. 28, 39). Earlier, in a preface to *Panic* (1935), Archibald MacLeish insisted that trochees had become more common than iambs, at least in American speech.

8 He started one sentence in marching anapaests but soon ran into a roadblock:
   x x /   x x   /x   x / x x /   x /
"But I think that it's going to be an enormous strain upon—uh—the facilities and logistics of Salisbury. . . ." The logistics of diplomatic statement continued to upset his rhythms.

9 Mr. Wain, who in 1960 had seemed ready to jettison verse drama, recently wrote: "All the metrical patterns that have served poets faithfully are still serving ordinary speakers," and in the same essay regretted the tendency of contemporary poetry to abandon clear rhythmic form. See "On the Breaking of Forms," in his *Professing Poetry* (Harmondsworth, Middlesex: Penguin, 1978), p. 111. In the same volume he prints his poem, "Furry Bundles," written without artificiality in dactylic hexameter.

10 In his history of drama, Allardyce Nicoll writes: "Of course, Yeats was absolutely correct in his realisation that the old blank verse tradition had lost its validity and that there was little or no hope for its resuscitation . . ." (*English Drama: 1900-1930* [Cambridge: Cambridge Univ. Press, 1973], p. 301). But Yeats' *The Death of Cuchulain,* written in his last year as a playwright, is in blank verse. *Purgatory,* in the same year, is not.

11 *Canto: Review of the Arts,* 3, No. 1 (1979), 127.

12 See Fraser, pp. 13-25, on "pure stress meters." Fraser shows that conventional analysis by feet and analysis by stress alone should sometimes supplement each other (pp. 24-25). He also reminds us that a full analysis cannot ignore quantity. Of course, verse, when read well, also involves pitch and pause.

13 Preface, *Helen in Egypt and Other Plays* (London: Oxford Univ. Press, 1958), p. ix.

14 *Selected Prose,* ed. John Hayward (Harmondsworth, Middlesex: Penguin, 1953), p. 70.

15 It is deeply significant of the modern theater that Beckett and Brecht, at opposite poles in fundamental ways, both shift their focus, intermittently, from stage world to audience. Each is asking the audience to re-examine the play in relation to the reality in the auditorium. For a study of drama as an art whose subject is acting in relation to life, see Michael Goldman, *The Actor's Freedom: Toward a Theory of Drama* (New York: Viking, 1975).

16 *The Workhouse Donkey* (London: Methuen, 1964), p. 16.

17 *Cain,* in *The Next Room of the Dream: Poems and Two Plays* (Chicago: Univ. of Chicago Press, 1962), p. 132.

The Mirror as Stage Prop in Modern Drama

Thomas P. Adler

I

The use of the mirror as an important stage prop is by no means peculiar to modern drama. A perhaps almost archetypal instance occurs near the end of Act IV of *Richard II,* when Shakespeare's narcissistic protagonist (essentially an actor who only plays at being a king) calls for a looking glass and then dashes it to the ground in disappointment when it fails to reflect his internal agony. But it is not until the Modernist movement that playwrights regularly employ the mirror as the dominant symbolic element of their stage setting. By examining in chronological order four dramas and three musicals which extensively use the mirror, we can chart the emergence and growing preponderance of a metatheatre—not only in the sense in which Lionel Abel applies the term to those works that capitalize on the life as dream/world as stage metaphors and on the audience's awareness of the play as play,[1] but also in the sense that the audience is consciously forced into a recognition of themselves *as audience.*

The mirror possesses rich symbolic as well as epistemological ramifications. For one thing, its presence is almost a hallmark of the Modernist age, signaling that the playwright has finally broken free from the language-bound orientation of the drama during the eighteenth and nineteenth centuries. To the extent that drama, by its very nature, is mimetic ("an imitation of an action in the form of an action"), the theatrical artifact mirrors life. If every play—to a greater or lesser degree—is a mirror of reality, then every prominent on-stage mirror serves as a metaphor for the nature of the dramatic work itself. Furthermore, every audience, even that which does not literally see itself in a mirror, ideally confronts an image of itself through experiencing

the play, so the space inhabited by the audience becomes a
"stage" for the action; the mirror simply renders this movement
of the action into the audience more explicit and emphatic. Yet
the precise effect of the mirror on the "characters/actors" both
on the stage and in the audience remains ambiguous. Gazing
into a mirror results in doubling, a fragmentation or dissociation of personality into the reflection and the thing reflected and
the person doing the reflecting. This may provide an occasion
for the person to reject the surface reflection and to see and
embrace the substance, to go deeper into himself and probe
what is not ordinarily perceived; but it might equally be a
confirmation of the mask, and thus an evasion and a source of
alienation of man from his true self. Since these seven works
have not previously been discussed together from this perspective, the methodology here is descriptive and analytical, intended
mainly to point out the dramatic function and theatrical effects
achieved through the use of the mirror—though this will indicate as well the dramatists' position on certain philosophical
issues and provide some speculative answers to the question of
how metadrama works.

The four dramas—Pirandello's *It Is So! (If You Think So)*
(1917); O'Neill's *A Touch of the Poet* (1939); Camus' *Caligula* (1945); and Genet's *The Balcony* (1958)—ranging in
time over four decades and in space over Italy, America, and
France—all pose metaphysical and/or ontological questions
that reflect some of the twentieth century's major philosophical
trends: relativism; skepticism; existentialism; absurdism. Three
of these works explore the nature and limits of human freedom,
either individual or social. Furthermore, all four 1) entail some
variation of the play-within-the-play, with the mirror becoming
the stage wherein the character, as his own audience, sees
himself; 2) imply a theory of the artist and/or the imaginative
process; and 3) violate the tidy sense of closure that audiences
expect even from modern plays.

Understandably, given his recurrent emphasis on the motifs
of illusion vs. reality and art vs. life, Pirandello employs mirrors—or stage props that function in much the same way as
mirrors do—in several of his plays. In *The Rules of the Game,*
for instance, mirrors underline the frequent disparity between
the reflection and the hidden truth it cannot begin to reveal,
while in both *As You Desire Me* and *Emperor Henry IV* the

full-size portraits are precise mirror images of the way characters
looked years ago. But at a point almost exactly midway through
It Is So! (If You Think So), a mirror takes center stage. When
Lamberto Laudisi, Pirandello's *raisonneur* who criticizes the
attempts of the meddling busybodies to impose their interpretation of events upon others as if it were the *only* interpretation
and laughs derisively at their folly in believing they can discover
the absolute truth about the puzzle of Signora Ponza's identity,
confronts himself in the "big mirror above the mantel"[2] he
expresses the well-nigh universal dissociation between an individual's self-conception and the image he presents to others, between what "I am" and what "they know." Pointing to "his image
in the glass"—which, of course, points back and returns his
smile—Laudisi verbalizes his belief that although he can get
in touch with his true self, with an essence or soul "inside himself," others see only the reflection that is but a shadow or a
mask:

> Between you and me, we get along very well, don't we! But the
> trouble is, others don't think of you just as I do. . . . As for
> me, I say that here, right in front of you, I can see myself with
> my eyes and touch myself with my fingers. But what are you for
> other people? . . . An image, my dear sir, just an image in the
> glass!   (p. 102)

The ideal, then, would be if others saw him exactly as he sees
himself; that they do not—or will not—should not be taken as
evidence, however, that Pirandello posits a radical skepticism
which sets mankind adrift from any possibility of certainty.

Rather than contend that since there exists no *one* truth all,
therefore, is in doubt, Pirandello—in a play that virtually begins
with Laudisi's challenges "How do you know that?" (p. 65),
and "What can we really know . . . ?" (p. 68)—suggests that
there exist multiple realities: one person's reality may not be
identical to that of those around him, but that does not render
his reality, or that of the others, any less real. The demonstration
of what might be called "subjective certainty" in the midst of
relativity occurs in the play's final moments with the arrival of
the mysterious Signora Ponza. Is she, as Signor Ponza insists,
his second wife, or is she, as Signora Frola claims, her daughter
and Ponza's first wife? Pirandello uses clothing expressionistic-
ally to indicate that Signora Ponza is as much a construct in
the minds of others as a creature of flesh and blood: "dressed

in deep mourning [with] her face concealed with a thick, black impenetrable veil" (p. 136), she is like an apparition—or, better still, like the outlines of a character that springs to mind to be filled in by the creative imagination of the artist. (Similarly, in a now-legendary *coup de theatre,* Georges Pitoëff, director of the original production of *Six Characters in Search of an Author,* had the six characters enter by descending in an old elevator, perhaps equating the theatre space with the mind of the artist.) Acclaimed by Signora Frola as "Lena!" and by Signor Ponza as "Julia," Signora Ponza tells everyone assembled: "I am nobody!" (p. 138). Though she exists, it remains for others to impose her essence—actually multiple essences—upon her: "I am she whom you believe me to be" (p. 138). Potentially all things that others need to make their lives bearable, she can be both "the daughter of Signora Frola . . . and the second wife of Signor Ponza" (p. 138). Fluid, not fixed, she possesses no essence apart from the way others perceive her, and yet no one perception can exhaust her complexity, while, at the same time, each of these multiple perceptions—"*a* truth" —becomes "*the* truth" (p. 117) for the one doing the perceiving.

Yet Pirandello, through Laudisi, cautions us against making *our truth* the only truth, as if it were all of reality, by imposing it upon others rather than compassionately responding to the desires of others as vulnerable and fallible as ourselves; in her absolute loss of ego, then, Signora Ponza in a sense becomes a model for emulation. When we accept or adopt a truth, hubristically we no longer consider it relative; for us it becomes an absolute certainty. The mirror, nevertheless, demonstrates that the co-existence of opposite truths is part of the human condition. As Robert Brustein diagnoses the "existential complaint" voiced in Pirandello's dramas, "[objective] truth cannot be grasped by the inquiring mind, since it is in a continual state of flux and varies with each individual."[3] So Pirandello expresses in drama the presuppositions inherent in the first person and rotating points-of-view in fiction, which implicitly question the knowability of others and even of ourselves, while he looks forward ultimately to the simultaneously opposing yet "correct" memories of the past held by the characters in Pinter plays such as *Old Times.*

O'Neill, in *A Touch of the Poet,* makes considerably more use of the mirror as stage prop than Pirandello, having his central character, Cornelius Melody, address his reflection four times, once in each act of the play. Melody's nickname, "Con," indicates that the essence of his character is to be an actor performing in a con-game that fools others less than it (at first anyway) fools himself. When he struts before the "large mirror"4 adorning the wall between the tavern dining room and barroom, Con consistently attempts to erase one aspect of his "real" self— that of the son of "a thievin' shebeen keeper" (p. 11)—by living out the more favorable memory of the courageous Major at the Battle of Talavera. (His daughter Sara's facial expression and voice, blending the aristocratic and refined with the coarse and sensual, also "mirrors" the split in Melody.) Striking an arrogant pose before the mirror, Con recites from his favorite Romantic poet, Byron, "who made of his disdain immortal music" (p. 44), including the line " 'Among them, but not of them' " (p. 43), with the mirror's image providing confirmation that this posture is the reality. By his third performance before the glass, Melody has added costume to his theatrical bag of tricks, having donned the Major's full-dress uniform to further the illusion. Thus the tavern becomes the stage for several little plays-within-the-play, the mirror's frame the proscenium arch, and the mirror itself throws back at him a view of the audience— which in this instance, of course, is identical to the actor.

But several other characters also function as audience and serve to undercut Melody's act. During the first mirror episode, Sara "stands watching him contemptuously" and then jeers "scathingly": "I hope you saw something in the mirror you could admire!" (p. 44); during the second, her prospective mother-in-law, Deborah Harford, "stares incredulously" and "smiles with an amused and mocking relish," accusing him of drinking too much and terming it an "absurd performance" (pp. 67, 72). His next playlet is preceded by O'Dowd's aspersion "play-actor" (p. 100) and then interrupted by the insistent knocking of the Harford family lawyer. In none of these instances, however, do we find any indication that the theatre audience is consciously to regard these characters as its own representatives on stage, even though it probably shares in their perception of his behavior.

As we know from O'Neill's other works—particularly *The Iceman Cometh* with which *Poet* has much in common—such exaggerations of and embroiderings on reality can be beneficial, for it is only the rare, perhaps only the heroic, individual who can, in Eliot's phrase, "bear very much reality"; yet such illusions become destructive if they harm another person or if the character fails to recognize that he or she is living in illusion. On the first count, Melody comes perilously close to ruining any possibility of marriage between Sara and Simon. On the second—and vastly more important—he has indulged in the illusion for so long that he has lost the ability to distinguish between the role and the reality: the stage directions indicate that "one soon feels that he is overplaying a role which has become more real than his real self to him" (p. 34); and, as Sara taunts him, "you can't tell any more what's dead and a lie, and what's the living truth" (p. 51). This appears to change when Melody stands before the mirror for the fourth and final time, now doing "a vulgar burlesque" of his earlier performance as Major. One of the "offstage" props buoying up that illusion was his treasured thoroughbred mare; but now having shot the horse, the Major is as good as dead himself, as is indicated by Melody's talking about the Major in the third person and "recit[ing] in mocking brogue" the lines from Byron (pp. 168, 176-77). Proclaiming—ironically as it turns out—"I'm fresh as a man new born" (p. 175), Melody associates himself now with "the crowd" as the noise of their comraderie wells up from the barroom beyond. And yet, rather than move from role playing to reality, he has simply replaced one illusion with another, this time assuming an exaggeratedly histrionic pose—though he denies it is a pose—of the Irish peasant. He has moved from mask to mask, neither role the total truth, but each containing a particle of reality; the stage directions indicate, "he appears to have no character left in which to hide and defend himself" and, to use Mary Tyrone's apprehensive words from *Long Day's Journey Into Night,* he has "lost [his] true self forever." As Travis Bogard remarks, "Melody is nothing without his dream. . . . He cannot rid himself of the need of a mask, for he has no substance without one."5

In this, he is perhaps like Charles Foster Kane in Welles' classic film. In one of the most famous shots late in that movie, Kane walks through a wide doorway having a mirror on both sides, with the effect that his image is reflected an infinite number of times as if in refracted prisms. Not only do those who "know" Kane and those in the film audience have a multitude of different, partially true—albeit incomplete—perceptions of his character; but also there exists little hope that Kane himself would ever have been able to recover his "true self," so distorted had it been by illusion piled upon illusion, either freely adopted or forced upon him by others. Assuming multiple roles might, in the beginning, be seen as a way of maintaining the fluidity and potentiality of becoming rather than succumbing to the fixity and limitation that would result from being some *one* thing. But to play the role for so long might mean that finally "the center does not hold" and the essential self can no longer be found. Signora Ponza, as an imagined construction in the minds of those who "see" her and impose her essence upon her from the outside, can bear to be nothing in her own right. Con cannot, and so must resort always to still another illusion. Neither can Caligula in Camus' play of that name.

During the time of wandering after his sister Drusilla's death, Caligula achieves a moment of enlightenment or lucidity —were is not that the vision is so dark, we might almost say an epiphany—into the condition of absurdity: "Men die and they are not happy."6 Rejecting either suicide or Sisyphean stoic endurance or the quietism of unquestioning acceptance as a response to this insight, he chooses instead the path of metaphysical revolt. Determining to activate an awareness of the human condition in those around him, he will create a persona which corresponds to and reflects his world view. Upon entering the stage, Caligula's first action is to become an audience, staring at himself in the mirror for assurance that his mask of cruelty and scorn is in place. As an artist figure whose own life becomes his major work, he both writes his own script and stars in it, as is evident from the two plays-within-the-play. In the first, acted out in "a curtained-off booth," Caligula appears as a "Grotesquely attired" Venus demanding adoration—an "absurd" role he plays "to perfection" (pp. 830-31). If one can become a god through play acting, then one can get even with the gods by being as cruel as they are. In the second, he performs "in shadow play" a "grotesque" ballet (p. 835), apparently mirroring the grotesquerie of the universe.

Yet since Caligula, displaying what Haskell Block and Robert Shedd call the "endless self-creation" of this actor who "delight[s] in the sheer pleasure of theatrical improvisation,"7 embroiders a role from almost first to last, perhaps the entire work should actually be regarded as a play-within-a-play. At the end of Act I, he "gongs" in his audience (composed of the other characters as well as of the theatre audience) for a show, and then shatters the on-stage mirror, effacing everything else but his own image. In his egomaniacal pursuit of power, he will be single-minded for evil. Like Shakespeare's Edmund, an example of extreme rationalism, Caligula, because of his recognition that the world possesses no value, thinks himself totally free, unbounded by any moral, ethical, or emotional considerations.

In following his insight to its logical conclusion, Caligula stage manages not only his own life but that of those around him as well. He dispatches people to their deaths at his whim, ultimately making "the curtain [fall]" (p. 839) on Caesonia's life by strangling her. At the close of the play, Caligula—by addressing himself in the mirror as "You" (pp. 839-40)—admits a split between the image reflected thereon and himself. Having discovered that he is not unbounded after all but that there are limits to his freedom (he has not, for example, succeeded in making grief everlasting, or in rendering "the impossible" possible so that "men will die no more and at last be happy" [p. 823]); that the road he has chosen, instead of laughing in the face of the void by challenging it on its own terms, has led finally to "nothing" (p. 840)—a word that reverberates a dozen and a half times throughout the play—, he smashes the mirror. When he obliterates his image in this fashion, it may at first seem a suicidal action. But that reflection, the "You," is not the totality of Caligula's being. "I'm still alive" (p. 840), Caligula's dying words as his enemies "stab his [real] face" after his mirrored image is no more, posit the reality of an essence—a "me"—beneath and beyond the existence captured in the reflection. The awareness of the Absurd that he was wearing as a pose, and his role as purveyor of that awareness, have penetrated down to the reality and become an ineradicable part of his essence, and part of the essence of the theatre audience as well. Of all the protagonists in these four dramas, Caligula alone might be called heroic. If the essence of the Absurdist is to continue to live in the face of the knowledge that life is without meaning, then part of that essence also is to see art, the imaginative act, for what it is: simply a mask that prevents acceptance of the Absurd, a placebo (which Genet will also show it to be) rather than the sentimental salvation that Con finds in illusion.

Genet's *The Balcony,* of all the dramas discussed here, uses the mirror most extensively to underline man's pervasive need not just to play roles but to receive as well the validation that can only come from being observed by an audience; for unlike *A Touch of the Poet* where the onstage audience were interlopers intruding on Con's performance, in *The Balcony* the role-playing to be complete depends on the willingness of other characters to be co-participants in or audience to the illusions. And, although none of the role-players acknowledges the presence of the larger audience sitting out in the theatre, there appears to be a tacit awareness all along that Madame Irma then makes explicit at the play's close. In a line reminiscent of Thornton Wilder and the *only* instance of a strictly non-representational technique among these four plays, she instructs the audience to see the world, where we are observers of the masks and roles assumed by others as well as abettors in creating and sustaining those illusions, as essentially no different from the theatre: "You must go home now, where everything—you can be quite sure—will be even falser than here."8 As Jerry Curtis writes, "we are what others see in us. They exist, on the other hand, because we see and recognize the roles they play. We *expect* them to act in a given way and they, in turn, act according to our expectation. This *jeu de glaces* is nothing other than the condition of man."9

There is, of course, nothing out of the ordinary in regarding the theatre as microcosm. But Genet is almost Jacobean—we think especially of Tourneur—in his casting of the theatre audience as voyeur. Just as Irma intrudes on her clients' sometimes de Sadean sexual fantasies by means of a closed circuit camera, the audience watches these same fantasies from their seats in the house. In this, she becomes the audience's representative up on stage, which forces them, in a sense, to "watch" themselves watching. Furthermore, since the prominent placement of the mirrors in the stage sets throughout the play, including "a large two-panelled mirror which forms the [rear] wall" in Scene Nine (p. 342), not only does not preclude but even makes likely the possibility of members of the audience catching sight of their own reflections—even though Genet's stage directions nowhere make this an explicit requirement— the potential is opened up for *The Balcony* to become metatheatre in the fullest sense of the term.

By regarding the fantasies that his characters act out as a sublimation of unfulfilled drives for political power and community adulation, Genet imparts a social dimension to his drama. When the chief patrons of Madame Irma's establishment first play out their fictive roles as Bishop, Judge, and General and look into the mirror, they never—unlike Con—totally lose sight of their real selves, nor do they want to. Their knowledge that this is a pretense largely created through costuming helps maintain the desired distance between role and reality; for if they could not consciously shed the fiction once the "scenario" for their little playlets was completed, then neither could they experience the pleasure of freely choosing to resume the play-acting at some later time. When, in fact, the revolutionaries outside kill the real Bishop, Judge, and General, these artists-in-little are unwillingly denied this freedom and traumatically forced to turn their temporary, private games into permanent, public poses.[10] They have moved from life to art, from flux to fixity. That the Revolution needs to retain these emblems of authority—either by actually perpetuating these higher roles or by mockingly aping them—suggests Genet's pessimistic attitude that most political and social reform is doomed from the start, as is further symbolized by Roger's "tak[ing] out a knife and, with back to the audience, mak[ing] the gesture of castrating himself" (p. 367).

The Revolution is further debilitated by continuing to function as a surrogate—as does the theatre itself—for organized religion as it caters to man's ritualizing impulse, which can be a protective shield against reality. The balcony/theatre becomes identified with the church: the fantasies played out therein are variously called "ceremonies," "rites," "liturgies"; and, at one point, an explicit analogy is drawn between "this sumptous theatre where every moment a drama is performed" and "the outside world [where] a mass is celebrated" (p. 309), which would again point directly at the theatre audience's use of art as a substitute for religion. The revolutionaries have yet to throw off the impetus to create icons that concretize abstract concepts such as ecclesiastical authority, civil justice, and military power; but these are false idols, really, that pretend to mythic proportions by wearing hidden cothurni. Hungry for a patron saint for their cause, they even romantically elevate the whore Chantel to a kind of Joan of Arc. The Chief of Police almost pitifully begs for someone to imitate him on one of the little stages in the brothel of illusions, for to be impersonated would signal that he had entered into the popular imagination and was assured of an existence beyond life in the realm of art/illusion. But that, from Genet's point of view, would be a facile escape rather than a fearless confrontation of the void. For neither this flawed attempt at revolution nor man's temporary escape into a "house of illusions" (p. 296)—whether it be Madame Irma's or the larger theatre itself where Genet's play, or any play, is being performed—achieves the radical breakthrough into reality/truth that Genet proposes, but rather provides what Albee (a disciple of Genet in a work such as *Tiny Alice*) would see as a crutch that man uses to get through life. So *The Balcony,* like *Caligula,* is against art as panacea.

What all four of these dramas share, then, is a concern with flux vs. permanence, with the fluidity of becomingness vs. the fixed essence of art. *It Is So!* is more epistemological than the others, since it approaches this problem from the viewpoint of the perceiver, demonstrating that sanity demands certainty, that of necessity each individual takes changing existence and, by forcing it into a—for himself—permanent mold, creates an artifact. Con Melody in *Poet* and the Police Chief in *The Balcony* each turns himself into an artifact, an image in a mirror, embracing illusion as an escape from selfhood and, ultimately, death. Only Caligula has the courage to break the mirror, to destroy the mask of art, to—in Robert Lowell's phrase—"choose life and die."

II

In *Between the Acts,* her last novel, Virginia Woolf provides an emblematic instance of the metatheatrical experience. Gathered at Pointz Hall to view a pageant created by Miss La Trobe, Woolf's characters are confronted by hand-held pieces of glass that throw back images of themselves and force them to see the moral connection between their own lives and civilization's decline. Such a confrontation between audience and itself through reflections in a looking glass—which remains a possibility in *The Balcony*—is realized in three recent major musicals: Leigh, Darion, and Wasserman's *Man of La Mancha* (1965); Kander, Ebb, and Masteroff's *Cabaret* (1966); and Bennett,

Kleban, Hamlisch, Kirkwood, and Dante's *A Chorus Line* (1975).

Looked at generically, the American musical play tradition-ally has been circumscribed by the form and structure of the romantic comedy, but this does not prevent it from being as serious in its intent as the four dramas already examined. Almost always dealing with love (under one of its many guises) and the conflicts that converge to delay its coming to fruition, the musical falls roughly into the tripartite movement that Northrop Frye has delineated for the comedy and the romance: the hero or heroine experiences rejection by an anticomic or antagonistic society—often represented by a harsh, authoritarian father figure; enters on a period of questioning-of-identity or testing away from society; and ends in a return to and reunion with the society, usually culminating in a formalized, ritual dance signifying regeneration.11 Furthermore, we might say that the characters' period of time away from society in the form's middle movement—often passed spatially in what has come to be called the "green world"—is analogous to the time that the audience spends in the library or the theatre: both characters and audience leave the real world (the first by force, the second by choice) to enter into a world of illusion or art where they undergo a process of learning; they cannot, however, remain forever in this world of the imagination, but must ultimately return to assume their proper roles in society.

Along with employing mirrors as a dominant symbolic and thematic stage prop, other similarities exist among these three musical plays. All of them, for instance, center on periods of social upheaval or decline: *La Mancha* occurs during the Spanish Inquisition; *Cabaret* focuses on the spiritual malaise and political disintegration of Germany on the eve of Hitler; and *A Chorus Line,* while not linked as outrightly to a specific historic phenomenon, pictures the surrender of America's abso-lute faith in the myth of success. Moreover, all three 1) depend, as already mentioned, on the audience's awareness of itself *as* audience for at least a part of their effect; 2) concern, as do the four dramas discussed previously, artists of one type or another and make use of the play-within-the-play—or, in these particular instances, the musical-within-the-musical; and 3) present differing versions of the "green world," thus partially or wholly thwarting the audience's normal expectations about romantic comedy in either or both of its second and third movements.

At the beginning of *La Mancha,* Miguel de Cervantes, incarcerated to await examination and judgment by the Inquisition, acts out part of his picaresque novel *Don Quixote* as his defense before the other prisoners. They become, then, an audience to his theatricale, and so those in the audience watch an audience watching. When Cervantes charges the prisoners "to enter into my imagination,"12 he challenges the theatre audience to do the same, since its doubts about the efficacy of illusion (or art) in the real world mirror the characters' own. By associating itself with the prisoners, the audience thus gazes upon *itself* responding to Cervantes. The prison has become a theatre, and the letting down and raising of the steps into the dungeon are equivalent to the raising and lowering of the curtain that signals the audience's journey away from the real world and its return back to it. If traditionally the "green world" is a place of losing oneself to find oneself, then *La Mancha's* prison/theatre is such a place: for while there, the audience learns, along with its surrogates up on the stage, that "Facts are the enemy of truth" (p. 74), that the dream or product of the imagination or work of art is truer than facts could ever be, and that the artist (madman though the world might deem him by its standards) is really a child of God who, in "com[ing] to terms with life" not "as it is" but as it should be "add[s] some measure of grace to the world" (pp. 99, 85). When the prisoners on stage assent to this insight, so, too, does the theatre audience.

This aesthetic of "truth" and "beauty" confronts a philosophy of empiricism when the Knight of the Mirrors and his attendants enter. The audience out front *may* catch glimpses of themselves in the mirrors that cover the chain-mail tunic of the Knight, or in his shield or those of his attendants; Don Quixote himself, who "reel[s] from one [mirror] to the other," is charged by the Knight to look into the mirrors and see in the multiple reflections an "aging fool, a clown" (p. 110), rather than the Knight of La Mancha. But the mirrors can reveal only the surface, not the substance. And the cure, like that perpetrated on Pirandello's Henry IV, may be worse than the disease, and is, in effect, rejected by the other prisoners who do not like this ending and demand that the redemptive power of the imagination—the reality of illusion—be assented to. This on-stage audience, then, is much like Nora in *A Touch of the Poet*. Yet the role of art espoused here is diametrically opposite to that expressed in *The Balcony* and *Caligula*. As in most "green worlds," reality is brought face to face with illusion, but with a difference: instead of the characters and audience escaping into a distant illusion for a pleasant interlude, here, because of the mirrors, they perceive that what is ordinarily thought of as reality *is* only an illusion, and that to live fully means to plunge into that illusion and remain there forever—a vision which makes the audience unfit for any comfortable accommodation with, or return to, a traditional society that values only the surface reflection or mask above all else.

Before *Cabaret* even begins, the audience sees a distorted image of itself in a tilted mirror, hanging high up on the back wall of the stage set, that "initially reflects the auditorium."13 Assured by the Emcee in the opening song of being "welcome" at the Cabaret—in this instance Berlin's Kit Kat Klub on New Year's Eve in 1930—the theatregoers (already reminded of themselves *as* an audience) now "join" the other patrons of the club on this stage-within-the-stage. The Cabaret itself (spelled out in neon lights) is, like the prison in *La Mancha,* a theatre, a place of illusion; in this case, however, its alleged "beauty" resides in its ability to make man forget—in the sense of being blinded to—the real world: "Why should I wake up?/ This dream is going so well" (p. 58), sings Cliff, the writer-in-search-of-a-subject who eventually turns life into art. So the audience has been simultaneously both distanced (aware of itself watching) and involved (by being placed up on the stage with the performers) through the use of the mirror, a distinctive prop of the self-reflexive Modernist drama whose use transforms this musical play into what might be called a "metatheatrical musical."

Cliff's initial lack of moral commitment is more than matched by Sally Bowles' apolitical as well as amoral stance: if, as she sings, "Life is a cabaret, old chum, only a cabaret" (p. 106), then the only thing to believe in is sensual pleasure, a detachment from any deeper responsibility. So she "preaches" hedonism as Caligula does absurdism. One lens of the theatre audience's double vision views from outside the events on stage, fully aware: ironically, the characters cannot foresee what will soon befall Germany, whereas the audience knows what will

happen—indeed, did happen; and yet, the other lens simultaneously becomes clouded over by the surface attractiveness of
the Emcee's tawdry promises of wealth, sensuality, diminished
moral concern, assuring them at the close, "your troubles now
[are] forgotten" (p. 113). But since at one point, in the Brechtian
commentative song "If You Could See Her Through My Eyes"—
sung to a gorilla in female costume—the audience is challenged
to see through the lens of the Emcee's eyes that all national
and racial and religious prejudice is only skin deep and therefore illusory, it seems that all along the Emcee's irony and
sardonic humor are meant to undercut these false values and
taunt the audience into a stance of commitment rather than
detachment; to make them recognize, perhaps, that American
racism is not all that dissimilar from German fascism.14 When
the mirror is readjusted at the end of the evening, the audience
again confronts itself, again watches itself watching. As watchers
of a musical and visitors to a cabaret, they expected to go on a
flight of fancy and harmless escape from cares. But they now
see that what this perverse "green world" offered instead was
a withdrawal from meaningful action. And so, in a sense,
Cabaret comments upon the form of the musical play itself,
urging that musical comedy as it has been understood traditionally—as entertainment disseminating an escapist ethic—be
rejected.

The kind of distorted, storybook world that the musical
comedy ordinarily posits is further undercut by the handling of
the love plots in Cabaret. Not only does Sally, having aborted
their child and thereby denied the essential "comic" resolution
of regeneration, finally break off with Cliff, but in the subplot
fear of racial violence prevents the marriage—with its promise
of symbolic beauty—of the German widow and the Jewish green
grocer. Their engagement party, which serves as the finale to Act
I, is shattered by the arrival of the Nazis: the music and dancing
are interrupted, and the guests join in a circle around the Swas-
tika-wearer and sing a patriotic hymn. Those who do not
participate in the dance of communal rebirth are not the
morally obtuse and inadequate ones who deserve to be left out
(as would be the case in the dance that ends traditional comedy
and romance), but instead are the two "engaged" couples with
whom the audience most identifies and who would ordinarily
most deserve to dance. Yet this is only appropriate, since what

the audience witnesses here is a perversion of the traditional celebratory dance, promising as it does death instead of birth. So the visual staging is a metaphor for the text.

This appears to be a far cry from the joyous dance/production number that concludes *A Chorus Line*—but is it really? For that dance, too, despite its surface glitter, is staged on an undercurrent of defeat. And although the physical mirror is not used importantly as stage prop until late in this "backstage" show, several of the motifs already noticed in *La Mancha* and *Cabaret* recur. The place is a theatre/audition hall; the characters are seventeen "gypsies" vying for the eight available places in the chorus of a Broadway-bound musical. The very nature of a chorus means that there will be no dancing "to a different drummer" or marching to variant tunes for those finally chosen: they must blend together into a whole, move in synchronization, "march in step." And virtually every song concerns this necessity of molding oneself into a socially and professionally acceptable person by masking individual idiosyncracies—in short, of fitting in by conforming to expectations imposed from without.

Although having the action occur on a stage without scenery contributes to the illusion that what is happening is an unplanned, improvised audition, the premise of the entire proceedings—namely, that the director (heard mostly as a disembodied voice) would put his potential chorus line on a couch as if he were a psychologist or a priest/confessor, is extremely artificial, even stilted at times. The photograph from his resumé that each of the dancers holds up in front of his face makes the same point about surface versus substance that the mirrors accomplished in *La Mancha,* since for each of them the resumé is "a picture of a person I don't know."15 And the song "Everything Was Beautiful at the Ballet" comments on the theatre as a place where reality can be forgotten by living the illusion. But if an actor/dancer ordinarily adopts the mask of a character when he goes out on the stage, here the dancers remove the masks that everyone (the audience included) wears to face the world. Once unmasked, the dancers' overriding desire to "find a place to fit in" becomes clear. Everyman and Everywoman will likely find elements of himself or herself somewhere up on the stage, a microcosm of the world as it was in *The Balcony,* or at the very least empathize with this enforced conformity. This central motif of the leveling-down inherent in egalitarianism, of the sameness that the democratic ideal has come to entail, reaches its apex in the conflict between Cassie, who in the past has been a lead dancer, and Zach, the director who has been her lover. Zach argues her inability to return to the chorus line: "You don't fit in. You don't dance like anybody else—you don't know how." Cassie counters that she has no desire to be unlike everybody else, that she can be special *within* the line, where "we're *all* special." And what Cassie is willing to agree to is what the audience must settle for as well.

In the old-fashioned production number that serves as the show's brilliant finale, all of the dancers, dressed in identical costumes of silver lamé top hat and tails, join in a precision dance in perfect unison; with no one out of step, they are like a well-oiled machine doing a show-stopping routine. And the song they dance to, entitled simply "One," accepts that dark underside, that leveling-down, of America's egalitarian ideal: there can be only "One singular sensation, and you can forget the rest." Those in the chorus line, and all those out in the audience, are among that "rest" who are "second best." The audience sees itself up on the stage, recognizing that its belief in unlimited opportunity and the probability for success is illusory, that they are *not* the "One." And the mirrors that serve as a backdrop for the finale reinforce this recognition. Not only do the rehearsal mirrors give the illusion of added size and dimension to the production number, but they also permit the audience to see itself as a mass of people reflected in the same image that catches the anonymity of the members of the line. So while the music makes this a celebratory occasion, a deeper and more somber resonance hints that for the majority ever being special is just a mirage. Individual fame eludes most people; they are part of the collectivity of common men, only a *part* of the dance and not the center of it.

And yet, the glamour and glory of this dance are themselves only another illusion, for this production number is being rehearsed to serve as the climactic showstopper spotlighting the star in an escapist musical comedy. But that this production number also provides, at one and the same time, the most thrilling moment of *A Chorus Line* perhaps suggests the unwillingness of many audiences to accept a Broadway musical play that has completely crossed the boundary into the realm of the metatheatrical. The creators of *Chorus Line*—unlike those of

Cabaret—evidently felt it prudent to step back from the insight to which they had led the audience through the use of the mirror. For the self-reflexivity peculiar to Modernist art and all things metatheatrical would seem to preclude the perennial popular appeal of the musical comedy, since in the metatheatrical musical—best exemplified by *Cabaret*—there can really be no "green worlds" anymore. Forcing an audience to confront itself in mirrors destroys the distance essential to comedy and turns the green world gray, or even black.

It is perhaps not surprising that creators of the musical, traditionally the theatrical form least bound by the confines and conventions of realistic drama, have taken their audiences that one extra step further, from simply being aware of themselves as audience to actually *seeing* themselves reflected in a mirror. And if most studies of metadrama have thus far focused on philosophical issues, then possibly an awareness of the centrality of the mirror as stage prop to metatheatre can suggest the beginning of a practical aesthetic theory in response to J. L. Styan's recent challenge that "the next task" is the "especially difficult" one of "demonstrat[ing] how metadrama works in practice."16

Purdue University

NOTES

1 *Metatheatre: A New View of Dramatic Form* (New York: Hill & Wang, 1963), p. 79.

2 *It Is So! (If You Think So)*, in *Naked Masks: Five Plays* by Luigi Pirandello, ed. Eric Bentley (New York: E. P. Dutton, 1952), p. 95. Further references appear within parentheses in the text.

3 *The Theatre of Revolt: An Approach to the Modern Drama* (Boston: Little, Brown, 1964), p. 295.

4 *A Touch of the Poet* (New Haven: Yale Univ. Press, 1957), p. 7. Further references appear within parentheses in the text.

5 *Contour in Time: The Plays of Eugene O'Neill* (New York: Oxford Univ. Press, 1972), pp. 391, 393.

6 *Caligula*, in *Masters of Modern Drama*, ed. Haskell M. Block and Robert G. Shedd (New York: Random House, 1963), p. 821. Further references appear within parentheses in the text.

7 "Albert Camus" in *Masters of Modern Drama*, p. 817.

8 *The Balcony*, in *Seven Plays of the Modern Theater* (New York: Grove Press, 1962), p. 370. Further references appear within parentheses in the text.

9 "The World is a Stage: Sartre versus Genet," *Modern Drama*, 17 (1974), 34.

10 Philip Thody (*Jean Genet: A Critical Appraisal* [New York: Stein and Day, 1968], p. 187) speaks of them as "deprived of the solace afforded by imagination," while June Schlueter (*Metafictional Characters in Modern Drama* [New York: Columbia University, 1979], p. 45) comments that "they can no longer step at will in and out of their roles nor enjoy the comfort of knowing their fantasies are fictive. . . ."

11 See, for example, Chapter III of *A Natural Perspective: The Development of Shakespearean Comedy and Romance* (New York: Harcourt, Brace & World, 1965).

12 *Man of La Mancha* (New York: Dell, 1968), p. 41. Further references appear within parentheses in the text.

13 *Cabaret* (New York: Scholastic Book Services, 1973), p. viii. Further references appear within parentheses in the text.

14 Martin Gottfried, *Broadway Musicals* (New York: Harry N. Abrams, 1979), p. 126.

15 No printed edition of *A Chorus Line* exists and, my efforts at obtaining a script having proved unsuccessful, quotations appear, therefore, as in my viewing notes. A synopsis of *Chorus Line* is, however, included in *The Best Plays of 1974-1975*, ed. Otis L. Guernsey (New York: Dodd, Mead, 1975), pp. 242 ff.

16 Review of *Metafictional Characters in Modern Drama*, *Modern Drama*, 23 (1980), 215.

Index

Abel, Lionel, 1, 181, 183n, 363
Adler, Alfred, 291n
Aeschylus, 4–7, 12, 15, 17, 20n, 85
Albee, Edward, 373
Alcmaeon, of Croton, 5
Alfred, William, 352, 354
Alpers, Boris, 220n
Amis, Kingsley, 28
Anaxagoras, 5
Anaximander, 4, 20n
Anderson, Maxwell, 352
Anderson, Robert, 30
Andrews, Harry, 338
Anouilh, Jean, 173–83
Antoine, André, 171
Appollinaire, Guillaume, 171
Archer, William, 66
Arden, John, 355–58
Arendt, Hannah, 201n
Aristotle, 164–65, 171
Arnheim, Rudolf, 16, 19n
Arnold, Matthew, 134
Artaud, Antonin, 171
Auden, W.H., 301–22, 347, 355
Augustine, Saint, 361
Austen, Jane, 332
Aylen, Leo, 55n

Bachelard, Gaston, 244
Bacon, Francis, 338
Barthel, Max, 205
Bashō, 325
Beckett, Samuel, 12, 15, 18, 21n,
   166, 223–53, 292n, 327, 346–48,
   362n

Bely, Audrey, 204, 210
Benedikt, Michael, 151
Benjamin, Walter, 207, 209–10, 212,
   218
Bentley, Eric, 182n
Berg, Alban, 320
Berger, Peter, 185
Berheimer, Martin, 303
Bernhardt, Sara, 305
Binswanger, Ludwig, 291n
Bishop, Thomas, 183n
Bjørnson, Bjørnstjerne, 54n
Blair, John, 301
Blake, William, 336, 339
Block, Haskell, 345, 369
Blok, Alexander, 205–06, 219
Blume, Bernhard, 201n
Bogard, Travis, 368
Boltzmann, L., 2–3, 11
Bond, Edward, 320, 323–43
Booth, Edmund, 305
Boulez, Pierre, 310
Brandes, Georg, 52, 54n
Bray, Barbara, 296
Brecht, Bertolt, 185–221, 323, 330,
   356, 362n
Brenck-Kalischer, Bess, 206
Brereton, Geoffrey, 1, 3, 21n
Breton, André, 171
Britten, Benjamin, 303
Bromberg, Victor, 181
Brook, Peter, 327–30
Brown, Norman O., 289, 291n
Browne, E. Martin, 345
Brustein, Robert, 366

Büchner, Georg, 346
Buckle, Henry Thomas, 73–74
Bulman, Joan, 86n
Byron, 305, 351, 358

Cabaret, 373–74, 376–78, 380
Calarco, N. Joseph, 7
Campbell, Joseph, 43, 255, 272n
Camus, Albert, 186, 276–78, 282,
   285, 291n, 292n, 364, 369–70,
   373, 376
Carnot, S., 2
Carrington, Lord, 349
Carter, Lillian, 350
Cassirer, Ernst, 43
Chayevsky, Paddy, 345
Chekhov, Anton, 1, 183n
Chorus Line, 374, 378–80
Clausius, R., 2, 19n
Coe, Richard, 175
Cohn, Ruby, 293n
Comte, Auguste, 73
Connolly, Cyril, 158
Corneille, Pierre, 166
Coward, Noel, 358
Craft, Robert, 302
Croce, Benedetto, 73
Cummings, E.E., 347
Curtis, Jerry, 371

Darwin, Charles, 28
Davidson, Patricia, 350
Deich, A.I., 221n
Descartes, René, 9
Dilthey, Wilhelm, 73
Diogenes, 5
Dionysus, 8, 15
Donizetti, Gaetano, 316
Donnington, Robert, 122n
Dowden, Edward, 127
Dudow, Slatan, 211
Dutschke, Rudi, 310–11

Eddington, Arthur, 3, 9
Eisenstein, Sergei, 204–05, 207
Eliot, George, 192
Eliot, T.S., 14–15, 43, 324, 345–47,
   355, 358
Empedocles, 5
Engels, Freidrich, 112
Erdman, N., 216

Esslin, Martin, 1, 13, 151, 190–91,
   276, 291n, 300n
Euripides, 7, 318, 346
Everyman, 347

Faiko, A., 216
Fanon, Frantz, 257–59
Felsenstein, Walter, 318
Fergusson, Francis, 141–42
Feuchtwanger, Lion, 209
Fischer-Dieskau, Dietrich, 302
Fjelde, Rolf, 60, 70
Fortner, Wolfgang, 310
Franc-Nohain, 168–69
Fraser, G.S., 362n
Freud, Sigmund, 28, 53, 69
Frost, Robert, 347
Fry, Christopher, 345
Frye, Northrop, 20n, 43

Gaskill, William, 338
Gay, John, 216
Geitel, Klaus, 315
Genet, Jean, 175, 255–73, 284,
   364, 370–73, 376, 378
Gide, André, 245
Gielgud, John, 345
Gignoux, Hubert, 182n
Giraudoux, Jean, 179
Goethe, Johann Wolfgang von, 1,
   10, 20n, 48, 99n, 303
Gogol, Nikolai, 207, 209, 216
Goldman, Michael, 362n
Goldmann, Lucien, 272n, 273n
Goodman, Paul, 297
Gordan, Louis G., 293n
Gourmont, Remy de, 154
Goya, Francisco, 338
Gozzi, Carlo, 311
Granville-Barker, Harley, 102
Gray, Ronald, 71
Gregory, Lady Augusta, 140n
Grimm, Reinhold, 186, 189
Guicharnaud, Jacques, 183n
Gussow, Mel, 295
Gutman, Robert, 102, 122n

Haakonsen, Daniel, 45
Hardy, Thomas, 192
Hart, Francis, 245–46
Harvey, John, 182n

Havel, Vaclav, 13, 15
Heath-Stubbs, John, 353–55
Hegel, 28, 73, 76
Hellman, Lillian, 31
Henstell, Bruce, 298
Henze, Hans Werner, 302–03, 306–20
Heraclitus, 4–5, 8
Herzfelde, Wieland, 213
Hesiod, 4
Hitchcock, Alfred, 46
Hoffmann, E.T.A., 303–04
Hofmannsthal, Hugo von, 309, 320
Holitscher, Arthur, 205
Holtan, Orley, 43
Homer, 15
Huneker, James, 103
Huppert, Hugo, 207
Huxley, Aldous, 16
Hyde, Douglas, 140n

Ibsen, Henrik, 1, 24–26, 30–31, 33, 36–41, 43–72, 305
Ionesco, Eugène, 12–13, 17, 166, 242
Isherwood, Christopher, 355

Jacobs, Arthur, 303, 316
Jakobson, Roman, 249
Jarry, Alfred, 151–72, 332
Jaspers, Karl, 291n
Jauss, Hans Robert, 249–52, 292n
Jeffers, R., 347
John, Saint, of Damascus, 154–55
Johnson, Samuel, 311
Johnson, Walter, 86n
Joyce, James, 43, 138, 152
Jung, C.G., 43

Kafka, Franz, 76
Kallman, Chester, 301–02, 310–11, 317
Kauffmann, Stanley, 297–98
Kaufmann, R.J., 19n, 75
Kaufmann, Walter, 1, 14, 20n
Kelvin, Lord, 10–11, 20n
Kenner, Hugh, 232
Kepler, Johannes, 9
Kerman, Joseph, 302
Kierkegaard, Søren, 291n
Kirby, E.T., 291n

Kirk, G.S., 4
Kitto, H.D.F., 183n
Kleist, Heinrich von, 311
Klitsch, Gustav, 319
Knust, Herbert, 219n
Kohlhase, Norbert, 186
Knopf, Jan, 213
Kommissarzhevky, Fedor, 208
Kopelev, Lev, 218
Kott, Jan, 327
Kreilisheim, Eva, 219n

Lacis, Anna, 207–10, 213, 217–18, 220n, 221n
Laing, R.D., 291n
Lance, Bert, 350
Landgraf, Ludwig, 313
Lan-fang, Mei, 213–14
Lautréamont, Compte de, 159, 165
Lévi-Strauss, Claude, 22n, 43–45, 54n, 55n
Liebowitz, René, 310
Lorca, Garcia, 141–42, 147–49
Losey, Joseph, 295–96, 298, 300n
Lowell, Robert, 347, 373
Lukács, Georg, 242–43
Lunacharsky, Anatoly, 17, 205, 207, 210, 215–18, 221n
Lunacharskaia-Rozenel, Nataliia, 216, 221n

MacLeish, Archibald, 347, 362n
Maeterlinck, Maurice, 165
Mallarmé, Stéphane, 165, 271
Man of La Mancha, 373–78
Mann, Thomas, 304
Manson, T. W., 187
Marinetti, F. T., 171
Marston, John, 347
Marx, Karl, 17, 28, 73, 198
Maxwell, J. C., 2
Mayakovsky, Vladimir, 210, 213
McLuhan, Marshall, 8, 22n
Meyerbeer, Giacomo, 102
Meyerhold, V., 203–21
Mill, J. S., 73
Miller, Arthur, 26, 30–31, 36–40
Miller, J. H., 361n
Milton, John, 134
Minkowski, Eugène, 291n
Molière, 166–67

Moltmann, Jürgen, 187, 189
Montensen, John, 86n
Moore, George, 140n
Moore, J. R., 132
Morris, William, 133
Mould, Daphne, 292n
Mozart, W. A., 102–03, 109, 313, 315, 320

Nathan, Leonard, 140n
Neher, Carola, 213
Nemerov, Howard, 347, 358–61
Newton, Isaac, 9
Nicoll, Allardyce, 362n
Niebuhr, Reinhold, 69
Nietzsche, Friedrich, 28, 109, 201n
Northam, John, 54n

O'Connor, Flannery, 23
Odets, Clifford, 30, 346, 348
Oliver, William J., 292n
O'Neill, Eugene, 364, 366–68, 373, 376
Ong, Walter J., 292n
Osborne, Conrad, 303
Osborne, John, 351

Parkinson, Thomas, 138–39, 140n
Parmenides, 4–5, 15
Parsons, Talcott, 187
Pater, Walter, 125–40
Péladan, Sâr Joséphin, 165
Pinero, Arthur Wing, 208
Pinter, Harold, 275–300, 366
Pirandello, Luigi, 75–76, 183n, 355, 364–66, 369, 373, 375
Piscator, Erwin, 207, 219n
Pitoëff, Georges, 366
Plato, 160–61
Poe, E.A., 28
Polak, Frederick, 198
Pope, Alexander, 9
Prévost, Abbé, 311
Prokofiev, Sergei, 205
Proust, Marcel, 295–300
Pynchon, Thomas, 21n

Racine, 1, 8–9, 166
Ranke, Leopold von, 73
Raphael, 45, 134
Raven, J.E., 4

Reich, Bernhard, 206–10, 212, 218, 220n
Rennert, Günther, 319
Robert, Paul, 156
Rousseau, Henri, 171

Sackler, Howard, 353
Sartre, Jean-Paul, 76, 273n
Schachteli, Werner, 313
Schechner, Richard, 45
Scheler, Max, 3–4
Schering, Emil, 74
Schlemmer, Oskar, 170
Schlueter, June, 381n
Schneider, Alan, 12
Schwarz, Peter Paul, 200n
Scofield, Paul, 327–28
Scriabin, Alexander, 205
Secunda Pastorum, 333
Sewall, Richard, 40
Shaffer, Peter, 29–30, 36
Shakespeare, William, 8–9, 24, 32–36, 40, 78, 85, 91, 125, 127–32, 135–36, 138, 169, 324–42, 353, 355, 363, 370
Shannon, C.S., 11
Shattuck, Roger, 151
Shaw, G.B., 53, 101–23, 309, 326, 347
Shedd, Robert, 345, 369
Shelley, Mary, 10
Shklovsky, Viktor, 204, 212–13, 220n, 221n
Sohlich, W.F., 272n
Sologub, Fedor, 208
Sophocles, 9, 15, 33–36, 39–40, 176, 180, 183n
Spears, Monroe, 301
Spender, Stephen, 302
Stanislavsky, Konstantin, 206, 208
Steiner, George, 1, 4, 9–10, 14, 17, 20n, 21n
Stephane, Nicole, 295
Stevens, Wallace, 138, 347
Stockhausen, Karlheinz, 310
Straus, Erwin, 142, 146
Strauss, Richard, 208, 320
Stravinsky, Igor, 301–03, 309, 315–17
Strindberg, August, 1, 73–99, 323
Stuckenschmidt, H.L., 316, 319

Styan, J.L., 181, 380
Sypher, Wylie, 2, 11, 19n

Tairov, Alexander, 205-06, 208,
  213, 216
Tate, Nahum, 342
Taylor, Simon Watson, 158
Thody, Philip, 381n
Thucydides, 7
Tillich, Paul, 198
Todhunter, John, 126-27
Tourneur, Cyril, 371
Tret'iakov, Sergei, 205-07, 210-15,
  218, 220n
Tynan, Kenneth, 346
Tzara, Tristan, 171

Ure, Peter, 138, 140n

Valéry, Paul, 145, 150n
Valgemae, Mardi, 21n
Verdi, Guiseppe, 102
Villiers de l'Isle-Adam, 126
Visconti, Luchino, 311
Voltaire, 9, 21n

Wagner, Richard, 21n, 65, 101-23,
  315, 318
Wain, John, 346-47, 362n
Walcott, Derek, 347
Walter, B.G., 18

Weaver, W. 11
Weber, Max, 28, 187
Webster, John, 347
Weigand, Hermann J. 54n
Weigel, Helene, 212
Weill, Kurt, 216
Weisstein, Ulrich, 301
Welles, Orson, 368
Wellwarth, George, 151
Whitman, Walt, 288
Whyte, Lancelot L., 7-8
Wilde, Oscar, 127
Wilden, Anthony, 54n
Wilder, Thornton, 371
Willett, John, 221n
Willey, Basil, 192
Williams, Betty, 350
Wisenthal, J.L., 112-14
Wolfit, Donald, 324-25
Woods, Barbara Allen, 186
Woolf, Virginia, 138, 373
Wordsworth, William, 134
Worth, Katharine, 337-38
Wright, Barbara, 151

Yeats, W.B., 26, 125-50, 293n, 345,
  347, 358, 362n

Zola, Émile, 28-29
Zuckmayer, Carl, 204